Bed & Breakfast

ALSO AVAILABLE IN THE COMPLEAT TRAVELER SERIES

☐ *Ferguson's* Europe by Eurail: *How to Tour Europe by Train*

☐ *Ferguson's* Britain by BritRail: *How to Tour Britain by Train*

☐ *Fistell's* America by Train: *How to Tour America by Rail*

☐ Bed & Breakfast: *The Great American Guest House Book*

☐ National & State Parks: *Lodges and Cabins*

☐ Country Inns & Historic Hotels of Great Britain

☐ Country Inns & Historic Hotels of Canada

☐ Country Inns & Historic Hotels of Ireland

☐ Country New England Inns

☐ Country Inns & Historic Hotels of the Middle Atlantic States

☐ Country Inns & Historic Hotels of the South

☐ Country Inns & Historic Hotels of the Midwest & Rocky Mts.

☐ Country Inns & Historic Hotels of California & the Northwest

☐ Guide to Country New England

☐ Guide to California and the Pacific Northwest

☐ Guide to Texas and the Southwest

☐ *Scheer's* Guide to Virginia

☐ *Scheer's* Guide to North Carolina

☐ *Scheer's* Guide to Tennessee

☐ *Scheer's* Guide to Florida

If your local bookseller, gift shop, or country inn does not stock a particular title, ask them to order directly from Burt Franklin & Co., Inc., 235 East 44th Street, New York, New York 10017, U.S.A. Telephone orders are accepted from recognized retailers and credit-card holders. In the United States, call 212-687-5250.

Bed & Breakfast America

John Thaxton

1984–85

The Great American Guest House Book

BURT FRANKLIN & COMPANY

Published by Burt Franklin & Company, Inc.
235 East Forty-fourth Street
New York, New York 10017

THIRD EDITION

Copyright © 1982, 1983, 1984 by Burt Franklin & Co., Inc.

All rights reserved
No part of this book may be reproduced
in whole or in part by any means
including any photographic, mechanical, or
electrical reproduction, recording, or information
storage and retrieval system
without the prior written consent of the publisher
except for brief quotations for the
purposes of review.

0-89102-301-1

Manufactured in the United States of America

1   3   4   2

CONTENTS

Introduction vii
Bed-and-Breakfast Reservation Services x

UNITED STATES

Alabama	1	Mississippi	258
Alaska	3	Missouri	261
Arizona	7	Nebraska	265
Arkansas	10	Nevada	267
California	13	New Hampshire	268
Colorado	115	New Jersey	275
Connecticut	124	New Mexico	291
District of Columbia	131	New York	293
Florida	133	North Carolina	325
Georgia	148	Ohio	330
Hawaii	158	Oregon	336
Illinois	165	Pennsylvania	345
Indiana	169	Rhode Island	358
Iowa	171	South Carolina	365
Kansas	177	Tennessee	371
Louisiana	182	Texas	376
Maine	189	Utah	387
Maryland	199	Vermont	390
Massachusetts	202	Virginia	405
Michigan	248	Washington	420
Minnesota	254	Wisconsin	437

CANADA

Alberta 441
British Columbia 442
Ontario 444
Quebec 447
INDEX with rates and credit-card information 450

INTRODUCTION

Experience people as well as places, pamper yourself, save money, look at Manhattan from a terrace high above, sleep in a lighthouse, on a houseboat, in a beautifully restored mansion listed in the National Register of Historic Places—these are just a few of the things I hope this book will help its readers enjoy. *Bed & Breakfast: The Great American Guest House Book* is the book smart travelers have been waiting for. It is the most comprehensive guide to one of the more comfortable and least costly forms of lodging: bed and breakfast. What has long been an English and European tradition seems almost overnight to have caught on in North America in a big way. This book is meant to help you learn how it works and how to make it work for you.

Guest houses vary tremendously, but the owners of nearly all share a desire to provide visitors with something special, with a form of lodging that's as old as it is new—spending the night in someone's home. Before World War II, guest houses, then frequently called "tourist homes," existed throughout the country as the principal lower-cost alternative to hotels along America's highways. Many of these guest houses have survived and are experiencing a resurgence in popularity, again as a lower-cost alternative to the high cost of hotels and the sterility of motels. Many guest houses are themselves historic buildings or were recently converted from historic structures; others are in popular locations near the mountains or seashore. During the past several years, thousands of Americans have opened their homes to guests while others have acquired and renovated homes far larger than they need with the express purpose of taking in guests. Recently bed-and-breakfast organizations—each of which acts as an agent for a number of guest houses, serving as a clearing house between guests and hosts — have sprung up in such places as Chicago, New York, San Francisco, the Napa Valley in California, Boston, the Hamptons on Long Island, Cape Cod in Massachusetts, Washington, D.C., and Vancouver, Montreal, and Toronto in Canada, to name just a few.

How to Use This Book

The guest houses described in this book fall into two broad categories—those you contact directly and those that accept reservations only through a referral service. As the bed-and-breakfast movement is new, the various referral services operate differently: Some require small membership fees, and others do not; some focus on a particular area or city, others cover the entire country; some collect fees for the host homes, others do not. The directors of the bed-and-breakfast referral services tend to be as friendly as the hosts they represent, and a brief phone call or letter will clarify exactly how a particular service currently operates.

In this book the guest houses that are represented by a referral service are briefly described, and each description is followed by the name and telephone number of the organization that should be contacted. Below is a listing—of all the bed-and-breakfast referral services mentioned in this volume.

The other type of accommodation represented in this book is more after the fashion of a small inn. Entries describing this type tend to be longer, and specific details are provided, including information on facilities for children and pets, driving instructions, and mention of such amenities as air conditioning and television.

Most of the referral services have many additional listings, and their staffs will be happy to help you find just the location you are looking for. When contacting these services, try to be as specific as possible about your requirements: If you will be traveling with children, be sure to mention that. If you will be traveling on business and may need the use of a private telephone or parking facilities, or need to be in a downtown location close to public transportation, remember to make that clear. If you'll be on vacation and would like access to a swimming pool, the beach, tennis courts, or a golf course, be sure to request those amenities. If you'll be bringing along the family dog and want a home that accepts pets or is near a kennel, most referral services will make an effort to fill that need. This book offers access to a very wide range of lodgings. Again, if you're clear and specific about your needs, you'll be likely to find just what you're looking for.

This book has been organized alphabetically by state or Canadian province and, within each state or province, alphabetically by city or town. Individually described guest houses follow those accommodations available through referral services in the same town.

Rates

Rates for those accommodations available through referral services have been listed at the end of each entry. Rates for guest houses you can contact directly have been listed in the Index, along with credit-card information. Rates vary widely, based on the number of persons sharing accommodations and on the particular season of travel. Holiday periods are generally more expensive. Be sure to confirm the rate you will be paying when making reservations.

A Word of Advice

Making a reservation at a bed-and-breakfast place is not like making a reservation at a motel, where you can call at any hour of the night or day and usually find a room available. A guest house tends to be more like someone's home. Most people who have opened their homes to guests will go out of their way to make you feel comfortable, but they cannot be expected to provide the services of a large hotel with bellhops, bartenders, and waiters. On the other hand, expect the unexpected: perhaps afternoon tea with your host's personal friends, sherry served on the porch upon your arrival, fresh flowers in your bedroom, or a hostess willing to baby-sit while you're off exploring the village. Be sure that your children or pets behave appropriately, and I am sure you will have fun and a pleasurable trip.

If you plan to stay at a guest house, you should make reservations as early as possible. If it's not their busy season, hosts may not be home the first time you call them, and referral services tend to operate only during regular business hours in their local time zones.

I hope my readers have as much fun meeting new people and staying in new places as I have. Since I revise and update this book on a regular basis, I want to hear from readers. A reader's report is printed on the last page of this book. I look forward to receiving your comments, suggestions, and recommendations of guest houses you believe might merit inclusion in future editions.

JOHN THAXTON

Bed-and-Breakfast Reservation Services

Please note: Some reservation services charge a small membership fee; others do not. Most will supply a complete list of their accommodations to those sending a self-addressed, stamped envelope. Several require a small fee to cover mailing expenses. Contact the individual services listed below for specific requirements.

Alaska Private Lodgings, P.O. Box 10135, Anchorage, AK 99502, (907) 345-222, Susie Hansen.

Alberta Bed and Breakfast, 330 Eighth Street SW #750, Calgary, Alberta T2R 1B6, Canada, (403) 233-8148; or 4327 Eighty-sixth Street, Edmonton, Alberta Y6K 1A9, Canada, (403) 462-8885.

American Bed and Breakfast Program, P.O. Box 983, St. Albans, VT 05478, (802) 524-4731. Bob Precoda.

American Family Inn, 2185-A Union Street, San Francisco, CA 94123. (415) 931-3083, Richard and Susan Kreibich.

The B & B Group (New Yorkers at Home), 301 East Sixtieth Street, New York, NY 10022, (212) 838-7015, Farla Zammit.

B & B in Iowa, 7104 Franklin Avenue, Des Moines, IA 50322, (515) 277-9018, Iona Ansorge.

Bed and Breakfast, Inc., 1236 Decatur Street, New Orleans, LA 70116, (504) 525-4640, Hazell Boyce.

Bed and Breakfast, Inc. of the Florida Keys, 5 Man-o-War Drive, Marathon, FL 33050, (305) 743-4118, Joan E. Hopp.

Bed and Breakfast Associates Bay Colony, Ltd., P.O. Box 166, Babson Park Branch, Boston, MA 02157, (617) 872-6990, Arline Kardasis.

Bed and Breakfast Atlanta, 1221 Fairview Road NE, Atlanta, GA 30306, (404) 378-6026, Madalyne Eplan.

Bed and Breakfast Birmingham, P.O. Box 31328, Birmingham, AL 35222, (205) 591-6406, Ruth Taylor.

Bed and Breakfast Brookline-Boston, 21 Monmouth Court, Brookline, MA 02146, (617) 277-2292.

Bed and Breakfast Cape Cod, P.O. Box 341, West Hyannisport, MA 02672, (617) 775-2772, Carla Smythe.

Bed and Breakfast Chicago, P.O. Box 14088, Chicago, IL 60614, (312) 951-0085.

Bed and Breakfast Co., 1205 Mariposa Avenue #233, Miami, FL 33146, (305) 661-3270, Marcella Schaible.

Bed and Breakfast Colorado, P.O. Box 20596, Denver, CO 80220, (303) 333-3340 1-5 P.M., Rick Madden.

Bed and Breakfast Down East, Ltd., Box 547, Eastbrook, ME 04634, (207) 565-3517, Sally B. Godfrey.

Bed and Breakfast Exchange, 1118 Pine Street, St. Helena, CA 94574, (707) 963-7756, Andee Beresini.

Bed and Breakfast Hawaii, Box 449, Kappa, Hawaii 96746, (808) 822-1582, Al Davis and Evelyn Warner.

Bed and Breakfast in Arizona, 8433 North Black Canyon Suite, Suite 160, Phoenix, AZ 85021, (602) 995-2831 or 939-2180. Bessie Lipinski.

Bed and Breakfast in Memphis, P.O. Box 41621, Memphis, TN 38174, (901) 726-5920, Helen Denton.

Bed and Breakfast in Minuteman Country, 8 Linmoor Terrace, Lexington, MA 02173, (617) 861-7063, Sally Elkind and Judy Palmer.

Bed and Breakfast International, 151 Ardmore Road, Kensington, CA 94707, (415) 525-4569 or 527-8836, Jean Brown.

The Bed and Breakfast League, 2855 Twenty-ninth Street NW, Washington, DC 20008, (202) 232-8718, Diana MacLeish.

Bed and Breakfast New Hampshire, RFD3, Box 53, Laconia, NH 03246, (603) 279-8348, Martha Dorais.

Bed and Breakfast of Los Angeles, 32074 Waterside Lane, Westlake Village, CA 91361, (213) 889-8870 or 889-7325, Angie Kobabe and Peg Marshall.

Bed and Breakfast Directory of Maine, 21 Monmouth Court, Brookline, MA 02146, (617) 277-2292.

Bed and Breakfast of Milwaukee, 3017 N. Downer Avenue, Milwaukee, WI 53211, (414) 342-5030.

Bed and Breakfast of Nebraska, 1464 Twenty-eighth Avenue, Columbus, NE 68601, (308) 564-7591, Marlene VanLent.

Bed and Breakfast of Philadelphia, P.O. Box 101, Oreland, PA 19075, (215) 884-1084, Janet Mochel.

Bed and Breakfast of the Palm Beaches, P.O. Box 322, Jupiter, FL 33468, (305) 746-2545, Eliza Hofmeister and Dolly Sherman.

Bed and Breakfast Rochester, P.O. Box 444, Fairport, NY 14450, (716) 223-8510.

Bed and Breakfast of Southeast Pennsylvania, Box 278, RD 1, Barto, PA 19504, (215) 845-3526, Joyce Stevenson.

Bed and Breakfast of Tidewater Virginia, P.O. Box 3343, Norfolk, VA 23514, (804) 627-1983 or 627-9409, Ashby Wilcox and Susan Hubbard.

Bed and Breakfast Pocono Northeast, P.O. Box 115, Bear Creek, PA 18602, (717) 472-3145, Patricia Mack and Ann Magagna.

Bed and Breakfast St. Louis, 16 Green Acres, St. Louis, MO 63137, (314) 868-2335, Evelyn Ressler.

Bed and Breakfast Society of Houston, 4432 Hoit, Bellaire, TX 77401, (713) 666-6372, Debbie Herman Seigel.

Bed and Breakfast Texas Style, 4224 West Red Bird Lane, Dallas, TX 75237, (214) 298-5433 or 298-8586, Ruth Wilson.

Bed and Breakfast U.S.A., Ltd., P.O. Box 528, Croton-on-Hudson, NY 10521, (914) 271-6228, Barbara Notarius.

Bed and Breakfast Upper Midwest, P.O. Box 28036, Minneapolis, MN 55428, (612) 535-7135, Maryann Kudalis.

Benson House of Richmond, P.O. Box 15131, Richmond, VA 23227, (804) 321-6277 or 648-7560, Lyn Benson.

Berkshire Bed and Breakfast Connection, 141 Newton Road, Springfield, MA 01118, (413) 783-5111. The Allens.

Blue Ridge B & B, Route 1, Box 517, Bluemont, VA 22012, (703) 955-3955, Sarah Genthner.

Carolyn's Bed and Breakfast Homes in the San Diego Area, P.O. Box 84776, (619) 435-5009 or 481-7662, Carolyn Waskiewicz.

Country Host, R.R. 1, Palgrave, Ontario K2H 7T9, (519) 941-7633.

Covered Bridge Bed and Breakfast, West Cornwall, CT 06796, (203) 672-6052, Rae Eastman.

Finger Lakes Bed and Breakfast Registry, 162 Hook Road, Macedon, NY 14502, (315) 986-4536, Diane M. Robinson.

Gîte Québec, 3729 Avenue LeCorbusier, Ste-Foy, Quebec GFW 4R8, Canada, (418) 651-1860, Thérèse Tellier.

Greater Boston Hospitality, P.O. Box 1142, Brookline, MA 02146, (617) 734-0807, Laura and Chris Simonelli.

Guesthouses Bed and Breakfast, P.O. Box 5737, Charlottesville, VA 22903, (804) 979-8327, Sally Reger.

Hampton B & B, Box 695, East Moriches, NY 11940, (516) 288-3390.

Historic Charleston Bed and Breakfast, 43 Legare Street, Charleston, SC, 29401, (803) 722-6606. Charlotte Fairey.

House Guests Cape Cod, 85 Hokum Rock Road, Dennis, MA 02638, (617) 398-0787, Allison Caswell.

Kansas City Bed and Breakfast, P.O. Box 14781, Lenexa, KS 66215, (913) 268-4214, Diane C. Kuhn.

Montreal Bed and Breakfast, 5020 St. Kevin Street, Suite 8, Montreal, Quebec H3W 1P4, Canada, (514) 735-7493, Marian Kahn.

Nashville Bed and Breakfast, P.O. Box 15651, Nashville, TN 37215, (615) 327-4546 or 292-2574.

Nashville Host Homes, P.O. Box 110227, Nashville, TN 37222, (615) 331-5244.

New Age Travel: The International Spareroom, 839 Second Street, Suite 3, Encinitas, CA 92024, (619) 436-9977, Pam Davis.

New England Bed and Breakfast, 1045 Centre Street, Newton, MA 02159, John Gardner.

New Orleans Bed and Breakfast, 3658 Gentilly Boulevard, P.O. Box 8163, New Orleans, LA 70812, (504) 949-6705, Sarah-Margaret Brown.

Newport Travel Center, 270 Main Post Office Building, Thames Street, Newport, RI 02840, (401) 846-1615, Robert Simmons.

North Country Bed and Breakfast Reservation Service, The Barn, Box 286, Lake Placid, NY 12946, (518) 523-3739, Lyn Witte.

Northwest Bed and Breakfast, 7707 Southwest Locust Street, Tigard, OR 97223, (503) 246-8366 or 246-2383, Laine Friedman and Gloria Shaich.

Nutmeg Bed and Breakfast, 56 Fox Chase Lane, West Hartford, CT 06107, (203) 236-6698, Phyllis Nova and Maxine Kates.

Ottawa Area Bed and Breakfast, P.O. Box 4848, Station E, Ottawa K1S 5J1, Canada, (613) 563-0161.

Pineapple Hospitality, Inc., 384 Rodney French Boulevard, New Bedford, MA 02744, (617) 990-1696.

Private Lodgings, Inc., P.O. Box 18590, Cleveland, OH 44118, (216) 321-3213.

Rest and Repast Bed and Breakfast Service, Pine Grove Mills, PA 16868, (814) 238-1484, Linda C. Feltman and Brent R. Peters.

Sand Dollar Hospitality Bed and Breakfast, 3605 Mendenhall, Corpus Christi, TX 78415, (512) 853-1222, Maureen M. Bennett.

Sharp-Adams, Inc., 33 West Street, Annapolis, MD 21401, (301) 269-6232 or 261-2233, B. J. Adams.

Suncoast Accommodations in Florida, 13700 Gulf Blvd., Madeira Beach, FL 33708, (813) 393-7020, Barbara Seligman.

Sweet Dreams and Toast, P.O. Box 4835-0035, Washington, DC, (202) 483-9191, Ellie Chastain.

Toronto Bed and Breakfast, Box 74, Station M, Toronto, Ontario M6S 4T2, Canada, (416) 233-3887 or 233-4041, Randy Lee.

Town and Country B & B, P.O. Box 301, Lambertville, NJ 08530, (609) 397-8399, Anita Impellizeri.

Town and Country Bed and Breakfast in B.C., Box 46544, Station C, Vancouver, British Columbia VGR 363, Canada, (604) 731-5942, Helen Burich and Pauline Scoten.

The Travel Tree, P.O. Box 838, Williamsburg, VA 23187, (804) 229-4037 or 565-2236 (evenings and weekends), Shiela R. Zubkoff.

Urban Ventures, 322 Central Park West, New York, NY 10025, (212) 662-1234, Frances Dworan and Mary McAulay.

"Forest Park" (*Bed & Breakfast Birmingham*); photo courtesy Neil Brake, *Birmingham News*

Birmingham Area **ALABAMA**

Classical Musicians. A restored 1920s house hosted by classical musicians, this guest house offers an accommodation with exposed-beam ceilings, a Murphy bed, a private bath, a semiprivate entrance, and a breakfast room. The hosts, a craftsman and a computer programmer, have traveled extensively in Britain and the United States. *Represented by:* Bed & Breakfast Birmingham, (205) 591-6406. $28-$32.

Red Mountain. A restored three-story frame structure, this bed and breakfast is on the side of Red Mountain. Furnished entirely with antiques, the guest rooms all have fireplaces, exposed-beam ceilings, Bahama fans, old tile baths, and working original lighting fixtures. The house has a 40-foot sitting room with two fireplaces, and the grounds include a swimming pool that guests are invited to use. *Represented by:* Bed and Breakfast Birmingham, (205) 591-6406. $65.

Children Welcome. Hosted by a couple who enjoy gardening, restoring antique clocks, and raising miniature horses and French chickens, this contemporary split-level structure is on 5 wooded acres. Guests may use the central parlor as well as the patio, and the hosts welcome children—and pets, too, as long as they can get along with the resident dog, cats, horses, and chickens. *Represented by:* Bed & Breakfast Birmingham, (205) 591-6406, $28-$32.

Forest Park. Hosted by an ex-schoolteacher, this accommodation is on a tree-lined street in the historic Forest Park neighborhood. The guest room, which has twin beds, opens onto a small porch. *Represented by:* Bed & Breakfast Birmingham, (205) 591-6406. $28-$32.

Sauna. With a living area surrounding a skylighted atrium, this white brick contemporary with floor-to-ceiling windows overlooking 3 wooded acres won awards for its architect. This guest house has a private entrance for guests, who are invited to use the pool and the sauna. The room has a kitchenette area. *Represented by:* Bed & Breakfast Birmingham, (205) 591-6406. $45-$50.

Scottsboro **ALABAMA**

The Brunton House

112 College Avenue, Scottsboro, AL 35768. (205) 259-1298.

Hosts: Norman and Jerry Brunton.

The Brunton House, painted a light blue Williamsburg and trimmed in ivory and rust, was built in the mid-1920s. Jerry and Norman bought the house from the original owner's grandson and have maintained as many of its original appointments as possible.

The dining room has a bay window at one end and a fireplace. The living room, decorated with Tudor motifs in the tradition of English pubs, features rough texture walls and beams. Jerry and Norman got the idea for a bed-and-breakfast place after spending some time in England, which they feel they experienced more fully for having stayed with local families. They have also begun a bed-and-breakfast service, for which they take reservations.

A second living room, there for the use of guests, has color television and a nonworking fireplace, whose artificial insert seems to give a pleasant glow to the room.

The first Monday of each month, and the Sunday before it, there is a First Monday Trade Day (one can find anything from soup to nuts and antiques as well) held two blocks from the Brunton House. This guest house is close to the Goosepond recreation area, which offers fishing, golf, swimming, and all manner of other outdoor activities.

Accommodations: 4 rooms with shared bath. *Smoking:* Permitted in living rooms only. *Children:* Permitted. *Pets:* Permitted outside if well behaved. *Driving Instructions:* Scottsboro is 41 miles from Huntsville on Route 72 and 30 miles from both I-24 and I-59.

"Six miles from downtown." (Alaska Private Lodgings)

ALASKA

Anchorage. Six miles from downtown Anchorage, on a wooded bluff above Cook Inlet, this bed and breakfast has views of Mt. Susitna, Fire Island, Mt. McKinley, and the Alaska Range. A private nature path leads from the hosts' property to adjoining wetlands, which in spring are rife with geese and goslings, and an occasional coyote. Three guest rooms are available, as well as a sitting room, adjoining the guest area, that is furnished with a sofa, a reclining chair, a television, a piano, and a fireplace. Forty-year residents of Alaska, with backgrounds in education and the Alaska Railroad, the hosts are interested in travel, hunting, fishing, and working their 2,000-acre gold claim. *Represented by:* Alaska Private Lodgings, (907) 345-2222. $30–$48.

Anchorage. A log structure with a steep roof and a gable and set on spacious grounds, this bed and breakfast was originally a pioneer's homestead. Now its accommodations consist of an efficiency apartment with a kitchen, a private bath, a private entrance, and bay windows overlooking "Sleeping Lady" Mountain and Mt. McKinley. Biking and hiking trails pass right in front of the house, and across the street is a small lake and a public picnic area. The

ALASKA

hosts run their antique-doll business out of a rustic log cabin adjacent to their house. The airport is a mile and a half away, and it's 4 miles to downtown Anchorage. *Represented by:* Alaska Private Lodgings, (907) 345-2222. $30–$45.

Talkeetna. This chalet-style log structure bed and breakfast was designed and built by the hosts. On 20 acres of forest, it has a stone fireplace flanked by carved totem poles, as well as exposed beams, log railings, a game room, and a sauna. The guest rooms, which share a bath, have hand-hewn log walls covered here and there with beaver pelts, and plank doors. Breakfast usually includes fresh eggs and home-baked breads or Alaska sourdough bread served with

birch syrup. You can see Peking ducks and ring-necked pheasants in the hosts' bird pen; and trumpeter swans and moose are often sighted in the marshes near the property. Talkeetna, a historic mining town, is the starting point for most Mt. McKinley climbing expeditions and close to Denali National Park. *Represented by:* Alaska Private Lodgings, (907) 345-2222. $25–$40.

Gustavus ALASKA

Gustavus Inn

Box 31, Gustavus, AK 99826. (907) 697-3311. *Hosts:* David and Joan Lesh.

Accessible only by airplane, the Gustavus Inn is a large structure that originally served as the homestead for a nine-child family. A generation later the building now functions as one of Alaska's few bed-and-breakfast places.

The Gustavus Inn is surrounded by Glacier Bay National Park, where you can observe icebergs, whales, seals sleeping on ice floes, mountain goats, and bald eagles. The park, which is the main attraction hereabouts, is awesomely beautiful.

The inn has a well-stocked bar and library, a working country kitchen, a wine and root cellar, and a greenhouse. The grounds run rife with wild berries, including strawberries, blueberries, and bog cranberries. The Salmon River, a hundred yards from the inn, yields plenty of cutthroat and Dolly Varden trout to fishermen.

The Leshes' rates include three meals, as well as airport-pickup service. They serve fresh food, which in this part of the country means salmon, halibut, and crab. The vegetables are grown on their property and harvested daily.

Accommodations: 7 rooms with shared bath. *Smoking:* Permitted in lounge areas only. *Children:* Permitted. *Breakfast:* Included. *Driving Instructions:* Accessible by plane only.

Skagway **ALASKA**

Skagway Inn

Seventh and Broadway, Box 129, Skagway, AK 99840. (907) 983-2289. *Hosts:* Wendell and Frances Long.

Originally a saloon and dance hall, the Skagway Inn was built in 1897 and moved four blocks in 1916 to its present location. The building was renovated, and the rooms were named after actual ladies of the evening, whose names had been culled from police records. Two of these ladies owned pieces of the land the hotel currently sits on.

The lobby has its 1916 wainscoting still intact, and the lounge features a player piano, a banjo, a guitar, and a television set. The guest rooms feature such items as iron beds, mirrored dressers and bureaus, and a built-in buffet.

The Longs don't serve meals, but their location is convenient to downtown Skagway, which is in the Klondike Gold Rush National Historical Park. Skagway (elevation 7,000 feet) has many nineteenth-century houses, curio shops, and gardens. The area's fishing and sight-seeing possibilities attract fishermen and naturalists from all over the world.

Accommodations: 15 rooms with shared baths. *Smoking:* Permitted. *Children:* Permitted. *Pets:* Not permitted. *Driving Instructions:* In downtown Skagway.

ARIZONA

Cottonwood. At the end of a private road and at the edge of a forest, this guest house is on 10 acres of terraced grounds where horses graze. The house has a large living room, a large paneled family room, and a glassed-in sun room. The host, a violinist and gourmet cook, operates a craft shop and an auto supply business. The ranch is ten minutes from Indian Monument and twenty minutes from Jerome, the ghost town. *Represented by:* Bed & Breakfast in Arizona, #7, (602) 995-2831. $25–$35.

Flagstaff. Ninety minutes from the Grand Canyon and twenty minutes from the Walnut Canyon Indian ruins, at the edge of a stand of pine trees, this guest house features an exterior of indigenous black rock, a greenhouse, wood paneling, and a large living room with a grand piano and a large fireplace. The hostess, who used to teach math at North Arizona University and works for a doctor part time, also offers a library and a good stereo. *Represented by:* Bed & Breakfast in Arizona, #24, (602) 995-2831. $25–$35.

Page. A contemporary wood structure with a great deal of glass and a sun patio, this guest house, on 4 acres of unspoiled desert, has a small yard with flowers. Furnished with contemporary pieces, it features wood paneling, wall-to-wall carpeting, and numerous works of American Indian art. The house is 10 minutes from Glen Canyon Dam and Lake Powell, where guests who wish to may sleep aboard the hosts' houseboat. *Represented by:* Bed & Breakfast in Arizona, #179, (602) 995-2831. $35–$45.

Payson. Something of a show place in Payson, this new three-story cathedral home is on a hill overlooking town. It features two decks, and a two-bedroom suite furnished with antiques for guests. The suite has a view, a sitting room, a private bath, and television. The hosts (one of whom heads Arizona Public Service) enjoy square dancing. *Represented by:* Bed & Breakfast in Arizona, #162, (602) 995-2831. $25–$50.

Phoenix. This 1926 Spanish-style structure features French doors, fireplaces, balconies, decks, and a Japanese garden. Each of the two floors of guest rooms has its own kitchen and laundry facilities; two apartments are also available, one of which has a silver shell basin in the bath, arcadia doors leading to a private deck patio, and a working fireplace. Furnished with a combination of antiques and contemporary pieces, the house features wood paneling and wall-to-wall carpeting. The host is a college professor. *Represented*

"Payson" *(Bed & Breakfast in Arizona #162)*

"Cottonwood" *(Bed & Breakfast in Arizona #7)*

ARIZONA

by: Bed & Breakfast in Arizona, #195, (602) 995-2831. $50–$100.

Prescott. Before he retired and she took to giving Chinese-cooking lessons, the host and hostess were teachers in the Orient. The decor here is primarily Oriental, and there's even a Japanese garden on the grounds of this brown two-patioed Victorian. The house, ten minutes from Sharlot Hall Museum, has a Grand Canyon den and many antique furnishings. *Represented by:* Bed & Breakfast in Arizona, #16, (602) 995-2831. $30–$40.

Scottsdale. This two-story contemporary home with three arches is in the exclusive McCormick Ranch area of Scottsdale, near Green Belt Park. The house features a sun deck, a swimming pool, a large stained-glass entry, and desert landscaping. An upstairs game room has a jukebox, a pool table, and a window seat. The hostess's background is in business and finance. She enjoys bicycling and church work. *Represented by:* Bed & Breakfast in Arizona, #202, (602) 995-2831. $35–$75.

Tucson. The centerpiece of this house is a large raised platform with hand-carved posts and steps that serves as a pavilion for the musical performers who often play here. A curved driveway leads to the house, which has a large pond in front and cactuses all around. The two master suites for guests have king-size beds, skylights, balconies, and Roman tubs. The house is 8 miles from Sabina Canyon and 5 miles from the University of Arizona. The host is fluent in Japanese. *Represented by:* Bed & Breakfast in Arizona, #97, (602) 995-2831. $35–$50.

Eureka Springs **ARKANSAS**

Dairy Hollow House

Route 2, Box 1, Eureka Springs, AR 72632. (501) 253-7444. *Hosts:* Ms. Crescent Dragonwagon, Mr. Ned Shank, Mr. Bill Haymes, and Ms. Carole McClearen.

Bill Haymes told me that since the 1880s Eureka Springs has had as its motto "Where the Misfits Fit," which may stem from the fact that so many artists live there. Several of them—some etching, some weaving, some painting, some tatting—had a hand in the restoration of Dairy Hollow House, an 1890 farmhouse that a writer, a historic preservationist, and a musician transformed into a carefully appointed bed-and-breakfast establishment.

The Rose Room is done entirely in shades of rose, pink, and raspberry. It has an Eastlake gentlemen's bureau made of cherry and topped with marble, a handmade Dutch Rose quilt on the bed, handwoven window shades, and an antique hooked rug. The bathroom features a skylight, etched glass, and a large claw-foot tub.

Done in blues, the Iris Room sports ornate iron beds covered with handmade quilts, as well as an oaken bureau, hooked rugs, handwoven window shades, and hardwood floors. The hosts provide fresh flowers in both rooms.

For breakfast there are German baked pancakes, fresh-baked whole-wheat butterhorns, fresh fruit in season, fresh-squeezed orange juice, and homemade jam. You can breakfast in your room if you like and the staff is responsive to special dietary needs.

Accommodations: 2 rooms with private bath. *Smoking:* Permitted. *Children:* Over 9 permitted. *Pets:* Not permitted. *Breakfast:* Included. *Driving Instructions:* Dairy Hollow House is within the Eureka Springs city limits, but guests should call for specific directions—the area has many side roads.

Hot Springs National Park **ARKANSAS**

Williams House Bed and Breakfast
   420 Quapaw Avenue, Hot Springs National Park, AR 71901. (501) 624-4275. *Hosts:* Mary and Gary Riley.
Encircled by magnolia, oak, maple, and black walnut trees, with large holly bushes bordering one side of the property, this 1890 brownstone and brick Victorian house showed up in the National Register of Historic Places in 1978.

   Inside the Williams House one discovers wainscoting, oak and walnut woodwork and doors, copper and brass antique lighting fixtures, beveled and stained-glass windows, Cupid wall sconces, a 12-foot beveled mirror, a Franklin stove, a black marble fireplace, and other antique appointments too numerous to list. The house features such diversions as a piano, a game room with a color television set (cable), and several wraparound porches. All the guest rooms, furnished with antiques and plants, are centrally air-conditioned.

   Mary and Gary serve a complimentary breakfast that's large enough for the biggest appetite—you can always have eggs with ham, bacon, or sausage and grits or hashed-brown potatoes; and when they're in the mood they rotate among eggs Benedict, baked toast amandine, omelets, waffles, pancakes, eggs fricassee, chipped beef, and other dishes.

Accommodations: 5 rooms, 2 with private bath. *Smoking:* Permitted in moderation. *Children:* Over 5 permitted. *Pets:* Not permitted. *Breakfast:* Included. *Driving Instructions:* From Little Rock, take Route I-30, then take Route 70 to Hot Springs.

Reminder: Rates and credit-card information are listed in the index.

CALIFORNIA

Anchor Bay. One hundred miles north of San Francisco, this accommodation has a private deck that overlooks the ocean. The hosts' hobbies include photography and Chinese cooking. *Represented by:* Northwest Bed & Breakfast, #500, (503) 246-8366 or 246-2383. $25–$40.

Berkeley. The hostess, who speaks French, as well as English and some German and Italian, has a large repertoire of occupations—documentary filmmaker, editor, photographer. Her home, a Mediterranean-style villa on a hillside, features a fine view of San Francisco and the bay. One room has a private patio, and the grounds, contiguous with the Berkeley hills, contain a cactus-and-succulent garden, a fern collection, and many fruit trees. *Represented by:* Bed & Breakfast International, (415) 525-4569. $36–$44.

Calistoga. The Larkmead offers four spacious guest rooms. The house is in a rural vineyard district, and a short walk will bring you to the Hans Kornell Champagne cellars or the Napa River. Breakfast is included. *Represented by:* Bed & Breakfast Exchange, (707) 963-7756. $85.

Chico. This contemporary home is beside a lake. The host is a fisherman, and the hostess plays banjo, piano, and guitar and sings with the "Sweet Adelines." Both are bridge players. They will pick up guests at the airport. *Represented by:* Northwest Bed & Breakfast, #509, (503) 246-8366 or 246-2383. $18–$30.

Healdsburg. Located in Healdsburg, one of the Sonoma Valley's smaller hamlets, the Grape Leaf is a Victorian guest house with four rooms, hosted by a young and vivacious lady who, in the afternoons, conducts casual wine tastings. The breakfast served to guests is a full one. *Represented by:* Bed & Breakfast Exchange, (707) 963-7756. $55–65.

Napa. A stunning Victorian guest house in downtown Napa, La Belle Epoque features elaborate stained-glass windows, a grand staircase, and a sun parlor. The hostess, a native of Chile, enhanced the decor of her home with many pieces of sculpture and oil paintings, as well as a collection of rare and unusual plants and handmade antique furniture. *Represented by:* Bed & Breakfast Exchange, (707) 963-7756. $65–$85.

St. Helena. A Victorian guest house, the Cottage is within walking distance of St. Helena, which has several good restaurants and

La Belle Epoque, Napa (*Bed & Breakfast Exchange*)

CALIFORNIA

a host of interesting shops. The Cottage has kitchen facilities, a barbecue area, and two bicycles available for guests. *Represented by:* Bed & Breakfast Exchange, (707) 963-7756. $55.

St. Helena. Furnished with antiques, Morgan House is a contemporary guest cottage with a swimming pool and garden that guests are invited to use. The hostess serves breakfast to her guests. *Represented by:* Bed & Breakfast Exchange, (707) 963-7756.$70.

Sonoma. Located smack in the middle of the Sonoma wine country, the Campbell Ranch, a contemporary house, has facilities that include a pool and a tennis court. One of the hosts is involved in the wine industry, which perhaps explains why guests are offered fruit wine before retiring. (They're also offered homemade pie.) *Represented by:* Bed & Breakfast Exchange, (707) 963-7756. $50–$70.

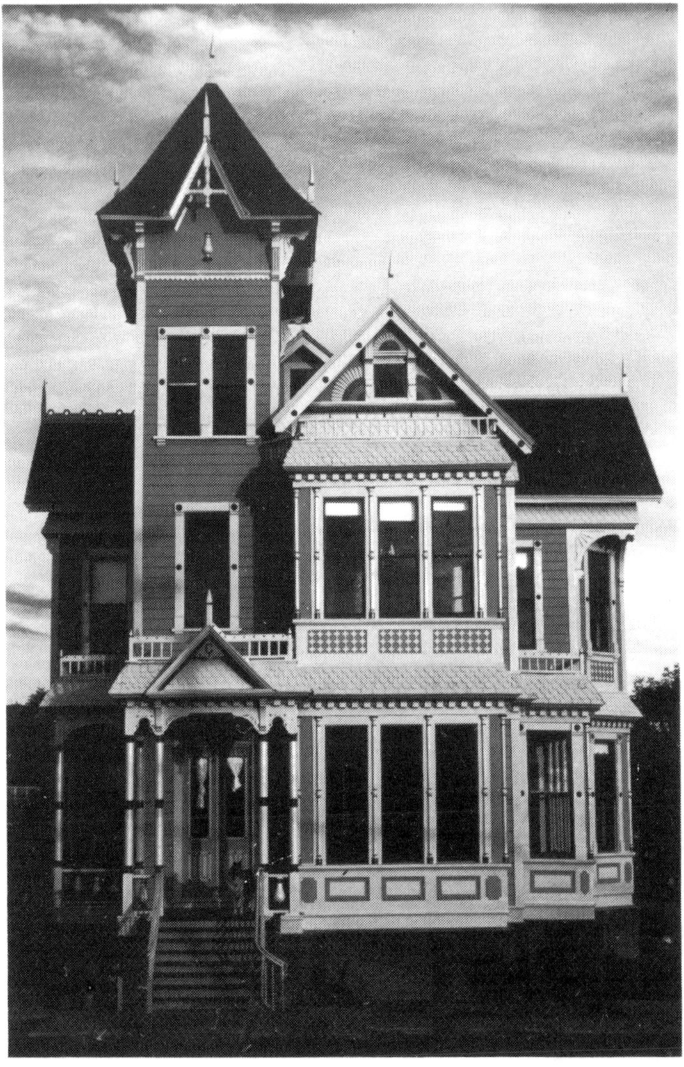

Arroyo Grande **CALIFORNIA**

The Rose Victorian Inn
 789 Valley Road, Arroyo Grande, CA 93420. (805) 481-5566.
 Hosts: Diana and Ross Cox.

The Rose Victorian Inn is an 1885 Victorian–Italian stick structure (essentially Victorian but characterized by strong vertical and horizontal lines). Painted in five shades of rose, the building takes up a full 1.5 acres, and the grounds include another 5 acres that haven't been, and won't be, developed.

The living room has an inlaid onyx fireplace with a Chinese design, burgundy carpeting, a dragon-legged armchair handcarved of ebony, a pump organ made of clear cedar stained dark, and a 13-foot ceiling with the house's original rosette and brass and a chandelier of hand-blown glass. The living room also has another fireplace, this one carved of oak, as well as a square rosewood grand piano that once belonged to General John C. Frémont. Off the living room there's a sun parlor done in white wicker with cushions upholstered in a burgundy fabric.

All the guest rooms are furnished with antiques. One room, which is 20 by 25 feet, has a mahogany armoire inlaid with oak and maple and is papered with silver, floral-print reproduction Victorian wallpaper. The bed is an antique, fashioned of brass and iron.

Hosts Diana and Ross met while in the third grade, but Diana tells me they didn't really become sweethearts until high school. Diana has a counseling and nursing background, and Ross used to be a contractor for Lion Country Safaris. (He built the largest natural-rock artificial waterfalls in the United States.)

Breakfast at the Rose Victorian is a treat: Such dishes as eggs Benedict and croissants stuffed with raisins and Parmesan cheese are parts of the typical morning meal. The restaurant is also open for dinner and Sunday brunch.

Accommodations: 6 rooms, 1 with private bath. *Smoking:* Permitted outside only. *Children:* Under 16 not permitted. *Pets:* Not permitted. *Driving Instructions:* Take Route 101 north and exit at Arroyo Grande, then turn left at the stop sign (Fair Oaks), go ¼ mile, turn left on Valley Road, and proceed for another ¼ mile.

Benicia **CALIFORNIA**

Union Hotel
   401 First Street, P. O. Box A-1, Benicia, CA 94510. (707) 746-0100. *Host:* Stan Siegel.

An 1882 structure, the Union Hotel has always been a hotel with a restaurant and a bar. It was also at one time a bordello, as were many establishments in this town. Benicia is now a rather historic town, probably because it was once, if only for a year, the state capital. The town, three sides of it surrounded by water, features many historic buildings and has plenty of antique shops and artists' studios.

Each guest room has a theme reflected by both its name and its decor. "Mei Lung," done in teals and grays, features a Chinese Chippendale armoire, a headboard that's actually a Coromandel screen, and an intricately carved Victorian seating arrangement. "Massachusetts Bay," a room with a view, has a rag rug in varying shades of plum covering an oaken floor, as well as stenciling and a spool bed. Other bedrooms may have oiled and stenciled pine woodwork, a marble-topped chest, armoires, lace curtains, a tufted headboard, inlaid period Empire pieces, a 7-foot-tall headboard, a canopy bed with a curved frame and a hand-knotted canopy. All guest rooms have private baths with Jacuzzi tubs.

Monday through Friday, the Union Hotel offers a complimentary Continental breakfast. Serious food buffs should try the hotel's restaurant, which has received a great deal of publicity. (James Beard described the food here simply but emphatically: "Delicious.") The hotel also features an elegant bar (hand carved in 1886) in a room with marble-topped tables and floor-to-ceiling stained- and leaded-glass windows.

Accommodations: 12 rooms with private bath. *Smoking:* Permitted. *Children:* Permitted though not encouraged. *Pets:* Not permitted. *Breakfast:* Included Wednesday through Sunday. *Driving Instructions:* From either Route I-80 or Route 680, take the Second Street exit—Union Hotel is one block over, on First Street by the water.

Berkeley **CALIFORNIA**

Gramma's Bed and Breakfast Inn

2740 Telegraph Avenue, Berkeley, CA 94705. (415) 549-2145.
Hostesses: Suzanne and Dorothy Jackson.

This 1902 Tudor mansion with nine fireplaces, inlaid floors, leaded-glass windows, multilevel decks, and a formal English garden, is a large stone house smack in the middle of Berkeley.

Many rooms have fireplaces, private decks, and access to the garden. Eight have private entrances. All the guest rooms are furnished with antiques, and each bed is covered by a handmade quilt.

Gramma's owners boast that "there are no surprises when it comes to comfort and convenience." Evenings, the staff serves guests complimentary sherry or, in a longtime Gramma's tradition, cookies and milk. Suzanne and Dorothy Jackson also offer a Continental breakfast that includes freshly baked croissants, homemade preserves, and a pot of coffee.

If Grammas's accommodations don't succeed in spoiling you, its location will. Next door to the University of California at Berkeley, across the bridge from San Francisco, and almost adjacent to Tilden National Park, Gramma's tends, as grammas do, to be close.

Accommodations: 19 rooms with private bath. *Smoking:* Permitted, but no cigars or pipes. *Children:* Over 6 permitted. *Pets:* Not permitted. *Breakfast:* Included. *Driving Instructions:* Take Route I-80 to Ashby turnoff, which runs into Telegraph Avenue; go three blocks.

Carmel CALIFORNIA

Holiday House

Camino Real at Seventh, Carmel, California. *Mailing Address:* P.O. Box 782, Carmel, CA 93921. (408) 624-6267. *Hosts:* Kenneth and Janet Weston.

A five-minute walk from the beach, Holiday House is a 1905 brown shingled cottage with dormered windows on its upper floor, a sun parlor, and a terrace that overlooks the garden. The house was originally built as a summer cottage by a professor from Stanford University, and in the 1920s two sisters from Kansas bought the place and began the guest-house operation that has been going on, under various owners, ever since.

The living room features a large stone fireplace, views of the ocean and the garden, a plethora of books and games, and a grand piano. The furnishings include antique pieces.

Three of the guest rooms have ocean views, and the other three overlook the garden. The upstairs rooms have slanted ceilings, and the hosts make sure that all the guest rooms have ample supplies of fresh flowers and jelly beans.

Kenneth and Janet serve guests complimentary sherry and offer a breakfast that comes with homemade coffee cake or muffins.

Accommodations: 6 rooms, 2 with private bath. *Smoking:* Permitted on the terrace. *Children:* Under 6 not permitted. *Pets:* Not permitted. *Breakfast:* Included. *Driving Instructions:* Take the Ocean Avenue exit off Route 1, continue on Ocean through town to Camino Real, turn left, and Holiday House will be on the right, just before Seventh Avenue.

Carmel CALIFORNIA

San Antonio House

P.O. Box 3683, Carmel, CA 93921. (408) 624-4334. *Host:* Bruce Levett.

San Antonio House is a large, shingled turn-of-the-century house with flowered patios and a sizable lawn. An old Monterey Pine, at least 4 feet in diameter, almost touches one corner of the house.

San Antonio House offers four guest suites, all of them with a private entrance, telephone, television set, and refrigerator. One suite, on the top floor, has three rooms and a view of the ocean. The guest-room furnishings include antiques, bright fabrics, and paintings and photographs. There are paintings by Van Gogh and Lautrec, photographs of Europe, and books everywhere.

Accommodations: 4 suites with private bath. *Smoking:* Permitted. *Children:* Permitted. *Pets:* Permitted. *Breakfast:* Included. *Driving Instructions:* Take Route 1 to Ocean Avenue in Carmel near the beach; the house is on San Antonio Avenue between Ocean and Seventh.

Castro Valley **CALIFORNIA**

Bergman's
22051 Betlen Way, Castro Valley, CA 94546. (415) 881-1533.
Hostess: Lore Bergman.

Lore's place is a pale olive California bungalow with dark olive trim, on a half acre planted with camellias, amaryllis, rhododendrons, azaleas, and tulips, and wooded with sweet gums, redwoods, ginkgos, and fir trees.

The house, furnished with a mixture of antique and contemporary pieces, has hardwood flooring throughout. Its living room has a pale beige area rug, two easy chairs upholstered with a handwoven gray wool fabric, a walnut bookcase with a mirrored bar, a German vase transformed into a lamp with a silken shade, and a walnut desk from Sweden. On the wall hang a burgundy, rose, black, and beige camel saddle and an original Dürer etching of a madonna.

One guest room has a king-size bed, a large window overlooking the garden, a teak bookshelf/chest/desk, teak end tables, an etching by a local artist, and a large abstract oil that Lore's son painted. The other guest room, done entirely in blues, has a blue Oriental rug.

Lore's idea of breakfast is elaborate: at least two types of imported cheese (brie and roquefort, for example), baguettes, black German bread, freshly-ground coffee, homemade jams and jellies, homemade waffles, and sour cream pancakes.

Lore's idea of going for a drive is to jump into her Saab 900 Turbo and take her guests on week-long tours of such places as the Grand Canyon, Bryce Canyon, Death Valley, Taos, and the Hopi Indian Reservation. If you like to drive yourself, Lore will rent you her car, which will do 50 mph in second gear.

Accomodations: 2 rooms with private bath. *Smoking:* Permitted. *Children:* Not permitted. *Pets:* Not permitted. *Breakfast:* Included. *Driving Instructions:* Call for specific directions.

Cloverdale **CALIFORNIA**

Vintage Towers
 302 North Main Street, Cloverdale, CA 95425. (707) 894-4535.
 Hosts: Tom and Judy Hayworth.

A Victorian, Queen Anne tower house with three turrets (one round, one square, and one octagonal), Vintage Towers is at the corner of two wide and quiet residential streets. A wisteria-covered veranda looks out on a garden that yields roses the size of grapefruits and whose pomegranate, persimmon, plum, apple, cherry, and other trees enclose the grounds almost completely. The garden also has a gazebo, which Tom built.

The ground-floor parlor has a golden oak piano, an antique mahogany Pianola, a solid-oak griffin rocking chair, and a maroon Oriental rug with a pattern in light blue and black. The entire ground floor is wainscoted in clear fir, and the library, with more than a thousand volumes, is always open to guests. The dining room, a rather formal one, has leaded-glass windows overlooking the garden and reflecting the fireplace on the wall opposite.

Each guest room has a theme. One actually has a carousel horse in it, another is done in dark reds and furnished with dark woods, and another has a private terrace and a sitting area. All the rooms are furnished with antiques.

Accommodations: 7 rooms, 4 with private bath. *Smoking:* Permitted on the veranda and the balcony only. *Children:* Under 10 not permitted. *Pets:* Not permitted. *Breakfast:* Included. *Driving Instructions:* Vintage Towers is one block east of Route 101 in the town of Cloverdale, at the corner of Third and Main Streets.

El Cajon (San Diego area) **CALIFORNIA**

Bud and Dot Shackelford

11532 Rolling Hills Drive, El Cajon, CA 92020. (619) 442-3164.

Hosts: Bud and Dot Shackelford.

This is the house that Bud built, and designed and architected. Dot considers it her husband's best work of art, although the Grumbacher and Strathmore companies, who sponsor Bud's annual demonstration and workshop tours throughout the United States, might disagree.

The grounds seem almost overrun by trees—eighteen avocados, six oranges, a lemon, a lime, a grapefruit, a tangelo, and a pecan, most of which produce year-round. A large wooden deck with a view in three directions runs around the house. The living room and family room walls have rough cedar paneling, and the exposed cedar-beam ceilings in the center of the house go as high as 15 feet. The house, most of it carpeted wall-to-wall, features large glass windows and sliding doors, a fireplace with Italian black marble trim, and an unobstructed view of 50 miles.

The Shackelfords provide a complimentary full breakfast including tree-fresh orange juice and homemade marmalade. Guests may swim in their pool.

Accommodations: 3 rooms, 1 with private bath. *Smoking:* Permitted. *Children:* Permitted. *Pets:* Not permitted. *Breakfast:* Included. *Driving Instructions:* Rolling Hills Drive is 10 minutes from El Cajon and 30 minutes from San Diego.

Eureka   **CALIFORNIA**

Carter House Inn

    1033 Third Street, Eureka, CA 95501. (707) 445-1390. *Hosts:* Mark and Christi Carter.

Even if being chauffeured around in a concourse-condition 1958 Bentley doesn't excite you; even if complimentary wine and hors d'oeuvres in the afternoon leave you cold, even if tea and cookies or cordials waiting when you return from dinner seems a bore; even if a breakfast prepared by someone who used to be a pastry chef fails to do it—Carter House Inn will still impress you.

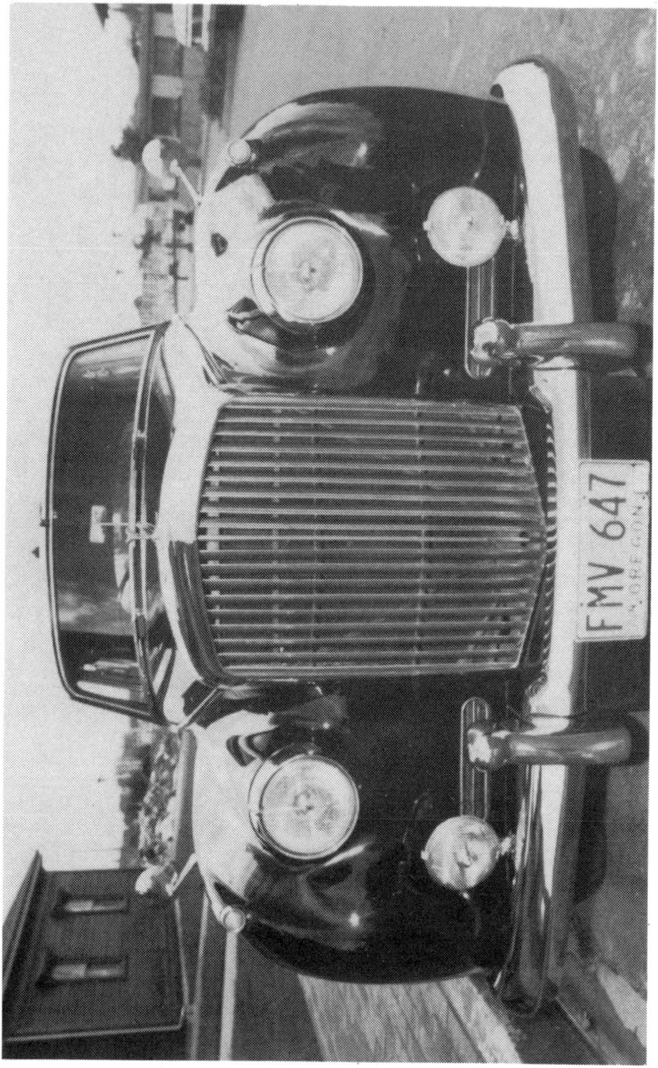
FMV 647

An 1884 Victorian stick structure with clear-heart redwood shingles and two 50-foot chimneys, Carter House Inn was built between 1980 and 1982—and built according to 1884 specifications. After discovering the original plans for the Murphy House, a San Francisco mansion designed by the same architects who created the Carson Mansion and the Pink Lady buildings, Mark Carter handpicked a construction crew and re-created the building (the original was destroyed in the 1906 earthquake).

The inside of the house is finished in polished redwood and oak. You can see your face in the floors, which are of oak. One bedroom features an old oaken headboard with a subtle hand-carved fleur-de-lis pattern, a blue down comforter, an inlaid oaken table, Scandinavian pine chairs with dragons carved into their backs, a Persian rug, and a view of Humboldt Bay. Another guest room has two double beds with hand-carved oaken headboards, Burgundy down comforters, Oriental rugs in blues and reds, an oaken sideboard, and a wardrobe made of flame mahogany.

For breakfast there are a fresh tart or pastry, fruit compote, homemade bran muffins, orange juice, tea or coffee, and bagels and lox when the salmon are running.

Accommodations: 3 rooms, 1 with private bath. *Smoking:* Permitted. *Children:* Permitted. *Pets:* Not permitted. *Breakfast:* Included. *Driving Instructions:* If entering Eureka from the south, take Fifth Street to L Street and make a left, then go two blocks. If entering town from the north, take Fourth Street to L Street and a make a right, then go one block.

Eureka   **CALIFORNIA**

Old Towne Bed and Breakfast

    1521 Third Street, Eureka, CA 95501. (707) 445-3951. *Hosts:* Agnes and Bob Sobrito.

Old Towne Bed and Breakfast is an 1871 gable-roofed Greek Revival house painted light blue and trimmed white with accents in dark blue. It was originally on the site of the Carson mansion and indeed was once inhabited by the Carsons. But William Carson gave the place to a man who'd beed injured in one of his mills, and then it was moved. If you're lucky, it will stay where it is, and under its current management.

    The house is surrounded by interesting plantings including a seventy-five-year-old rhododendron that's 20 feet tall and 8 inches in diameter, a tree-sized camellia, an old lilac bush, and the leaning peach tree of Eureka, which is supported by a brick.

    The central living room has raspberry-colored wall-to-wall carpeting, a brick fireplace fronted by a hand-hooked wool rug that picks up the colors in the carpet, a traditional sofa upholstered in beige mohair, a cherry coffee table, cherry end tables with brass lamps whose shades have translucent shells, an antique rocker covered with a beige fabric, and easy chair upholstered in white.

    The Raspberry Parfait room has a brass bed, two birch hand-carved antique chairs, a small walnut table, a Tiffany lamp, and a large oaken Victorian dresser.

    Breakfast here is generous—homemade muffins, peaches and cream, French toast, quiche, and eggs Benedict. The Sobritos serve complimentary wine between four and six in the afternoon. Bob and Agnes own ten bicycles, which guests are invited to use.

    Accommodations: 5 rooms, 3 with private bath. *Smoking:* Not permitted. *Children:* Not permitted unless quiet and well-behaved. *Pets:* Not permited. *Breakfast:* Included. *Driving Instructions:* Call for specific directions.

Fort Bragg **CALIFORNIA**

Country Inn

632 North Main Street, Fort Bragg, CA 95437. (707) 964-3737.
Hosts: Helen and Don Miller.

Surrounded by a white picket fence, Country Inn is a late-nineteenth-century redwood structure, a little more than two and a half blocks from the Pacific Ocean. Fort Bragg is along a ruggedly beautiful stretch of the Pacific, and the town is flanked by two state parks.

The Millers have a sunlit sitting room with a potbellied stove backed and supported by brick, contemporary Colonial-style furnishings upholstered with print fabrics, dark brown wall-to-wall carpeting, an owl, and an eagle. The owl, which Don carved out of white poplar, sits on the table where guests find coffee and breakfast in the morning and wine in the afternoon. The eagle, also carved by Don out of a block of black walnut, measures 54 inches. Other pieces of wood sculpture (a bas-relief of a mermaid, a madonna and child, an abstract) as well as Don's photographs dress up this room and the hallways.

Each guest room has a chandelier-type fixture with a dimmer, floral-print wallpapers, and redwood woodwork. Six rooms feature wainscotting. Granny's Attic has a sloping ceiling, wainscotting, a queen-size bed built into the wall, delicate floral-print wallpaper, and a clawfooted tub in its bath.

The breakfast includes coffee or tea, juice, fresh fruit, and from two to five kinds of nut- and fruit breads. (Helen has three sources for the berries she puts into her breads.)

There's plenty to do in and around Fort Bragg. The area is rife with galleries and restaurants, and the natural attractions include whales and sea lions.

Accommodations: 8 rooms with private bath. *Smoking:* Permitted in guest rooms only. *Children:* Not permitted. *Pets:* Not permitted. *Breakfast:* Included. *Driving Instructions:* Country Inn is on Main Street in Fort Bragg.

Geyserville **CALIFORNIA**

Hope-Merrill House
21253 Geyserville Avenue, Geyserville, CA 95441. (707) 857-3945. *Hosts:* Rosalie and Bob Hope.

Built between 1870 and 1885, Hope-Merrill House is a Victorian Eastlake stick-style structure with a wraparound porch filled with plants and furnished with 1920s rattan pieces from the Philippines. In restoring the house, Rosalie and Bob sought out elegant period wallpapers and had them reproduced by a hand silk-screen process.

The central living room's 6-inch-wide redwood plank floor is partially covered by a Kurman-design rug in blues and cranberries. It has hand-carved walnut Eastlake furniture upholstered in cranberry velvet, and a hand silk-screened reproduction William Morris wallpaper entitled "Bird and an Enemy." Pocket doors 10 feet high connect the living room and the dining room, which is papered with a hand silk-screened P.D. White design titled "The Lily" and features bay windows and a cast-iron fireplace painted to look like Italian marble.

One guest room features a 24-inch frieze of stylized peacocks, a fireplace, a small walnut table and matching pair of side chairs, and an ecru coverlet on the bed. Another guest room has a 9½-foot-tall, elaborately carved walnut headboard from 1865, a Victorian chaise longue covered in linen and velvet, and a marble-topped dresser. One room is done entirely in wicker.

Rosalie and Bob serve a full country-style breakfast, and offer complimentary wine each afternoon.

Accommodations: 5 rooms, 2 with private bath. *Smoking:* Permitted on porch area. *Children:* Check in advance. *Pets:* Not permitted. *Breakfast:* Included. *Driving Instructions:* Take Route 101 into Geyserville and follow Geyserville Avenue through town—Hope-Merrill House is on the west side of the road.

Geyserville **CALIFORNIA**

Isis Oasis Lodge and Cultural Center

20889 Geyserville Avenue, Geyserville, CA 95441. (707) 857-3524. *Hosts:* Lorna Vigne and Paul Ramses.

When the San Francisco city legislature passed a law forbidding its residents to harbor exotic animals, Lorna Vigne—who happened to own six ocelots, three bush babies, and a tarantula—decided to move. She has led a life that seems to strain coincidence: her achievements in San Francisco include presiding over the birth of the first ocelot ever born in that city, as well as running, out of a work-home complex of buildings, the Nori Enamelcraft Company.

The Isis Oasis comprises several buildings on a large parcel of land. The grounds include a mini-zoo, a pool, a sauna, and a meditation tree—a four-hundred-year-old Douglas fir whose trunk has divided three times. The parlor, with a fireplace in the middle and a view of the pool, features a billiard table and other diversions.

The guest rooms are furnished, as Lorna says, in country exotic. There's plenty of bamboo, plants, wood, white walls, and Indian bedspreads. A recent addition to the lodge is a wine-barrel room that is, one hears, popular with honeymooners.

In addition to running a guest house that offers complimentary wine and breakfast, Lorna has founded a group called the Isis Society for Inspirational Studies. She and the society's director—Paul Ramses, a Past Life Therapist—conduct workshops.

Lorna calls her facilities "not a motel, but rather a sharing of a very special place on our planet."

Accommodations: 12 rooms with shared baths. *Smoking:* Permitted. *Children:* Permitted with advance permission. *Pets:* Tolerated. *Breakfast:* Included. *Driving Instructions:* From San Francisco, take Route 101 to the Geyserville exit; the lodge's driveway is the second on the left.

Healdsburg **CALIFORNIA**

Camellia Inn

211 North Street, Healdsburg, CA 95448. (707) 433-8182.

Hosts: Ray and Del LeWand.

Named for the thirty varieties of camellias that grow in its garden, the Camellia Inn is an 1869 Italianate town house with a villa-style swimming pool behind it and a tiled fishpond near the front. Owned at one time by a physician, the building served as Healdsburg's first hospital.

Furnished with antiques, the Camellia Inn features such appointments as inlaid hardwood floors, chandeliers hanging from high ceilings, and many Oriental rugs. The parlor has twin marble fireplaces, and in the dining room there's an imposing carved and tiled mantel.

The "Firelight" room has a fireplace with a carved oak mantel, a Queen Anne bay window, a silk-screened frieze, an Oriental rug, an antique armoire, a queen-size brass bed, an antique shaving mirror that used to belong to Del's grandfather, a private bath, and a private entrance. The "Royalty" room, originally the dining room, features tall, arched windows that overlook the veranda, a huge maple tester bed, brass fixtures, a medallioned ceiling, a private bath, and a private entrance.

Other guest rooms, all done in warm salmon tones, have such appointments as a claw-foot tub-shower, lace curtains, a marble-topped dresser, a hand-crocheted bedspread, and armoires. All rooms contain fresh flowers, and guests are offered complimentary wine.

Accommodations: 6 rooms, 4 with private bath. *Smoking:* Reluctantly permitted. *Children:* Not permitted. *Pets:* Not permitted. *Breakfast:* Included. *Driving Instructions:* From Santa Rosa, take Route 101 north and exit at the second Healdsburg exit; then turn right at North Street.

Blackthorne Inn

266 Vallejo Road, Inverness, CA. *Mailing address:* P.O. Box 712, Inverness, CA 94937. (415) 663-8621. *Hosts:* Judith Pollack, Susan Hemphill, Bill Hemphill, and Sarah Scott-Mitchell.

Built of redwood, cedar, and a 180-foot Douglas fir cut and milled at the building site, Blackthorne Inn is a 1976 tree house. That's right, a tree house. Fragrant bay trees surround the structure, which has four levels connected by a spiral staircase that rises through an octagonal tower. A 2,500-square-foot deck wraps around the main level, which features a glass solarium, whose inside walls are made of doors salvaged from the old San Francisco railroad depot, and an A-frame living room with a large stone hearth.

One flight up from the main level is a room with stained-glass windows, a queen-size bed, and two balconies; a garret room on the same floor has an antique brass bed and a private bridgeway to another deck, which features a hot tub and a cold tub installed there for guests' use.

Still higher up the rising spirals, one comes to an octagonal-shaped room that's almost entirely enclosed by glass. Called "The Eagle's Nest," it features a private sun deck on its roof and a skywalk that leads to the hot-tub deck.

For acrophobes, lovers of shade, night-life buffs, or late sleepers, there's a secluded room with a private entrance below the main floor.

Blackthorne Inn, on the Point Reyes Peninsula, is very close to the Point Reyes National Seashore and a little more than an hour from San Francisco.

Accommodations: 4 rooms with shared bath. *Smoking:* Permitted. *Children:* Permitted. *Pets:* Not permitted. *Breakfast:* Included. *Driving Instructions:* From San Francisco take Route 101 north to Lucas Valley Road and proceed through Nicasio and Point Reyes Station; turn right at Green Bride and proceed 1¼ miles to Vallejo Road (a dirt road) and look for number 266.

Ione   **CALIFORNIA**

The Heirloom

214 Shakeley Lane, Ione, CA 95640. (209) 274-4468. *Hostesses:* Patricia Cross and Melisande Hubbs.

The Heirloom is an 1863 two-story brick Colonial structure, situated on 1.5 acres of private grounds. Magnolia, crepe myrtle, chinaberry and walnut trees totally enclose the lawn, which has four sets of chairs and umbrellaed tables and a small white gazebo.

The ground-floor parlor—where complimentary sherry, tea, or coffee is always available for guests—contains a rosewood piano that once belonged to Lola Montez, a 400-year-old refectory table from Italy, an elaborately hand-carved chest made entirely of teak in China, and a wood-burning fireplace surrounded by overstuffed sofas and wing chairs upholstered in a brillant Williamsburg blue.

One guest room has a private bath, a working fireplace with a reproduction of an early Degas hanging from the brick wall above it, a walnut Eastlake bed with a matching dresser, and two French doors that open onto a semiprivate balcony, which overlooks the lawn. Another room has a brass bed and a private balcony, with chairs, a love seat, and a table, that faces the tops of 75-year-old trees.

Pat (a former housewife, missionary, and business manager) and Sandy (previously a registered nurse and a housewife) serve a generous complimentary breakfast. The fare includes cheese and sour-cream crepes, hot popovers, freshly squeezed orange juice, fresh fruit, and home-ground coffee. Pat and Sandy, in period costumes, serve their guests breakfast in bed.

Accommodations: 4 rooms, 1 with private bath. *Smoking:* Permitted. *Children:* Permitted. *Pets:* Not permitted. *Breakfast:* Included. *Driving Instructions:* The Heirloom is in the center of Ione.

Jackson **CALIFORNIA**

Ann Marie's Lodgin and Gallery

410 Stasal Street, Jackson, CA 95642. (209) 223-1452. *Hostess:* Ann Marie Joseph.

Ann Marie, a pretty and seemingly indefatigable hostess, has an 1892 country-Victorian house with bay windows and a gable embellished with a fish-scale motif. An artist who works in acrylics, charcoal, pencil, and pen and ink, and also writes articles for *Off Road* magazine, she sometimes sketches on the baseboards of her house. Ann Marie also grows most of her own food and puts up her own preserves. The "grub ... 9 A.M." is a complimentary breakfast that includes fruits in season, juice, meat pie, and coffee or tea.

The 1892 Victorian house is furnished mostly with pieces from her grandparents' farm. Her paintin's and sketchin's cover the holes in the walls, she observes.

Ann Marie serves complimentary wine each afternoon, and brandy is always available in the parlor and on the guest rooms' side tables.

Unlike the many hosts who don't allow children, Ann Marie will provide baby-sitting for her guests.

Accommodations: 3 rooms with private bath. *Smoking:* Permitted in the parlor only. *Children:* Permitted. *Pets:* Not permitted. *Breakfast:* Included *Driving Instructions:* Take Route 49 to North Main Street; turn right at the first stoplight, and right at the first intersection, which is Stasal Street.

Jackson CALIFORNIA

The Court Street Inn
 215 Court Street, Jackson, CA 95642. (209) 223-0416. *Hostess:* Mildred Burns.

The California State Historic Resources Commission recently designated the Court Street Inn a "State Point of Historic Interest" and placed it in the National Register of Historic Places. The facade is typical of nineteenth-century gold-country architecture; but once you step inside, you won't encounter anything merely typical.

The parlor, where guests are served complimentary sherry, has a white marble fireplace, a black ebony Chinese screen with a bird pattern inlaid in stones of various shades (jades and soap-stones primarily), a hand-carved Belter couch upholstered in a pink brocade fabric, a beige-and-pink Oriental rug, a marble-topped Eastlake table, and a Hong Kong chest made of camphor wood with hundreds of tiny figurines carved at least half an inch in relief.

One ground-floor guest room contains Eastlake spoon-carved furniture, a beige Oriental rug with a tree-of-life pattern in shades of rust, a wood-burning fireplace, a marble-topped dresser with a mirror, an antique desk, and a collection of antique photographs. Another ground-floor guest room is furnished with Queen Ann pieces, and has a magenta Oriental rug and a floral-design rose-colored wallpaper. The room also has a sun-parlor sitting area with three exposures, furnished with rattan and carpeted in a brilliant green. Of the seven guest rooms, three have private baths, and the others share two.

The complimentary breakfast here is as varied and sumptuous as the furnishings.

Accommodations: 7 rooms, 3 with private bath. *Smoking:* Permitted. *Children:* Not permitted. *Pets:* Not permitted. *Breakfast:* Included. *Driving Instructions:* From Jackson take Main Street to Court Street and drive up the hill.

Laguna Beach **CALIFORNIA**

Carriage House

1322 Catalina Street, Laguna Beach, CA 92651. (714) 494-8945.

Hosts: Vernon and Dee Taylor.

A designated historical landmark, the Carriage House is a 1920 Colonial-style structure. The cupola on the roof was added by Louis B. Mayer (the second *M* in MGM) when he owned the building, which is a five-minute walk from the Pacific Ocean.

The Carriage House features a central courtyard with a brick floor and a profusion of plants and flowers—some on hanging planters, some in ornate ground-level pots, some in huge built-in brick planters. Moss hangs from a gnarled carrotwood tree.

Each guest suite has a sitting room and a separate bedroom—some have two bedrooms, some have fully equipped kitchens. Decor combines antiques and modern furnishings, and plants everywhere.

Guests find a complimentary bottle of California wine and bowl of fresh fruit waiting for them in their suites. Afternoon refreshment is always available in Grandma Fean's Dining Room, whose carved-wood chairs and antique chests seem the perfect backdrop for the family-style complimentary breakfast.

Accommodations: 6 suites with private bath. *Smoking:* Pemitted. *Children:* Permitted. *Pets:* Permitted if well behaved. *Breakfast:* Included. *Driving Instructions:* From Laguna take the Coast Highway south to Cress Street, turn east to Catalina Street.

Little River **CALIFORNIA**

Glendeven

8221 North Highway 1, Little River, CA 95456. (707) 937-0083.
Hosts: Jan and Janet De Vries.

Two miles south of Mendocino and adjacent to Van Damme State Park, Glendeven is an 1867 New England-style house. Eucalyptus trees shade the garden, where such flowers as camellias, princess flowers, and a rare acacia bloom in their proper seasons. A path winds through the state park to the ocean, its shore ruggedly beautiful in this part of the country.

Jan and Janet De Vries both have backgrounds in art and contemporary crafts, and their house shows it. Tasteful posters—a Georgia O'Keeffe here, the Cloister's unicorn series there—as well as strong contemporary paintings and ceramics, catch the eye continually. The artwork blends effortlessly with the many green plants.

The sitting room, where Janet serves a complimentary breakfast of freshly baked muffins, fresh fruit, juice, coffee, and eggs, has a dark mahogany baby-grand piano, a sofa-and-chair set covered in Belgian linen, a fireplace, and some 20-odd feet of windows facing south. Oriental rugs lie on a subtle puce-gray carpet. One guest room has a fireplace and French doors that open onto a private balcony; another has a slanted wall with two skylights.

Accommodations: 6 rooms, 4 with private bath. *Smoking:* Permitted in the sitting rooms only. *Children:* Permitted only by prior arrangement. *Pets:* Not permitted. *Breakfast:* Included. *Driving Instructions:* On Route 1, located 2 miles south of Mendocino.

Little River   **CALIFORNIA**

Victorian Farmhouse
P.O. Box 357, 7001 Highway 1, Little River, CA 95456. (707) 937-0697. *Hosts:* Tom and Jane Szilasi.

The Victorian Farmhouse was built in 1877 by John and Emma Dora Dennen, who came to this area from Maine, as many pioneers did. The grounds, which occupy several acres, include an apple orchard and flower gardens.

The inn is several hundred yards from the ocean, and some of the rooms, two of which feature redwood ceilings, have ocean views. Another room overlooks a private flower garden, and one suite features a French wood-burning stove and a sitting room. All rooms, as well as the public areas, are furnished with antiques. All bedrooms have either king- or queen-size beds.

The main parlor has a fireplace and, not far away, a decanter of sherry to keep guests warm. The Victorian living room upstairs overlooks the flower garden.

The Szilasis bring a complimentary breakfast of juice, coffee or tea, fresh fruit, and hot breads and muffins to their guests' rooms each morning.

Accommodations: 4 rooms with private bath. *Smoking:* Permitted. *Children:* Over 16 permitted. *Pets:* Not permitted. *Breakfast:* Included. *Driving Instructions:* On Route 1, 2½ miles south of Mendocino.

Los Angeles Area **CALIFORNIA**

Beverly Hills (near). The host, a social worker, has two rooms for guests; but one of these is available only when her daughter is away at college. The house, on Comstock Avenue a short walk from Wilshire Boulevard, Beverly Hills, and UCLA, has a garden, which the main guest room overlooks. *Represented by:* Bed & Breakfast International, (415) 525-4569. $38–$46.

Burbank. A retired teacher of music and art, the host of this accommodation frequently guides guests around the Hollywood studios, about which he knows a great deal. The house, on a quiet residential street, is a mile from the NBC studios. *Represented by:* Northwest Bed & Breakfast, #651, (503) 246-8366 or 246-2383. $25–$40.

Camerilla. In an avocado orchard, this turn-of-the-century ranch house features a large living room with an exposed-beam ceiling and a huge stone fireplace. Guests are invited to use the large wine-barrel spa in back of the house, and there's a play area for children in front. The hostess will prepare gourmet meals for a slight charge and gives guests limited kitchen privileges as well as full use of the laundry facilities. *Represented by:* Bed & Breakfast of Los Angeles, #2C, (213) 889-8870 or 889-7325. $30.

Hermosa Beach. The host, a high-school teacher interested in music and theater, has a home right on the Pacific shore. The ocean is just outside the front door, and the house's porch is perfect for watching sunsets. One guest room has a king-size bed and a private bath with a Jacuzzi. *Represented by:* Bed & Breakfast International, (415) 525-4569. $28–$48.

Huntington Beach. This accommodation, 3 miles from the ocean and 30 minutes from Disneyland, features an outdoor pool, a covered patio, and parakeet aviaries. The hosts cultivate such hobbies as bridge, gardening, and golf. *Represented by:* Northwest Bed & Breakfast, #652, (503) 246-8366 or 246-2383. $18–$34.

La Habra. Ten miles north of Disneyland, slightly east of Los Angeles, this contemporary house is done in various shades of peach, and matching pink and green-print fabrics cover much of its furniture. The living room has a fireplace and television, and the grounds include a large patio and a swimming pool, as well as tennis courts that are lighted for night play. The hosts, fluent in Spanish and French, offer two guest rooms with shared bath. *Represented by:* Bed & Breakfast of Los Angeles, (213) 889-8870 or 889-7325. $35.

Los Angeles Area **CALIFORNIA**

Malibu. This new, contemporary-style home high in the hills overlooking Malibu features several decks and two-story, windows with a spectacular view of the California coastline. Appointments include large exposed beams, deep brown carpeting, Mexican floor tiles, and an extensive collection of folk art. The guest room features a king-size bed, a sitting area with television, a private bath, and a private balcony overlooking the mountains. *Represented by:* Bed & Breakfast of Los Angeles, #6C, (213) 889-8870 or 889-7325. $40.

Newport Beach. Two hundred yards from a private swimming beach and an easy walk from the ferry to Catalina Island or Disneyland, this guest house is hosted by an attorney and his wife. The guest suite, which has a private entrance, includes two bedrooms and a sitting area with a fireplace and a refrigerator. *Represented by:* Bed & Breakfast International, (415) 525-4569. $36–$46.

Ventura. This restored, 1930s traditional-style home has two guest rooms available—one with a king-size bed, and another with a queen- and a twin-size bed. An elevator affords easy access to the second floor and a protected patio and loggia with Ping-Pong and shuffleboard facilities. The hosts invite guests to share their television and refrigerator and can arrange for baby-sitting. *Represented by:* Bed & Breakfast of Los Angeles, #1C, (213) 889-8870 or 889-7325. $25–$35.

Westlake Village. Surrounded by greenbelts and bike paths, and within easy walking distance of movies and shops and restaurants, this large two-story home is in Westlake Village's exclusive First Neighborhood. Guests are invited to use the pool, patio, Ping-Pong table, and barbecue. The hosts have bicycles available for guests and can arrange for baby-sitting. *Represented by:* Bed & Breakfast of Los Angeles, #3C, (213) 889-8870 or 889-7325. $30–$35.

Little South Fork. A manufacturer and a former public relations professional are hosts at this sprawling single-story contemporary structure. It is on grounds with numerous patios, a gazebo with a barbeque/wet bar, a swimming pool and stables complete with eight horses. Available are three guest rooms, as well as a master suite with a king-size bed, private bath, a sitting room with a fireplace and television, and sliding doors that open onto the pool. *Represented by:* Bed & Breakfast of Los Angeles, (213) 889-8870 or 889-7315. $40–$60.

Malibu **CALIFORNIA**

Casa Larronde

22000 Pacific Coast Highway, Malibu, CA 90265. (213) 456-9333.

Hosts: Jim and Charlou Larronde.

A thirty-year-old, 4,000-square-foot house, Casa Larronde has had many tenants, including Lee Marvin, Ben Gazzara, Laurence Harvey, Jayne Mansfied, Connie Stevens, Judy Garland, John Travolta, and Rodney Dangerfield. Perhaps these movie stars moved into the house because of the neighbors: Johnny Carson, Flip Wilson, Jennifer Jones, and Carol Burnett have homes in the same strip of beach. Locals call the area Millionaire's Row.

If show business bores you, you can look at the stars overhead or watch the sun sink into the Pacific. Even those who loathe California's tinsel and glamour have to admit the place looks gorgeous when you have your back to it and are squinting at an ocean horizon bisecting a blood-orange sun.

Jim and Charlou have plants growing two stories high in the stairwell. The living room has a fireplace, a library, and exposed beams in the ceiling. The master bedroom also has a fireplace, as well as 40 feet of windows facing the ocean. The property features a 60-foot private beach overlooked by an ocean porch where you may have your complimentary breakfast if you like.

Accommodations: 1 room with private bath. *Smoking:* Permitted. *Children:* Permitted. *Pets:* Permitted occasionally, check first. *Breakfast:* Included. *Driving Instructions:* Drive 12 miles north from Santa Monica on the Pacific Coast Highway.

Mendocino CALIFORNIA

The Headlands Inn
 44950 Albion Street, Mendocino, CA 95460. (707) 937-4431.

Hosts: Pete Albrecht, Lynn Anderson, and Kathy Casper.

A few hundred yards from the Pacific Ocean, on a hill that overlooks it, is The Headlands Inn, a restored 1868 Victorian building painted ivory and trimmed in brown. It was originally a barber shop but was reincarnated over the years as a saloon, a hotel annex, a private residence, and, currently, a bed-and-breakfast inn.

The three front guest rooms—all have fireplaces, and one has bay windows—face directly on the ocean and the Mendocino coastline with its blue water and white surf and rugged mountains. The third-floor guest rooms feature redwood window seats in dormer windows, and a second-floor room has a parlor stove on a round hearth backed by glistening copper. Another room, with a wrought-iron parlor stove, opens onto a private balcony that overlooks the village of Mendocino.

Beige carpeting runs throughout the halls and the guest rooms, framed antique maps hang everywhere, and tiny Victorian print wallpapers and dark woods are prominent in the decor. Every quilt in the place was made by hand; fresh flowers are on every breakfast tray and in every room.

Pete, Lynn, and Kathy bring a complimentary breakfast to your room; if you like, they will start a fire for you if your room has a fireplace. "It's a lot of work," says Lynn, "but the people are worth it."

Accommodations: 5 rooms with private bath; 1 cottage room with private bath and fireplace. *Smoking:* Permitted. *Children:* Over 16 permitted. *Pets:* Not permitted. *Breakfast:* Included. *Driving Instructions:* From Cloverdale, take Route 128 to Route 1 North; exit at Mendocino and proceed to Albion Street.

Monterey **CALIFORNIA**

The Jabberwock

598 Laine Street, Monterey, CA 93940. (408) 372-4777. *Hosts:* Jim and Barbara Allen.

Named after Lewis Carroll's famous poem, the Jabberwock is a 1911 neo-Victorian gabled structure painted cream and forest green. The house, which was a Roman Catholic convent during its first thirty years, has several porches, one of which wraps around its bay side and overlooks the water. The grounds contain two 20- by 50-foot waterfalls, one of which has five streams feeding three tiered pools.

The living room has a brick fireplace, forest-green wall-to-wall carpeting, furnishings from the 1920s, and wainscoting painted cream. The dining room, which faces Monterey Bay, also has a fireplace, as well as an oaken floor on which is an Oriental rug in shades of maroon.

The 15- by 35-foot Borogrove Room ("All mimsy were the borogroves") features a mahogany king-size bed with four down pillows, a down comforter, and percale sheets with lace borders; a fireplace; dark forest-green wall-to-wall carpeting; and a Victorian love seat and chair upholstered in a delicate tapestry fabric. The third-floor guest rooms, which overlook the bay, have slanted ceilings covered with reproduction Victorian print wallpapers.

Host Jim Allen, who has been involved in at least thirty restorations, is a fireman; and Barbara has been active in the hotel business for 15 years. Jim and Barbara supply guests with bathrobes, complimentary wine and hors d'oeuvres, fresh flowers, and other amenities such as shoe-polishing service.

Accommodations: 5 rooms, 2 with private bath. *Smoking:* Permitted. *Children:* Not permitted. *Pets:* Not permitted. *Breakfast:* Included. *Driving Instructions:* Take Route 68 west to Route 1 South, exit at Monterey, and then turn right at Camino Aguajito, left at Del Monte, and left again at Hoffman.

Murphys   **CALIFORNIA**

Dunbar House

P.O. Box 1375, 271 Jones Street, Murphys, CA 95241, (209) 728-2897. *Hosts:* John and Barbara Carr.

Surrounded by seven 50-foot-tall elms, some small pines, and lots of plantings left behind by a previous owner who was president of a local gardening club, Dunbar House is an 1880 Italianate painted white with blue shutters. It is a hop, a skip, and a jump from Angels

Camp—the site each May of the Mark Twain Frog Jumping Contest—and from Calaveras Big Tree State Park, an extensive stand of giant sequoias.

The central living room, carpeted wall to wall, has contemporary teak furnishings including a pair of couches upholstered in a blue and ivory swirl fabric and a wall unit full of books on regional subjects, Hummel figures, and a record collection with everything from jazz to Brazilian to romantic selections. The common rooms as well as the guest rooms are decorated with the work of local artists, and delicate Brazilian lace scarves show up throughout.

One guest room has an oaken queen-size bed with matching armoire and a white down comforter with a floral pattern in pale green and pink. Its walls are decorated with the work of local artists as well as some framed dried-flower arrangements. A few steps up from this room is a shared bath that has wide-board pine floors, a 15- by 22-inch sink set into a hollowed-out oaken buffet, a 1920s beveled mirror vanity, a white wicker chair, plenty of green plants, and lace curtains over louvered windows.

John and Barbara serve a Continental breakfast each morning, and iced tea, lemonade, and sherry each afternoon.

Accommodations: 5 rooms with shared bath. *Smoking:* Permitted. *Children:* Over 10 permitted. *Pets:* Not permitted. *Breakfast:* Included. *Driving Instructions:* From Angels Camp take Route 4 east for 8 miles, then turn left onto Main Street and proceed to the first stop sign—Dunbar House is 200 yards from here, on your left.

Napa CALIFORNIA

The Beazley House

1910 First Street, Napa, CA 94558. (707) 257-1649. *Hosts:* Jim and Carol Beazley.

Nicely shaded by the large, mature maple trees distributed about its front lawn, the Beazley House is a 1902 Colonial Revival house with a hipped roof. A large oak tree shades the entire backyard, where guests often relax.

The ground-floor parlor, where guests are always welcome, has a fireplace, two Prussian blue wing chairs, an overstuffed couch covered in beige linen with a blue-and-green floral pattern, and a brass serving cart stocked with complimentary sherry and a variety of teas. Adjoining the parlor is a library and music room. Guests are invited to use the stereo (except in the morning, when it plays Mozart during breakfast) or to read any of the more than four hundred volumes in the library, which, Jim being a former photo journalist, contains an extensive collection of photography books.

The foyer is dominated by the blue Persian rug on its hardwood floor and the large oaken staircase leading to the second floor. The stairs are carpeted in a dark powder blue, and six steps or so above the foyer, on the staircase's landing, there's a stained-glass inset of rich orange roses on a Tiffany blue background 6 feet in diameter.

Accommodations: 4 rooms with shared baths; 4 carriage-house rooms with private bath and fireplace, 2 with hot tub. *Smoking:* Not permitted. *Children:* Under 12 not permitted. *Pets:* Not permitted. *Breakfast:* Included. *Driving Instructions:* The house is in central Napa, at the corner of First and Warren streets.

Napa **CALIFORNIA**

Gallery Osgood

2230 First Street, Napa, CA 94559. (707) 224-0100. *Hosts:* Joan Osgood and Howard Moehrke.

Situated on grounds featuring a ninety-year-old fig tree, three 60-foot birches, and fifteen rose and camellia bushes, Gallery Osgood is an 1889 Queen Anne structure. As its name implies, it functions as an art gallery as well as a bed-and-breakfast place. Here, guests enjoy fresh flowers in their rooms, complimentary wine whenever they feel like it, and a complimentary breakfast (Joan's a gourmet cook) served in a room filled with original art. The work of twenty-five artists is on display throughout the house, as well as Joan's work, mainly silkscreens, and Howard's stained glass.

The living room has a pair of down-filled love seats; a combination gas-electric brass chandelier; a dragon-design Persian rug in shades of brown, gold, peach, and blue on an apricot background; a brass fire-extinguisher lamp with a handmade stained-glass lampshade; an original Leroy Nieman serigraph, lithographs, watercolors, and a piece with the title "One Hundred Birds Paying Homage to the Queen."

The Blue Room, furnished entirely with period antiques, has an 8-foot walnut bed with a matching dresser, a decorative 6-foot hand-carved crucifix from Mexico, a late-nineteenth-century tapestry complete with falcons, and a mahogany Victrola. The Rose Room has an Art Nouveau stained-glass window depicting a blue and purple bird against a background of reds and roses; Bill Blass bedding; wicker furniture; and a collection of photographs.

Breakfast is served in one of the gallery rooms, which has a bay window with an off-white Austrian valence and all manner of artwork—lithographs, serigraphs, ceramics, silkscreens, stained glass, and photographs.

Accommodations: 2 rooms with shared bath. *Smoking:* Permitted. *Children:* Not permitted. *Pets:* Not permitted. *Driving Instructions:* Take Route 29 to the Napa/First Street ramp; proceed one block left on Second Street, one block left on Seymour Street, then turn left on First and watch for Gallery Osgood on the right.

Napa **CALIFORNIA**

Yesterhouse Inn

643 Third Street, Napa, CA 94559. (707) 257-0550. *Hosts:* Susan and Jack Harrison and Paula Weir.

Yesterhouse Inn is an 1896 Queen Anne Victorian house with small orange trees in its yard and a rose garden between its main building and two guest cottages.

One host used to be an electronics draftsman with Hewlett Packard, and another runs a group interested in antiques that meets each week at the inn.

The front parlor has a chandelier, a white marble fireplace, a red Victorian loveseat, red-floral-on-white Victorian wallpaper, red-on-red drapes over white linen curtains, and a red, ivory, and turquoise Oriental rug. The library, likewise furnished with antiques, contains more than six hundred books on antiques. The sun porch has a brown and tan Persian rug on the floor, many hanging plants, and a lace-covered table surrounded by four bentwood chairs. Hand-carved beds appear in most guest rooms, and every quilt and afghan in the house is handmade.

The rates here include a complimentary breakfast of pastries and breads, fresh fruit, and coffee or tea. Complimentary wine is served each evening.

Accommodations: 6 rooms, 3 with private bath. *Smoking:* Permitted. *Children:* Tolerated. *Pets:* Not permitted. *Breakfast:* Included. *Driving Instructions:* From Silverado Trail, take Third Street west to its intersection with Burnell.

Orosi CALIFORNIA

Valley View Citrus Ranch

14801 Avenue 428, Orosi, CA 93647. (209) 528-2275. *Hosts:* Tom and Ruth Flippen.

Surrounded by three olive trees, twenty-six bougainvillea vines, and a hundred or so geranium plants, the Valley View Citrus Ranch is a 1964 structure, with Spanish or Mexican design overtones. Several of the bathrooms and the kitchen have Spanish tiles. Encircled by orange, peach, and avocado orchards, the grounds contain two patios and a 70-foot porch. The Valley View is a working orchard ranch that produces, primarily, oranges and ruby-red seedless grapes.

The living room, which has a brick fireplace, overstuffed furniture upholstered in shades of green, and wood-paneled walls, overlooks a valley, and on a clear day you can see the ocean. One

61

guest room features Indian wall hangings, a private entrance, a private bath, a king-size bed, and wall-to-wall carpeting.

On the grounds are a clay tennis court and a trailer, which Ruth told me she and Tom stayed in during a period when they had an overflow of guests. There's also a 15-foot gazebo.

Ruth serves either a Continental or a full breakfast, depending on her guests' preferences.

Accommodations: 4 rooms, 2 with private bath. *Smoking:* Permitted. *Children:* Permitted. *Pets:* Permitted if arranged for *far* in advance. *Breakfast:* Included. *Driving Instructions:* The house is 8 miles east of Denuba on El Monte (Avenue 416). Follow El Monte to Route 144, then go north 2 miles to Avenue 428, turn right, and go ¾ mile to the house on the hill.

Pacific Grove **CALIFORNIA**

The Gosby House Inn

643 Lighthouse Avenue, Pacific Grove, CA 93953. (408) 375-1287.

Hosts: Roger and Sally Post.

In search of a climate warmer than that of his native Nova Scotia, P. F. Gosby traveled to California and decided to settle in Pacific Grove, a small city on the Monterey Peninsula. Gosby built this Victorian mansion in 1887, and operated it as a boardinghouse for Methodist church members who attended summer retreats in Pacific Grove. When the only other hotel in the area burned down, Gosby began to expand his house.

The house, now in the National Register of Historic Places, has been totally restored—its original stained glass and wood moldings seem almost new. Guest rooms, several of which have fireplaces, are all furnished with antiques and have quilts, silk flowers, ruffled curtains, and reproduction wallpapers.

A Continental breakfast is served each morning in the parlor, or guests may want to take their breakfasts to the backyard, the front porch, or their rooms. Each afternoon, complimentary sherry, apple cider, and tea are served.

Accommodations: 19 rooms, 13 with private bath. *Smoking:* Not permitted. *Children:* Over 12 tolerated. *Pets:* Not permitted. *Driving Instructions:* Take Route 1 to the Pebble Beach—17 Mile Drive turnoff; turn right onto Route 68 and follow it to Forest Avenue in Pacific Grove; continue on Forest to Lighthouse Avenue, then turn left and go three blocks.

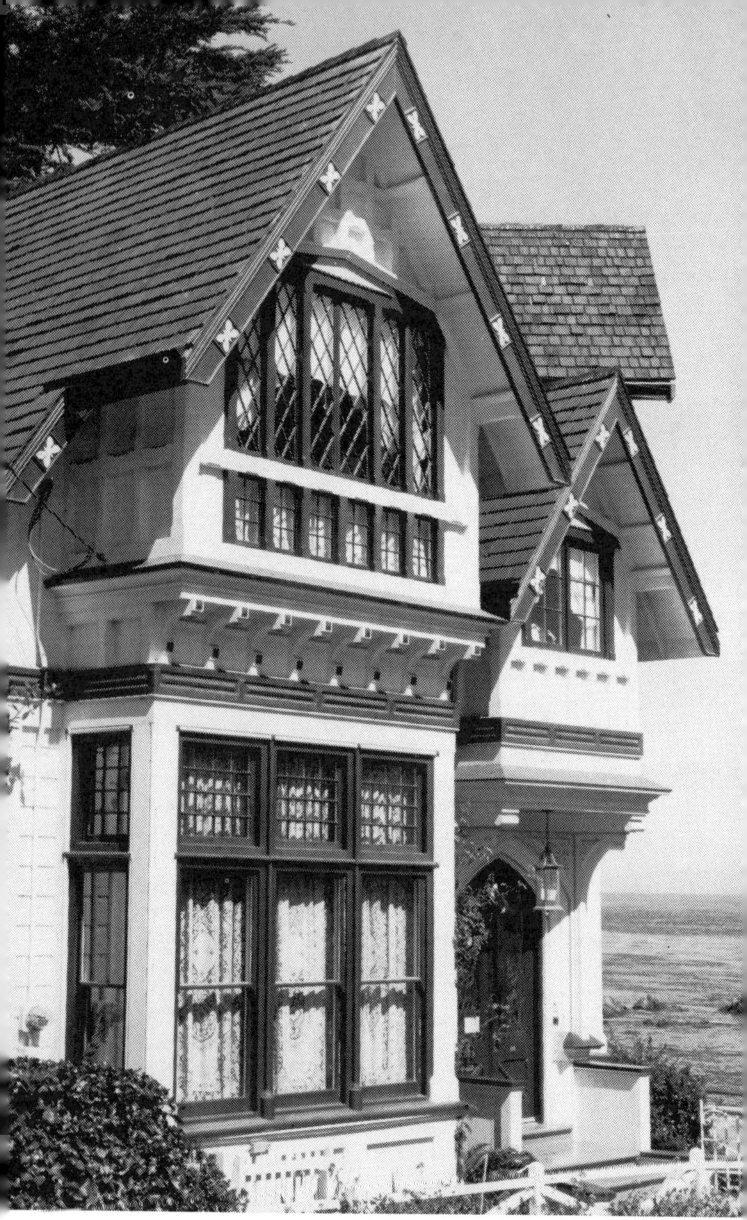

Pacific Grove **CALIFORNIA**

Green Gables Inn

104 Fifth Street, Pacific Grove, CA 93950. (408) 375-2095. *Hosts:* Sally and Roger Post.

This 1888 Victorian building is, as its name suggests, a many-gabled structure with leaded-glass windows here and there and an intricate brickwork chimney and chapel. The house overlooks Monterey Bay, one of the Pacific Ocean's more pacific inlets. A small cove beach is directly across the road from the inn.

The guest rooms, decorated with antiques and reproduction wallpapers, contain such niceties as window seats. One room has a ladder leading to a small attic that faces the ocean. The downstairs rooms—a large living room for guests, a den, a dining room, and a kitchen—feature high ceilings, stained-glass windows, and breathtaking views.

Sally and Roger Post serve a complimentary breakfast each morning, serve sherry and homemade appetizers each afternoon, happily make dinner reservations for guests, and always make sure to direct them to areas of special interest.

Accommodations: 5 rooms with shared baths plus 1 suite with private bath; open June 15 through August 1. *Smoking:* Not permitted. *Children:* Over 12 tolerated. *Pets:* Not permitted. *Driving Instructions:* Take Route 1 to the Pebble Beach—17 Mile Drive exit; turn right onto Route 58; continue to Forest Avenue in Pacific Grove; follow it to Ocean View Boulevard and turn right; continue to Fifth Street.

Placerville   **CALIFORNIA**

The Fleming Jones Homestead

3170 Newtown Road, Placerville, CA 95667. (916) 626-5840.
Hostess: Janice Condit.

In 1883, Fleming Jones, a homesteader who seldom gambled, won a great deal of money. Slapping the cash down on the table, the story goes, he said to his wife, "There, go build your new house." Fleming and Florence Jones transformed their gambling windfall into a farmhouse built entirely of clear lumber and surrounded it with a large lawn bordered by a wall of hand-hewn stones. The homestead comprises 11 acres of meadows and woods.

From the outside the Fleming Jones Homestead appears to be a working farm, and it is. Chickens and hens roam the property, either ignoring guests or looking for a handout; two antique burros and a Welsh pony, willing to be ridden after they've dined, graze in the meadows. To keep it from awakening the guests at 4:30 A.M., the owner locks the rooster in the barn.

From the inside the homestead appears to be a rare cache of

antiques and artwork. The dining room has a 54- by 138-inch oaken table supported by carved griffin legs. The central parlor, where guests gravitate toward complimentary sherry, has two Morris rockers upholstered in a fabric of dusty rose, a curved Chinese bed-table made entirely of teak, and several paintings by Olga de Chica, the celebrated Colombian primitive artist.

One guest room combines a 6-foot carved-oak headboard, walls covered with pale yellow wainscoting, and a series of etchings the owner picked up while teaching English in South America.

Another guest room has walls covered almost entirely by framed pressed-flower collages assembled by the owner's great-uncle, a botanist. The walls in the Lovers Fancy room are peach and match the peach and ivory fabric of the room's two corner screens as well as the comforter that covers an iron and brass bed.

Janice Condit tries to make her place "A retreat, where city people can escape the craziness, wander in the woods, get back in touch with themselves, you know."

Accommodations: 5 rooms, 3 with private bath. *Smoking:* Permitted. *Children:* Under twelve not permitted. *Pets:* Not permitted. *Breakfast:* Included. *Driving Instructions:* Take Route 50 to Newtown Road and turn right just past the pond.

Placerville CALIFORNIA

Morey House

805 Lilac Lane, Placerville, CA 95667. (916) 621-1186. *Hosts:* Jim and Marlene Moore.

Morey House, a white 1859 farmhouse with a column-supported brick porch, is on 1 ½ acres that are heavily wooded with more than seventy 75- to 100-foot incense and deodar cedars, three Ponderosa pines, black and red locust trees, and a few hundred-year-old rose bushes.

The central living room, roughly 24 feet square, features ivory wall-to-wall carpeting, an oaken Victorian secretary, a 1917 Victrola, an oaken waiting bench from a train station, a corner fireplace with a rosewood mantel, two wing chairs upholstered in a burnt sienna velvet, an oaken Morris chair, and Marlene's great-great-grandfather's sword, with which he fought in the Civil War.

One typical guest room has wall-to-wall carpeting, a marble fireplace, a brass and iron bed covered with a down comforter, a walnut burl dresser topped with marble, a watercolor by Evelyn Chamberlain, and a private bath with a marble vanity. The dining room has a brick fireplace as well as an oaken dining table with pressed-back chairs made of oak, an antique Singer sewing machine cabinet full of silverware, a heavily carved oaken china closet, and a turn-of-the century nickel-plated National cash register.

The Moores serve a full breakfast—eggs Benedict, thickly sliced French toast with real maple syrup, crepes, home-baked muffins, freshly ground coffee, fruit compote, juice, and . . .

Accommodations: 3 rooms with private bath. *Smoking:* Permitted in parlor and on porch only. *Children:* Over 12 permitted. *Pets:* Not permitted. *Breakfast:* Included. *Driving Instructions:* Take the highway north into Placerville, turn right on Coloma Avenue, then go one block to High Street and turn right—High Street becomes the Moores' private drive.

St. Helena **CALIFORNIA**

Hotel St. Helena

1309 Main Street, St. Helena, CA 94574. (707) 963-4388. *Host:* Ralph Usina.

Built in 1881, the Hotel St. Helena, which once entertained Lily Langtry, deteriorated over the years to little more than a hangout for derelicts. Owner Carl Johnson, a Santa Barbara restorer, redecorated the hotel tastefully inside and out and runs it today as a bed-and-breakfast place.

The furnishings are a subtle blend of antique and contemporary pieces. The burgundy, tan, and brown wallpaper throughout the hallway sets the color scheme for the rooms, which are painted in burgundy, mauve, chocolate brown, dark tan, or pale gold. There's a burgundy love seat on either side of a fireplace in the sitting room at the top of the hall stairs. The patterns of the quilted bedspreads pick up the colors of the rooms.

The larger guest rooms feature brass or carved-wood headboards, armoires, cloth-covered tables, and lounge chairs; the smaller rooms have ladder-back chairs and painted iron headboards. The four rooms without private baths have bent-willow headboards and marble-topped commodes. All rooms have white shutters and wall-to-wall carpeting. One of the two suites features a sitting room with a fireplace.

Guests tend to congregate in the lobby-reception area, where a fire blazes when it's cold, and wine flows regardless of the climate.

Accommodations: 18 rooms, 14 with private bath. *Smoking:* Permitted. *Children:* Not permitted. *Pets:* Not permitted. *Breakfast:* Included. *Driving Instructions:* The hotel is right on Main Street in St. Helena (you can't miss it).

San Diego Area **CALIFORNIA**

Mission Bay Beach. Directly on Mission Bay Beach, this three-story suite has an uninterrupted view of the bay and the ocean and consists of two bedrooms, a kitchen, a living room, a deck, and a private entrance. For a nominal fee guests may use the health club managed and owned by the host, who is interested in sports. The suite is conveniently near San Diego's restaurants and shopping areas. *Represented by:* Carolyn's Bed & Breakfast Homes, (619) 435-5009 or 481-7662. $50–$125.

La Jolla. The hostess, a high-school business teacher who works part time in real estate, offers guests a room, with a private bath, in her condominium, which has a pool and a Jacuzzi that guests may use. She enjoys sports and cooking, and her home is close to the University of California at San Diego and two new shopping centers. *Represented by:* Bed & Breakfast International, (415) 525-4569. $32–$40.

Stained-Glass—Woodburning Stove. Twenty-five minutes from downtown San Diego, in a stand of pines overlooking a valley, this bed and breakfast features a screened-in porch, exposed-beam ceilings, a fireplace, a woodburning stove, and lots of stained glass. There are a large garden and an orchard on the grounds, over which strut the chickens who provide the eggs for breakfast. The hosts, who own a well-known Lemon Grove restaurant, are interested in quilting, antique restoration, weaving, and, of course, stained glass. *Represented by:* Carolyn's Bed & Breakfast Homes, (619) 435-5009 or 481-7662. $28–$40.

Near Theaters. This *ca.*-1900s canyon bungalow bed and breakfast is a short walk from the restaurants, theaters, and other San Diego attractions. Accommodations consist of a suite with a private entrance, garden patio, and deck, as well as cable television and an efficiency kitchen. The host works in fashion and entertainment planning and production, and has interests in classic cars, motorcycles, antiques, music, and the theater. *Represented by:* Carolyn's Bed & Breakfast Homes, #23, (619) 435-5009 or 481-7662. $50–$125.

La Mesa Canyons—Swimming Pool. This bed and breakfast in the hilly canyons of La Mesa has grounds with a swimming pool overlooking the canyon beyond the house and running fountains in the back and front yards. The hostess, a legal secretary who speaks Spanish and German, welcomes children providing they can

House #24 (Carolyn's Bed & Breakfast Homes)

House #1 (Carolyn's Bed & Breakfast Homes)

San Diego Area **CALIFORNIA**

swim, and she has guest rooms with both private and shared baths. Fiesta Dinner Theater is minutes away. *Represented by:* Carolyn's Bed & Breakfast Homes, #3, (619) 435-5009 or 481-7662. $30–$40.

Near La Jolla Beach. On a hill above the ocean, this large custom-designed house is a short walk from downtown La Jolla and the famous La Jolla Shores beach. Sea World, the San Diego Zoo, and the Del Mar racetrack are short drives away. Accommodations consist of a suite with two bedrooms, a private bath, a living room with a fireplace, and a private deck overlooking the ocean, as well as color television, a Jacuzzi, and a large patio. The hosts will arrange to meet guests at the airport. *Represented by:* Carolyn's Bed & Breakfast Homes, #1 (619)435-5009 or 481-7662. $50–$125.

Town Houses. Surrounded by trees and walkways, this contemporary town house is convenient to shopping, restaurants, and the bus line. The hostess, an educational coordinator for the regional vocational program, also plans and directs tours, primarily to the garment district of Los Angeles. She collects art and has interests in travel, dance, and reading. For a small fee she will pick up guests at the airport and extend them laundry privileges. *Represented by:* Carolyn's Bed & Breakfast Homes, (619) 435-5009 or 481-7662. $30–$40.

Beach and Jacuzzi. The hosts of this bed and breakfast across the street from a secluded ocean beach are a couple interested in tennis, golf, traveling, and art collecting. They invite guests to use their beach equipment; and, in case the ocean's too rough, guests may use their Jacuzzi and patio. A private television room for guests has cable and HBO, and there is a private entrance to the guest quarters. The beach here is popular with surfers. *Represented by:* Carolyn's Bed & Breakfast Homes, #25, (619) 435-5009 or 481-7662. $40–$70.

San Diego **CALIFORNIA**

Britt House

406 Maple Street, San Diego, CA 92103. (619) 234-2926. *Hosts:* Daun Martin, Charlene Brown, and Robert Hostick.

Britt House, a white 1887 Victorian building, was built by an attorney and has served over the years as everything from a teahouse to a chiropractor's office. The grounds contain a formal garden, from which come the flowers that decorate every room.

The entrance hall has an ornate staircase, and behind it there's a stained-glass window the size of a wall—a triptych that depicts morning, afternoon, and evening primarily with blue, red, green, and opal glass. The window catches the afternoon sun and lights the entrance way like a Chinese lantern. The parlor has a nonworking tiled fireplace, a carved Victorian couch upholstered in a rust velour, and light and dark rust reproduction Victorian print wallpaper.

The guest rooms have reproduction Victorian wallpapers, hardwood floors, and antique furnishings. One guest room has a sofa that used to belong to Ludwig, the "mad" king of Bavaria. There's also a small cottage, which has a kitchenette, a private bath, and quite a few antique pieces, primarily made of oak. One of the bathrooms has a sauna, which guests are invited to use.

Guests are greeted with a complimentary glass of wine, and each room contains fresh fruit and candies. Breakfast (juice, breads, a soft-boiled egg, and coffee) is brought to your room.

Accommodations: 8 rooms with shared baths; cottage. *Smoking:* Permitted. *Children:* Check in advance. *Pets:* Not permitted. *Breakfast:* Included. *Driving Instructions:* From I-5 take the airport exit onto Kettner Boulevard, go 1 mile, turn left on Laurel and again on third, and turn right on Fourth, which runs into Maple.

San Diego **CALIFORNIA**

The Cottage

3829 Albatross Street, San Diego, CA 92103. (619) 299-1564.

Hosts: Robert and Carol Emerick.

Painted terra-cotta and trimmed in various shades of sienna, The Cottage is a 1944 clone, albeit smaller, of a 1916 California barn bungalow, painted the same colors and on the same grounds. The house, as well as the cottage, which is for guests, are on property dressed up with begonias, lilies, impatiens, morning glories, and other flowers, and wooded with black locust, pine, avocado, and lime.

The guest cottage, a self-contained little house furnished entirely with antiques, has a living room, bedroom, full kitchen, and complete bath. The living room has fir flooring, a woodburning stove, a Wilton wool rug, an antique oaken pump organ, an oaken rocker with a cane seat, and brass lamps with etched or milk-glass shades.

The bedroom has a king-size bed, a filigreed brass nightstand, fir flooring, a dresser fashioned of cherry, mahogany, and maple, an oaken frame mirror, and serveral turn-of-the century hand-colored photographs.

The kitchen has everything you need for preparing meals, including a commercial coffee-grinder and fresh roasted beans; a Continental breakfast of fresh fruit, home-baked breads, juice, and coffee is delivered to the cottage each morning.

Accommodations: 1 cottage with private bath. *Smoking:* Permitted. *Children:* Permitted. *Pets:* Not permitted. *Breakfast:* Included. *Driving Instructions:* From Route 5 South, exit at Washington; turn left and go half a mile to University Avenue; take University east for a mile to Front Street; turn right on Front and go one block to Robinson; turn right again and go one block to Albatross; turn right again and look for The Cottage on your right.

"Pier 39" (*American Family Inn*)

San Francisco **CALIFORNIA**

Pier 39, Fishermans Wharf. This 45-foot sailboat docked at San Francisco's Fisherman's Wharf offers a captain's cabin, a mate's cabin (both large enough for two), two heads, and a galley-sitting area. The entire interior is paneled in mahogany. Fisherman's Wharf is rife with shops and restaurants. The host doesn't stay on the boat with his guests. *Represented by:* American Family Inn, (415) 931-3083. $100 per couple per night.

Sixth Avenue. A short walk from Golden Gate State Park, this turn-of-the-century three-story house features a 12- by 24-foot combined bedroom and sitting room with antique furnishings, a private

Golden Gate Park (American Family Inn)

San Francisco **CALIFORNIA**

bath, and television. Another room features a stereo, television, and a sitting area. Street parking is available. *Represented by:* Bed & Breakfast International, (415) 525-4569. $36–$48.

Golden Gate Park. This English Tudor mansion bed and breakfast is furnished entirely with antiques. The guest rooms have marble fireplaces and private baths, and one bed has an 8-foot-high hand-carved headboard. The central living room features a grand piano and a fireplace, and the entrance has cast-iron doors. *Represented by:* American Family Inn, (415) 931-3083. $55–$75.

Noe Valley. A 1900 Victorian structure with a wisteria-covered archway in front and a deck with a hot tub in the back garden, this guest house is a fifteen-minute walk (five minutes by bus) from downtown San Francisco. The host, a restaurateur in both Quebec and France, speaks fluent French. The house is furnished with period

San Francisco **CALIFORNIA**

antiques, most of them from France. A gourmet breakfast is served. *Represented by:* American Family Inn, (415) 931-3083. $40–$55.

Sutter Street. Built in 1889 by Colonel Isaac Trumbo, this house is one of San Francisco's historic homes. The guest suite has a private bath, a dining room with television, and a kitchen. The hosts are a school principal and an educational-agency worker, and their home is within walking distance of downtown San Francisco. *Represented by:* Bed & Breakfast International, (415) 525-4569. $34–$46.

Cow Hollow. Hosted by a retired professional ice skater who's now a free-lance photographer, this guest house is a recent Victorian-style structure with bay windows. Many of the furnishings are antique, such as the huge carved oaken bed in one of the guest rooms (the other guest rooms have brass beds). The host speaks English, French, German, and Russian. A full breakfast is served. *Represented by:* American Family Inn, (415) 931-3083. $40–$55.

San Francisco Victorian
(Bed & Breakfast International)

San Francisco **CALIFORNIA**

The Bed and Breakfast Inn

4 Charlton Court, San Francisco, CA 94123. (415) 921-9784.

Hosts: Marily and Bob Kavanaugh.

On a quiet, mews-type street in the middle of one of San Francisco's most fashionable areas, The Bed and Breakfast Inn is a beautifully restored pair of adjacent Victorian town houses.

One suite has a private balcony, a living room, a kitchen, and a carpeted spiral staircase that leads to the bedroom, which overlooks the Golden Gate Bridge. Another guest room features a sunken bathtub large enough for two. Several rooms overlook the scrupulously tended garden. Each guest room contains antiques, books that you should have read, a complimentary carafe of sherry, and fresh flowers.

The complimentary breakfast is brought to your room on a tray set with Copeland, Spode, or Wedgwood china. At bedtime, look before you lie down: Whoever turns the beds down places fortune cookies on the pillows, and you might have to shake the crumbs out of your hair while reading a fortune like "The cistern contains, the fountain overflows."

Advance reservations are strongly recommended.

Accommodations: 9 rooms, 5 with private bath. *Smoking:* Permitted. *Children:* Under twelve not permitted. *Pets:* Not permitted. *Breakfast:* Included. *Driving Instructions:* Take Court Street to Charlton Court, a half-block street.

San Francisco **CALIFORNIA**

Bock's Bed and Breakfast

1448 Willard Street, San Francisco, CA 94117. (415) 664-6842.
Host: Laura J. Bock.

Bock's Bed and Breakfast is a 1906 Edwardian-style structure that was built immediately after the San Francisco earthquake. On a hill in the Parnassus Heights area (adjacent to Sutro Forest), the house has a spectacular view of San Francisco and the hills surrounding it. The front yard is full of flowering Japanese plum trees.

The living room, carpeted in a warm shade of green, has a piano and a pair of French doors that open onto a deck overlooking the city. Each guest room, carpeted wall to wall, features twin beds, fresh flowers, a small refrigerator, and an electric coffeepot. Laura recently completed renovating the house's Edwardian entry room, dining room, and staircase, stripping away old paint and exposing the redwood-paneled walls. The dining room, where Laura serves a Continental breakfast (fresh juices and fruit in season, fresh rolls with English marmalade and jams, and coffee and tea), also affords a splendid view.

Laura, a free-lance business-services consultant, invites guests to share her garden, which has a patio and lawn furniture. The garden, which used to be quite a formal one, is frequented by Pokey McTavish, a Scottish terrier not at all undisposed to visitors.

Accommodations: 2 rooms, 1 with private bath. *Smoking:* Permitted. *Children:* Permitted. *Pets:* Not permitted. *Breakfast:* Included. *Driving Instructions:* Three blocks from Golden Gate Park.

San Francisco **CALIFORNIA**

Casa Arguello

225 Arguello Boulevard, San Francisco, CA 94118. (415) 752-9482. *Hostess:* Emma Baires.

Located a few blocks from the Golden Gate Bridge in the Presidio Heights section of town, Casa Arguello is an extremely large apartment. At one time it was an annex for Lone Mountain College and Emma Baires had twenty-four coeds living with her. Mrs. Baires, obviously, loves company.

The apartment contains electrified wall sconces, chandeliers, French doors, curved windows, and antique furnishings. There are brass beds, gilded mirrors, heavily tufted chairs, numerous plants, and molded walls and ceilings.

Emma has a large living room with a long couch covered in an elegant floral print fabric, two tufted chairs upholstered in beige, two other tufted chairs and a matching tufted love seat, and an antique coffee table usually bedecked with flowers.

The apartment has a two-room master suite on the main floor, as well as four bedrooms on the upper floor. The upstairs bedrooms overlook the gardens of surrounding homes.

Visitors from all over the world come to stay here, and one would be hard pressed to tell if they come for the elegance, the warmth, the convenience, or all three.

Accommodations: 4 rooms, 1 with private bath. *Smoking:* Permitted. *Children:* Under 7 not permitted. *Pets:* Not permitted. *Breakfast:* Included. *Driving Instructions:* Arguello Boulevard is in Presidio Heights, three blocks from the Golden Gate Bridge.

San Francisco **CALIFORNIA**

Casita Blanca
330 Edgehill Way, San Francisco, CA 94127. (415) 564-9339.
Hostess: Joan M. Bard.

Built about 1920, Casita Blanca is a small West Coast cottage that is completely separate from the main house and that has a location unique for San Francisco—it's on top of a hill that overlooks parts of the city and the bay (it has a view of the Golden Gate Bridge), and it's surrounded by hundred-year-old pine trees.

Essentially a large studio room, the cottage features a painted brick fireplace, an alcove with a small desk, a dining area, a completely equipped kitchen, and a private bathroom with shower only. The French prints on the walls, the hardwood floors, the wool rug, the painting over the fireplace and the leather couch in front of it, give the cottage the feeling of a sitting room.

Joan doesn't serve breakfast but does leave condiments around on a "take a little, leave a little" basis. Guests are greeted by Tinkerbelle, a white bull terrier who appears to be ferocious, but is "really a love and won't eat you up."

Joan also operates three other bed-and-breakfast places: a three-bedroom townhouse with two decks and a fireplace on Lake Tahoe, a two-bedroom redwood home with a deck and a fireplace in Carmel Valley, and a redwood-shingled two-bedroom house with a fireplace in Sonoma Valley.

Accommodations: 1 room (cottage) with private bath. *Smoking:* Permitted. *Children:* Permitted if accompanied by only one adult. *Pets:* Not permitted. *Driving Instructions:* Take Kensington to Vasquez, which turns into Garcia and then Edgehill Way; take a sharp right hairpin turn at the top of Edgehill Way.

San Francisco **CALIFORNIA**

Inn on Castro

321 Castro Street, San Francisco, CA 94114. (415) 861-0321. *Host:* Joel Roman.

The Inn on Castro is a 1910 Victorian structure with buttressed eaves that follow the contours of the facade's bay windows. Inside one finds very little Victorian because Joel Roman, a painter and interior designer, has filled the old house with sleek modern furnishings and appointments. A series of tufted chocolate-brown seating modules line the walls of the living room, which features a bold kilim rug, a chrome and brass table, track lighting, a fireplace with a mirrored mantel, lots of plants, and a large, lush painting by Joel.

Papier-mâché parrots, soft sculptures, paper umbrellas suspended from the ceiling, a white oval table encircled by chairs upholstered in white, modular rattan storage cases, a handmade patchwork quilt, coolie hats hanging from the ceiling, a white lacquer headboard with matching chests.

The lovely rooms are the more so for such appointments as fresh flowers and chocolates waiting on the pillows of turned-down beds. Joel serves a complimentary breakfast on handpainted plates that, guests gradually notice, he rotates each day.

Accommodations: 5 rooms with shared baths. *Smoking:* Permitted in guest rooms only. *Children:* Not permitted. *Pets:* Not permitted. *Breakfast:* Included. *Driving Instructions:* The Inn on Castro is at the intersection of Castro, Market, and Seventeenth.

San Francisco **CALIFORNIA**

Jackson Court City Share
 2198 Jackson Street, San Francisco, CA 94115. (415) 929-7670.
 Hostess: Kathy Odsather.
With part of the fortune they amassed while dabbling in the railroad business, the Calahan family built this red stone mansion in 1904. Two years later, as the great San Francisco earthquake of 1906 was shaking the city into pieces, a totem pole Mrs. Calahan picked up during an Alaskan cruise tipped over and knocked her Chinese servant unconscious. Abandoned by even the foggiest notion of what to do, Mrs. Calahan took tea in her bedroom, wondering, one imagines, how properly to sip tea in a trembling mansion. When her servant finally came to, she passed out.

Jackson Court is decorated with a dazzling and eclectic mixture of antiques and modern pieces. A sleek modern couch upholstered in white Haitian cotton, with a brass coffee table in front of it and a turquoise and gold Persian rug beneath it, faces the fireplace. A handmade patchwork quilt covers the brass bed to the right of the couch, and three colors of paint cover the walls and molding.

Each floor of Jackson Court has a kitchen where a complimentary Continental breakfast is served. In the afternoons, complimentary sherry flows in the parlor, which has exposed-beam ceilings and a fireplace with male and female heads in bas-relief.

There is a minimum stay of two nights.

Accommodations: 10 rooms with private bath. *Smoking:* Permitted. *Children:* Not permitted. *Pets:* Not permitted. *Breakfast:* Included. *Driving Instructions:* In the heart of San Francisco.

Santa Barbara **CALIFORNIA**

Bayberry

111 West Valerio Street, Santa Barbara, CA 93101. (805) 682-3199.

Hosts: Keith Pomeroy and Carlton Wagner.

Surrounded by shrubs, flowers, and orange, lemon, and avocado trees, Bayberry is a 1904 two-story slate-roofed house painted Williamsburg blue and trimmed white. Its east side has a sun porch as well as a deck where, weather permitting, Keith and Carlton serve breakfast. The deck has tables with umbrellas, and the sun porch has tables and chairs, bookshelves, plants, and zebra finches who add a little music.

The central living room features wall-to-wall carpeting, a Chesterfield sofa upholstered in leather, two Italian armchairs covered with a tapestry fabric, a baby grand piano, a fireplace, and an elaborate bouquet of flowers—which are also in evidence in the entranceway and the dining room.

Three of the six guest rooms have fireplaces. One, the Bayberry Room, has a king-size bed, an eighteenth-century Morris-type chair from England, a modified wing chair upholstered in Belgian tapestry, a dark walnut English armoire, beige wall-to-wall carpeting, and views of the mountains and the garden.

Keith and Carlton have backgrounds in interior design, and their house shows it.

Accommodations: 6 rooms, 3 with private bath. *Smoking:* Permitted on the deck only. *Children:* Over 12 permitted. *Pets:* Not permitted. *Breakfast:* Included. *Driving Instructions:* From Route 101, take Charles Street north into Valerio Street; turn left, and proceed one block—the Bayberry is on your right.

Santa Barbara **CALIFORNIA**

The Blue Quail Inn

1908 Bath Street, Santa Barbara, CA 93101. (805) 687-2300.
Hostess: Jeanise Suding.

Situated under a large oak tree, The Blue Quail Inn is an early-twentieth-century redwood frame house, with a secluded backyard complete with a picnic table and chairs. Jeanise used to be involved in the aerospace industry but exchanged the world of high tech for a bed-and-breakfast place in her home town.

Jeanise offers guests two rooms in the main house and three other rooms in two nearby cottages. One of the cottages has a bedroom, a living room, a dining area, a kitchen, and a bath. All the rooms feature something special—one has bay windows with a comfortably upholstered window seat, another has a canopied bed with quilted pillows and a white comforter. Guests are invited to use the living room in the main house.

Each morning in the dining room Jeanise serves a complimentary Continental breakfast that usually includes juice, coffee, popovers, and bran muffins. Later in the evening, Jeanise is wont to share a brandy or some hot cider with her guests.

Accommodations: 8 rooms, 2 with private bath. *Smoking:* Permitted. *Children:* Under 13 not permitted. *Pets:* Not permitted. *Driving Instructions:* From U.S. 101 South, take the Mission Street off-ramp and turn left; go two blocks and turn right onto Bath Street.

Santa Barbara **CALIFORNIA**

The Parsonage

1600 Olive Street, Santa Barbara, CA 93101. (805) 962-9336. *Hostess:* Hilde Michelmore.

Originally a rectory for the Trinity Episcopal Church, the Parsonage is an 1892 Queen Anne Victorian structure painted tan and trimmed in blue. The building has a sun deck from which you can descry the ocean, as well as a front porch embellished with intricate woodwork.

The living room has a striking purple Oriental rug with a floral pattern in greens and roses at its corners, and fringes the color of wheat; a fireplace carved out of bird's-eye redwood; and windows that extend almost from floor to ceiling with hand-carved redwood moldings. The dining room features bay windows with bird's-eye redwood moldings and lace tieback curtains; a gray Oriental rug with blue trim and wheat-colored fringes, and a glass-doored hutch displaying hostess Hilde Michelmore's crystal-and-china collection.

One guest suite has a king-size canopied bed, a light blue Oriental rug with a beige, tan, and apricot design at its corners, a mahogany armoire with a mirror, and an antique brass chandelier with hand-blown fluted glass. The suite opens into the solarium, which features rattan furniture covered in a wheat-colored fabric, 180 degrees of windows, and a floor covered by a dhurrie rug from India. The bathroom has a pedestal sink, a claw-footed tub, and shower curtains that match the wallpaper.

Hilde used to own a Volkswagen dealership but got involved with a guest house because she loves to decorate and entertain. She does both well.

Accommodations: 5 rooms with private bath. *Smoking:* Permitted. *Children:* Not permitted. *Pets:* Not permitted. *Breakfast:* Included. *Driving Instructions:* From Los Angeles take the Ventura Freeway and continue on U.S. 101 to Santa Barbara Street; turn right, go 1 mile to Arrellage Street, turn right again, and go four blocks to Olive Street.

Santa Cruz **CALIFORNIA**

Cliff Crest

407 Cliff Street, Santa Cruz, CA 95060. (408) 427-2609. *Hostess:* Mae Lund.

At the crest of Beach Hill, which overlooks Monterey Bay and the boardwalk, Cliff Crest is an 1887 Queen Anne Victorian painted light blue, accented in teal, and trimmed with antique gold. John McLaren, who designed Golden Gate Park, landscaped the grounds for a friend, the lieutenant governor of California, who lived here is the 1890s. The yard has a pair of 100-year-old ginkgos, a redwood, a Monterey cypress, a persimmon, Japanese camellias, four small maples, and an apricot tree.

Cliff Crest features a good deal of stained glass, which dates from 1904 and resembles in mood and color Gauguin's paintings. The front door is generously inlaid with stained glass, and the six-sided solarium/living room, which gives the feeling of sitting in the garden, has a stained-glass border running along the top of each of its six glass walls.

One guest room has an Eastlake queen-size bed and a fireplace; another has white wicker furnishings, views of the bay and the mountains, and a Victorian claw-footed tub. The Pineapple Room has a carved pineapple four-poster bed, oaken flooring, and a stained-glass window.

Mae's Continental breakfast can be taken either in the solarium or your room, and she offers guests complimentary wine or champagne each evening.

Accommodations: 6 rooms with private bath. *Smoking:* Not permitted. *Children:* Over 12 permitted. *Pets:* Not permitted. *Breakfast:* Included. *Driving Instructions:* Take Route 17 to Ocean Street in Santa Cruz, then follow Ocean Street until it ends at San Lorenzo Boulevard; turn right onto San Lorenzo and go to the traffic light, then turn left onto Third Street—follow Third to Cliff Street and turn left.

Reminder: Rates and credit-card information are listed in the index.

Sonoma **CALIFORNIA**

Thistle Dew Inn

171 West Spain Street, Sonoma, CA 95476. (707) 938-2909. *Hostess:* Lisa LaBoskey.

Thistle Dew Inn consists of two houses, both single-story Victorians, that were built in 1900 and 1910. One building was moved here some five years ago, at which time a 4-foot-high stone wall was erected in front of the property. The stone wall is planted with succulents, giant hibiscus, and Old World roses; the grounds comprise two large lawns (one of them bordered by a row of roses), three mimosa trees, an olive tree taller than either house, some plum trees, and a few Norway spruces. The two buildings are separated by a garden.

Both buildings accommodate guests, and both have central living rooms with fireplaces—brick in one house, soapstone in the other. All the rooms here have slate-blue wall-to-wall carpeting, and each is furnished with authentic Mission pieces fashioned of oak (the furniture was constructed by either the Stickley or Limhert workshops). Each guest room comes with fresh flowers and has a queen-size bed, a ceiling fan, a chair, and a desk.

A Continental breakfast includes melon or fruit, cheeses from a local cheese factory, three to five kinds of home-baked goods, juice, and coffee or tea. It is served each morning, buffet style, around a table that seats twelve. Guests may help themselves to sherry at any time.

Accommodations: 6 rooms, 4 with private bath. *Smoking:* Not permitted in bedroom. *Children:* Not permitted. *Pets:* Not permitted. *Breakfast:* Included. *Driving Instructions:* From San Francisco, take Route 101 to Ignacio; then take Route 37 east to Route 121, which runs into Sonoma—the inn is three houses away from the northwest corner of Plaza.

Soulsbyville   **CALIFORNIA**

Willow Springs Country Inn
   20599 Kings Court, Soulsbyville, CA 95372. (209) 533-2030.
   Hosts: Marty and Karen Wheeler.

Willow Springs Country Inn is an 1880 ranch-style structure, painted beige and trimmed white, that was built by Ben Soulsby, the founder of Soulsbyville. Soulsby no doubt founded the town because he discovered a mine nearby and, during the last half of the nineteenth century, extracted from it some $7 million. The house is at an elevation of 3,000 feet, in something of a country development that has very few houses and a lot of land, tennis courts, horseshoe and shuffleboard facilities, and a pond that is adjacent to the Wheelers' property.

The central living room has an old Franklin stove, forest-green wall-to-wall carpeting, two large rattan couches upholstered in a green floral print fabric, a number of Karen's dried flower arrangements, and a collection of Marty's photographs (primarily nature studies, mostly of the Sierra Nevadas). Part of the entranceway serves as a library and sitting area, and the expansive kitchen has a brick fireplace.

One guest room has a canopied bed draped with handmade curtains, wall-to-wall blue-on-blue carpeting, an oaken dresser, an antique wicker chair, a reproduction bowl-and-pitcher stand with a mirror, a private bath, and a private entrance.

Breakfast here includes homemade zucchini, banana, and pumpkin breads, homemade pastries, crepes with a quiche lorraine filling, fresh fruit, and, from time to time, hot egg nog or hot apple cider.

Accommodations: 4 rooms, 1 with private bath. *Smoking:* Not permitted. *Children:* Permitted. *Pets:* Not permitted. *Breakfast:* Included. *Driving Instructions:* From Sonora, take Route 108 east for 7½ miles to the Soulsbyville exit; take your first left onto Kings Court, and continue two blocks.

Sunnyvale **CALIFORNIA**

Sunnyside, an Urban Inn

435 East McKinley Avenue, Sunnyvale, CA 94086. (408) 736-3794. *Hosts:* Byrd and Phyllis Helligas.

A 1930s Italianate peasant-style building with a stucco entrance on a low, broad frame, Sunnyside used to be a potato-chip factory. Byrd and Phyllis incorporated many remnants of the factory into decorative or functional pieces. The sculpture on the front lawn is its old stapling machine, and the glass-topped table in the atrium used to be the candy cooker.

Byrd and Phyllis bought Sunnyside in 1976 and have brought into it numerous pieces of urban archaeology—the iron lamps with burlap covers that hang in the keeping room used to be San Jose streetlamps; the knob and tube light in the atrium was once a City of Santa Clara light; an old "account safe" is now a storage bin.

The house still has the old hydraulic freight elevator, which huffs and puffs its way from the basement to the second floor.

The guest rooms, which have private entrances, are furnished eclectically, with antiques and memorabilia setting the tone. One room has sliding glass doors that open into the atrium, and another features a kitchen area, as well as a hall dressing and sitting area. The patio, which guests are welcome to use, has a fireplace.

"Breakfast is served at the time and place of the guest's choice."

Accommodations: 2 rooms with private bath. *Smoking:* Permitted. *Children:* Not permitted. *Pets:* Not permitted. *Breakfast:* Included. *Driving Instructions:* Take U.S. 101 south from San Francisco; exit at Mathilda Avenue; turn left on Washington, right on Bayview, and then left on McKinley.

Sutter Creek **CALIFORNIA**

The Foxes in Sutter Creek

77 Main Street, P. O. Box 159, Sutter Creek, CA 95685. (209) 267-5882. *Hosts:* Pete and Min Fox.

The Foxes' 1857 New England-style house contains Pete Fox's real estate office, Min Fox's antique shop, the couple's private residence, and two guest suites with private baths.

A 9-foot-tall Victorian headboard, entirely of walnut, and a matching tall dresser, with a white marble top at table level, dominate one bedroom, which features a 1797 Louis XVI tapestry woven in grays, pale pinks, and antique burgundies. A brass chandelier hangs from the bedroom's ceiling, and an auburn wall-to-wall carpet covers the floor. The sitting room is furnished with a Queen Anne love seat covered in fawn velvet.

The other suite features a cathedral ceiling with two brass chandeliers, a Victorian bedroom set with a 10-foot-plus armoire, four Louis XV side chairs, a queen-size bed, and a daybed.

A complimentary breakfast of fresh fruit juice, freshly baked breads, and coffee is brought to the guest suite's door on a Towle silver serving tray strewn with fresh flowers. Each evening the Foxes provide a complimentary carafe of wine.

Accommodations: 3 suites with private bath. *Smoking:* Tolerated. *Children:* Not permitted. *Pets:* Not permitted. *Breakfast:* Included. *Driving Instructions:* Take Route 49 into Sutter Creek, where it becomes Main Street.

Sutter Creek   **CALIFORNIA**

The Hanford House

3 Hanford Street, P.O. Box 847, Sutter Creek, CA 95685. (209) 267-0747. *Host:* Ron Van Anda.

On grounds planted with liquidambars, redwoods, crepe myrtles, daisies, and devil's walking sticks, The Hanford House is an 1898 home with a mixture of gold-country and Victorian motifs. It has a side porch embellished with gingerbread trim, and a 73-foot redwood deck that overlooks the town of Sutter Creek. The building also contains Ron's antique shop.

Guest rooms vary, with a mixture of contemporary and antique pieces. The 20- by 30-foot honeymoon suite has an iron and brass bed covered with a lace bedspread, two Victorian tables made of mahogany, a corner fireplace (gas) with a Douglas fir mantel, sloping ceilings, a wicker settee, and wicker chairs. Other guest rooms have such appointments as a leather wing chair, a seventeenth-century oaken coffer chest, a teak chest from China, a 1910 bronze bank table with a glass top, and an 1820s Spanish door transformed into a headboard. Each room has either a queen-size sofa bed or a pair of love seats or easy chairs. Each guest room has an antique pine armoire.

The central living room has wall-to-wall charcoal-gray carpeting and exposed-beam ceilings painted white. Ron serves guests a Continental breakfast and greets them when they arrive with a complimentary bottle of chilled Montevina Zinfandel.

Accommodations: 9 rooms with private bath. *Smoking:* Permitted in some areas. *Children:* Over 12 permitted. *Pets:* Not permitted. *Breakfast:* Included. *Driving Instructions:* The Hanford House is at the intersection of Route 49 and Main Street in Sutter Creek.

Tahoe City **CALIFORNIA**

Mayfield House

236 Grove Street, Tahoe City, CA 95730. (916) 583-1001. *Hostess:* Janice Kellermyer.

A stone-and-wood structure built in 1932 by a successful Lake Tahoe contractor, Mayfield House is marked by steep gables, a stone path that runs through the garden, and a convenient location: You can walk anyplace in Tahoe, and a shuttle bus stops yards away to take you where your feet can't.

The living room has a large stone fireplace flanked on either side by windows looking over the lawn, plus wood paneling, large buttressed pine beams on the ceiling, two love seats covered with a fabric of blue and gray, and a dark brown plush carpet.

All of the Mayfield House guest rooms have down comforters; one has a sitting area with a view of the lake (a few hundred yards from the house), and another features a network of eaves covered in a tiny-print Victorian wallpaper.

While light classsical music plays in the background, Janice Kellermyer serves a complimentary breakfast of fresh orange juice, fresh fruit, coffee, and homemade pastries.

Accommodations: 6 rooms sharing 3 baths. *Smoking:* Permitted if smoker is considerate. *Children:* Over 12 permitted. *Pets:* Not permitted. *Breakfast:* Included. *Driving Instructions:* From Truckee, take Route 89 South; turn left at Grove Street.

Templeton **CALIFORNIA**

Country House Inn

91 Main Street, P.O. Box 179, Templeton, CA 93465. (805) 434-1598. *Hosts:* Barbara Ford and Nick Milovina.

Built in 1886 for the developer of the town of Templeton, Country House Inn is a Victorian farmhouse on grounds with 50-foot palm trees, old oaks, fifty rose bushes, and camellias and other flowers. Designated a San Luis Obispo County historic site, the house still has its original woodwork and wrought-iron decor around the roof line, as well as its original hardware and shutters. The woodwork and the better part of the house are made of redwood, which was originally painted to look like walnut.

The guest rooms, with their 11-foot ceilings with gold-leaf molding, vary in color scheme and design. One is done in blues and whites and has a white iron bed; one has a brass bed and a rose and burgundy color scheme. An 8-foot-tall oaken headboard is in another guest room.

The house is furnished with a mixture of antique and contemporary pieces including canopied beds, a few crystal chandeliers, some fireplaces, a copper sink, and an oaken player piano.

There is plenty to do in and around Templeton, especially if one enjoys touring wineries and looking at historic houses. The Hearst Castle is thirty minutes away.

Accommodations: 6 rooms with shared baths. *Smoking:* Not permitted. *Children:* Sometimes permitted—check in advance. *Pets:* Not permitted. *Breakfast:* Included. *Driving Instructions:* Country House Inn is 5 miles south of Paso Robles on Route 101.

Reminder: Rates and credit-card information are listed in the index.

Truckee **CALIFORNIA**

Bradley House

P.O. Box 2011, Truckee, CA 95734. (916) 587-5388. *Hosts:* Donna and Larry Bradley.

This 1880 Victorian structure, its decorative trim painted gray and white, was built by a man who exported ice taken from a nearby river. The house has been lovingly restored by Donna and Larry Bradley, who have furnished it with their extensive collection of antiques.

The parlor has a Franklin stove, and a 9-foot oak and stained-glass back bar that, a hundred years or so ago, refreshed the guests of a Kansas City hotel. Hand-carved oak beds with handmade Amish quilts appear in most of the guest rooms. Period reproduction wallpapers, chosen to complement the quilts, cover the guest-room walls. Most of the furnishings are antiques, and most are made of golden oak—even the toilet seats, the towel racks, and the toilet-tissue holders.

Bradley House features such other niceties as a staircase with a carved banister and leather wainscoting; a large, rare rolltop table;

several wood and glass display cabinets housing Larry's collection of ceramic figurine liquor decanters; and a color television set with cable and a video-recorder complete with several movies on tape.

The Bradleys serve a complimentary breakfast that includes—depending on whether Donna or Larry bake—homemade strudel or blueberry muffins. Each evening between 5 and 6, guests are offered complimentary wine and cheese.

Accommodations: 6 rooms with private bath. *Smoking:* Not permitted. *Children:* Under 11 not permitted. *Pets:* Not permitted. *Breakfast:* Included. *Driving Instructions:* Take Route I-80 to the Central Truckee exit; follow Donner Pass Road into town; take Spring Street up the hill.

Tuolumne **CALIFORNIA**

Oak Hill Ranch

P.O. Box 307, 18550 Connally Lane, Tuolumne, CA 95379. (209) 928-4717. *Hosts:* Sanford and Jane Grover.

Although the main house at Oak Hill Ranch was completed in 1980, the better part of its components are of Victorian buildings, which Sanford and Jane collected over the years, hauled here by truck, and refinished over the course of two years. The house, on 55 acres of rolling hills and pastureland, is at an elevation of 3,000 feet and overlooks the foothills of the Sierra Nevadas, which are sprinkled with ponds and streams and wooded primarily with oaks and Ponderosa pines.

The grounds also include a 200-square-foot Victorian cottage that used to be a milking barn. It is furnished almost entirely with antiques, including Victorian lamps with Tiffany shades, an oaken sideboard and dining table, and a Spanish chandelier of brass. The living room has a fireplace fashioned of native slate, and the rest of the cottage includes a full kitchen, a bath, and a bedroom with an iron and brass queen-size bed and oaken furniture.

The main house has numerous antiques and heirlooms, including an oaken player piano in the hallway. The sitting room has a fireplace with an 8-foot-tall mahogany mantel, a walnut pump organ, overstuffed couches and chairs, and marble-topped tables. The staircase dates from 1870 and features mahogany and walnut turned woodwork—refinishing that must have been some job!

The guest rooms vary, but all are decorated with Victorian antiques. One room is furnished with Eastlake pieces and has a private balcony; another has a canopied bed; another, an iron bed with scrollwork.

The Grovers serve a gourmet breakfast, which often includes an egg dish of green peppers, mushrooms, scallions, tomatoes, and parsley cooked in layers and garnished with a sherry-based sauce, and fresh juice and fruit.

Accommodations: 3 rooms with shared bath; 1 cottage with private bath. *Smoking:* Permitted outdoors only. *Children:* Permitted in cottage. *Pets:* Not permitted. *Breakfast:* Included. *Driving Instructions:* Oak Hill Ranch is off Route 108, west of Yosemite National Park (call for specific instructions).

Venice **CALIFORNIA**

The Venice Beach House
   15 Thirtieth Avenue, Venice, CA 90291. (213) 823-1966. *Hostesses:* Elaine Burke and Vivian Boesch.

Half a block from the ocean, The Venice Beach House is a 1911 California bungalow painted gray and trimmed in dark gray. The building has a porch furnished with wicker pieces, and a trellised veranda. The gardens are rife with subtropical palms and ferns.

   The central living room has oaken floors partially covered by a Persian rug with a pattern in mauves and blues, exposed-beam oaken ceilings, an antique French Provincial mahogany coffee table and a matching chair upholstered with a dusty rose fabric. A pair of wing-back chairs upholstered in a mauve wool and a brick fireplace with an oaken mantel complete this room, which adjoins the dining room with its bay window.

Immediately above the dining room's bay window is another bay window overlooking the ocean and the Venice Pier. This one is in the sitting area of a suite the has an overstuffed sofa and chair covered in herringbone, a fabric that also covers the walls and the blinds on the bay window. The suite also has a king-size bed, an antique desk with leaded-glass insets, an antique oaken dresser with a mirror, and a white brick fireplace at the foot of the bed. Other rooms here feature canopied or brass beds, fireplaces, a balcony, and ocean views.

Famous for roller skating, Venice is also popular for its beautiful beach and, of course, people-watching.

Accommodations: 8 rooms, 4 with private bath. *Smoking:* Not permitted. *Children:* Over 10 permitted. *Pets:* Not permitted. *Breakfast:* Included. *Driving Istructions:* Take the Marina Freeway exit off the San Diego Freeway and proceed west to Lincoln; turn right on Lincoln and continue to Washington; then turn left on Washington and drive toward the ocean. Turn right on Speedway, then drive past Thirtieth Avenue and turn right onto Twenty-ninth Place, where guest parking is available.

West Covina **CALIFORNIA**

The Hendrick Inn
   2124 East Merced Avenue, West Covina, CA 91791. (213) 919-2125. *Hosts:* George and Mary Hendrick.

A U-shaped ranch-style house with a large deck overlooking a 20- by 40-foot swimming pool, the Hendrick Inn is full of decorative and creature-comfort surprises. The house was photographed, inside and out, for *Life* magazine. The deck, carpeted and done in rattan furniture upholstered in duck, has a Jacuzzi that holds six people.

One of the living rooms has a white marble fireplace, European reproductions of paintings by Velázquez, El Greco, and Van Gogh, a beige carpet that matches the color of the fireplace, and fabrics blended predominantly of cool colors—blues, greens, and lavenders. The other living room is suffused with warm colors and features a white brick fireplace.

The master suite, which has sliding glass doors that open onto the deck, has a walnut secretary with glass doors, a walnut chair upholstered in a beige, olive green, and blue fabric, and a teak-paneled wall. One guest room is done entirely in rainbow motifs, which are reflected in everything from the towels to the bedspread, and furnished in French provincial style. Mary and George's decorative eclecticism reaches its height in the "booze bath," which is wallpapered with more than three thousand labels removed from foreign liquor bottles.

Mary and George serve complimentary wine to their guests, as well as a complimentary liqueur on the first night of their stay. For an irresistibly reasonable price, they will serve guests a hard-to-forget dinner.

Accommodations: 4 rooms, 1 with private bath. *Smoking:* Permitted. *Children:* Under 6 not permitted. *Pets:* Not permitted. *Driving Instructions:* From Los Angeles take Route I-10 to West Covina, and go south on Citrus Avenue to East Merced Avenue.

Yountville   **CALIFORNIA**

Burgundy House Country Inn

    6711 Washington Street, Yountville, CA 94599. (707) 944-2855. *Hosts:* Mary and Robert Kennan.

Burgundy House is an 1872 brandy distillery with 22-inch-thick fieldstone walls. Mary Kennan won an Award of Merit for its restoration. Her husband, Robert, an architect, designed and built an annex called Bordeaux House—a formal red-brick structure all but hidden behind two old Italian stone pines—where every room offers a fireplace and a patio.

    Burgundy House, convenient to some 120 Napa Valley wineries, is decorated with the antiques, mostly French country, that Mary and Robert have accumulated over the years. There are antique brass beds, colorful comforters, and decanted complimentary wine and glasses on the bureaus. Each room is air-conditioned.

Around the hearth in one of Burgundy House's common rooms, Mary and Robert serve a complimentary breakfast; in the late afternoon, and sometimes into the evening, they offer complimentary wine.

Accommodations: 16 rooms, 11 with private bath; 1 suite. *Smoking:* Permitted. *Children:* Permitted in cottages. *Pets:* Not permitted. *Breakfast:* Included. *Driving Instructions:* From Napa, go north on Route 29 to Yountville; turn right on Madison Street; turn right on Washington Street.

Yountville CALIFORNIA

Oleander House

7433 Saint Helena Highway, Yountville, CA 94599. (707) 944-8315. *Hostess:* Jean A. Brunswick.

Oleander House is a contemporary California cottage painted French blue and trimmed in white, situated between the Domaine Chandon and Robert Mondavi wineries. Jean recently planted the grounds with lots of white oleanders.

Each guest room has a fireplace, a private bath, and period antiques. The overall tone of the rooms is perhaps suggested by the Laura Ashley wallpapers and coordinated bedspreads and dust ruffles. One guest room has wheat-colored wall-to-wall carpeting, a brass queen-size bed, a fireplace inlaid with handmade Indian tiles, an antique pine dresser, and a private balcony that overlooks a vineyard. Each guest room also has a sitting area, where Jean serves breakfast, and a private balcony. On an antique Welsh pine sideboard in the library at the top of the stairs, Jean sets out cheeses and wine each afternoon.

A typical breakfast consists of orange juice, pineapple with honey and Tripple Sec, scrambled eggs, jams, and croissants.

Yountville is centrally located in the California wine country, which offers any number of activities—shops, restaurants, hot-air ballooning, and, of course, tours of the wineries—and in my experience, a tour of a winery can make you even more light-headed than a ride in a balloon.

Accommodations: 4 rooms with private bath. *Smoking:* Not permitted. *Children:* Not permitted. *Pets:* Not permitted. *Breakfast:* Included. *Driving Instructions:* Oleander House is on Saint Helena Highway (Route 29), between Yountville and Oakville.

COLORADO

Beulah. Part of a 67-acre working horse ranch, this four-bedroom home has sweeping views of mountains, two creeks running through the property, and a neighboring 600-acre park. The host enjoys restoring antique carriages and welcomes children and dogs. *Represented by:* Bed & Breakfast Colorado, (303) 333-3340. $28–$33.

Denver. This ninth-floor condominium, which includes a king-size bed and a private bath, is in a building with tennis courts, an indoor swimming pool, a Jacuzzi, and racquetball courts. The apartment has spectacular views of Denver and the nearby mountains, especially from the balcony, which is furnished in white wicker. *Represented by:* Bed & Breakfast Colorado, (303) 333-3340. $35–$40.

Denver. Furnished with many antiques and with a lot of bird's-eye maple trim, this *ca.* 1900 "Denver Square" structure has one guest room available. The room features a maple fireplace, a walnut antique vanity, a king-size bed, and a small sitting area. The house, three minutes from Denver Botanical Gardens, is decorated with many plants; the foyer is done in white wicker. *Represented by:* Bed & Breakfast Colorado, (303) 333-3340. $35–$40.

Durango. This circa-1898 Victorian farmhouse is situated on 160 acres. There's a lake on the property, and the hosts are a writer and a social worker. The house, furnished with period antiques, features a four-poster in the guest room, a country kitchen, a solarium, and a patio. Downtown Durango is fifteen minutes away, and it's 20 miles from the house to the Purgatory Ski Area. You can ski cross-country right on the property or swim in the lake. *Represented by:* Bed & Breakfast Colorado, DRO #01, (303) 333-3340. $35–$40.

Eaton. Situated at the planting line of a large farm, this ranch-style house is hosted by people interested in railroads, the Southwest's Indians, computers, and bridge. The living room has a fireplace, as well as windows with mountain views. There are bicycles for guests who request them, and the hosts are willing to cook meals for guests. *Represented by:* Bed & Breakfast Colorado, (303) 333-3340. $25–$30.

Evergreen. Situated in a secluded wooded area above town, this four-story redwood contemporary house has sweeping views of the Rocky Mountains. There's a suite with a queen-size bed, a desk, plenty of books, and a panoramic view. Guests may occupy the entire floor. The hosts—with interests in stained glass, sewing, and

"Evergreen" (*Bed & Breakfast Colorado*)

COLORADO

reading—have furnished their home with contemporary pieces. Evergreen, forty-five minutes from Denver, is a quaint little town with plenty of shops and restaurants. *Represented by:* Bed & Breakfast Colorado, EUE #01, (303) 333-3340. $20–$40.

Loveland. Furnished with a combination of period and reproduction antiques, this contemporary suburban home is one block from Boyd Lake. The hosts' interests include travel, interior design, flowers, waterskiing, hiking, and camping. They have bicycles for guests and laundry facilities. Trail Ridge Road, the highest paved road in the world, is 30 miles from here. *Represented by:* Bed & Breakfast Colorado, LOV #01, (303) 333-3340. $30–$35.

Mancos. This two-story contemporary structure on 36 wooded acres is in southwest Colorado, about 11 miles from Mesa Verde National Park. The hostesses, retired health administrators, enjoy hunting, fishing, woodworking, and music. They can make arrangements for fishing trips and are willing to pick up guests at the airport and provide for additional meals. The two guest rooms that are available have queen-size beds and share a bath. *Represented by:* Bed & Breakfast Colorado, (303) 333-3340. $24–$30.

"Durango" (*Bed & Breakfast Colorado*)

COLORADO

Vail/Beaver Creek. This bed-and-breakfast condominium is right across the street from the free shuttle to the Beaver Creek ski area. The host who is interested in traveling, skiing, cooking, and writing, offers guests a small bedroom with a private bath and a large picture window that overlooks the mountains. Guests are invited to use the washer/dryer facilities. Advance lift tickets and rent-a-car service are available. *Represented by:* Bed & Breakfast Colorado, (303) 333-3340. $35–$40.

Boulder COLORADO

Briar Rose Bed and Breakfast

2151 Arapahoe, Boulder, CO 80302. (303) 442-3007. *Host:* Emily Hunter.

Shaded by a 70-foot tulip tree, Briar Rose is a brick Victorian structure trimmed in dusty rose, gray-green, and beige. There are apple, cherry, and peach trees in the side yard, a trumpet vine climbing up the north side of the house, roses clinging to a small balcony, and Concord grapevines trying to enclose the enclosed sun porch more fully.

The living room features 15-foot ceilings, an oaken floor partially covered by a pale mauve carpet, a fireplace, a wing chair covered in a deep rose velvet, a couch with down pillows, an adjustable-back crewel Victorian oaken chair with a footrest, and ceramic and brass lamps. Double doors lead from the living room into the dining room, which has an oval gilt mirror hanging above a walnut upright piano; a window seat dressed up with a basket of apples and an antique crystal decanter and glasses on a silver tray (the decanter's always full of sherry for the guests); a Queen Anne highboy that belonged to Emily's grandmother; oaken floors; and a mahogany dining table with antique English hoop-back chairs.

One of Emily's guest rooms has a small balcony; a bed with a pleated and padded headboard and a white eyelet dust ruffle that matches the curtains; and a small Italian lady's desk with an enamel-and-gilt Victorian brush and mirror set. Another room has a Victorian chaise longue upholstered in gray-blue velvet.

Guests find their beds turned down and chocolate mint truffles on their pillows, fresh flowers and a basket of fruit in their rooms, which also feature feather quilts.

Breakfast—fresh croissants and pastries, yogurt, orange juice and coffee or English tea—is served between 7:00 and 10:30 A.M., in your room on a tray with china and linen, on the sun porch, or in the dining room.

Accommodations: 11 rooms, 6 with private bath. *Smoking:* Permitted. *Children:* Welcomed. *Pets:* Permitted. *Breakfast:* Included. *Driving Instructions:* From Denver, take Route 36 into Boulder. Route 36 becomes Twenty-eighth Street—turn west at the intersection of Twenty-eighth and Arapahoe. Briar Rose is on the corner of Twenty-second and Arapahoe.

Buena Vista **COLORADO**

Blue Sky Inn

719 Arizona Street, Buena Vista, CO 81211. (303) 395-8862. *Hosts:* Hazel and Bill Davis.

On 25 acres bordering the Arkansas River and Cottonwood Creek, which merge here, Blue Sky Inn is a 1964 split-level contemporary constructed primarily of Philippine mahogany. The property—wooded with pinion and Ponderosa pines, and shimmering aspens the Davises planted—is at an elevation of 8,000 feet and includes 1,150 feet of Arkansas River shore, which two of the guest rooms overlook. The other two rooms overlook the Elk Mountain range; the living room, flanked by sliding glass doors, has views of both river and mountains.

The central living room has an oaken parquet floor partially covered with Oriental rugs, mahogany paneling, a stone fireplace, several seventeenth-century French antiques, and an antique desk over which there has been some controversy: One expert claimed it was made in France near the Italian border; another, that it was made in Italy near the French border. The recreation room, carpeted in earth tones and painted lighter-than-lemon yellow, holds a generous collection of handsomely bound books (Shakespeare, Homer, Melville, Gibbon), and the backyard comes complete with a joggling board, a Southern invention conducive to romance and other antigravity experiences.

The guest rooms share baths and range in decor—one has mahogany twin beds, another mahogany paneling—and are dressed up with many antiques. Two of the rooms function nicely as a suite.

Accommodations: 4 rooms with shared bath. *Smoking:* Permitted on terrace only. *Children:* Permitted, but check in advance. *Pets:* Permitted, but not in house. *Driving Instructions:* From Colorado Springs, take Route 24 west to Buena Vista; turn east at the traffic light (Main Street), then turn south at Court Street, which becomes Arizona Street—Blue Sky Inn is half a mile on the left.

Green Mountain Falls — COLORADO

Outlook Lodge
P.O. Box 5, Green Mountain Falls, CO 80819. (303) 684-2303.
Hosts: The Ahern Family.

Originally built in 1889 as a summer parsonage for a church, the Outlook Lodge is a large Victorian structure with a wide veranda running across the better part of its front. Green Mountain Falls was a stopping place on the Old Ute Indian Trail. The Utes, after a season of hunting in what is now western Colorado, used to cross the Rockies at this point, stopping for a while to cure their sick and wounded in the hot springs now called Manitou Springs. "Manitou" is the Ute name for God, Whom they thought dwelled there.

The house, furnished with Victorian country antiques, features a large, sun-filled dining room (complete with a piano, games, toys, and an elaborate 1860s base-burner wood stove) that runs across one entire side. The small parlor has a fireplace and an antique desk, which Impy Ahern considers the perfect place for writing letters or cards. The large parlor has a color television set with Home Box Office.

The lodge features picnic and barbecue facilities in a forested area behind it; the view includes mountains and a small village.

The Aherns offer a complimentary breakfast and will put together a pack lunch for hikers, fishermen, or explorers.

Accommodations: 10 rooms, 2 with private bath. *Smoking:* Permitted. *Children:* Permitted. *Pets:* Permitted. *Breakfast:* Included. *Driving Instructions:* Green Mountain Falls is 15 miles west of Colorado Springs on Route 24 West.

Nederland **COLORADO**

Goldminer Hotel

Eldora Star Route, Nederland, CO 80466. (303) 258-7770. *Hosts:* Dwight Souder and Jean Bell.

An 1897 log building, the Goldminer Hotel has something of a Dodge City facade. "Originally, the rooms were rented in eight-hour shifts, but a bullet hole in one of the doors attests to someone's desire for a longer snooze," explains Dwight. As far as its grounds are concerned, suffice it to say the Goldminer is located in the Roosevelt National Forest, not far from the Continental Divide.

All of the guest rooms, furnished with antiques, have views of the surrounding mountains; one room features five large windows overlooking the Indian Peaks Wilderness Area.

The lobby, where the guests usually congregate, has a wood-burning stove that helps take the edge off the cold (the elevation here exceeds 9,000 feet). Dwight and Jean serve a complimentary breakfast each morning.

The Eldora area is rife with streams, lakes, and waterfalls. The Eldora Ski Area is 3 miles from the Goldminer, and cross-country skiing is even closer.

Accommodations: 5 rooms with shared baths. *Smoking:* Permitted. *Children:* Permitted. *Pets:* Not permitted. *Breakfast:* Included. *Driving Instructions:* The Goldminer is 3 miles west of Nederland, in the townsite of Eldora.

Ouray **COLORADO**

Baker's Manor Guest House

317 Second Street, Ouray, CO 81427. (303) 325-4574; off season: (303) 325-4496. *Hosts:* John and Nancy Nixon.

Baker's Manor Guest House is a Victorian structure painted yellow with white trim. It was built in 1881, when local mines were active, but was deserted suddenly and remained empty until the 1950s. A woman named Mrs. Baker took over the property and turned it into a boardinghouse. Situated at an elevation of 8,000 feet, the building, which has landscaped grounds rife with wildflowers, has views of the San Juan Mountains.

Nancy, who runs a nursery school, and John, an architect, restored the house, furnishing it with some antiques and a collection of heirloom furniture. The guest rooms, four of which offer views of the mountains, contain such items as oaken dressers, iron beds, Oriental rugs, and an antique oaken armoire. The living room has a brick-and-tile fireplace and an antique couch upholstered in red velvet, and the halls are lined with family photographs, old and new, in antique frames.

Nancy and John serve a Continental breakfast that includes freshly baked breads. This guest house is open June 1 through October 1.

Accommodations: 6 rooms with shared baths. *Smoking:* Permitted. *Children:* Permitted. *Pets:* Not permitted. *Breakfast:* Included. *Driving Instructions:* From Montrose go 35 miles south of U.S. 550; Baker's Manor is a block west of Ouray's Main Street, between Second and Third avenues.

CONNECTICUT

Essex. If you plan to come here by boat, the hostess, a boating enthusiast, will invite you to dock at a nearby marina. Her house is right on the Connecticut River, and every one of its rooms has a water view. Breakfast is served on the enclosed sun porch. *Represented by:* Nutmeg Bed & Breakfast, (203) 236-6698. $55.

Falls Village. An architect-designed home with a steep, sloping roof, a cupola, and a stone fireplace, this bed and breakfast is on a winding road not far from Lime Rock Racetrack. The hosts, whose business revolves around gourmet delicacies, have two rooms available—one has a queen-size bed, a private bath, and a sitting area; the other is a suite that features a fireplace, a king-size bed, and a sitting room. *Represented by:* Nutmeg Bed & Breakfast, #54, (203) 236-6698. $35-$65.

Guilford. This eighteenth-century Colonial in the historic town of Guilford is mostly furnished with period antiques from France. Its guest quarters have a private bath, a private entrance, and a fireplace. The house, convenient to plenty of restaurants and a nature trail, is hosted by an avid sailor willing to charter a 33-foot sailboat on a daily basis. *Represented by:* Bed & Breakfast, Ltd., (203) 469-3260, $35-$40.

Hartford (West). Adjacent to the University of Connecticut Law School and Hartford College for Women, this brick Georgian structure is on landscaped grounds. Manicured bushes surround three sides of the house, and there's a pool in the backyard. Interior appointments include elaborately carved wood moldings and fireplaces. A double guest room has a private bath and an adjoining den with stenciled floors. Two single rooms on the third floor share a bath. *Represented by:* Nutmeg Bed & Breakfast, #2, (203) 236-6698. $50-$65.

Hartford. In the middle of downtown Hartford, this urban brownstone has an elaborate wrought-iron entry gate and an enclosed tiled garden. Appointments include period antiques, a huge kitchen with a fireplace, and many area rugs and paintings. The host is fluent in Spanish and French. *Represented by:* Nutmeg Bed & Breakfast, (203) 236-6698. $55.

Kent. An eighteenth-century Federal structure, this house is one of the oldest in Kent. One guest room features a canopied four-poster bed, and another has a fireplace. The hosts have set aside for guests a private living room whose decor centers around a

Falls Village (Nutmeg Bed & Breakfast)

West Hartford (Nutmeg Bed & Breakfast)

125

CONNECTICUT

generous use of textiles, which one host designs for a living. Weather permitting, breakfast is served beneath the trees. *Represented by:* Covered Bridge Bed & Breakfast, (203) 672-6502. $40–$50.

Killingsworth. Near the Long Island shore and within earshot of the owners' horses, this 1830s Colonial farmhouse has two rooms available for guests. Both rooms are filled with antiques, always contain fresh flowers, and one features a four-poster covered with a patchwork quilt. Breakfast includes fresh fruits, cereals, and homemade breads and muffins, served on a fastidiously set table. *Represented by:* Nutmeg Bed & Breakfast, (203) 236-6698. $28–$35.

Lake Waramaug. This large white Colonial with black shutters is high on a hill that overlooks Lake Waramaug. The grounds include 200 feet of lakefront property. Convenient to skiing, sailing, and antiquing, the house, whose hosts are former innkeepers, is furnished with many antiques. *Represented by:* Nutmeg Bed & Breakfast, (203) 236-6698. $33–$48.

Lime Rock. Currently hosted by a couple who manufacture gourmet foods, this bed and breakfast is a former icehouse that was restored by a well-know architect. It features exposed beams and a pair of foot-thick doors that lead into a cathedral-ceilinged living room. The guest room, done in shades of silvery gray, has a private bath and entrance, and overlooks a lawn with a brook flowing through it. *Represented by:* Covered Bridge Bed & Breakfast, (203) 672-6502. $50.

New London. Directly on the ocean, this two-story clapboard structure painted white and trimmed blue features a widow's walk and a patio, as well as a view of a lighthouse. New London, Mystic, and Connecticut College are all close by. *Represented by:* Nutmeg Bed & Breakfast, (203) 236-6698. $35–$48.

Penwood State Forest. This rambling contemporary structure has a glass wall with a view of the Connecticut Valley (on a clear day you can see 70 miles). The house, on 5.6 acres of land adjacent to Penwood State Forest, is on grounds with two hundred varieties of daffodils, a profusion of wildflowers, and eleven lawn mowers—all of them goats who answer to their names. Guests are invited to use the pool when it's warm and, when it's cold, may commence their ski outings at the front door. *Represented by:* Nutmeg Bed & Breakfast, (203) 236-6698. $35–$55.

CONNECTICUT

Sharon. This restored Victorian structure faces north overlooking the foothills of the Berkshires, and there is a particularly good view from its large terraces. A pull-out double bed converts a sunny sitting room into a bedroom, adjacent to which is a private bath. One host is an entrepreneur who runs three businesses; the other is an occupational therapist. Two cats and a teen-ager complete the personnel. *Represented by:* Covered Bridge Bed & Breakfast, (203) 672-6502. $45–$50.

Groton Long Point   **CONNECTICUT**

Shore Inne

54 East Shore Road, Groton Long Point, CT 06340. (203) 536-1180. *Hostess:* Helen Ellison.

A *circa*-1915 Colonial-style structure, the Shore Inne was built by a couple who used to live next door to it. Show-business people, the couple, so the story goes, built the Shore Inne to accommodate an overflow of guests. Even though the current zoning laws prohibit inns in this area, the Shore Inne exists because of a "grandfather clause," which basically says, "What's already here can stay."

The house is on the shore of the Long Island Sound, and the living room, dining room, and sun parlor all have views of the water. The living room is furnished with white wicker, with cushions covered in a yellow, green, and bittersweet floral fabric. The sun parlor, also a library, features television and hand-stenciled walls. The dining room features a maple hutch and a china cupboard. Of the seven guest rooms, six have views of the water and all have patchwork coverlets.

The Shore Inne's location is eminently convenient: Mystic is 3.5 miles away, Groton 8 miles, and New London 10 miles. The area features, as well as its natural beauty, plenty of restaurants and other attractions.

Accommodations: 7 rooms, 3 with private bath. *Smoking:* Permitted. *Children:* Permitted. *Pets:* Not permitted. *Breakfast:* Included. *Driving Instructions:* Take I-95 to exit 88, follow Route 1 to Route 215, turn onto Groton Long Point Road, and take the first left after the Yankee Fisherman Restaurant.

Mystic **CONNECTICUT**

1833 House

33 Greenmanville Avenue (Route 27), Mystic, CT 06355. (203) 572-0633. *Hostess:* Joan Brownell Smith.

1833 House was erected in the year of its name, probably by someone involved in the construction of whaling vessels, which was a thriving industry in Mystic 150 years ago. The house is right next door to the Mystic Seaport Museum.

The living room, originally the kitchen, has hardwood floors, a Victorian love seat upholstered in pink brocade, a dark-wood lady's writing desk, and other comfortable furniture.

Two guest accommodations have views of Mystic Seaport, another consists of two bedrooms and serves as something of a family unit: The children's room, which has attached white beds, adjoins the parents' bedroom, which has a painted pine double bed, an antique blanket chest with a television set on top of it, and a private bath.

Joan used to work at the local tourists' information center and, consequently, knows a great deal about the area. She's willing to pick up guests at the Amtrak station.

Joan serves a Continental breakfast with a choice of three kinds of juice, muffins with jam, and coffee.

Accommodations: 4 rooms, 2 with private bath. *Smoking:* Permitted. *Children:* Permitted. *Pets:* Permitted. *Breakfast:* Included. *Driving Instructions:* From I-95 take exit 90 and go 1 mile south, just past the south entrance to the Mystic Seaport Museum.

New Haven Area **CONNECTICUT**

Woodburning Stove. An eclectic 1911 home five minutes from Yale University and downtown New Haven, this bed and breakfast is hosted by a couple prominent in the arts. Numerous nineteenth-century oil paintings done by one of the host's ancestors decorate the house, which is furnished with many antiques and has a wood-burning stove, air conditioning, and a deck overlooking a secluded backyard. For a highly negotiable fee, the host will prepare gourmet dinners. *Represented by:* Bed & Breakfast, Ltd., (203) 469-3260. $35.

Eighteenth Century. A fully restored eighteenth-century home, this bed and breakfast is in a historic New Haven neighborhood, five minutes from Yale. The guest room has antique furnishings, a fireplace, and a piano; the house features views of the Housatonic River and a private breakfast patio for guests. *Represented by:* Bed & Breakfast, Ltd., (203) 469-3260. $50.

Fireplace and Piano. A *ca.*-1900 home, this bed and breakfast is in the heart of the Yale University area. The guest room has a private bath and a private sitting area. The double living room contains a fireplace and a piano, and a large deck adjoins the country kitchen. The host, who enjoys history and design, has decorated the house with many antiques. *Represented by:* Bed & Breakfast, Ltd., (203) 469-3260. $22.50–$35.00.

Washington Area **DISTRICT OF COLUMBIA**

Chevy Case section of D.C. Just off Rock Creek Parkway, ten minutes from the Smithsonian Institution, this is a modern town house in an exclusive complex. Well traveled, the hosts here speak Spanish and Portuguese, as well as English and some Italian. The house is furnished with contemporary Spanish-style pieces, and there are two guest rooms—one with a private and the other with a semiprivate bath. *Represented by:* Sweet Dreams & Toast, (202) 483-9191. $35–$45.

Capitol Hill. A restored Victorian structure, this guest house is a mile from Union Station and the Capitol. The host, a retired government employee, has lived in many parts of the United States and is active in D.C. politics. The Smithsonian Institution is ten minutes from here. *Represented by:* Sweet Dreams & Toast, (202) 483-9191. $35–$45.

Georgetown. A three-year-old Federal town house, this bed and breakfast is near Chain Bridge, which allows easy access to the McLean and Tysons Corner areas of Virginia. A guest room with twin beds and private bath is available, and guests may use the recreation room, which features television and a fireplace. *Represented by:* Sweet Dreams & Toast, (202) 483-9191. $33–$45.

Georgetown. This brick three-story Victorian bed and breakfast was built in 1887. The hosts are in the continuing process of restoring this large home, and if you enjoy such projects, they'll appreciate any help. The guest room has a double bed and private bath, and guests are invited to use a small sitting room. The grounds feature a pool that guests may use, and the interior of the house is patrolled by a resident cat and an English setter. *Represented by:* Sweet Dreams & Toast, (202) 483-9191. $35–$65.

Washington **DISTRICT OF COLUMBIA**

The Kalorama Guest House

1854 Mintwood Place, N.W., Washington, D.C. 20009. (202) 667-6369. *Hosts:* Roberta Pieczenik and Jim Mench.

Constructed of dark bricks, the Kalorama Guest House is a *circa*-1890 Victorian row town house on a quiet, tree-lined street. Roberta and Jim spent nine months restoring and furnishing it. They did a splendid job.

The central parlor features a white-tiled fireplace surrounded by a white-painted mantel with a built-in mirror, a beige Oriental rug with a pattern in blues and reds, two antique couches, a crystal and brass chandelier suspended from a ceiling medallion, an oaken floor, and antique coffee and side tables. On an elaborately carved antique desk/bureau is a decanter of sherry, which guests are invited to enjoy.

All guest rooms have brass beds, oaken floors, Oriental-style rugs, wing chairs upholstered in chocolate brown or Prussian blue crushed velvet, antique writing desks, subtle but colorful quilts and pillow covers that match the curtains, live plants, washstands and unobtrusive working sinks, and plenty of lamps. Rooms are painted cream and are air-conditioned. The back rooms, one of which has a private, enclosed porch, overlook a park.

The skylit central hallway is carpeted wall-to-wall and decorated with framed pages from such turn-of-the-century magazines as *Ladies' Home Journal,* prints that are also featured in the guest rooms.

The Kalorama offers several services not usually available at bed-and-breakfast places—a telephone-answering service that will take messages for guests, and a washer and dryer and soft-drink vending machine that are all well-hidden. In a downstairs dining room, Jim puts out a Continental breakfast for the guests. The Kalorama operates by *reservation only.*

Accommodations: 6 rooms with shared baths. *Smoking:* Permitted. *Children:* Permitted. *Pets:* Not permitted. *Breakfast:* Included. *Driving Instructions:* Coming from the south, take Route I-95 to the Memorial Bridge, bear right, and get on Rock Creek Parkway; take the Connecticut/Cathedral exit and bear left when you see (at a point where the exit forks) the Calvert Street part of the exit; turn right and follow Calvert to Columbia; turn right on Columbia and take the second right turn onto Mintwood.

Amelia Island **FLORIDA**

1735 House

584 South Fletcher, Amelia Island, FL 32034. (904) 261-5878.

Hosts: David and Susan Caples.

1735 House consists of two buildings: a 1920s frame home painted white with black shutters and an eight-year-old four-story reproduction of the Amelia Island lighthouse. Both have guest accommodations, and both are immediately on the Atlantic Ocean at the northeasternmost tip of Florida, almost contiguous with Cumberland National Seashore in Georgia.

All the rooms here are suites that include a bedroom with private bath and a living-entertainment area. The living areas overlook the ocean and have contemporary wicker and rattan furnishings, color cable television, parquet floors partially covered with area rugs, and dark Georgia pine tongue-and-groove paneling. Each of these rooms has a work area with a table, of either oak or mahogany, and a supply of reading material. The bedrooms, which are on the street side of the building, are furnished with antiques—one has a captain's chest fashioned of pecan; another, a marble-topped mahogany dresser; another, a period brass bed; and another, a large mahogany buffet now doing duty as a dresser. Each room has a small refrigerator.

The lighthouse, which has a kitchen-living area, is designed to be occupied by a couple—it's quite popular with honeymooners—or a family. It too has tongue-and-groove woodwork, a staircase that winds around the interior, a bath with a sunken shower, and a glassed-in crow's nest fitted out with captain's chairs and opening onto an observation platform. Rooms in both structures are decorated with nautical appointments.

A Continental breakfast in a basket, as well as a newspaper, are delivered to the guest rooms each morning; guests are invited to use the kitchen any time they like.

Accommodations: 7 rooms with private bath. *Smoking:* Permitted. *Children:* Permitted. *Pets:* Not permitted. *Breakfast:* Included. *Driving Instructions:* Take I-95 south to the Amelia Island exit (Route A1A); proceed for 15 miles and look for the inn, which is on the beach.

East Coast **FLORIDA**

Boynton Beach. This guest house in a quiet neighborhood has a swimming pool and a separate entrance for guests. The host, who conducts painting classes, has a pottery studio behind his house. *Represented by:* Bed & Breakfast of the Palm Beaches, (305) 746-2545. $35.

Cape Kennedy. Involved in public relations and real estate (and, therefore, a Cape Kennedy booster), the host here gives guests a complimentary box of grapefruits or oranges, as well as a poster commemorating the first moon walk. This one-story home has two rooms for guests. *Represented by:* Sun Coast Accommodations in Florida, (813) 360-1753. $30.

Delray Beach. Hosted by a librarian hooked on tournament bridge, this town house has a guest room overlooking the ocean. Guests are invited to swim in the ocean or the heated pool, and children are welcome. The house is in a quiet residential area within walking distance of shopping and restaurants. *Represented by:* Bed & Breakfast Company, #275, (305) 661-3270. $40–$45.

Fort Lauderdale. Surrounded by and filled with tropical plants, this contemporary ranch-style house is on Commercial Boulevard, an easy walk to restaurants and shopping. The hosts serve a Continental breakfast, including homemade bread and rolls, by the pool, which overlooks a tropical landscape and the waterway. *Represented by:* Bed & Breakfast Company, #290. (305) 661-3270. $28–$40.

Fort Lauderdale. Half a block from Route 1, this bed and breakfast is hosted by a couple of retired professionals who enjoy pointing their guests in the right directions and who decorate the guest room with fresh flowers. The house is convenient to everything in Fort Lauderdale, and the grounds feature a swimming pool that guests are invited to use. *Represented by:* Bed & Breakfast Company, #265, (305) 661-3270. $30–$45.

Hollywood. Across the street from a large, open shopping mall with restaurants, shops, and a theater, this bed and breakfast is a town house on Sheridan Street. The grounds include tennis courts and swimming pool that guests may use. The hosts also extend kitchen and laundry privileges. *Represented by:* Bed & Breakfast Company, #270, (305) 661-3270. $28–$40.

Jupiter. The host, retired from the lumber business, has a modern ranch-style house directly on an inlet, 150 feet from the ocean. He offers a pool, a fireplace, and excellent opportunities to fish for

Pompano Beach (Bed & Breakfast Company)

Pompano Beach (Bed & Breakfast Company)

snook in the inlet. There are tennis courts next door to the house. *Represented by:* Bed & Breakfast of the Palm Beaches, (305) 746-2545. $65.

Jupiter. This guest house is furnished with antiques such as a rosewood piano and a walnut desk from the host's grandfather's hardware store in Tennessee. The house has a pool, and every bed is covered by a handmade quilt. Homemade sourdough English muffins are part of the breakfast. *Represented by:* Bed & Breakfast of the Palm Beaches, (305) 746-2545. $35–$45.

Jupiter West. An Englishwoman devoted to the bed-and-breakfast concept, the hostess has a ranch-style house on several acres of grounds. She also has a riding stable and quite a few horses. *Represented by:* B & B of the Palm Beaches, (305) 746-2545. $35.

Pompano Beach. A brick house that features a whirlpool bath, this accommodation is hosted by someone with a green thumb. Antique bowls filled with freshly cut flowers appear all over the house, which is furnished in Oriental motifs. The host has a greenhouse, where he grows orchids and African violets, and the house has a patio. *Represented by:* Bed & Breakfast of the Palm Beaches, (305) 746-2545. $40–$55.

Pompano Beach. A retired airlines pilot currently into antique cars and sport fishing is host of this bed and breakfast, which is half on land and half in water. A guest room is available in the host's home on the Intercoastal Waterway. There are also accommodations in the host's boat, a 58-foot Hatteras yacht with three bedrooms, three heads, a full galley, and two sitting rooms—one inside and one on deck. In the pool/patio area between the house and the boat, the host serves a Continental breakfast. *Represented by:* Bed & Breakfast Company, #280, (305) 661-3270. $30–$60.

Pompano Beach. Across the street from the Pittsburg Pirates' spring-training camp, these bed-and-breakfast accommodations include a room in a private house, or a completely equipped cottage with an entrance less than 5 feet from the swimming pool. Golf and tennis are two blocks away; the beach is a twenty-minute walk or a five-minute drive away. The hosts welcome children, and they serve a Continental breakfast on the patio. *Represented by:* Bed & Breakfast Company, (305) 661-3270. $28–$50.

West Palm Beach. This guest house on the shore of a lake in the heart of West Palm Beach has a pool and a large screened-in patio. The host extends kitchen privileges to guests. *Represented by:* Bed & Breakfast of the Palm Beaches, (305) 746-2545. $30.

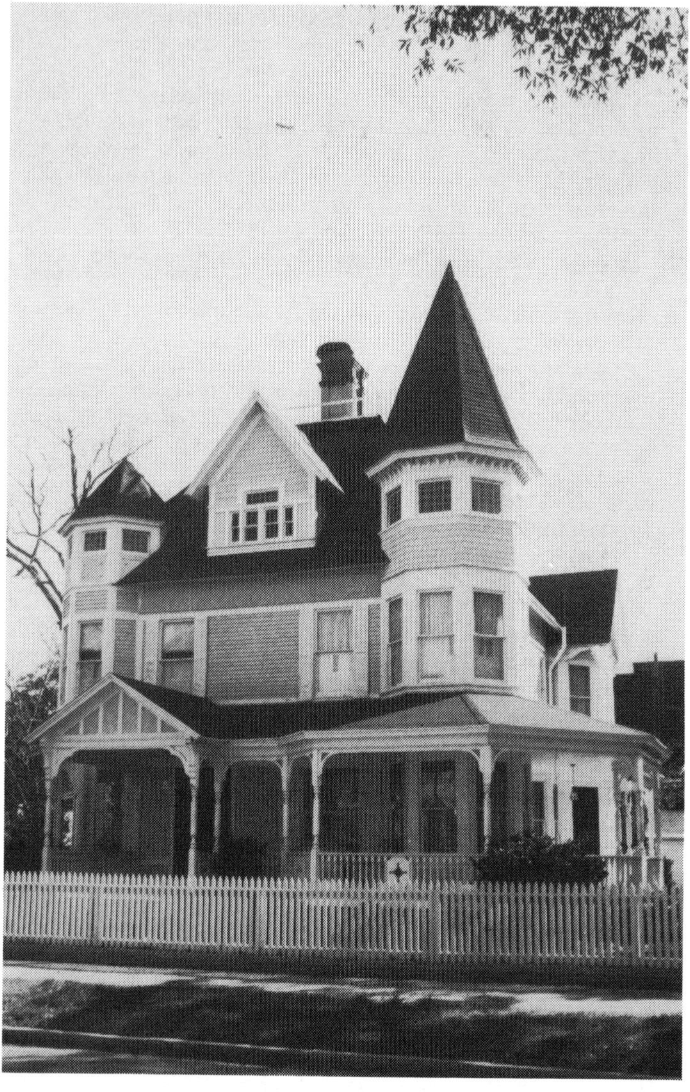

Fernandina Beach **FLORIDA**

The Bailey House

28 South Seventh Street, Fernandina Beach, FL 32034. (904) 261-5390. *Hosts:* Tom and Diane Hay.

Pale cream yellow trimmed in white, The Bailey House is an 1895 Queen Anne structure with two towers. It was built by Effingham W. Bailey, a steamship agent who, rumor has it, used a team of Danish shipbuilding carpenters from his industry to work on his home. The building's elaborate woodwork, all of it in heart pine, lends the rumor credibility.

The house is furnished with period Victorian pieces, most of them walnut—an 8-foot étagère, heavily carved and featuring turned-wood lacework and open filigree; a huge marble-topped oval table; a pump organ; a French sofa upholstered in pink brocade; and a marble-topped washstand with a tilt mirror. There are also some oaken pieces, such as the 9-foot double-mirrored wardrobe in the Rose Room, which also features a 26-foot Oriental rug and a bay window with six panes of glass covered with lace curtains.

The 30- by 18-foot reception hall takes up half the ground floor and has a fireplace with an engraved heart-pine mantel; bay windows with beveled and stained glass; a walnut Gramophone; an Oriental-style rug in navy and light blue and several shades of mauve; and an English davenport desk with a lift-up lid.

The house, listed in the National Register of Historic Places, has six fireplaces, footed tubs and pedestal sinks, a widow's walk, and 9-foot pocket doors of heart pine that separate several of the downstairs rooms.

The Continental breakfast is served on lace place mats with china coffee cups.

Accommodations: 4 rooms with private bath. *Smoking:* Permitted on veranda only. *Children:* Over 10 permitted. *Pets:* Not permitted. *Breakfast:* Included. *Driving Instructions:* From the Route I-95 exit on Centre Street, turn left on Seventh Street; The Bailey House is on the left.

The Keys **FLORIDA**

Big Pine Key. This bed and breakfast is a California-style guest cottage separate from the main house and directly on the ocean. Surrounded by tropical plants, the cottage has a queen-size convertible sofa and a kitchen with a dishwasher and a washer and dryer, as well as a complete supply of breakfast ingredients. *Represented by:* Bed & Breakfast, Inc. of the Florida Keys, (305) 743-4118. $45.

Big Pine Key. This California-style contemporary bed and breakfast is directly on the ocean, which guests get to view while eating breakfast in the screened-in garden atrium. The hosts offer three guest rooms, two with private bath, and they invite guests to use their hot tub. *Represented by:* Bed & Breakfast, Inc. of the Florida Keys, #5, (305) 743-4118. $40.

Key Largo. Particularly suited for two couples traveling together, this bed and breakfast has two rooms available for guests. One room directly overlooks the water and has a separate entrance, a private bath, and a queen-size bed; the other has twin beds. The hosts don't serve breakfast but leave all the ingredients for one in the kitchen, which they invite their guests to use. *Represented by:* Bed & Breakfast, Inc. of the Florida Keys, #50, (305) 743-4118. $40–$75.

Marathon. A half mile from Marathon Beach and Marathon's restaurant and shopping area, this bed and breakfast has two rooms available for guests. Both rooms face the ocean; each has twin beds, television, a Bahama fan, air conditioning, a private entrance, and a private bath. The hosts serve a full breakfast. *Represented by:* Bed & Breakfast, Inc. of the Florida Keys, #1, (305) 743-4118, $30–$35.

Marathon. If you arrive here by boat, the hosts invite you to tie up at their dock, about 20 feet from the living room of this bed and breakfast. Their oceanfront apartment has two guest bedrooms, one with a king-size bed, and the other with twin beds. The apartment has a complete kitchen as well as color television and directly overlooks the ocean. *Represented by:* Bed & Breakfast, Inc. of the Florida Keys, #6, (305) 743-4118. $75–$90.

Marathon. A short walk from the beach, this efficiency apartment is on a 100-foot-wide canal. Its screened-in porch overlooks the canal, and its small kitchen is stocked with all the ingredients for a full breakfast. *Represented by:* Bed & Breakfast, Inc. of the

Marathon #1 (Bed & Breakfast, Inc. of the Florida Keys)

The Keys **FLORIDA**

Florida Keys, #36, (305) 743-4118. $40.

Ramrod Key. A half hour from Key West, this bed and breakfast on a 3-acre estate is a large home with arched windows and a private deck overlooking a lagoon. Guests are invited to swim or snorkel in the lagoon. The hosts, who speak German, offer guests three rooms, and they serve a full breakfast. *Represented by:* Bed & Breakfast, Inc. of the Florida Keys, #23, (305) 743-4118. $40.

Tavernier. This bed and breakfast on the Gulf of Mexico has a private swimming area and a fenced-in yard. The guest suite is a complete apartment with one bedroom, a living room, a kitchen area, a screened-in patio, and docking facilities. *Represented by:* Bed & Breakfast, Inc. of the Florida Keys, #55, (305) 743-4118. $50–$75.

"Dock, pool and sauna" (Bed & Breakfast Company #210)

Private Island in Biscayne Bay (Bed & Breakfast Company #201)

Miami Area **FLORIDA**

Private Island. Something of an Art Deco mansion, this bed and breakfast on a private residential island in Biscayne Bay features a 40-by-28-foot living room with a series of 14-foot-tall windows overlooking a patio/garden area. The hosts, sailors by profession as well as inclination, offer three guest rooms, each with a private bath. They also have a 28-foot sailboat tied up at their dock. The Miami Beach Convention Center and the Theater of the Performing Arts are nearby. *Represented by:* Bed & Breakfast Company, (305) 661-3270. $28–$40.

Dock, Pool, and Sauna. A real estate professional who also manages a marina is host of this bed and breakfast a few yards from Biscayne Bay. The house has a dock, a patio, a pool, and a sauna. One of the guest rooms, on the second floor, has a private bath and a large balcony overlooking the Miami and Miami Beach skylines. In her family kitchen beside the pool, the hostess serves a Continental breakfast that includes a specialty of hers—fresh fruit compote. *Represented by:* Bed & Breakfast Company, #210, (305) 661-3270. $28–$48.

Coconut Grove. A studio guest room with a cathedral ceiling, a private bath, and a private entrance, this bed and breakfast is in a verdant section of Miami where yuccas, palmettos, and dieffenbachias abound. The area is also rife with historic landmarks as well as craft shops, the Biscayne Bay marinas, galleries, and restaurants. The hosts serve a Continental breakfast in their landscaped sculpture garden. *Represented by:* Bed & Breakfast Company, (305) 661-3270. $28–$40.

Art Deco. In an older residential section roughly 3 miles north of downtown Miami, this bed and breakfast is a block from Biscayne Boulevard. A block in the other direction takes you to a quiet park on the shore of Biscayne Bay. The house is convenient, even by public transportation, to the Port of Miami and the airport, and its decor is Art Deco. Well-traveled and well-acquainted with bed-and-breakfasting, the hostess is a journalist. *Represented by:* Bed & Breakfast Company, #500, (305) 661-3270. $26–$35.

Apartment. In a third-flor condominium apartment not far from Biscayne Bay, Coconut Grove, and Coral Gables, this bed and breakfast has a sun deck, a heated pool, and a sauna. Lots of major attractions are nearby, and public transportation is a short walk away. The hostess here is an attorney. *Represented by:* Bed &

Miami Area **FLORIDA**

Breakfast Company, (305) 661-3270. $28–$40.

Pineapples. The hosts of this bed and breakfast are enthusiastic organic gardeners. Over Continental breakfast, guests often get to sample the hosts' exotic fruits and vegetables; and the hostess, a gourmet cook, will provide, on request, additional meals for her guests. The hosts' latest project is a mini-pineapple plantation, which can have as many as a hundred or so plants bending toward the sun. The house is convenient to recreational as well as shopping and eating possibilities. *Represented by:* Bed & Breakfast Company, (305) 661-3270. $28–$40.

Pool. Furnished with a definite European flavor, this bed and breakfast is hosted by a pair of transplanted Germans. One of them picked up most of the furnishings during a career as a travel representative. The U-shaped house wraps around a pool beside which the hosts often serve a Continental breakfast. *Represented by:* Bed & Breakfast Company, (305) 661-3270. $30–$40.

North **FLORIDA**

Gainesville. The hosts—who speak Finnish and Portuguese, as well as English—have three bedrooms available for guests. The house, located in a college town, features lawns, lounge chairs, and a patio area. You may be able to cajole the hosts into taking you on a tour of the area. *Represented by:* Sun Coast Accommodations in Florida, (813) 360-1753. $30.

Saint Augustine. This restored Spanish-style house in the historic St. George area has five rooms available for guests. A buffet breakfast is served in a large meeting room with a fireplace. The hosts give honeymooners a complimentary bottle of champagne and bowl of fruit. *Represented by:* Sun Coast Accommodations in Florida, (813) 360-1753. $35–$45.

Seminole. One of the hosts is a member of the local industrial council, and the other is an avid kayaker, canoer, and white-water rafter willing to take guests on outings. The house is furnished with a combination of contemporary and early-American furniture, and the hosts speak Swedish and Norwegian, as well as English. For a small fee, guests may use the hosts' beach club facilities. *Represented by:* Sun Coast Accommodations in Florida, (813) 360-1753. $30–$35.

Tarpon Springs **FLORIDA**

The Livery Stable

100 Ring Avenue, Tarpon Springs, FL 33589. (813) 938-5547.

Hosts: Marvin and Ingrid Jones.

Built around the turn of the century out of hand-hewn concrete blocks, The Livery Stable originally functioned as a livery stable, but the advent of the automobile eliminated the need for a large livery stable in Tarpon Springs. The horse and mule stalls were converted into a lobby, and the building turned into a boarding-house that catered primarily to the Greek fishermen who worked in the sponge-gathering industry.

Most guest rooms face south and even in winter admit plenty of Florida sunshine. Large and high-ceilinged, the guest rooms are simply but comfortably furnished and feature cable television sets.

The Livery Stable has for the guests' use a living room, dining room, and kitchen. The Joneses serve approximately three evening meals per week as well as a complimentary breakfast.

Close to the Gulf of Mexico, The Livery Stable is five minutes away from white sand beaches, golf courses, tennis courts, and picnic facilities. Horse and greyhound racing takes place the year round, and deep-sea boats sail daily from local docks.

Accommodations: 12 rooms with shared baths. *Smoking:* Permitted. *Children:* Permitted except in winter. *Pets:* Permitted if small. *Breakfast:* Included. *Driving Instructions:* In the center of downtown Tarpon Springs.

West Coast **FLORIDA**

Apollo Beach. This contemporary home has a golf course in front of it and a canal behind it. The house has its own dock, and the host has a boat on which he's willing to take guests out. (He knows the best fishing holes in Florida.) Guests have a choice between a room with a private bath and one with a shared bath. Continental breakfast is served. *Represented by:* Sun Coast Accommodations in Florida, (813) 360-1753. $30.

New Port Richey. A white two-story brick structure, this guest house, on a country road and surrounded by generous amounts of undeveloped land, is hosted by a retired couple willing to lend their guests bicycles and fishing rods. The guest rooms have private baths and television. The decor—typified by wicker furniture and a yellow, lime green, and white color scheme—lends the place a summery feeling. *Represented by:* Sun Coast Accommodations in Florida, (813) 360-1753. $45.

Tampa. The hosts—involved in real estate, investments, and a temporary-help agency—have three guest rooms in their brick contemporary home on a corner lot. A pool, sauna, and private beach are available to guests. The house is furnished with sleek modern pieces (a mirrored wall in the den is representative of the decor). The hosts often prepare guests' meals, for an extra charge. *Represented by:* Sun Coast Accommodations in Florida, (813) 360-1753. $35.

Tampa. Overlooking the bay and with biking and jogging trails right outside its door, this Victorian house contains antique furnishings such as four-poster beds. An extensive antique-doll collection is housed in a small upstairs anteroom. Other features include a large foyer and reception room, wide-paneled wooden floors, and two upstairs bedrooms with fine views. *Represented by:* Sun Coast Accommodations in Florida, (813) 360-1753. $30–$35.

Atlanta Area **GEORGIA**

Historic Area. A renovated early-1900s home in a designated historic area, this guest house features a room with a queen-size bed, a large sitting area, and an adjoining bath. The house has a large deck and a backyard swimming pool. Hosted by a corporate executive and a nurse, this accommodation is two blocks from Atlanta's Cultural Art Center, which has a museum and a theater, where the Atlanta Symphony plays. *Represented by:* Bed & Breakfast Atlanta, (404) 378-6026. $36–$40.

Atlanta Northwest. A late-nineteenth-century Victorian structure, this guest house is hosted by a medical doctor and a doctor of musicology. They offer guests two bedrooms, each with a private bath. The location has excellent expressway connections to all local points of interest. *Represented by:* Bed & Breakfast Atlanta, (404) 378-6026. $40–$44.

Peachtree Road. Ten minutes from downtown Atlanta, on a tree-arched street of older homes, this guest house is a two-story, traditional-style home with a patio and terraces, set amid many varieties of flowers. The guest room is furnished with antiques, and the hosts, a retired contractor and his wife, are active in the local art scene. *Represented by:* Bed & Breakfast Atlanta, #11, (404) 378-6026. $36–$44.

Morningside. Hosted by a young female graphic designer and three hospitable felines, this contemporary two-story brick cottage is a few minutes from Emory University. The house is furnished with bright contemporary pieces, and the guest room has a private bath. *Represented by:* Bed & Breakfast Atlanta, #12, (404) 378-6026. $32–$36.

Historic Area. Painted gray with white trim, this large, rambling Victorian house is on a hill in Atlanta's historic district. The building, which is within walking distance of Colony Square and the Cultural Arts Center, features a wraparound porch. Both guest rooms are furnished with antiques. *Represented by:* Bed & Breakfast Atlanta, #3, (404) 378-6026. $36–$44.

Columbus   **GEORGIA**

The De Loffre House
  812 Broadway, Columbus, GA 31901. (404) 324-1144. *Hosts:* Shirley and Paul Romo.

Once inhabited by a steamship baron who claimed to be directly descended from William the Conqueror, this 1883 Italianate town house is on the brick-paved parkway that runs through Columbus's Historic District.

The De Loffre House has been thoroughly restored and modernized—its antique furnishings and modern conveniences ride comfortably at anchor. Each guest room has a fireplace, a private bath, a color television set, and toilet accessories for those who forget their own. No one forgets Shirley and Paul's complimentary breakfast, which is served on antique china with candles burning on the tables.

Some guest rooms have four-poster beds, some have carved spool beds, some have chandeliers, some have Oriental and Persian rugs. In each, a complimentary bottle of sherry and a bowl of fruit are set out.

  Accommodations: 4 rooms with private bath. *Smoking:* Permitted. *Children:* Under twelve not permitted. *Pets:* Not permitted. *Breakfast:* Included. *Driving Instructions:* Take Route 280 into Columbus (the house is four blocks from the highway).

Savannah **GEORGIA**

Eliza Thompson House
 5 West Jones Street, Savannah, GA 31401. (912) 236-3620.
 Host: Jim Widman.

This town house was built in 1847 for Miss Eliza, a pretty redhead with seven children who, on her kitchen's large hearth, baked corn cakes to sell to General Sherman's soldiers. Legend has it that Sherman didn't destroy Savannah because he couldn't resist Miss Eliza's corn cakes.

Owners Jim and Laurie Widman see to it that breakfast includes Miss Eliza's corn cakes, the recipe for which they still follow. The past reappeared recently during an elaborate restoration undertaken by the Widmans. Breaking through a wall of an upstairs bathroom, they discovered a fireplace; in the living room they found a hand-hewn, 2-foot-square and 20-foot-long oak log, which they decided to leave exposed—albeit cleaned up—over the windows; and after scraping away paint and wallpaper, they uncovered 20-inch-wide clear cedar paneling over the fireplaces in the parlor and foyer.

The inn features an enclosed private courtyard, a garden with an 8-foot-high copper sculpture and a fountain. Fireplaces, heart pine floors, Oriental rugs, and a large collection of Vanity Fair prints suggest the Widmans' taste.

Guests are welcomed with a glass of complimentary sherry, and later in the evening they frequently gather around the bar, where they mix their own drinks.

Accommodations: 26 rooms with private bath. *Smoking:* Permitted. *Children:* Permitted. *Pets:* Not permitted. *Breakfast:* Included. *Driving Instructions:* Take Liberty Street to Whittaker and make a right; then turn left on West Jones Street.

Savannah   **GEORGIA**

The Halsam-Fort House
   417 East Charlton Street, Savannah, GA 31401. (912) 233-6380.
   Host: Alan Fort.

Every so often, late in the evening, the ghost of its original owner stomps around on the third floor of the Halsam-Fort House. A minstrel-show impresario unfortunately lynched by an irate Ohio audience for whom he failed to produce a show, John Halsam left behind him an 1872 brick Italianate home. It's now a landmark building, as well as a bed-and-breakfast inn, in the middle of Savannah's Historic District.

   Alan Fort, the current owner, lives on the top two floors—with the ghost, many antiques (he has an interest in an antique business), and an extensive collection of antique dolls and toys. The entire garden level is a guest accommodation. With a living room, two bedrooms, a full bath, and a "country kitchen," the guest suite can accommodate one or two couples or a medium-sized family. Mr. Fort never asks strangers to share the suite.

   The living room has a Savannah-gray brick fireplace; an 1840 Pennsylvania pine apothecary cabinet; two wing chairs covered and quilted in a light navy blue broadcloth with bird and flower patterns in beiges, whites, and yellows; and views through two windows of the English Regency townhouses across the street.

One bedroom has twin brass beds and a fireplace, another has a double bed and walnut Victorian furnishings. For parties of guests that require more sleeping room, the sofa in the living room is a convertible with a queen-size mattress.

Although Mr. Fort doesn't prepare breakfast, he provides fresh pastry, coffee, tea, and juice for his guests to enjoy at their leisure. The suite's kitchen has plenty of cookware, a dinner service and flatware for eight, a coffee maker, and a refrigerator stocked with soft drinks.

Mr. Fort, who traditionally invites guests for a tour of his home and a small libation of an evening, reports that his average guest tends to be an "explorer kind of person."

Accommodations: 1 suite with private bath; 2 rooms with shared bath. *Smoking:* Permitted. *Children:* Permitted. *Pets:* Permitted but with a charge. *Driving Instructions:* Between Habersham and Price streets, just off Troup Square, in the Historic District.

Savannah **GEORGIA**

Liberty Inn, 1834

128 West Liberty Street, Savannah, GA 31401. (912) 233-1007.
Hosts: Janie and Frank Harris.

The Liberty Inn was built in 1834 by a militia colonel named William Thorne Williams. The colonel was also a bookseller, a publisher, and a six-term mayor of Savannah. Constructed of bricks overlaid with clapboard, the Federal-style building survived the numerous fires that devastated early Savannah.

Somewhere in the middle of reconstructing the house, Frank Harris, nervously perusing estimates that had quadrupled, thought there was no way he could afford that much house. So he and his wife, Janie, both of whom operate restaurants in Savannah, decided to open their doors to guests, which they had thought about doing anyway.

The Harrises have four guest suites, two of them with three rooms. Each suite has a private entrance, individually controlled air conditioning, a telephone, a color television set with Home Box Office, laundry facilities, and a complete kitchen. Although they no longer function—which perhaps explains why the house escaped so many fires—earthen-fired brick fireplaces appear in all but one suite.

Exposed ceiling-beams are found throughout the house, and the landscaped courtyard, with fruit trees and a grape arbor, features a solar spa with a whirlpool bath (great except in the winter—"last year we had two inches of ice on it"). For those not in the mood to take advantage of their suite's kitchen, the Harrises serve a complimentary breakfast of orange juice, coffee, and Danish.

Accommodations: 4 suites with private bath. *Smoking:* Permitted. *Children:* Permitted. *Pets:* Not permitted. *Breakfast:* Included. *Driving Instructions:* Take Route I-16 to Ogelthorpe Avenue; turn south and go one block on Barnard Street to Liberty Street.

Savannah **GEORGIA**

Mary Lee Guest Accommodations

117 East Jones Street, Savannah, Georgia. *Mailing Address:* P.O. Box 607, Savannah, GA 31402. (912) 232-0891. *Hostess:* Mary Lee.

"They seem to feel my presence even though I'm not visible," says Mary Lee of her guests. The presence they feel wanders around among old iron beds, handmade quilts, a wicker immigrant's trunk from Bulgaria, fresh flowers, afghans, exposed beams, fireplaces, and bowls of fruit.

This 1854 tabby-over-brick Savannah town house has a courtyard—complete with a bougainvillea-covered statue of Saint Francis—that is totally enclosed by a foot-thick wall of Savannah-gray brick. The carriage house at one end of the courtyard contains two of Mary Lee's three guest suites. Each suite has a living room, a bedroom, and a kitchen, which Mary stocks with coffee, juice, and fresh fruit. The suites have telephones and central air conditioning.

Mary Lee always keeps a bottle of cold champagne around in case some honeymooners show up, or a couple celebrating an anniversary comes, or it turns out to be a guest's birthday.

Accommodations: 3 apartments with private baths. *Smoking:* Permitted. *Children:* Permitted. *Pets:* Not permitted. *Breakfast:* Food for preparation by guests included. *Driving Instructions:* Take I-16 into Savannah; turn right on Liberty; turn right on Abercorn; then right on Jones Street.

Savannah **GEORGIA**

Remshart-Brooks House

106 Jones Street West, Savannah, GA 31401. (912) 236-4337.

Hosts: Martha and Charles Brooks.

In 1854, Mr. Remshart built Remshart's Row—a series of four red-brick Savannah town houses. He had three sons and one daughter—hence, the four units, Martha Brooks explains.

Martha and Charles Brooks have one guest-accommodation—a garden suite with a bedroom, a living and dining room, and a full kitchen. The bedroom has a four-poster bed, shuttered windows, many green plants, and a working fireplace. The living room also has a fireplace (which is unusually large because this room originally served as a kitchen), late-nineteenth-century furnishings, paintings by local artists, and a sofa that opens into a double bed. The living room also has a color television set with cable, and a library offering everything from Nancy Drew and the Hardy Boys to tomes on Savannah history.

The guest suite has two private entrances, one of which opens onto a walled courtyard, which Martha recommends for afternoon coffee or cocktails.

The Brookses consider sharing their home with guests "one of life's extras." Their rates include a complimentary Continental breakfast and private off-street parking.

Accommodations: 1 apartment with private bath. *Smoking:* Permitted. *Children:* Permitted. *Pets:* Not permitted. *Breakfast:* Food for preparation by guests included. *Driving Instructions:* Take Route I-95 to Route I-16; take exit 37B. Make a right turn at the first traffic light, a right at the next traffic light (Whitaker Street), and a right on Jones Street West.

HAWAII

Hawaii. On a cliff overlooking Hilo Bay and the Pacific, this guest accommodation has a private entrance and a shaded lanai (veranda). Twenty minutes from the airport. *Represented by:* Bed & Breakfast Hawaii, H-1A, (808) 822-1582. $25–$30.

Hawaii. On landscaped property in the hilly area of Hilo, this A-frame home offers two bedrooms to guests. Close to the airport and near the ocean, this accommodation is convenient to beaches and parks. *Represented by:* Bed & Breakfast Hawaii, H-2, (808) 822-1582. $20–$30.

Hawaii. Near Boiling Pots, a Hilo attraction, this designer home enjoys a view of Mauna Kea and the ocean. The host, who knows the island well, frequently acts as a tour guide for guests. *Represented by:* Bed & Breakfast Hawaii, H-3, (808) 822-1582. $20–$30.

Hawaii. Decorated with curios from around the world and surrounded by 20,000 square feet of tropical plants, this accommodation, which has a private bath, is in the Hilo Hills area. *Represented by:* Bed & Breakfast Hawaii, H-5, (808) 822-1582. $20–$25.

Hawaii. Convenient to shopping and dining areas, this accommodation is at the edge of the golf course. A pool, Jacuzzi, and tennis courts are available; your host has a car and a moped for rent. *Represented by:* Bed & Breakfast Hawaii, H-7, (808) 822-1582. $25–$30.

Hawaii. A mile or so from Kailua town center, this accommodation on landscaped property is close to tennis courts and a pool. *Represented by:* Bed & Breakfast Hawaii, H-8, (808) 822-1582. $25–$30.

Hawaii. A completely furnished condominium apartment, this accommodation features a 7-by-20-foot veranda that overlooks Snug Harbor. The building has washers and dryers, a pool, a Jacuzzi, and a parking lot. *Represented by:* Bed & Breakfast Hawaii, H-9, (808) 822-1582. $58–$80.

Hawaii. Each guest room has a private entrance and a private bath. This recently built home also offers a tennis court, a pool, and a view of the Pacific. *Represented by:* Bed & Breakfast Hawaii, H-10, (808) 822-1582. $32–$35.

Kauai. This accommodation, minutes from Poipu Beach, features a private entrance and small back patio. The room has a small refrigerator and a color television set. The grounds are marked by well-tended gardens. *Represented by:* Bed & Breakfast

HAWAII

Hawaii, K-1, (808) 822-1582. $22–$27.

Kauai. Located behind Sleeping Giant Mountain, this studio apartment is separate from the main house and features a large lanai (veranda). The Wailua River is nearby, as are several parks and hiking trails. *Represented by:* Bed & Breakfast Hawaii, K-3, (808) 822-1582. $25–$30.

Kauai. This bungalow-style house in Kapaa Heights is a mile and a half from an ocean beach. Its guest room has a private bath and a separate entrance as well as a small refrigerator, and its grounds include flower, fruit, and vegetable gardens. *Represented by:* Bed & Breakfast Hawaii, K9, (808) 822-1582. $22–$27.

Kauai. In Kapaa, this completely self-contained studio, separate from the main house, overlooks the Valley of Rainbows and Mt. Waialeale, the wettest spot on earth. The studio can accommodate four adults downstairs and perhaps half a dozen children in the loft area, and comes with a sink, a refrigerator, and service for eight. Guests are invited to use the hosts' hot tub on the main deck, which is where breakfast is served. *Represented by:* Bed & Breakfast Hawaii, K-25, (808) 822-1582. $35.

Kauai. In Koloa, on grounds surrounded by gardens, these accommodations consist of a guest room with a private bath, a private patio, color television, and a refrigerator. Poipu Beach, minutes from here, offers excellent swimming, snorkeling, and surfing. *Represented by:* Bed & Breakfast Hawaii, K-1, (808) 822-1582. $22–$27.

Kauai. On a half acre of landscaped property, this accommodation is in a residential area 4 miles from the beach. Two guest rooms are available, and both offer limited use of the kitchen. *Represented by:* Bed & Breakfast Hawaii, K-4, (808) 822-1582. $15–$22.

Kauai. Your host, a marathon runner, is involved in many island activities and looks forward to sharing them with guests. The house is 2 miles from the ocean and the Wailua River, and guests here are offered limited use of the kitchen. *Represented by:* Bed & Breakfast Hawaii, K-5, (808) 822-1582. $15–$20.

Kauai. This one-bedroom condominium on Hanalei Bay with a view of Bali Hai features tennis courts, two pools, and nightly movies. You can rent the studio only or the entire apartment. *Represented by:* Bed & Breakfast Hawaii, K-6, (808) 822-1582. $42–$60.

(Bed & Breakfast Hawaii O-4)

HAWAII

Kauai. Your hostess, active in community affairs, has a three-bedroom home in the hills above the Wailua River. The property, located on a dead-end street, is quite rural. *Represented by:* Bed & Breakfast Hawaii, K-7, (808) 822-1582. $22–$27.

Kauai. Two miles from Poipu Beach, this accommodation features a private entrance, a pullman kitchen, a television set, and a patio. The host, who enjoys hiking, tennis, golf, and swimming, is willing to accompany guests on excursions. *Represented by:* Bed & Breakfast Hawaii, K-8, (808) 822-1582. $22–$27.

Kauai. This accommodation offers a 180-degree view of the mountains and the ocean, as well as a private entrance and a kitchenette. The house is situated in the Lawai hills, on several acres. Your hosts own horses and dogs. *Represented by:* Bed & Breakfast Hawaii, K-10, (808) 822-1582. $42.

Kauai. An old plantation worker's house, this accommodation is on the northern coast of Kauai. A secluded beach is a short walk away. Your hosts, and their dog, are marathon runners. *Represented by:* Bed & Breakfast Hawaii, K-12, (808) 822-1582. $15–$20.

Kauai. This accommodation is a two-bedroom condominium in Princeville. Large windows and glass doors provide lovely views, and the apartment provides linens, cooking utensils, and a washer and dryer. Available for a minimum of four nights, the apartment is in a complex that has tennis courts, a swimming pool, and a golf course. *Represented by:* Bed & Breakfast Hawaii, K-13, (808) 822-1582. $70 (4 nights minimum), $342 weekly (6 nights).

Kauai. Located in Kilauea, a sleepy town on Kauai's lush northern shore, this accommodation features a private bath, a patio, and full kitchen privileges. *Represented by:* Bed & Breakfast Hawaii, K-15, (808) 822-1582. $20–$25.

Maui. Two acres of land surround this house, from whose deck you can watch the Pacific Ocean. Minutes from an uncrowded beach, this accommodation offering two rooms will appeal to hikers and countryside explorers. *Represented by:* Bed & Breakfast Hawaii, M-4, (808) 822-1582. $25–$35.

Maui. The grounds of this accommodation are landscaped with fruit trees, berries, vegetables, and local flowers. A patio has a table and chairs, and a sitting-room has a television set. *Represented by:* Bed & Breakfast Hawaii, M-7, (808) 822-1582. $27.

HAWAII

Maui. Furnished with mats, pillows, and low tables, this Japanese teahouse-style home is three blocks from the ocean. The beds are *futons* (Japanese sleeping quilts), and each guest room has a private outdoor area. Tea ceremony breakfast; outdoor shower. *Represented by:* Bed & Breakfast Hawaii, M-8, (808) 822-1582. $18–$23.

Maui. A large banyan tree shades the garden of this accommodation, which is a short walk from the beach and also convenient to shops, restaurants, and cafés. Limited use of kitchen. *Represented by:* Bed & Breakfast Hawaii, M-9, (808) 822-1582. $19–$24.

Molokai. This studio cottage, 18 miles east of Kaunakakai, has a refrigerator, cooking facilities, a private bath, and a walk-in closet. On a sandy beach near Halawa Valley this accommodation features a sun porch that overlooks the ocean. *Represented by:* Bed & Breakfast Hawaii, MO-1, (808) 822-1582. $40–$50.

Oahu. Situated in the Oiea Hills overlooking Pearl Harbor this guest house is 15 minutes from downtown Honolulu and Waikiki. The house features a swimming pool, a garden, and a lanai. Guests are invited to use the pool table and Ping-Pong tables. *Represented by:* Bed & Breakfast Hawaii, O-1 (808) 822-1582. $25.

Oahu. In Hawaii Kai, on a cliff a short walk from Hanauma Bay, this bed and breakfast has an English hostess who offers guests a master bedroom with an adjoining bath. The living/dining room has two exposures, and through its glass walls there's a sweeping view of the ocean, the mountains, and the southern section of Honolulu. A bus stops nearby, and shopping is within walking distance. *Represented by:* Bed & Breakfast Hawaii, O-19, (808) 822-1582. $30–$38.

Oahu. Five minutes from Waikiki in the Honolulu hills, this studio apartment, separate from the main house, features large windows, a kitchen area, and a private patio with a barbecue. *Represented by:* Bed & Breakfast Hawaii, O-2, (808) 822-1582. $30–$35.

Oahu. With views of Waikiki, Pearl Harbor, and the ocean, this house is high in the hills, 15 minutes from downtown Honolulu (and 10 degrees cooler). *Represented by:* Bed & Breakfast Hawaii, O-4, (808) 822-1582. $23–$28.

Oahu. The entire top floor of this elegantly furnished two-story house is reserved for guests. Each room has television. One has a

Kauai (#10) (*Bed & Breakfast Hawaii*)

HAWAII

half bath; and the other, a full bath down the hall. The house features a sitting room, a lanai, and a swimming pool. *Represented by:* Bed & Breakfast Hawaii, O-5, (808) 822-1582. $25.

Oahu. A short walk from this home will get you to a large shopping mall, and an even shorter walk, a few steps in fact, will bring you to a small private beach. The house has a large lanai. *Represented by:* Bed & Breakfast Hawaii, O-9, (808) 822-1582. $25–$40.

Evanston Historic District (*Bed & Breakfast Chicago*)

Glencoe Cape Cod (*Bed & Breakfast Chicago*)

Chicago Area **ILLINOIS**

Marina City. On the forty-third floor of a high-rise building, facing south, this condominium apartment has views of Lake Michigan, the Chicago River, the Loop, and the Chicago Yacht Basin. It is furnished with contemporary pieces, such as a glass dining-room table surrounded by six leather chairs, and it has two balconies—one off the living room, another off one of the bedrooms. Guests are invited to use the building's exercise-and-beauty salon, and the building also has shops, restaurants, and discotheques. *Represented by:* Bed & Breakfast Chicago, (312) 951-0085. $70–$90.

North Michigan. One-half block from the beach and a short walk from the Chicago Institute of Art, this guest house is hosted by a painter with an interest in theater. The guest room has a private bath, wall-to-wall carpeting, and antiques. The building has a 24-hour doorman and a garage attendant, and guests are invited to use the roof deck. *Represented by:* Bed & Breakfast Chicago, (312) 951-0085. $50–$60.

Evanston. The hosts, who buy and sell estates, have a Tudor-style home that faces a forest preserve. They offer guests a suite with two bedrooms—one of which has wood paneling and an exposed-beam ceiling—and a single bedroom, with a private bath, that overlooks their yard and patio. The Loop is only 20 minutes away. *Represented by:* Bed & Breakfast Chicago, (312) 951-0085. $30–$45.

Evanston. Built in 1892, this row house is owned by a professional caterer who will prepare dinners for guests who so request. Two bedrooms, done in Colonial motifs, are available for guests, and the sitting room has a fireplace. Public transportation is nearby. *Represented by:* Bed & Breakfast Chicago, (312) 951-0085. $30–$45.

Evanston. Two blocks from Lake Michigan and five from Northwestern University, this accommodation is in an 1890s townhouse in Evanston's historic district. The hosts are a professional couple who have traveled a great deal. *Represented by:* Bed & Breakfast Chicago, (312) 951-0085. $30–$45.

Glencoe. This Colonial-style home has a private beach and a host whose hobbies—quilting and needlework—contribute substantially to the home's decor. The guest room, which has a fireplace, overlooks Lake Michigan. *Represented by:* Bed & Breakfast Chicago, (312) 951-0085. $35–$50.

Eldred **ILLINOIS**

Hobson's Bluffdale

Eldred, IL 62027. (217) 983-2854. *Hosts:* Bill and Lindy Hobson. Hobson's Bluffdale is a 320-acre working farm. The farmhouse, an 1828 stone structure, was built by Bill Hobson's great-great-great-grandfather, an American officer who fought in the War of 1812. The house has six fireplaces made of local limestone. Very local limestone: you can see the limestone bluffs, on the other side of the river, from the Hobsons' front yard.

The backyard has a heated swimming pool, a whirlpool bath, a basketball court, a bonfire area, and, for swingers, rope-swings hanging from large trees. The backyard blends into thick woods where hikers or joggers or horseback riders find miles of scenic trails.

The Hobsons enjoy organized activities like bonfires or hayrides or picnics: It's not uncommon for them to prepare a box lunch for everybody and take guests motorboating or canoeing down the Illinois River.

Rates here, based on weekly occupancy, include all meals. Once a week the Hobsons roast a hog.

Accommodations: 3 suites and 5 family-size rooms, all with private bath. *Smoking:* Permitted except in the main house. *Children:* Permitted. *Pets:* Not permitted. *Breakfast:* Included. *Driving Instructions:* From Carrouton proceed west; at Eldred go north for 3½ miles.

Galena ILLINOIS

Colonial Hotel
   1004 Park Avenue, Galena, IL 61036. (815) 777-0336. *Hostess:* Mary Keller.

The Colonial Hotel, a large 1826 Greek Revival structure, has two

36-foot screened-in porches and columns in front. It is fronted by two large pine trees and gaslights imported from England. Its Victorian antique furnishings include a great deal of art and pattern glass and china and silver. Mary Keller has been in the antique business all her life and operates a shop on the premises. Her home, photographed by *P.M.* Magazine, appeared on national television. Oriental rugs, Victorian furniture upholstered in velvet, and chandeliers and similar appointments characterize the kind of furnishings one would expect to find in an antique dealer's home. Mary doesn't serve breakfast, but coffee is always available. Each guest room has a private entrance.

Mary's front windows have a panoramic view of the city of Galena, which has several museums as well as theaters and antique shops. General Ulysses S. Grant's home is nearby, as are the Chestnut Mountain Ski resort and several public golf courses.

Accommodations: 4 rooms with private bath. *Smoking:* Permitted. *Children:* Permitted. *Pets:* Permitted only if small. *Driving Instructions:* On Route 20, at the Eastend Bridge.

Westfield **INDIANA**

Camel Lot

    4512 West 131st Street, Westfield, IN 46074. (317) 873-4370.

    Host: Moselle Schaeffer.

You won't run into Launcelot or Guinevere or Merlin as you wander about the 50-acre grounds of Camel Lot, but you will very likely bump into Jane Doe, a resident deer. A working animal-breeding farm, Camel Lot has (in addition to what the pun implies) llamas, zebras and other exotic quadrupeds.

    Moselle has one guest accommodation—a three-room suite with a bedroom, a television room, and a private bath. The bedroom is furnished with antiques including a grand old four-poster bed. A complimentary breakfast includes freshly squeezed orange juice, coffee, and homemade bread. When the weather is good, Moselle serves breakfast on the terrace, which overlooks Ivan's cage. Ivan is a Siberian tiger. What's Moselle like? You have to Noah to love her. A guest who stayed at Camel Lot put it this way: "It worked out great—she's into breeding tigers, and I'm into breeding fresh air."

    Accommodations: 1 suite with private bath. *Smoking:* Permitted. *Children:* Over 10 permitted. *Pets:* Permitted by prior arrangement. *Driving Instructions:* Take Meridian Street to 131st Street (proceeding north); turn west on 131st Street and go 4½ miles.

McGregor (Bed & Breakfast in Iowa)

IOWA

Burlington. This brick 1854 Federal guest house, listed in the National Register of Historic Places, is a block and a half from the Mississippi River, right where the *Delta Queen* docks. The house, filled with Federal-period antiques, still has its original windows. One in the living room features a set of initials carved by the engagement ring given to the original owner's daughter. One guest room has a four-poster canopied bed and a white marble fireplace. Another, with twin beds, also has a marble fireplace. The hosts, who speak a little German, serve a full breakfast. *Represented by:* Bed & Breakfast in Iowa, (515) 277-9018. $25–$40.

Des Moines. Listed in the National Register of Historic Places, this restored Victorian guest house has gables, a turret, and a front porch. The grounds, an acre encircled with hedges, contain a formal garden and numerous mature shade trees. The house is furnished entirely with period antiques and has a winding staircase with a built-in dormer seat. The hosts, who speak French as well as English, serve a full breakfast. *Represented by:* Bed & Breakfast in Iowa, (515) 277-9018. $33–$49.

McGregor. This two-story contemporary house among cliffs and bluffs is part of a working farm that raises primarily Hampshire pigs. From a knoll on the property you can see the Mississippi. The living room, furnished largely with antiques, is done in greens and whites and golds and has a fireplace. There are also a large formal dining room and a porch. *Represented by:* Bed & Breakfast in Iowa, (515) 277-9018. $30–$40.

Monana. This large Colonial-style house with an attached greenhouse is close to Effigy Mounds National Monument and the Iowan Pikes Peak. It is on a working farm, which the hosts lease out. One of the hosts, an interior designer who hails from Chicago, furnished it with a mixture of antique and contemporary pieces—there are a four-poster canopied bed, a grandfather clock, a couple of chandeliers, and wall-to-wall carpeting; its sunken living room has a brick fireplace. For a nominal fee the hosts, who have a boat, take guests for a ride on the Mississippi. *Represented by:* Bed & Breakfast in Iowa, (515) 277-9018. $25–$45.

Orange City. Decorated primarily with period antiques, this contemporary wooden farmhouse is on a 400-acre farm. You can hand-feed the lambs if you like. The hosts raise mainly sheep and pigs, and grow corn and soybeans. The beautifully decorated house has

Adel (Bed & Breakfast in Iowa)

IOWA

some formal, some informal, rooms, which vary in decor. The parlor has comfortable, casual furniture, a large brick fireplace, a wagon-wheel chandelier, a pair of deer heads, and an antique rifle. Breakfast here often includes *sauajasebroodges,* a Scandinavian delicacy of pork and beef in a rich pastry. *Represented by:* Bed & Breakfast in Iowa, (515) 277-9018. $25–$35.

Bentonsport   **IOWA**

Mason House Inn

Front Street, Bentonsport, IA. *Mailing address:* c/o Keosauqua, IA 52565, (319) 592-3133. *Host:* Herbert K. and Burretta Redhead.

Bentonsport, population 32, started operating on electricity in 1951. In 1972 the U.S. Department of the Interior designated the place a National Historic District, probably because every building in the town, except for six, was more than 100 years old.

Mason House Inn, dating from 1846, was built originally as a luxurious inn for steamboat passengers and still contains its original furnishings, although a series of floods necessitated refinishing work on the lower level's hardwood floors. The structure, which operated as a museum from 1956 to 1981, is a stone's throw from the Des Moines River.

The entire lower level is there for guests' use. The parlor/kitchen area is 36 feet long and has Williamsburg-blue walls. Iron pots and skillets hang over a brick fireplace with its pine mantel;

there are country scatter rugs, Boston rockers, and a double-rocker bench. The dining room, 40 feet long, features leaded glass, brass kerosine chandeliers, hardwood floors, and an old-time fiber rug. The bedrooms contain such appointments as marble-topped dressers, hardwood floors, a 9½-foot-tall, intricately carved and shaped mahogany headboard, and handmade quilts.

Breakfast varies but is always substantial—you might have scrambled eggs and sausages, fresh-baked cinnamon rolls, orange juice and tea or coffee, and quiche on some mornings.

Accommodations: 8 rooms with shared bath; private cottage with private bath. *Smoking:* Permitted on the first floor only. *Children:* Not permitted. *Pets:* Not permitted. *Breakfast:* Included. *Driving Instructions:* Bentonsport is 7 miles southeast of Keosauqua, Iowa.

Brooklyn IOWA

Hotel Brooklyn
 154 Front Street, Brooklyn, IA 52211. (515) 522-9229. *Hostess:* Kathryn Lawson.

The Hotel Brooklyn is an 1875 brick Victorian structure with buttressed gables, a three-story tower, and four Doric columns supporting its porch and pediment. The building, in the National Register of Historic Places, was originally erected as a home but later served as a hospital. The sitting room has a marble fireplace, mahogany and walnut furniture, and handpainted murals. Fine woodwork is found throughout the house, which features a grand old central staircase.

 Two of the nine guest rooms have private baths; all have television sets and air conditioning. Each guest room features at least one genuine antique—a 100-year-old dresser here, a 125-year-old easy chair there.

 Kathy has been in the hotel business since 1940 and told me that this year her establishment has entertained guests from twenty-two different countries. Can city-dodgers find something to do in Brooklyn? Yes, provided they enjoy lakes, swimming pools, golf courses, and parks. The Hotel Brooklyn is a half hour from the Amana colonies, a group of small villages formed by mid-nineteenth-century German emigrés who came to this country to escape persecution.

Accommodations: 9 rooms, 2 with private bath; family units available. *Smoking:* Permitted. *Children:* Permitted. *Pets:* Not permitted. *Driving Instructions:* Two miles from Route I-80, or a mile from Route 6.

Kansas City Area **KANSAS**

Shawnee Mission. Surrounded by manicured shrubs and hedges, this contemporary house is convenient to Route I-35, which takes you into the downtown area in about twenty minutes. The host is interested in horses and sports cars, which he puts together and refurbishes in his spare time; the hostess is a gourmet cook who has a weakness for quiches. The hosts, who serve a full breakfast, have two rooms available for guests, both with private baths. *Represented by:* Kansas City Bed & Breakfast, (913) 268-4214. $30–$35.

Shawnee Mission. A forty-year-old home in a wooded residential area, this bed and breakfast is hosted by a woman who is active in community affairs and considers among her specialties her homemade bread and muffins. The house, convenient to restaurants and shopping, is furnished with a mixture of contemporary and antique pieces and features a fireplace. Prairie Village is a mile away; Country Club Plaza is ten. *Represented by:* Kansas City Bed & Breakfast, (913) 268-4214. $25–$30.

Shawnee Mission. This wooden, contemporary ranch-style bed and breakfast is in a wooded cul-de-sac. One of the hosts, a retired air-traffic controller, teaches; and the other spends her time seeing to church and community activities. The house, fifteen minutes from downtown Kansas City and Royal Stadium, is furnished with contemporary pieces. Route I-35 is three quarters of a mile from here, and Country Club Plaza is fifteen minutes farther. *Represented by:* Kansas City Bed & Breakfast, (913) 268-4214. $29–$32.

Shawnee Mission. Guests, as many as three adults, have this entire apartment to themselves, except perhaps when the hosts appear with a gastronomic specialty or two. The apartment's bedroom features an antique double brass bed, and it comes with such amenities as a piano, books, and the use of indoor and outdoor swimming pools, a sauna, tennis courts, and an exercise room. Guests prepare their own breakfasts here, and there is a two-night maximum stay. *Represented by:* Kansas City Bed & Breakfast, (913) 268-4214. $32–$35.

Shawnee Mission. Custom-designed for a famous movie-producer, this bed and breakfast has a beamed entry hall that was once a screening room. Furnished generously with antiques, the house features living space on five different levels. The guest room and its private bath, for example, are on a separate level and have

Kansas City (Missouri) (Kansas City Bed & Breakfast)

Shawnee Mission (Kansas) (Kansas City Bed & Breakfast)

Shawnee Mission (Kansas) (Kansas City Bed & Breakfast)

Kansas City Area **KANSAS**

a private entrance. The hosts serve breakfast in a sunny dining room, on a pine table 8 feet long. *Represented by:* Kansas City Bed & Breakfast, (913) 268-4214. $30–$35.

Shawnee Mission. Hosted by a magazine editor, this bed and breakfast is in a condominium. The guest room features a king-size bed, a private bath, and a private balcony. The condominium is accessible to Route I-35 and has a pool and tennis courts that guests are invited to use. The hosts serve a full breakfast, either in the dining room or on the shaded patio. *Represented by:* Kansas City Bed & Breakfast, (913) 268-4214. $35.

Manhattan **KANSAS**

Kimble Cliff

R.D. 1, Box 139, Manhattan, KS 66502. (913) 539-3816. *Hosts:* Betty and Neil Anderson.

Kimble Cliff is an 1894 stone farmhouse built partially into the side of a cliff. Like the large stone barn also on the property, the main house was built out of limestone, which was quarried nearby and fashioned into shape by hand. The house and barn sit on slightly less than 7 acres—wooded mostly with cedar, black walnut, and pine—that include an orchard with peach, apple, and pear trees, and raspberry bushes. The part of the house that was dug into the cliff now serves as a fruit cellar and storm shelter.

The house features a "summer" and a "winter" parlor, which are separated by French doors. The winter parlor has a corner fireplace with a fieldstone hearth and a walnut and oak mantel; wall-to-wall carpeting the color of sand; an oaken church pew and hymn board; an antique rocker of walnut, pine, and pecan; and an oaken bentwood rocker, two antique kerosene lamps, and other similar appointments. The summer parlor has a piano, an old Victrola, a sofa upholstered in a brown floral-print fabric, an antique basinette, and some antique baby quilts.

One guest room has a private entrance, an oaken dresser, an antique pine rocker, a pedestal table, an overstuffed chair covered with a floral print in greens and browns, and four windows—two overlooking Wildcat Valley, the other two overlooking the stone barn.

Accommodations: 2 rooms with shared bath. *Smoking:* Not permitted. *Children:* Permitted. *Pets:* Not permitted. *Breakfast:* Included. *Driving Instructions:* Kimble Cliff is on Country Route 412, 5 miles west of Manhatan.

Wakefield **KANSAS**

Bed and Breakfast on Our Farm

Route 1, Wakefield, KS 67487. (913) 461-5596. *Hosts:* Rod and Pearl Thurlow.

"We're not a guesting ranch," says Pearl Thurlow, "but just a plain farm family who really like people, and especially children." Rod and Pearl live in a hundred-year-old midwestern farmhouse, situated on 160 acres of land. The Thurlows raise wheat, soybeans, oats, pigs, cattle, and chickens. They grow just about all of their own food and grind their own wheat flour for baking. Rod and Pearl serve a hearty breakfast each morning; and for late sleepers they leave about the kitchen all the makings of a morning meal.

Pearl's and Rod's farm is close to the Eisenhower home, the Tuttle Creek and Milford dams' water facilities, Fort Riley, and one of the country's most important archeological sites—a prehistoric Indian burial pit near Salina.

Accommodations: 3 rooms with shared bath. *Smoking:* Permitted. *Children:* Permitted. *Pets:* Permitted. *Breakfast:* Included. *Driving Instructions:* From Junction City or Salina take Route I-70; take exit 286; proceed 10 miles north to the county line; then go 1 mile east and ⅓ mile north, to the first farm on the west side of the road.

Asphodel Village

Route 2, Box 89, Jackson, LA 70748. (504) 654-6868. *Host:* Mack Couhig.

William Carlos Williams began what sensible critics consider his best poem with these lines: "Of Asphodel, that greeny flower, I have come to speak." The asphodel, according to Greek mythology, was the flower of heaven, the Greeks' Elysian fields.

Asphodel Village consists of five buildings. The main antebellum plantation house, which took ten years to build, was completed around 1830. When the Couhigs took over the property, they moved to it from the nearby town of Jackson a structure called the Levy House, built in 1780. In order to be moved, it had to be cut into three pieces and then reassembled.

Asphodel Village has 500 acres of grounds, with trails winding among hills and creeks. The property also has three guest houses, designed by Mrs. Couhig, who incorporated into the structures antique doors and windows that she acquired in New Orleans. All the guest rooms, some of which are cottages surrounded by pine trees and flowering dogwood, have individually controlled air conditioning and heat, and eight have fireplaces.

The Couhigs serve a complimentary full country breakfast to guests. Their facilities include a gift shop and a restaurant where, for a price, items like beef balls Burgundy or crabmeat crepes are available.

Accommodations: 18 rooms with private bath. *Smoking:* Permitted. *Children:* Permitted. *Pets:* Not permitted. *Breakfast:* Included. *Driving Instructions:* From Baton Rouge, proceed north on Route 61; turn right onto Route 68 and follow it for 8 miles.

New Orleans Area **LOUISIANA**

1880 Creole. Hosted by a young entrepreneur who is currently restoring it, this 1880 Creole structure is fifteen minutes from downtown New Orleans. In an area where many historical renovations are taking place, the block this house is on is almost entirely unchanged. Some of the furnishings are original to the house, which has large rooms with ceiling fans, fireplaces, and air conditioners. The house also has a side porch and a walled side garden that's softly illuminated at night. *Represented by:* New Orleans Bed & Breakfast, #5, (504) 949-6705. $45.

Eight-room Cottage. Painted pink and trimmed white, this 8-room cottage is in a quiet uptown residential area convenient to several universities. Hedges and palm trees decorate the front lawn. The host, a retired science teacher and seasoned traveler, has furnished his home with many antiques and heirlooms. Each guest room has a private bath. *Represented by:* New Orleans Bed & Breakfast, #7, (504) 949-6705. $40.

Pink Stucco. Located uptown, this large, pink stuccoed structure is convenient to the downtown, University, and Audubon Park-Zoo areas. Well traveled, the hostess is a knowledgeable tour guide.

New Orleans Area **LOUISIANA**

The house, which features one double and one triple room, is furnished with many antiques. *Represented by:* New Orleans Bed & Breakfast, #2, (504) 949-6705. $20–$25.

Oak-lined Street. A white 1920s New Orleans raised bungalow, this house sits on a lot 220 feet deep, on a residential street lined with large oak trees. A former teacher, gardener, and traveler, the hostess is now an active businesswoman. Her house, which has three bedrooms and two apartments available to guests, contains much of its original furniture, which she has refurbished, with colorful fabrics setting the tone. *Represented by:* New Orleans Bed & Breakfast, #1, (504) 949-6705. $25–$50.

New Orleans   **LOUISIANA**

Cornstalk Fence Guest House
    915 Royal Street, New Orleans, LA 70116. (504) 523-1515. *Hosts:* David and Debbie Spencer.

Once upon a time, about 150 years ago, as a matter of fact, a wealthy man from Iowa built a cast-iron fence for his new bride. He brought her from Iowa to live with him in New Orleans, and he wanted her to see, through the windows of her new home, cornstalks entwined with morning glories, which is what she had grown up seeing. Everybody knows there ain't no cornstalks in New Orleans, so the wealthy man from Iowa had incredible facsimiles thereof cast in iron. The fence must be seen to be believed. You can almost hear it growing. Many years later, a writer stayed in this house, and while she was there she wrote a novel—*Uncle Tom's Cabin*.

    The house is a *circa*-1780 Georgian, with four large Ionic columns holding up the second-floor balcony, where you may have your complimentary breakfast if you like. All rooms have high ceilings, fireplaces, and antique furnishings.

    Accommodations: 14 rooms with private bath. *Smoking:* Permitted. *Children:* Permitted. *Pets:* Not permitted. *Breakfast:* Included. *Driving Instructions:* Take Route I-10 to the French Quarter; proceed to Royal Street.

New Orleans **LOUISIANA**

Lafitte Guest House

1003 Bourbon Street, New Orleans, LA 70116. (504) 581-2678.

Host: Steve Guyton.

Built in the grand old tradition of brick French Quarter houses, the Lafitte Guest House was completed by master builder Joshua Peebles in 1849. The house, on the corner of Bourbon and Saint Phillip streets, has wrought ironwork on its balconies, 14-foot ceilings, black marble and carved-mahogany mantels, crystal chandeliers, and many antiques.

Some guest rooms feature entrances to the landscaped courtyard, windows overlooking it, or, in some cases, private entrances. All guest rooms are carpeted and air-conditioned (a must in New Orleans) and have telephones. The Guytons offer a complimentary breakfast (freshly squeezed orange juice, French-roast coffee, a croissant or a brioche), which is served to you in your room. The Lafitte Guest House also has parking facilities (as badly needed as air conditioning in New Orleans's French Quarter).

As lovely as this guest house is, its location is even lovelier—it is within walking distance of but not intruded upon by the frenetic activity of Bourbon Street. Food and jazz are always close at hand.

Accommodations: 14 rooms with private bath. *Smoking:* Permitted. *Children:* Permitted. *Pets:* Not permitted. *Breakfast:* Included. *Driving Instructions:* Take Route 1-10 to the French Quarter; proceed to the intersection of Bourbon and Saint Phillip streets.

New Orleans **LOUISIANA**

Park View Guest House

7004 St. Charles Avenue, New Orleans, LA 70118. (504) 861-7564. *Host:* Zafer B. Zaitoon.

A large, rambling Victorian structure with steep gables and column-supported balconies on two floors, the Park View Guest House was built in 1892. Inspired, rumor has it, by the 1884 World's Fair, held across the street in Audubon Park, the building first functioned as Widow Corey Taylor's Boarding Home. The house today is replete with Victoriana, such as mahogany woodwork, crystal chandeliers, stained glass, beveled glass, and fireplaces. Guest rooms are furnished with a combination of period reproductions and genuine antiques. Several rooms have fireplaces, some have private or shared balconies, and some feature large, low-silled windows overlooking Audubon Park.

The Park View Guest House is on historic Saint Charles Avenue, immediately across the street from Tulane and Loyola universities and Dominican College. The oldest surviving streetcar system in the country runs along Saint Charles Avenue, and in twenty minutes it will take you from the Park View's front door to the French Quarter.

Each morning, in the central dining room, the hosts serve a complimentary Continental breakfast.

Accommodations: 25 rooms, 14 with private bath. *Smoking:* Permitted. *Children:* Permitted. *Pets:* Not permitted. *Breakfast:* Included. *Driving Instructions:* Take Saint Charles Avenue uptown toward the Univer-Section, to the corner of Audubon Park and Saint Charles.

New Orleans **LOUISIANA**

623 Ursulines

623 Ursulines Street, New Orleans, LA 70116. (504) 529-5489.

Hosts: Jim Weirich and Don Heil.

Having purchased the property from Ursuline nuns, Joseph Guillot, a New Orleans contractor, built this 1825 French Quarter town house. The facade features iron railings and gateways. Flagstone-paved alleyways lead from the street to the large private courtyard, which each guest suite opens onto. It is lushly planted with magnolias and orchids, and azaleas, palms, and other subtropical plants. All manner of birds congregate around the courtyard's feeders and birdbath. Each guest suite has a bedroom, a sitting area, a private bath, and a kitchenette and is air-conditioned.

Jim and Don do not include breakfast in their rates, but they do offer a morning paper. Like any interesting city, New Orleans can be baffling to visitors, so they make a point of directing their guests to the many places most worth visiting in this town.

Accommodations: 7 rooms with private bath. *Smoking:* Permitted. *Children:* Over 12 permitted. *Pets:* Permitted if well-behaved. *Driving Instructions:* Take Route I-10 to the French Quarter and proceed to Ursulines Street.

MAINE

Bar Harbor. Close to Acadia National Park, this contemporary, gambrel-roofed structure is on 4½ wooded acres. The hosts, one of whom is a retired chef trained at the Culinary Institute of America, enjoy hiking, sailing, canoeing, camping, and photography. They grow their own fruits and vegetables, and their house has an exercise room and a small library of ornithological and culinary books. *Represented by:* Bed & Breakfast Down East, Ltd., #110, (207) 565-3517. $32–$44.

Bucksport. Eighteen miles from Bangor International Airport, Blue Hill, Castine, and Ellsworth, this frame town house is one of four such homes on a residential street a block from Bucksport's Main Street. The hostess, an octogenarian who does part-time consulting work on aging, enjoys reading, gardening, and chamber music. Buthksport offers visitors plenty of eating and shopping possibilities. *Represented by:* Bed & Breakfast Down East, Ltd., #127, (207) 565-3517. $20–$40.

Camden. A five-minute walk from Camden Harbor, the home base of the windjammers that cruise the Penobscot Bay, this bed and breakfast is hosted by a couple who enjoy sailing, tennis, bridge, skiing, music, and knitting. The house is walking distance from Camden's many shops, restaurants, and galleries. *Represented by:* Bed & Breakfast Down East, Ltd., #121, (207) 565-3517. $35–$45.

Dresden. Surrounded by acres of fields and orchards, this 1826 Colonial is on a hill that overlooks the Kennebec River. Five guest rooms, furnished with a mixture of antique and contemporary pieces, share two baths. The house features wide board floors, and stenciling in the foyer and hallways. One guest room features a piano, and there is a guest parlor available. *Represented by:* Bed & Breakfast Directory of Maine, (617) 277-2292. $30–$35.

Eliot. A large 1736 Colonial built by a sea captain, this bed and breakfast is on the side of a hill. The Maine Beaches are 6 miles away, as are the Portsmouth whale-watching excursions. Breakfast is served either on the porch or the terrace, where guests are always invited to lounge. The house has a private den for guests; and the grounds have a game-room complete with setups. *Represented by:* Bed & Breakfast Directory of Maine, (617) 277-2292. $35–$40.

Ellsworth. An hour's drive from Acadia National Park and the Blue Hill Peninsula, this 1830 Cape Cod farmhouse is hosted by a retired teacher with weaknesses for traveling, reading, and garden-

MAINE

ing. It features a glassed-in porch, and accommodations include a two-room suite with a private bath. *Represented by:* Bed & Breakfast Down East, Ltd., #125, (207) 565-3517. $40.

Ellsworth. Four miles from the center of Ellsworth, on a back road that goes to Bar Harbor, this bed and breakfast is a split-level contemporary structure. The grounds feature a swimming pool, a patio, and a fenced-in backyard (children and well-behaved pets are welcome here). Guests are invited to enjoy the hosts' collection of video-cassette movies as well as their piano. *Represented by:* Bed & Breakfast Down East, Ltd., #101, (207) 565-3517. $10–$35.

Kennebunkport. When the double bed in the guest room here is set in its reclining position, the view is of the ocean as seen through sliding-glass doors and over the small private deck a few steps in front of it. The room has a private bath and high ceilings; halfway up is a loft suitable for an adolescent to sleep in. Breakfast is served either in the dining room or on the private deck. *Represented by:* Bed & Breakfast Directory of Maine, (617) 277-2292. $40–$60.

Moody. A mile and a half from Moody Beach and 2 miles from the Ogunquit art colony, this ranch-style house is at the end of a cul-de-sac. Its guest suite has a private bath and entrance, and the house comes with a hot pot for late-evening tea as well as a refrigerator that guests are free to use. A former New York City investment broker, the host currently serves on the local library board and has interests in art and photography. *Represented by:* Bed & Breakfast Directory of Maine, (617) 277-2292. $30–$40.

Newcastle. Hosted by an antique dealer interested in genealogy and the history of his house, this bed and breakfast is a mile from Route 1, on grounds covered with mature trees. The house is furnished entirely with antiques, including the matresses, which are filled with horsehair. Both guest rooms have fireplaces, and one has its original exposed beams. *Represented by:* Bed & Breakfast Directory of Maine, (617) 277-2292. $25–$35.

Nobleboro. A few miles north of Damariscotta, this large restored farmhouse is on 45 acres of meadow. Furnished with many antiques, the house features some hand-stenciling, handmade quilts, and handmade dust ruffles. The hosts serve a full breakfast in their dining room and offer afternoon wine and snacks in the guest parlor. Five double rooms are available for guests. *Represented by:* Bed & Breakfast Directory of Maine, (617) 277-2292. $35–$47.

MAINE

Portland. A Victorian town house in Portland's West End, this bed and breakfast is near Maine Medical Center and the Museum of Art. Its three guest rooms share a bath, although each has a marble sink. The hosts, one fluent in French, the other interested in architectural design, are vegetarians who favor natural foods. *Represented by:* Bed & Breakfast Directory of Maine, (617) 277-2292. $30–$40.

Southwest Harbor. This 1860s house in town is a short walk from Southwest Harbor's shops, restaurants, and the Wendell Gilley Museum of Bird Carvings. One of the hosts is the town manager of Southwest Harbor, and the other is a self-employed entrepreneur. The hosts enjoy sailing, cross-country skiing, and gardening—which guests can observe from the patio or the porch. Breakfast here comes complete with popovers. *Represented by:* Bed & Breakfast Down East, Ltd., #102, (207) 565-3517. $25–$35.

Winter Harbor. Half a mile from the Schoodic Point section of Acadia National Park, immediately next to a golf course, is this bed and breakfast, a restored farmhouse. The hosts, one a retired engineer and writer, the other a quilter and needleworker, enjoy music and traveling, and have an Afghan hound. They serve a Continental breakfast. *Represented by:* Bed & Breakfast Down East, Ltd., #104, (207) 565-3517. $40.

Camden **MAINE**

Goodspeed's Guest House

60 Mountain Street, Camden, ME 04843. (207) 236-8077. *Hosts:* Linda and Don Goodspeed. Open: Mid-June through October. An 1878 Federal structure painted gray with white trim and black shutters, Goodspeed's Guest House is five blocks from Camden Harbor, from where the well-known Windjammer tour ships leave on tours of the Penobscot. You can't see the harbor from the house, but you can see mountains and, if you carefully inspect the 3- by 10-foot stained-glass window in the living room, Tiffany's signature.

The living room here is furnished with white rattan pieces upholstered in a white, green, and turqouise print fabric and has deep forest-green wallpaper with a tiny pattern in beige. The living room also features a Franklin stove, an antique trunk, and a good part of the Goodspeeds' antique clock collection.

One guest room, the Oak Room, has red and white print wallpaper, Priscilla curtains, a white eyelet spread, wide-board pine floors partially covered with a throw rug, and turn-of-the-century piecrust furnishings—a bed, chest, table, and chair.

Linda and Don have traveled quite a bit and have lived in Europe. When they showed up in Camden and found out the only guest house in the area had closed, they got to thinking, and, well . . .

Accommodations: 9 rooms with shared bath. *Smoking:* Permitted. *Children:* Over 12 permitted. *Pets:* Not permitted. *Breakfast:* Included. *Driving Instructions:* Take Route 1 north to Route 52; turn left and proceed five blocks—the inn is on your left.

Damariscotta MAINE

The Brannon-Bunker Inn
 Box 045, Route 129, Damariscotta, ME 04543. (207) 563-5941.
 Hosts: Dave and Char Bunker.

The Brannon-Bunker Inn, which is open May through October, consists of an 1820 Cape-style house, an attached barn, and a small carriage house on the other side of an old footbridge. During the 1920s the barn was a dance hall called La Hacienda.

Furnished for the most part with period antiques, the house contains such features as pineapple-post beds, an Empire chest and mirror, a corner cabinet filled with antique Strawberry dishes and pewter, a sleigh bed, reproduction period wallpapers, and an old ice chest that's been converted into a bar. Dave and Char don't serve liquor, but they provide guests with all the setups they need, and sometimes they bring out hors d'oeuvres.

Several of the guest rooms—including the two new rooms in the old carriage house—have views of the Damariscotta River. One of these new rooms features a pineapple-post bed, and the other comes complete with a kitchen area.

Accommodations: 6 rooms, 3 with private bath. *Smoking:* Permitted. *Children:* Permitted. *Pets:* Permitted if well behaved. *Breakfast:* Included. *Driving Instructions:* Follow Business Route 1 through the town of Damariscotta, then take Route 129 south.

Kennebunkport **MAINE**

The Chetwynd House
 Chestnut Street, Box 130, Kennebunkport, ME 04046. (207) 967-2235. *Hostess:* Susan Knowles Chetwynd.

The Chetwynd House is an 1840 Colonial structure originally built by Captain Matthew Seavey. Abbott Graves, the artist, owned it in the early twentieth century. The house features a handsome staircase, floor-to-ceiling windows, and pumpkin-pine floors. The rooms are furnished in country Colonial, with predominantly mahogany and cherry four-poster beds. Susan Chetwynd characterizes the color scheme as consisting of "lots of blues and white, with touches of red, gold, and celery."

A former high school English teacher who moved to Maine from Connecticut, Susan has a large collection of books, and she keeps the oral tradition alive at her breakfast table. She claims many of her guests get so full at breakfast that they have no choice but to skip their lunch. Hot chocolate and tea are available when it's cold, and Susan serves wine and cheese in her garden when it's warm.

Accommodations: 5 rooms, 2 with private bath. *Smoking:* Permitted. *Children:* Not permitted. *Pets:* Not permitted. *Breakfast:* Included. *Driving Instructions:* From Kennebunkport's Dock Square, follow the signs for Ocean Avenue—Chestnut Street is the second street off it.

Kennebunkport **MAINE**

The 1802 House

Box 774, Locke Street, Kennebunkport, ME 04046. (207) 967-5632. *Hosts:* Robert and Charlotte Houle.

The 1802 House, a large structure whose top half is painted marine blue and whose bottom half is covered with natural cedar shingles, used to be 20 miles from where it now stands. A team of oxen dragged the house all the way from Waterboro to Kennebunkport, and they must have pulled the house gently because its original walnut staircase is still intact.

The house is furnished with reproduction Colonial pieces, and each guest room has reproduction wallpaper color-coordinated with the bedspreads, linens, and curtains. All these rooms are carpeted wall to wall, and each has a private bath. One guest room has a fireplace with an antique oval mirror hanging above it and a large sitting pillow immediately in front of it, two maple double beds, reproduction Colonial ship-print wallpaper, and a view of the river. Each of the guest rooms has at least one green plant in it, and there's a profusion of plants in front of the glass doors in the dining-and-sitting area, which has a rust and brown carpet that matches the colors of the couch's upholstery. At a large table in this room a full country breakfast is served every morning.

The 1802 House has a lawn with umbrellaed tables and plenty of room to relax. Guests would do well to forsake their cars and either bicycle or walk around the area, which offers many attractions, including an eighteen-hole golf course next door

Accommodations: 8 rooms with private bath. *Smoking:* Permitted. *Children:* Under 13 not permitted. *Pets:* Not permitted. *Breakfast:* Included. *Driving Instructions:* Take exit 3 off the Maine Turnpike, then Route 35 into Kennebunkport; turn left at the Sunoco station, then left on North Street, and look for the red-and-white sign just after passing the church.

North Waterford **MAINE**

Olde Rowley Inn

Route 35, Junction of Route 118, North Waterford, ME 04267. (207) 583-4143. *Hosts:* Michael and Debra Lennon and Peter and Pamela Leja.

Built in 1790 by stagecoach driver John Rice, the Olde Rowley Inn is a clapboard building that used to service the White Mountains stagecoach line. The living room has a large brick fireplace, a beehive oven, wide-board pine floors, and a mixture of genuine antiques and period reproductions. The room has an overstuffed reproduction Colonial sofa, antique oaken tables and rockers, and a bookcase dating back to the mid-nineteenth century.

A tightwinder staircase leads up to the guest rooms, which have exposed-beam ceilings and pumpkin pine floors and are lighted by electrified tin lanterns. The guest rooms feature reproduction wallpapers and, like the living room, are furnished with a combination of period reproductions and genuine antiques, such as a four-poster and oaken dressers from the early nineteenth century. One room has a four-poster, antique Windsor chairs, crocheted pillows, and white Cape Cod curtains that soften the morning sun.

The inn also has a bar constructed of wood from a barn, as well as a dining room with a wood-burning stove.

Accommodations: 4 rooms with shared baths; 1 with half bath. *Smoking:* Permitted. *Children:* Check in advance. *Pets:* Not permitted. *Breakfast:* Included. *Driving Instructions:* The Olde Rowley Inn is in North Waterford a hundred yards or so from the junction of Routes 35 and 118.

Ogunquit   **MAINE**

High Tor

Frazier Pasture Road, Ogunquit, ME 03907. (207) 646-8232.

Hostesses: Julie O'Brien and Cleda Farris Wiley.

A 1913 New England–style house with a column-supported overhang forming a veranda, High Tor is constructed entirely of natural wood. The building, on an acre of pines and wild bushes and berries, overlooks a mile-long coastal footpath known as the Marginal Way. The property's 190-foot artesian well draws 100 percent–tested pure springwater.

The central living room, which is 30 feet long, features a fieldstone fireplace and exposed ceiling-beams. Of an afternoon, Julie and Cleda often start a fire and serve complimentary wine to their guests. All guest rooms have ocean views, private baths, and individually controlled heating. They all have comfortable beds and are furnished with New England country antiques.

High Tor's location is at once convenient and secluded—the towns of Ogunquit and Perkins Cove are short walks away, and a 500-foot-long path leads from the property to the ocean. Julie and Cleda don't serve breakfast, but the guest rooms have hot plates, refrigerators, and all the ingredients for morning coffee.

Accommodations: 3 rooms with private bath. *Smoking:* Permitted. *Children:* Not permitted. *Pets:* Not permitted. *Breakfast:* Not included. *Driving Instructions:* Proceed south from Ogunquit a half mile to Stearns Road; turn left, then take first right onto Cherry Lane; take first left on Frazier Pasture Road; watch for the sign on a pine tree.

South Brooksville **MAINE**

Breezemere Farm

South Brooksville, ME 04617. (207) 326-8628. *Hosts:* Jim and Joan Lipke.

Breezemere Farm consists of an 1850 farmhouse with an attached shed and barn. The 60-acre property, in the beautiful Penobscot Bay area, also has six guest cottages, each with a private bath and a Franklin stove or a fireplace. On the grounds are a pine forest, an apple orchard, and a meadow that runs down to the sea. If you don't feel like playing badminton or croquet or horseshoes, the Lipkes will gladly let you take out a rowboat or a sailboat or a bicycle. It's amazing how many smog-bound urbanites have never seen the Milky Way or a sky exploding with stars, Joan notes.

The farmhouse is furnished with genuine early American antiques. A fieldstone fireplace in the lodge burns 3-foot logs. The complimentary breakfast includes Breezemere granola and blueberry pancakes with real maple syrup. A nearby charter boat will take you to where seals play, or you can explore Arcadia National Park.

Accommodations: 13 rooms, 6 with private bath. *Smoking:* Permitted. *Children:* Permitted. *Pets:* Permitted in cottages only. *Breakfast:* Included. *Driving Instructions:* Take Route 176 from North Brooksville to South Brooksville.

MARYLAND

Annapolis. Furnished with Victorian antiques and reproductions, this house is in the heart of Annapolis. All of that city's attractions are within walking distance, as is public transportation. *Represented by:* Sweet Dreams & Toast, (202) 483-9191. $40.

Annapolis. Without making you feel the slightest bit guilty, the hosts of this fifth-floor apartment will welcome you and then move onto their sailboat for the duration of your visit. The apartment includes a room with a king-size bed, a living room, and a cooking and dining area. It also has a balcony with unobstructed views of Chesapeake Bay and the Bay Bridge. *Represented by:* Sharp-Adams, (301) 269-6232 or 261-2233. $58.

Annapolis. An artist and a physics professor are hosts at this bed and breakfast three-story town house. Guests get the run of the entire third floor, which has a room with a double bed, a private bath, and a balcony that overlooks the Severn River, Chesapeake Bay, and the Bay Bridge. Historic Old Annapolis is a short walk away, and the hosts serve guests a Continental breakfast. *Represented by:* Sharp-Adams, (301) 269-6232 or 261-2233. $48.

Annapolis. This 1838 mini-mansion is on 7 acres of land. The hosts have two cats, two German shepherds, and six peacocks. *Represented by:* Sweet Dreams & Toast, (202) 483-9191. $40–$50.

Annapolis. A new Colonial structure furnished entirely with antiques, this guest house is located directly on the South River. The house is ten minutes from Annapolis, an hour from Washington, D.C., and close to the Chesapeake Bay recreation areas. The guest room has a private bath and a daybed for a child. *Represented by:* Sweet Dreams & Toast, (202) 483-9191. $45.

Annapolis. Ten minutes from the center of Annapolis and a mile from the Chesapeake Bay Bridge-Tunnel, this contemporary home overlooks the bay. There's a water view from almost every room in the house, which is furnished with contemporary pieces and offers a pool and two guest rooms. *Represented by:* Sweet Dreams & Toast, (202) 483-9191. $55.

Annapolis (South River). Situated on 8 acres planted with boxwood and holly, this eighteenth-century mini-mansion features a deep-water pier and a swimming pool. It is ten minutes from downtown Annapolis and an hour from Washington, D.C. The hosts are fluent in both French and English. *Represented by:* Sweet Dreams & Toast, (202) 483-9191. $50.

MARYLAND

Baltimore. A 36-foot Trojan, that is, a cabin cruiser, this bed and breakfast features a 360-degree view of Inner Harbor and, for those who feel queasy away from land, a safe mooring. Heated as well as air-conditioned, the craft is suitable for year-round use, can sleep six, and comes complete with a Continental breakfast. Television is available on request. *Represented by:* Sharp-Adams, (301) 269-6232 or 269-2233. $68.

Baltimore. In one of Baltimore's historic neighborhoods, this bed and breakfast is a restored three-story brick town house on Federal Hill. The guest room features a king-size bed, a private bath, a sitting room, and a deck that overlooks the waterfront. The house is a short walk from the Convention Center and Harborplace. The hosts serve a Continental breakfast. *Represented by:* Sharp-Adams, (301) 269-6232 or 261-2233. $58.

Bethesda. A licensed tour guide who has written numerous brochures on Washington, D.C., and its environs is host at this bed and breakfast twenty minutes from downtown Washington (the Metrobus stops two and a half blocks from here). Furnished entirely with antiques, the house features a game room with Ping-Pong and pool tables, and the host extends golf and tennis privileges to guests. *Represented by:* Sweet Dreams & Toast, (202) 483-9191. $33–$45.

Chevy Chase. This contemporary structure is in a heavily wooded area one mile from Chevy Chase Circle. It features an indoor swimming pool, a sun deck, and a fireplace. The house is very open in its design—there aren't many doors but the rooms are separated by pull-down shades. The hosts, who speak French and Hebrew, as well as English, offer one guest room, which includes a loft for children. *Represented by:* Sweet Dreams & Toast, (202)483-9191. $40.

New Market **MARYLAND**

Strawberry Inn

17 Main Street, Box 237, New Market, MD 21774. (301) 865-3318. *Hosts:* Ed and Jane Rossig.

An electrical engineer who tired of serving in corporate management, Ed Rossig decided to open an inn. He and his wife, Jane, restored this mid-nineteenth-century Victorian home. Ed and Jane have a picture-framing business and an interest in an antique business. There are some forty-six antique stores in the small town of New Market, and the Strawberry Inn looks like one of them.

The building is furnished with antiques and period reproductions. Brass beds, wide-plank floors, reproduction wallpapers, hand-stenciled baseboards and ceiling moldings, bay windows—touches like these appear throughout the inn. Another nice touch is the Rossigs' complimentary breakfast, which you may have in the dining room or served to you in bed. The Rossigs, at an hour you specify, place a breakfast tray at your door.

Accommodations: 10 rooms with private bath. *Smoking:* Permitted. *Children:* Over 5 permitted. *Pets:* Not permitted. *Breakfast:* Included. *Driving Instructions:* From Frederick, take Route I-70 east for 7 miles; take exit 60 and follow the signs to New Market.

The Berkshires — MASSACHUSETTS

Berlin (New York). Two hundred years old, this bed and breakfast home is fifteen minutes from Williamstown. Its 260 acres of grounds include seven ponds—in which guests are invited to swim or fish—and a mountain that overlooks an extensive valley. The hosts, fluent in Swiss, German, French, English, Italian, and Spanish, have one guest room, with a double bed and a private bath. Guests here get to sample the hostess's home-baked Swiss farmer bread. *Represented by:* Berkshire Bed & Breakfast, (413) 783-5111. $45.

Great Barrington. An 1820 Greek Revival structure, this bed and breakfast is fifteen minutes from Tanglewood, the summer home of the Boston Symphony. The hosts, classical musicians and antique dealers, offer guests five rooms that share two baths. Breakfast here is hearty and includes eggs, fruit, bacon, and other early-morning essentials. *Represented by:* Berkshire Bed & Breakfast, (413) 783-5111. $35–$45.

Lanesboro. A 1780 Colonial farmhouse, this bed and breakfast is on the road that winds to the summit of Mt. Greylock, the highest point in Massachusetts. The hosts raise lambs, AKC-registered Labrador retrievers, and registered Morgan pleasure horses. One of the three guest rooms has an adjoining sun-room that in summer turns the room into a family suite. Guests are invited to use the den, which has color television, and breakfast here includes home-baked fruit breads—cranberry, blueberry, and raisin. *Represented by:* Berkshire Bed & Breakfast, (413) 783-5111. $20–$25.

Lenox. On 20 acres, this bed and breakfast is convenient to October Mountain, which is very popular with cross-country skiers. The grounds include lawns, fields, mature trees, blackberries, and many species of wild flowers. One guest room has its own fireplace. *Represented by:* Berkshire Bed & Breakfast, (413) 783-5111. $40–$65.

Pittsfield. Six miles from Tanglewood, which offers many entertainment, dining, and shopping possibilities, this Colonial structure is on 5 acres adjacent to the Pittsfield State Forest; the house itself overlooks Onota Lake. One guest room has a queen-size bed and a private bath. Another has a king-size bed, a half-bath, and a marble fireplace. The hosts offer guests ice, coffee, or tea anytime they want it, and can even arrange for babysitting. *Represented by:* Berkshire Bed & Breakfast, (413) 783-5111. $45–$60.

Sheffield. High on a hill, surrounded by fields and woodlands, this bed and breakfast features a panoramic view of the Berkshires.

The Berkshires **MASSACHUSETTS**

The hostess, an actress, built this authentic log house herself. Her lawn mower, a horse, grazes near the house, from which there's a short walk to a swimming hole beyond the fields. The hostess has two guest rooms with shared bath and serves a full breakfast—on the porch, weather permitting. *Represented by:* Covered Bridge Bed & Breakfast, (203) 672-6502. $58.

Stockbridge. An old Colonial 2 miles from Tanglewood, this bed and breakfast has wide-board floors and exposed beams throughout and a fireplace in every room. The host offers two guest rooms, one with twin beds and the other with a four-poster double; the guest bath has wide-board paneling. A full breakfast is served on Limoges china. *Represented by:* Covered Bridge Bed & Breakfast, (203) 672-6502. $45.

Williamstown. High on a knoll overlooking the foothills of the Berkshires and the Green Mountains of Vermont, this bed and breakfast is a 52-acre working farm. The property is adjacent to the Appalachian Trail and the Long Trail, and features a pond that guests may use for either swimming or fishing for trout. Various museums, theaters and restaurants are close by, as are 5 miles of well-cared-for cross-country skiing trails. *Represented by:* Berkshire Bed & Breakfast, (413) 783-5111. $30–$45.

Williamstown. A working farm that raises cows, sheep, and chickens, this bed and breakfast is high in the Berkshires. Its grounds include a large pond suitable for swimming, boating, or skating. Furnished with many antiques, the second floor bedroom overlooks the pond. The breakfast here is a full one, and homemade; weather permitting, it is served on a screened-in porch with a view of two states and who knows how many mountains. *Represented by:* Covered Bridge Bed & Breakfast, (203) 672-6502. $25–$45.

15 Minutes from Downtown (*New England Bed & Breakfast*)

Near Boston College (*New England Bed & Breakfast*)

Boston Area **MASSACHUSETTS**

Near Boston College. Myra, who teaches art and paints, and Richard, who works in a high-technology industry, invite guests into their split-level contemporary home on a tree-lined dead-end street. They offer a large bedroom with a queen-size bed and a private bath. Their home is furnished with modern pieces, and there is a marked exotic feeling about the place. Although there's no telling what their Siamese cat enjoys, Myra and Richard are fond of music and art, as well as gourmet cooking, of which guests, for far less than what an average restaurant charges, can take advantage. *Represented by:* New England Bed & Breakfast, (617) 498-9819 or 244-2112. $26–$43.

15 Minutes from Downtown. The nearest subway station is a 1-minute walk from Margaret's house in Newton Centre, and you can get to downtown Boston in 15 minutes. Born in Nova Scotia, Margaret used to run a delicatessen in Newton, and of late she's been spending the better part of her free time doing work for the Catholic Church. Margaret bakes her own muffins and offers guests a room with twin beds. *Represented by:* New England Bed & Breakfast, (617) 498-9819 or 244-2112. $24–$43.

Stone House. Mildred is a retired schoolteacher who lives in a stone house 5 minutes from the subway. Her living room has a fireplace and a stereo Mildred acquired because she loves classical music. The house is filled with artifacts and objets d'art from all over the world. Mildred's interests include mountain climbing, backpacking, and scuba diving. Another hobby is sharing wine with guests while Mozart's music plays in the background. *Represented by:* New England Bed & Breakfast, (617) 498-9819 or 244-2112. $24–$43.

Margaret's Room. John and Margo own and operate the New England Bed and Breakfast guest-house agency. John is also executive director of a private social-service agency, and Margo is a travel-promotion specialist. The room they offer guests used to be the quarters of their maid Margaret and has a private bath and a private entrance. A gourmet cook, John tells me his favorite pastime is sitting on the porch while drinking wine and talking about food and travel. I've never tasted his cooking, but I've always enjoyed John's conversation. *Represented by:* New England Bed & Breakfast, (617) 498-9819 or 244-2112. $25–$40.

Fifteen-Room Colonial. Situated on an acre filled with trees

Lexington—"Small, gabled..." (Bed & Breakfast in Minuteman Country)

Margaret's Room (*New England Bed & Breakfast*)

Boston Area **MASSACHUSETTS**

and large, stately homes, this fifteen-room Colonial house has been painted white and trimmed in black. Four large guest rooms are available (some with private bath), and the house offers several sitting rooms and a formal living room. *Represented by:* Bed & Breakfast Associates, Bay Colony, Ltd., #13, (617) 872-6990. $35–$50.

Large and Victorian. This large Victorian guest house, in one of Boston's older single-family neighborhoods, was completely restored. A retired couple, the hosts have maintained a register of guests that includes photographs as well as written remembrances. *Represented by:* Bed & Breakfast Associates, Bay Colony, Ltd., #5, (617) 872-6990. $25–$35.

Boston Balcony. Almost entirely obscured by evergreens, Jennie's house is a short drive from downtown Boston and within easy walking distance of the subway. She has a thick Austrian accent, and her taste in silver and crystal seems to reflect the Old World heritage her voice evokes. Jennie offers guests a suite of rooms with a balcony, where many of them like to eat breakfast. The living room is quite large, with big vases filled with dried flowers here and there and many mirrors. *Represented by:* New England Bed & Breakfast, (617) 498-9819 or 244-2112. $25–$43.

Brookline, Salisbury House. This turn-of-the-century Victorian house has nine fireplaces, each with a unique mirrored mantel. Members of the Museum of Fine Arts, the hosts are seasoned travelers, both fluent in Spanish and French as well as English. One guest room has a brass double bed and an antique cradle, and guests are invited to use the game room, which contains a pool table. *Represented by:* Bed & Breakfast Brookline/Boston, (617) 277-2292. $45.

Brookline, Colonial Revival. This 1883 Colonial Revival guest house has a Japanese garden complete with a small pool and a teahouse. The building still has its original woodwork, stained-glass windows, and fireplaces. The hosts, who welcome children, are amateur Thespians with careers in insurance and library science. *Represented by:* Bed & Breakfast Brookline/Boston, (617) 277-2292. $25–$45.

Brookline, Victorian Row House. Hosted by the proprietor of Bed and Breakfast Brookline/Boston, this 1876 brick Victorian row house features marble fireplaces, chestnut woodwork, and heirloom

"Fifteen-Room Colonial" (*Bed & Breakfast Associates Bay Colony, Ltd., #15*)

"Brookline, Salisbury House" (*Bed & Breakfast Brookline/Boston*)

Boston Area **MASSACHUSETTS**

antiques. Guests have a choice of two baths, one with a Victorian tub and another with a stall shower. An outdoor person, the hostess usually serves home-baked muffins and jam along with her freshly brewed coffee. The house is within walking distance of Boston University and the Harvard Medical School. *Represented by:* Bed & Breakfast Brookline/Boston, (617) 277-2292. $45.

Cambridge. This two-family home, 10 minutes from Harvard Square by bus, is on a quiet residential street. Naomi is in the health-food field, and Elain is a psychiatric social worker. Both women enjoy music and cooking, and they share a penchant for observing the flutter of activity around the bird feeder on their front porch. Naomi and Elain's guest room has a private bath. *Represented by:* New England Bed & Breakfast, (617) 498-9819 or 244-2112. $26-$40.

Cambridge. A short walk from Harvard Square, this guest house offers a room with a private bath. The hostess and host are Jane, who has a career as a nurse, and Bob, who is a school psychologist in the Cambridge school system. They have four children, two of whom are usually away at college. Their home features an open back porch where they serve breakfast when the weather's nice. *Represented by:* New England Bed & Breakfast, (617) 498-9819 or 244-2112. $26-$40.

Ipswich. This restored antique Colonial with a stone fence in front and trees behind is twenty minutes by car from Rockport and Gloucester; Ipswich itself is known for the dunes at Crane's Beach. The hosts, a nurse/midwife and an artistic researcher/optometrist, offer a second-floor bedroom that shares a bath and has a private entrance. The hostess invites guests to join her on her jog to Newburyport. *Represented by:* Bed & Breakfast Associates, Bay Colony, Ltd., #675, (617) 872-6990. $40-$45.

Lexington. A wooden, gambrel-roofed structure with a Colonial-style appendage, this bed and breakfast is in a private woodland broken up by only gardens and brick paths. The hosts researched 1820-40 Colonial America and have designed and decorated their home accordingly—low-ceilings, woodburning stoves, fireplaces, brick and pine floors, braided rugs, antique glass, pewter, tin, and ironware. The hosts, whose craft pieces show up all over the house, have interests in gardening, travel, sailing, and camping. Children are welcome, and guests traveling with infants are invited to use the laundry facilities. *Represented by:* Bed & Breakfast in Minuteman

Ipswich (Bed & Breakfast Associates, Bay Colony, Ltd.)

Lexington—"A wooden..." (Bed & Breakfast in Minuteman Country)

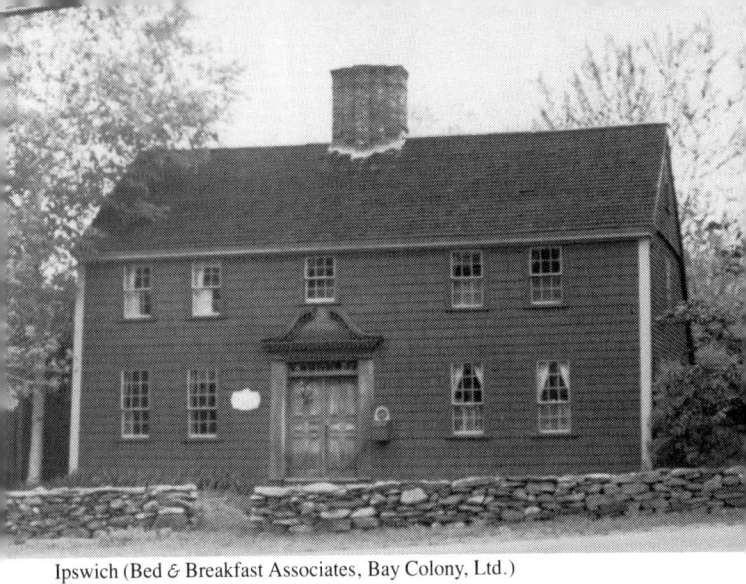

Boston Area **MASSACHUSETTS**

Country, (617) 861-7063. $35–$40.

Lexington. Small, gabled, and painted red, this 1884 Victorian structure is a short walk from Lexington Center and its many historic sites, specialty shops, galleries, and restaurants. Guests tend to congregate in the central living room, where period chairs are arranged around an old coal stove. The hostess, a long-time resident of the area, has interests in local history, art, music (choral singing), wild flowers, and writing. She published an article on bed and breakfast in a national magazine and also wrote one on "big breakfasts," which around here are served in the greenhouse. *Represented by:* Bed & Breakfast in Minuteman Country, (617) 861-7063. $35–$40.

Lunenburg. An environmental engineer who enjoys gourmet cooking is host at this bed and breakfast offering a solarium with a hot tub and a newly designed recreation room for children. One guest room has a king-size waterbed, color television, and a private bath; the other has a queen-size four-poster, color television, and a shared bath. Crotched Mountain, a popular skiing area in New Hampshire, is forty-five minutes away. *Represented by:* Bed & Breakfast Associates, Bay Colony, Ltd., #681, (617) 872-6990. $30–$50.

North of Boston. Situated on 30 acres of land planted with 850 tall bush blueberries, apple trees, 52 varieties of herbs, vegetable and flower gardens, and a formal garden, this guest house is a fourteen-room 1830 Colonial. The mantels (the house has eight working fireplaces) date from 1660, and there is 20 inch wide-board pine flooring, exposed corner posts and beams, and a 30-foot-long living room with two fireplaces. The grounds include a swimming pool, a greenhouse with a conservatory and a fountain, a tennis court, and a three-story barn. Boston is thirty-five minutes away. *Represented by:* Bed & Breakfast Associates, Bay Colony, Ltd., #1, (617) 872-6990. $40–$55.

West of Boston. Forty-five minutes west of Boston, this guest house was built in 1690. The house, which was purchased in 1932 by Henry Ford, has been partially restored to its original condition. It is situated on 150 acres of rural countryside. The hostess, a retired United Press correspondent, enjoys taking guests to the hillside tomb of a Revolutionary War soldier. *Represented by:* Bed & Breakfast Associates, Bay Colony, Ltd., #3 (617) 872-6990. $35–$40.

"East Sandwich" (*Bed & Breakfast Cape Cod #10*)

Hyannis (Bed & Breakfast Cape Cod #5)

Cape Cod **MASSACHUSETTS**

Dennis Port. This guest house features a private beach on Nantucket Sound, a picnic table and barbecue, and a Florida-type room for relaxing at day's end. In addition to the swimming, facilities for golf, biking, and fishing are nearby. The hostess is fluent in French and German, as well as English. *Represented by:* Houseguests Cape Cod, Host Home #2, (617) 398-0787. $42 (2-night minimum).

East Orleans. An artist with interests in golf, shells, and books is the host of this contemporary house with a large sun deck and private upper-level guest quarters. The guest room has twin beds and a private bath, as well as a sitting room with a sofa bed. Nauset Beach is five minutes away, and a short walk brings you into East Orleans, a scenic, informal town with numerous shops and restaurants. *Represented by:* Bed & Breakfast Cape Cod, #6, (617) 775-2772. $45–$50.

East Sandwich. This new Cape Cod–style structure with an attached woodcarving workshop overlooks a cranberry bog. The guest room has a canopy bed and a skylight. The hosts—one of whom is a consultant to a nearby museum on the restoration of old objects—have beehives and raise chickens. The house is ten minutes from the Heritage Plantation, which has a museum, an authentic Shaker barn, a working windmill, and a profusion of hybrid rhododendrons. *Represented by:* Bed & Breakfast Cape Cod, #10, (617) 775-2772. $24–$44.

Forestdale. Almost entirely surrounded by trees and by ponds in which to swim, this home offers two guest rooms, which share a bath. The arrangement is ideal for a pair of couples traveling together. From the patio, where guests are invited to relax, one can see the sun set over the water. Sandwich, the Cape's oldest settlement, is nearby; and Falmouth, where you can catch a ferry to Nantucket or Martha's Vineyard, is a short drive away. *Represented by:* Houseguests Cape Cod, Host Home #2, (617) 398-0787. $35–$55.

Harwich Port. Two blocks from the beach and a short walk from many restaurants, this house has three rooms for guests. The guest room on the top floor used to be a sailmaker's loft. Guests returning from the beach are invited to shower and dress in an area beside the patio, which has a fountain around which breakfast is served. *Represented by:* Houseguests Cape Cod, Host Home #2, (617) 398-0787. $25–$40.

Hyannis. A contemporary ranch-style structure painted white

Yarmouth Port (Bed & Breakfast Cape Cod #2)

Hyannisport (Bed & Breakfast Cape Cod #28)

Cape Cod **MASSACHUSETTS**

and trimmed black, this bed and breakfast is in a wooded residential area. The house features a sun deck in the rear, and from there can be seen the hostess's special interest—flowers. Two guest rooms are available, one with a queen-size bed and shared bath, the other with twin beds and a private half-bath. Craigville Beach is five minutes away. *Represented by:* Bed & Breakfast Cape Cod, #41, (617) 775-2772. $28–$36.

Hyannis. This bed and breakfast, a Cape Cod–style structure, has a rear sun deck overlooking flower gardens. The hostess, a social worker fluent in Spanish and French as well as English, enjoys music, art, and children. The house is a convenient five-minute walk from Hyannis, and from Sea Street Beach, a three-minute walk. One of the two guest rooms has a queen-size waterbed; guest rooms share a hall bath. *Represented by:* Bed & Breakfast Cape Cod, #5, (617) 775-2772. $40.

Hyannis Port. An architectural hybrid, this twenty-room estate has a gambrel roof on one side and, over a connecting walkway, a hexagonal, many-windowed water tower on the other. The house is on a bluff overlooking the Kennedy compound, Hyannis harbor, Squaw Island, and Nantucket Sound. The hostess, a real estate broker and a registered nurse, has furnished the house with period antiques. Downtown Hyannis is a short drive away, and beaches are within walking distance. *Represented by:* Bed & Breakfast Cape Cod, #28, (617) 775-2772. $50–$60.

Marston Mills (the Boat House). A converted boat house suspended over a pond with a gaggle of geese, this accommodation has a boat-shaped kitchen and a large sun deck. The main house, far away enough for privacy, has additional rooms for guests. *Represented by:* Houseguests Cape Cod, House Guest Home #3, (617) 398-0787. Weekly only; rates on request.

Sagamore Beach. A rambling New England–style house built in 1906 by a travel writer, this bed and breakfast is on a small cliff overlooking the hosts' private beach. The grounds are thick with pines and cedars, and the house has a sheltered patio with an unobstructed view of Cape Cod Bay. The original tongue-and-groove paneling has been preserved in the house, and the guest rooms, which share a bath, have views of the bay. *Represented by:* Bed & Breakfast Cape Cod, #10, (617) 775-2772. $30–$44.

South Chatham. With a university administrator as host, this

Cape Cod **MASSACHUSETTS**

traditional Cape Cod structure is next to a salt marsh where snowy and great egrets, great blue herons, green- and black-crowned night herons, greater yellowlegs, belted kingfishers, and similar species stalk or hover about. The house features wide-board flooring usually partially covered by braided rugs, many antiques, and dried flower arrangements. The guest floor has a private bath, a living area, and a view of the water. *Represented by:* Bed & Breakfast Cape Cod, #11, (617) 775-2772. $32–$44.

Truro. A historic Cape Cod building, this bed and breakfast was the homestead of Truro's founder. The house, on grounds covered with flowering shrubs, is across the street from the Castle Hill Arts Center, which holds summer workshops in various media. The grounds also include a converted cottage barn and a sheltered porch where breakfast is served. The hostess is a professional artist, and her eye for design is evident throughout the house. *Represented by:* Bed & Breakfast Cape Cod, #9, (617) 775-2772. $32–$40. Cottage $50.

Yarmouth Port. This Cape Cod structure is a short walk from a picturesque town beach on Cape Cod Bay. The hostess deals in antiques, particularly in American pattern glass. The house, featuring a sun deck that guests are invited to use and a guest wing with a private entrance and bath, is near many restaurants and shops. *Represented by:* Bed & Breakfast Cape Cod, #2, (617) 775-2772. $28–$36.

Hyannis (Bed & Breakfast Cape Cod #41)

Concord MASSACHUSETTS

Hawthorne Inn

462 Lexington Road, Concord, MA 01742. (617) 369-5610.
Hosts: Gregory Burch and Marilyn Mudry.

The Hawthorne Inn is an 1870 Colonial structure on 1.5 acres of wooded land that was owned, in turn, by Nathaniel Hawthorne, Ralph Waldo Emerson, and the Alcott family. A pine tree Hawthorne planted still stands on the property, which is immediately across the road from the master's homesite. Recently George and Marilyn planted seven hundred spring-flowering bulbs around the goldfish pond. The grounds already boast numerous flowering trees and bushes and a vegetable garden.

The rooms, with hardwood floors covered by Oriental and rag rugs, are furnished with antiques. Original artworks, ranging from antique Japanese ukiyo-e prints to contemporary sculpture, appear throughout the building. The rooms contain books of poetry, magazines, AM-FM clock radios, and sometimes bowls of fruit.

Gregory and Marilyn serve a complimentary breakfast of home-baked breads, fresh fruit, juice, and tea, and their own special blend of coffee. In season, raspberries and grapes grown on the property show up on the breakfast table. The Hawthorne Inn is close to such treasures as Emerson's house, the Old North Bridge, and Walden Pond.

Accommodations: 5 rooms with shared bath. *Smoking:* Permitted in guest rooms only. *Children:* Permitted. *Pets:* Not permitted. *Breakfast:* Included. *Driving Instructions:* Located ¾ mile east of Concord's town square.

Falmouth **MASSACHUSETTS**

Sea Gull Lodge

41 Belvidere Road, Falmouth, MA 02541. (617) 548-0679.
Hosts: John D. and Doris L. Gouliamas.

Situated on grounds planted with pines and maples, the Sea Gull is a 1948 Cape Cod structure with gables and shutters. The Sea Gull, operated by the Gouliamases since 1953, has a backyard patio with chaise longues, and a picnic area complete with a brick-and-stone fireplace.

John and Doris own some genuine heirloom furniture: several antique Swedish pieces were hand-carved out of heavy oak as long ago as 1679. The living room has two davenports, six chairs, two coffee tables, and a large table—all of hand-carved oak. The walls are paneled with wide pine boards, and a fireplace warms the room in chilly weather. Several paintings and a wood sculpture hang on the living-room walls, and the floor, its planks laid diagonally, is covered with a heavy area rug.

All the guest rooms have wood floors covered by small rugs, and cedar-lined closets. All rooms but one have television.

Doris and John don't serve breakfast but are more than happy to serve guests iced tea on the patio.

Accommodations: 8 rooms with shared bath. *Smoking:* Permitted. *Children:* Permitted. *Pets:* Not permitted. *Driving Instructions:* From Boston, take Route 28 to Scranton Avenue in Falmouth on Cape Cod, then turn right at Lowry.

Falmouth Heights **MASSACHUSETTS**

Schofield's Guest House

335 Grand Avenue, Falmouth Heights, MA 02540. (617) 548-4648. *Host:* Clyde E. Schofield.

Clyde, who's been in the guest-house business for twenty years, observed: "People are people no matter where you go." Clyde's matter-of-factness about the nature of travel and people hasn't deflected potential guests, who, he assures us, arrive after consulting with the Cape Cod Chamber of Commerce. "They just keep on sending them, and most of them keep coming back year after year because my rates are reasonable and I own a beautiful piece of the ocean."

Clyde has a large sundeck 100 feet from the ocean and facing it. His beach is a private one for guests only. "I don't need to be fancy, people who like the ocean like my place." Guests who want to may watch television in the lobby, with its numerous lounge chairs, which "shuts down automatically—at eleven."

The four guest rooms share two baths. Although Clyde doesn't serve breakfast, he says "There's food close enough."

Accommodations: 4 rooms with shared baths. *Smoking:* Permitted. *Children:* Permitted. *Pets:* Not permitted. *Driving Instructions:* Take Route 90 into Falmouth and stay on Main Street until you see the ocean; turn left, and keep your eyes open.

Great Barrington **MASSACHUSETTS**

The Ellings' Guest House
R.D. 3, Box 6, Great Barrington, MA 01230. (413) 528-4103.
Hosts: Ray and Josephine Elling.

A 1746 Colonial structure, The Ellings' Guest House was built by Stephen King, the owner of a woolen mill. The house is surrounded by cornfields, mountains, gardens, and a large lawn. Tall pines and maples shade the grounds, which feature a tree swing and badminton and horseshoe facilities.

Across the road, a river that runs through cornfields forms, at a bend, a swimming hold complete with a sandy beach. The central parlor (furnished, like the guest rooms, in antiques and Colonial reproductions) has a large fireplace and a writing desk that will please those who enjoy looking first at words they've put on paper, and then, an instant later, at a field of corn.

The guest rooms, two with private baths and four others sharing two baths, offer pretty views of cornfields or mountains or spreading lawns with gardens. Ray and Jo, who believe in privacy and in knocking before they enter rooms, serve a complimentary breakfast that usually consists of homemade muffins and jams, and all the coffee or tea you require.

Accommodations: 6 rooms, 2 with private bath. *Smoking:* Permitted. *Children:* Permitted. *Pets:* Not permitted. *Breakfast:* Included. *Driving Instructions:* On Route 23-41, a half mile west of Route 7 in Great Barrington.

Martha's Vineyard **MASSACHUSETTS**

Oak Bluffs. Situated directly on the ocean shore, this guest house has seven rooms with shared baths available for guests. The village of Oak Bluffs is two minutes from the house, and a five-minute walk will bring you to a shop that rents out bicycles. *Represented by:* Houseguests Cape Cod, Guest House #1, (617) 398-0787. $45–$55.

Vineyard Haven. Three-quarters of a mile from the beaches, this guest house has a swimming pool and mopeds guests can rent. There are eleven guest rooms—four with semiprivate and seven with shared bath. *Represented by:* Houseguests Cape Cod, Guest House #1, (617) 398-0787. $40–$47.

Martha's Vineyard **MASSACHUSETTS**

Amherst House

38 Ocean Avenue, Oak Bluffs, MA 02557. (617) 693-3430. *Hosts:* Don and Ricky Blair. Closed October through the day before Memorial Day.

Situated next to a park on Martha's Vineyard and directly facing the ocean, Amherst House is an 1869 Victorian structure. It was owned for years by a wealthy Philadelphia family, the daughter of which, the locals say, was a recluse who had her birds flown up to spend the summer with her. When the previous owners bought the house, they discovered an elaborate collection of fancy hats, some still with price stickers, that guests can see in the Hat Room. They also came across a great deal of wicker furniture and several Oriental rugs. The decor throughout Amherst House is a combination of wicker and wood, with Oriental rugs here and there.

A special treat the Amherst House offers: good seats for the concerts that take place each Sunday evening (in season) in the park next door.

Accommodations: 4 rooms, 1 with private bath. *Smoking:* Permitted. *Children:* Permitted. *Pets:* Permitted. *Breakfast:* Included. *Driving Instructions:* On Ocean Park, near the dock of the Woods Hole ferry and the bandstand.

Martha's Vineyard **MASSACHUSETTS**

Haven Guest House

P.O. Box 1022, Vineyard Haven, Martha's Vineyard, MA 02568. (617) 693-3333. *Hosts:* Karl and Lynn Buder.

The Haven Guest House—architecturally something of a classic American bungalow with a neo-Williamsburg interior—was built in 1918 as a wedding present for one of the Colgate daughters and accommodated guests at the Colgate estate. The house, just outside a Martha's vineyard town, is near the summer homes of William Styron, Art Buchwald, and Lillian Hellman.

Each guest room has a private bath and a sitting area, and two have private decks. Furnishings vary from room to room, as do the predominant woods for which several rooms are named: There are The Walnut, The Mahogany, The Oak, and The Maple rooms. Decor includes Victorian, Colonial, and Art Deco; eclecticism is more the rule than the exception.

The public areas of the house include an unusually large foyer and central staircase, a living room with a fireplace, and a sunny screened-in porch where guests partake of a morning paper and a complimentary breakfast with homemade breads and muffins.

Accommodations: 9 rooms with private bath. *Smoking:* Permitted in guest rooms only. *Children:* Over 12 permitted. *Pets:* Not permitted. *Breakfast:* Included. *Driving Instructions:* From Falmouth, follow signs for Woods Hole ferry (advance auto reservations required).

Martha's Vineyard **MASSACHUSETTS**

The Oak House

Seaview and Pequot Avenue, Box 299, Oak Bluffs, Martha's Vineyard, MA 02557. (617) 693-4187. *Hosts:* Marcia and Stuart Haley.

This 1872 Queen Anne structure on Martha's Vineyard was built, as its name implies, of oak. In 1876 Governor Claflin, who owned it then, added wide porches as well as leaded glass (some with stained-glass trim) in more that fifty-five windows. The bathrooms have tin walls and ceilings, and many original marble sinks and fixtures still remain.

Five guest rooms have balconies, and several have views of Cape Cod or the ocean. A number have antique beds, some have intricate oak paneling, one has open-beamed ceilings, and another has an ocean view interrupted handsomely by a window whose top is stained glass. Antique furnishings and lovely woodwork appear in most guest rooms. The Haleys' living room, spacious and furnished with some antiques, has a grand piano and an electric organ.

Marcia and Stuart do not serve breakfast but do offer their guests coffee each morning on a sun porch overlooking the ocean.

Accommodations: 10 rooms with shared bath. *Smoking:* Permitted. *Children:* Discouraged. *Pets:* Not permitted. *Driving Instructions:* Two blocks south of the Oak Bluffs Steamship Dock.

Martha's Vineyard **MASSACHUSETTS**

The Victorian

24 South Water Street, Edgartown, Massachusetts. *Mailing Address:* P.O. Box 947, Edgartown, Martha's Vineyard, MA 02539; P.O. Box 251, Wilmington, VT 02363. (617) 627-4784; off season: (802) 464-3716. *Hosts:* Marilyn and Jack Kayner. Although the back part of The Victorian was built in the early eighteenth century, the front part of the house was not completed until around 1820. The building is Victorian, with widow's-walk balconies off several rooms and with bay and dormer windows.

The guest rooms are furnished with antiques such as marble-topped dressers and tables and eighteenth-century canopied four-posters. Decorator touches such as matching sheets and wallpaper characterize the rooms. Some rooms have views of the harbor, and Marilyn and Jack make sure that each guest room is stocked with fresh flowers and mints.

The sitting room, which has a color television set and a marble fireplace, is always available for use by guests, as is the enclosed lawn and garden area, where cocktails and conversation often precede dinner. In a breakfast room with a fireplace, Marilyn and Jack serve a complimentary breakfast.

Accommodations: 14 rooms with private bath. *Smoking:* Permitted. *Children:* Permitted during off season (November 2 through March 31) only; check in advance. *Pets:* Not permitted. *Breakfast:* Included. *Driving Instructions:* Take the ferry from Woods Hole to Martha's Vineyard, and then follow the signs to Edgartown.

Nantucket **MASSACHUSETTS**

Carlisle House

26 North Water Street, Nantucket, MA 02554. (617) 228-0720.

Hosts: John and Susan Bausch.

Built in 1765, the Carlisle House is a large, typically New England structure with a sun porch and a shaded veranda. John and Susan have maintained the original appointments, which include wide pine floors and a number of fireplaces. Several guest rooms feature fireplaces, as does the living room, which is decorated with original artworks.

The Bausches serve a complimentary breakfast, weather permitting, on the sun porch, which has a cable color television set that guests are invited to watch. The veranda, shaded by trees and flowers and complete with summer furniture, is a place where, says Susan, guests may partake of everything from packed lunches to their favorite cocktails.

Accommodations: 14 rooms, 4 with private bath. *Smoking:* Permitted. *Children:* Not encouraged. *Pets:* Not permitted. *Breakfast:* Included. *Driving Instructions:* On Water Street, near the center of town.

Nantucket **MASSACHUSETTS**

The Chestnut House

3 Chestnut Street, Nantucket, MA 02554. (617) 228-0049. *Hosts:* Jerry and Jeannette Carl.

"The wart," a term some Nantucketers use when they mean "cottage," didn't become an addition to the house until 1950, but the Chestnut House itself dates back to about 1856. A first addition appeared on the house in 1905, and the three-part structure strikes one now as rambling and roomy.

And friendly—Jerry and Jeannette Carl make a point of meeting all their guests personally. "This is one of our pleasures," as Jerry put it. Meeting guests always compels Jerry and Jeannette to hold forth on the idiosyncrasies of their cat, a Russian Blue with a will of iron (all attempts at feline reconditioning have failed miserably) who occupies room 11—whether guests like it or not. "So far it's working out," they say.

The Carls have five guest rooms with private baths and four others sharing two baths. The wart has a complete kitchen, a bedroom with a double bed, and a living room with a convertible sofa. Claudia, Jerry and Jeannette's daughter, makes quilts by hand that complement the rugs her father hooks. Jeannette's paintings cover the walls: "Don't shudder," Jerry says, "she's good." (Her paintings are figurative, neo-impressionistic studies of flowers and animals and people.)

Accommodations: 9 rooms, 4 with private bath. *Smoking:* Permitted. *Children:* Over 5 permitted. *Pets:* Not permitted. *Driving Instructions:* Three blocks from the steamboat wharf.

Nantucket **MASSACHUSETTS**

Grieder Guest House

43 Orange Street, Nantucket, MA 02554. (617) 228-1399. *Hosts:* Ruth and William Grieder. Closed mid-October through mid-May.

It sometimes seems that every house in New England was owned by a whaling captain, but this one, built in the early eighteenth century, probably actually was. Orange Street used to be called the "street of captains," and appropriately enough, Ruth is a third-generation Nantucketer with sea captains on both sides of her family. William's father was once a lighthouse keeper on the island. They have been operating their guest house since 1952, and, in a tone suggesting understatement, Ruth says they "enjoy the business immensely."

The guest rooms have exposed beams on the ceilings, "ship's knees" in the corners, pineapple four-poster beds, sea chests, and braided rugs.

Ruth and William don't serve any meals, but their being in the center of Nantucket compensates for that—you can walk to a restaurant or the ocean. Picnic facilities in the shaded back yard are available for guests.

Accommodations: 2 rooms with shared bath. *Smoking:* Permitted. *Children:* Permitted. *Pets:* Not permitted. *Driving Instructions:* In the center of town, adjacent to Main Street.

Nantucket **MASSACHUSETTS**

House of the Seven Gables, Inc.

32 Cliff Road, Nantucket, MA 02554. (617) 228-4706. *Hostess:* Suzanne Walton.

The House of the Seven Gables, a large 1880s Victorian building with seven gables, is not the one immortalized by Nathaniel Hawthorne. This building originally served as the annex for one of Nantucket's oldest hotels, which was destroyed in 1972.

Several guest rooms have views of the Nantucket Harbor, and all are decorated with a combination of genuine antiques and period reproductions. The parlor, always available for guests to relax in, features a color television set.

Richard serves guests a complimentary breakfast of coffee or tea, juice, and freshly baked Danish. The house overlooks Nantucket Harbor and is a ten-minute walk from Main Street. It is open from June 14 through September 7.

Accommodations: 10 rooms, 8 with private bath. *Smoking:* Permitted. *Children:* Permitted sometimes (check in advance). *Pets:* Not permitted. *Breakfast:* Included during the summer season. *Driving Instructions:* On Cliff Road about three blocks from Main Street.

Nantucket **MASSACHUSETTS**

Martin's Guest House

61 Centre Street, Nantucket, MA 02554. (617) 228-0678. *Hosts:* Anne and Frank Berger.

Originally built in 1803 by a man Frank Berger refers to as a "mariner and gentleman," Martin's is a large, typically Nantucket structure with two gables on the roof and one over the doorway. The house has several fireplaces—one in the parlor for the use of guests and five more in the guest rooms, several of which are furnished with genuine antiques and period reproductions.

Minutes from downtown Nantucket and all its attractions, Martin's offers guests a large lawn and a complimentary Continental breakfast each morning, with homemade muffins and breads. Commenting on Nantucket's many attractions, Frank concludes that "mostly, Nantucket's meant for long, leisurely strolls along winding roads with rose-covered cottages, or along miles of open, unspoiled, clean beaches."

Accommodations: 12 rooms, 8 with private bath. *Smoking:* Permitted. *Children:* Permitted. *Pets:* Not permitted. *Breakfast:* Included. *Driving Instructions:* Near the center of town.

Nantucket **MASSACHUSETTS**

Nantucket Landfall

4 Harbor View Way, Nantucket, MA 02554. (617) 228-0500. *Hostess:* Dorothy M. Mortenson.

Built on the site of an old whaling business, the Nantucket Landfall is a 1928 Cape Cod structure with a porch tucked under an overhanging gable. Beside the porch is an old weathered fence that in the summer seems almost to be holding back the roses and hydrangeas that Dorothy grows. In June and July there are flowers everywhere.

Amid profuse shrubbery and flowers, Dorothy has managed to find room for a barbecue and a picnic table, which guests are invited to use. With the ocean right across the street, Dorothy's veranda offers nothing less than a panoramic view of Nantucket Harbor. She claims Nantucket's moors are "like Scotland's own."

Dorothy doesn't serve breakfast, but she helps her guests ease into the day by offering them coffee in the morning. She describes her place as informal, congenial, and comfortable. She quotes Conrad: "But if you have sighted it on the expected bearing, then the landfall is good."

Accommodations: 6 rooms, 4 with private bath. *Smoking:* Permitted. *Children:* Permitted. *Pets:* Not permitted. *Driving Instructions:* The center of town.

Nantucket **MASSACHUSETTS**

Royal Manor Guest House

31 Centre Street, Nantucket, MA 02554. (617) 228-0600. *Hosts:* Leon Macy Royal and Eleanor Jewett Royal.

Leon Macy Royal says the Royal Manor was one of the first houses built after the great Nantucket fire of 1846. He also says the house is one of Nantucket's best built, pointing to its 18- by 20-foot-high studded recessed windows with lovely panel work surrounding them and the wooden shutters on the inside. The house has elaborate cornice work and was constructed in the backplaster method (an inside and an outside wall of plaster, with 10 inches of airspace between them. It is on a 12,000-square-foot lot landscaped with shrubbery and trees, with a border of flowers. Its two porches, one open and one closed, are surrounded by flower boxes.

Each guest room has a fireplace with an Italian marble mantel, antique door knobs, an Oriental rug, and antique furnishings and fixtures.

The Royals have been operating the Royal Manor for thirty-seven years, and most of their guests, says Leon, are repeat lodgers or people recommended by them. Their confidence in satisfying guests is such that they don't even have a brochure. Leon and Eleanor don't serve any meals, but the Royal Manor is convenient to several good eating places.

Accommodations: 7 rooms, 5 with private bath. *Smoking:* Permitted. *Children:* Over 10 permitted. *Pets:* Not permitted. *Driving Instructions:* In the center of town.

New Bedford Area **MASSACHUSETTS**

Families. Hosted by a technical engineering manager and a school counselor, this bed and breakfast has a guest room that will accommodate a family (it has a private sitting area). The house, built in 1859, is in a residential area near a park, the beaches, and the historic district. *Represented by:* Pineapple Hospitality, #MA126, (617) 990-1696. $20–$44.

Historic Home. A half mile from the downtown historic district and a park with tennis and jogging facilities, this bed and breakfast is hosted by an antique-car buff and architect. The host restores houses, and has renovated four in New Bedford, including this one, which is in New Bedford's historic residential district, about ten minutes from the beach. *Represented by:* Pineapple Hospitality, #MA114, (617) 990-1696. $25–$35.

Georgian Colonial near Beach. Two minutes from the beach, this Georgian Colonial is across the street from a park that has a pond, a zoo, tennis courts, jogging paths, and cookout facilities. An apartment available for guests has a bedroom, a living room with a sofa, and a full kitchen. Children are welcome, and the host invites guests to use the laundry facilities. *Represented by:* Pineapple Hospitality, #MA118, (617) 990-1696. $35–$55.

Fireplace. This home was built in 1857 by a genuine descendant of a passenger on the *Mayflower,* as an 1857 plaque on the house attests. It is in the residential historic district, quite close to the Martha's Vineyard ferry, and one of its guest rooms has a fireplace. The host is interested in historic preservation, teaching, and computer science. *Represented by:* Pineapple Hospitality, #MA123, (617) 990-1696. $23–$33.

Historic District. This bed and breakfast in the historic district overlooks the New Bedford harbor. The house is convenient to everything in New Bedford, and guests can walk to the best restaurants, all the historic attractions, and the various ferries that leave from the port. The host is a young professional. *Represented by:* Pineapple Hospitality, #MA122, (617) 990-1696. $25–$33.

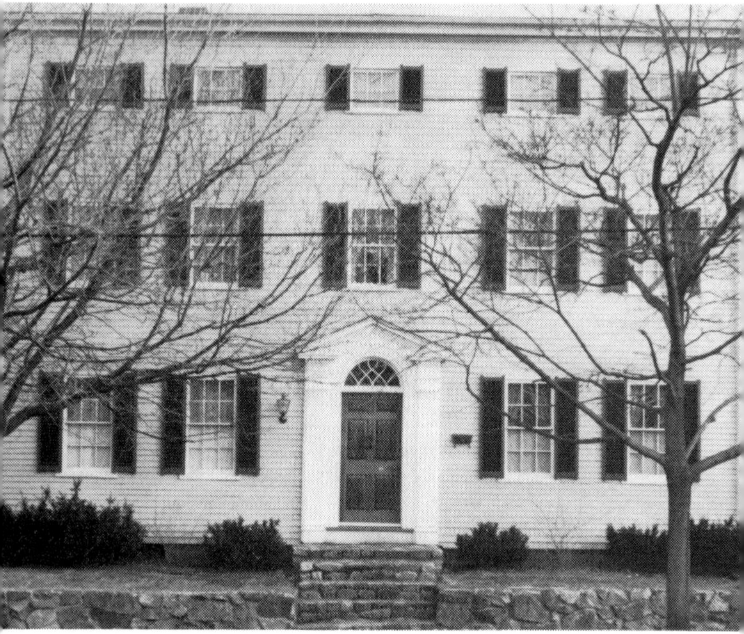

Newburyport **MASSACHUSETTS**

The Benjamin Choate House

25 Tyng Street, Newburyport, MA 01950. (617) 462-4786. *Host:* Herbert A. Fox.

Situated at the crest of Tyng Street (overlooking the Merrimack River, the boats tied up by Towle Silversmiths, and the North End Boat Club), the Benjamin Choate House is a three-story Federal structure. Several rooms in the house retain their original Indian shutters on the windows. The kitchen features antique paneling and the largest residential hearth in Newburyport.

Furnished with antiques, the beds made with hand-ironed designer sheets, the guest rooms feature Oriental rugs and an extensive collection of artwork that Mr. Fox accumulated during his twenty years as a master printer for such artists as Leonard Baskin, Saul Steinberg, and Joseph Albers. Mr. Fox's collection also includes many museum-quality old masters' prints.

Mr. Fox encourages his guests to join him in a glass of wine in front of one of the fireplaces, and provides wine and bar glasses for guests' private use. A full complimentary home-cooked breakfast is served each morning in the kitchen. Cloth napkins, antique lace tablecloth, and fresh flowers set the tone.

Accommodations: 5 rooms, 2 with private bath. *Smoking:* Permitted. *Children:* Permitted. *Pets:* Permitted, but check in advance. *Breakfast:* Included. *Driving Instructions:* Take Route I-95 to the exit for Newburyport onto Route 113; follow Route 113 for 1 ½ miles, then turn left on Tyng Street.

Provincetown MASSACHUSETTS

Asheton House

3 Cook Street, Provincetown, MA 02657. (617) 487-9966. *Hosts:* Jim Bayard and Les Schaufler.

Asheton House consists of two early-nineteenth-century houses (1806 and 1840) erected by the Cook family, which owned a fleet of whaling vessels. The grounds feature Japanese temple trees, a semiformal English boxwood garden, and sun decks that overlook Cape Cod Bay. The sunsets of the bay fall, say Jim and Les, into the never-to-be-forgotten category. So does their collection of antiques.

One guest room, furnished with period French pieces, has a fireplace, a view of the bay, and a large private bath. Another room, overlooking the garden, is done in natural wicker and bamboo. There is also a three-room apartment with a living room, a bedroom, and a spacious kitchen–dining area (complete with washer and dryer).

To prepare you for exploring Provincetown's shopping areas or its vast expanse of dunes, Jim and Les serve a complimentary breakfast.

Accommodations: 8 rooms, 2 with private bath. *Smoking:* Permitted. *Children:* Not permitted. *Pets:* Not permitted. *Breakfast:* Not included. *Driving Instructions:* Proceeding north on Route 6, take the first left after the town line; go to the water and turn right; then go half a mile.

Rockport **MASSACHUSETTS**

Eden Pines Inn
 Eden Road, Rockport, MA 01966. (617) 546-2505. *Hostess:* Inge Sullivan.

The Eden Pines Inn—a large shuttered and shingled New England structure with an upper porch and a brick sundeck—borders directly on the ocean. For those more inclined toward smooth old rocks than chaise longues, huge boulders begin where the sundeck ends. The view from both is spectacular—lobstermen and ocean liners and the famous twin lighthouses of Thatcher's Island.

The view during Inge Sullivan's complimentary breakfast, with Scandinavian pastries, is also marvelous, especially to those who enjoy seeing the rim of the ocean's horizon over the rims of their coffee cups.

All guest rooms have a private bath and a sitting area. Two rooms feature private decks, and of the six rooms, only one lacks an ocean view. The parlor has a fireplace, books, and a television set. Inge serves tea at 3 P.M., and at 5 P.M. glasses and ice are set out for guests, who may store beverages in a conveniently located refrigerator.

Inge also has a cottage for rent on Bearskin Neck, a strip of land with an outstanding view of Rockport harbor.

Accommodations: 6 rooms with private bath. *Smoking:* Permitted. *Children:* Young children not permitted (check first). *Pets:* Not permitted. *Breakfast:* Included. *Driving Instructions:* Take Route 128 North; turn left onto Route 127, then right onto Route 127A (Mt. Pleasant and South Street); drive 1 mile to Eden Road and turn left. The inn is on the ocean.

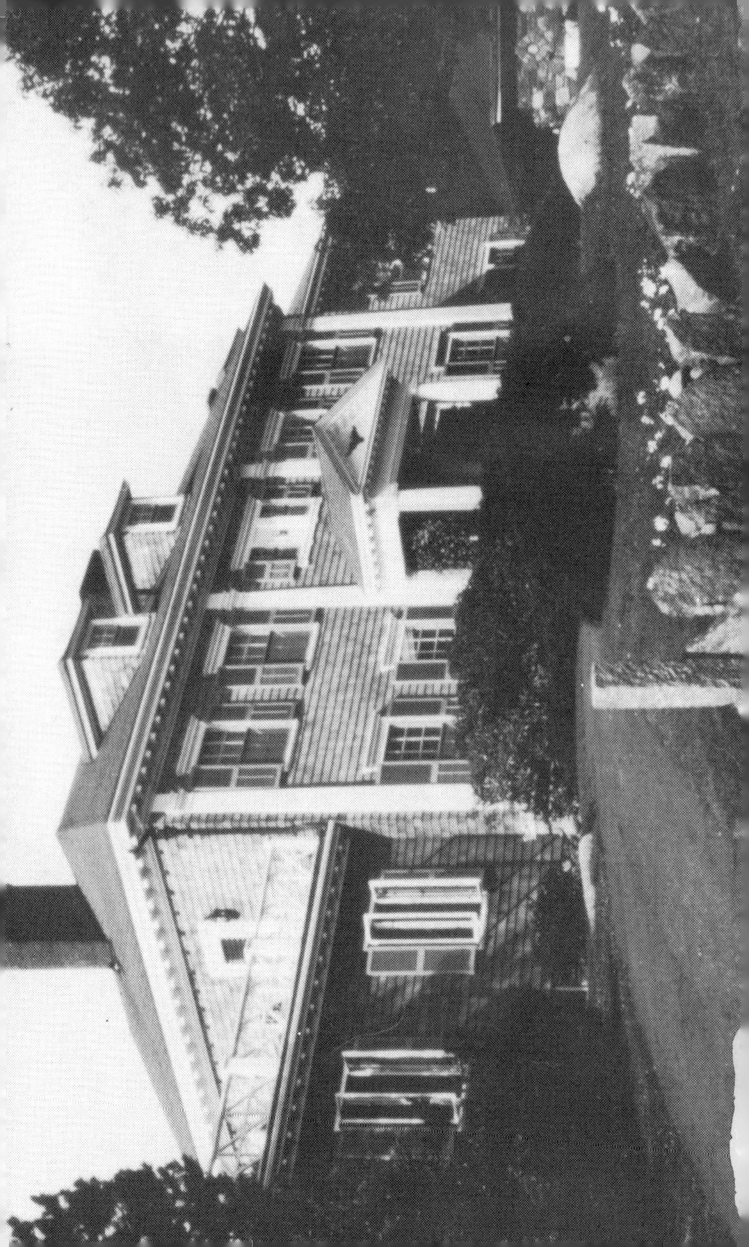

Rockport **MASSACHUSETTS**

Seacrest Manor

131 Marmion Way, Rockport, MA 01966. (617) 546-2211. *Hosts:* Leighton T. Saville and Dwight B. MacCormack. Closed January. An early nineteenth-century Colonial structure to which an eastern wing and a sun deck were added in the 1960s, Seacrest Manor is on a rocky Cape Anne crag. The view from the sun deck is extraordinary, encompassing almost 180 degrees. The strong of sight can discern Mount Agamenticus, 40 miles away in Maine. Straitsmouth Island, with its picturesque house and light, and the famous twin lights of Thatcher's Island are both easily visible from the sun deck.

Inside, the library, which includes several hundred volumes, has leather wing chairs, gray walls, a white door and ceiling moldings, and a fireplace. The living room, where afternoon tea is served, has a Colonial chandelier, a couch in front of a large window overlooking the garden, and a set of Colonial chairs.

The guest rooms are furnished with a combination of antiques and contemporary pieces. Some of these rooms have solid-wood doors, all are carpeted, and several afford ocean views. The rooms also feature fresh bouquets of flowers, turned-down beds with mints left on the pillows, a morning paper waiting outside the door, and if you remembered to leave them in the hall, your shoes freshly polished.

Leighton and Dwight serve a full breakfast, and when it's cold the dining room's hearth has a fire to warm things up. Seacrest Manor is closed in January.

Accommodations: 8 rooms, 4 with private bath. *Smoking:* Permitted. *Children:* Under 16 not permitted. *Pets:* Not permitted. *Breakfast:* Included. *Driving Instructions:* From Rockport Center, take Route 127A (Mount Pleasant Street) south; Marmion Way is the second left after the Delmar Nursing Home.

Rockport   **MASSACHUSETTS**

Lantana House

22 Broadway, Rockport, MA 01966. (617) 546-3535. *Hostess:* Cyndie Sewell.

The Lantana House, which hostess Cyndie Sewell reckons to be about 150 years old, is almost directly in the middle of Rockport. Through the windows on one side of the house you can see Saint Mary's Episcopal Church, slightly obscured by trees in the summer; and from the staircase's landing window you can see the docks area and the ocean beyond it. On the ground floor, beneath the building's porch, there's a bookstore, which provides extra reading material for guests.

The living room is decorated with paintings, primarily watercolor seascapes, and furnished with dark walnut traditional pieces covered in a green velvety material. Cyndie is proud of the rooms' numerous objects d'art and is especially pleased with an aluminum sculpture that sits in the living room.

Cyndie serves a Continental breakfast of juice, coffee, rolls, and homemade muffins. When it's warm, guests usually prefer having breakfast on the sun deck.

Accommodations: 7 rooms, 6 with private bath. Two rooms have kitchens and can be rented as efficiencies. *Smoking:* Permitted. *Children:* Permitted. *Pets:* Permitted. *Breakfast:* Included. *Driving Instructions:* From Boston, take Route 128 to its end, then turn left onto Route 127; the guest house is two blocks from the five-corner intersection in Rockport.

Rockport **MASSACHUSETTS**

The Seafarer Guest House

86 Marmion Way, Rockport, MA 01966. (617) 546-6248. *Hosts:* Mary and Gerry Pepin. Open April through mid-November. The Seafarer Guest House is an 1893 gambrel-roofed structure with column-supported porches formed by the roof's overhangs. The guest house, originally constructed to be part of a planned summer colony, was almost immediately incorporated into the Straitsmouth Inn complex of buildings.

The Seafarer, at the western edge of Gap Cove, is surrounded by the ocean, and each guest room has an ocean view. Mary and Gerry, intent on capturing a feeling of the sea, have scoured about and found many maritime ships' fittings, salvage pieces, and reproductions. Brass fittings, brass and teak towel racks, ships' lamps, and many kinds of nautical paraphernalia are found all over the house.

Each guest room has at least three original oil paintings by local artists; two of the rooms, both on the third floor, have kitchenettes, breakfast nooks, and private baths. A large old-fashioned porch leads into the living-sitting room, which has a fireplace, lovely antique furnishings, plenty of books and magazines, and a stereo that usually softly plays classical or contemporary music. Over the living room's fireplace is a large painting of a ship; other paintings hang in the hall and on all the landings. Mary and Gerry serve a complimentary breakfast that includes, as well as juice and coffee, cranberry nutbread.

Accommodations: 8 rooms, 6 with private bath. *Smoking:* Permitted. *Children:* Small children not permitted (check first). *Pets:* Not permitted. *Breakfast:* Included. *Driving Instructions:* Take Route 127 North to Rockport Center, then take Route 127A for a mile to Marmion Way.

Sheffield **MASSACHUSETTS**

Ivanhoe Country House
   Route 41, Sheffield, MA 01257. (413) 229-2143. *Hosts:* Carole and Dick Maghery.

The Ivanhoe Country House is a large 1780 New England farmhouse located between the foot of Mount Race and the shores of Berkshire Lake (its guest rooms overlook either one or the other). The 25-acre grounds contain, in addition to the splendid Berkshire landscape, a lighted sleighing slope and a swimming pool.

The parlor—called the Chestnut Room because of its wood paneling—features a fireplace, a library, a color television set, and Ping-Pong and other game tables. Three of the nine guest rooms have working fireplaces, two have kitchenette units (refrigerators are available to guests who bring perishables or wine and spirits).

The Magherys include a complimentary Continental breakfast (muffins and coffee, tea, or cocoa), which they serve at your bedroom door. The house is convenient to Butternut ski basin, the Appalachian Trail, Tanglewood, and the Jacob's Pillow dance festival.

Accommodations: 9 rooms, 6 with private bath. *Smoking:* Permitted. *Children:* Permitted. *Pets:* Dogs permitted. *Breakfast:* Included. *Driving Instructions:* Located 7 miles south of Great Barrington on Route 41.

Ware   **MASSACHUSETTS**

The Wildwood Inn

121 Church Street, Ware, MA 01082. (413) 967-7798. *Hosts:* Margaret and Geoffrey Lobenstine.

When the autumn foliage is at its peak, driving down Church Street is like driving through a stained-glass window. As if out of central casting, the street is arched with maples. There are a few maples on the grounds of the Wildwood Inn, too, but the real attractions are the many firs, the rare chestnut, and the pair of flowering apple trees right outside the dining-room window. Margaret and Geoffrey, assisted in just about all matters by their twin teenage-daughters, operate an 1881 Victorian establishment with a wraparound porch. It is on 2 acres that adjoin a wooded park (separated from the property by a stone fence) that has a swimming hole and a river.

The house is filled with American primitive antiques, most of them family heirlooms. The living room features three antique cradles, one of them containing a doll dressed in Geoffrey's great-great-aunt's christening outfit. An antique heirloom quilt covers each bed in the house. One bedroom has a queen-size pine four-poster bed covered with a hand-embroidered blue and white quilt and eyelet pillows; a bay window with four panes of glass, all of them covered with eyelet curtains; an antique cherry and mahogany chest; and a night table made from an old sewing machine.

The parlor, lit in winter by hurricane lamps and a fire, has two bay windows. One of these looks out on the chestnut tree, transplanted here from a nearby area that was flooded to make the Quabbin Reservoir (which resembles a combination of a lake and a Norwegian fjord and serves as a winter home for American bald eagles). The parlor also has oaken floors covered by braided rugs; a Victorian tiled fireplace; and a hand-pegged carpenter's chest.

Margaret's complimentary breakfast includes fresh popovers, homemade peach butter, homemade breads, juice, and tea or coffee. For those still hungry. she'll throw together, for a nominal fee, concoctions like puff pancakes.

Accommodations: 5 rooms with shared bath. *Smoking:* Permitted. *Children:* Over 6 permitted. *Pets:* Not permitted. *Breakfast:* Included. *Driving Instructions:* From the Massachusetts Turnpike take exit 8 and go left on Route 32, which bears right and becomes Ware's Main Street; turn left at the third traffic light (by the fountain) onto Church—the Wildwood Inn is ¾ mile up.

Yarmouth Port **MASSACHUSETTS**

One Centre Street Inn

One Centre Street and Old King's Highway (Route 6A), Yarmouth Port, MA 02675. (617) 362-8910. *Hosts:* Barbara Mutchler, Donald Mutchler, and Jack Williams.

An 1824 Colonial house painted white with black trim and shutters, and with an attached carriage shed, One Centre Street Inn is surrounded by manicured shrubs and shaded by a couple of old maples. It is furnished mostly with period antiques.

Mahogany bookshelves line the walls of the library, which has wide-board pine floors partially covered by an Oriental rug. The living room features a chestnut Governor Winthrop desk, a mahogany chair upholstered in needlepoint, more wide-board pine floors partially covered with an Oriental rug, a contemporary spinet piano made of cherry, and an overstuffed sofa upholstered in a chocolate-brown fabric. The room is lighted by oil lamps.

Guest rooms vary, but each has some antiques—one has a mahogany four-poster, another has a bed of white iron. They all have wide-board pine floors, Oriental rugs, and antique chests or dressers. Four of the six rooms have private baths.

Breakfast here is a full one and includes omelets with bacon, French toast, fruit juices, and homemade jams and jellies.

Yarmouth Port, centrally located on Cape Cod, makes a fine home base for explorers. The ferries to Martha's Vineyard and Nantucket are 8 miles away, as is the Cape Cod National Seashore. Pedalers will be pleased to know the inn lends bicycles to guests.

Accommodations: 6 rooms, 4 with private bath. *Smoking:* Permitted in living room only. *Children:* Permitted. *Pets:* Not permitted. *Breakfast:* Included. *Driving Instructions:* From Route 6 (the mid-Cape highway), take exit 8; go north to Route 6A (Old King's Highway) and proceed east; the inn is at the intersection of Route 6A and Centre Street, on the left-hand side of the road.

Horton MICHIGAN

Wellman General Store Guest Apartment
 205 Main Street, Horton, Michigan. *Mailing Address:* P.O. Box 58, Horton, MI 49246. (517) 563-2231. *Hostess:* Karen D. Gauntlet.

This 1886 brick structure, listed in Michigan's Historic Registry, used to be a general store. When the wreckers were just about ready to tear it down, Karen Gaunlet threw down the gauntlet, restored the building, and opened her doors to guests.

Karen has one guest accommodation—an apartment. The bedroom used to be a storage area for canned goods; the kitchen once served as a meat cooler; and years ago the bathroom functioned as a post office.

Karen, an interior designer by trade, decorated her guest apartment with wall-to-wall carpeting, a leather card table and chairs, a sofa and rocker, and a color television set. The apartment features antique artwork and appointments, and a shell collection. It has two private entrances—one in front and one in the rear garden.

Karen doesn't serve breakfast but for an additional charge will stock the apartment's refrigerator with juice, eggs, sausages, fresh bread, Colombian coffee, and fruit and cheese. For a charge, she will serve dinner, which might include beef bourguignon with potatoes amandine and carrots Grand Marnier.

Accommodations: 1 apartment with private bath. *Smoking:* Permitted. *Children:* One or two permitted, but only in apartment with parents. *Pets:* Not permitted. *Breakfast:* Food for preparation by guests provided for an additional charge. *Driving Instructions:* Take Route 60 to Spring Arbor Road, then take Moscow Road South to the village of Horton; turn right on Main Street.

Saugatuck **MICHIGAN**

Wickwood

510 Butler Street, Saugatuck, MI 49453. (616) 857-1097. *Host:* Laur Statler.

A Federal-style structure built in the 1940s, Wickwood is in downtown Saugatuck. Saugatuck? It is on the Kalamazoo River, which flows into Lake Michigan, less than 5 miles away.

Inspired by a stay at a small, elegant hotel in London, the owners, who also own a gift shop and a women's-sweater shop in town, dedicated themselves to establishing an elegant bed-and-breakfast.

You enter through a foyer featuring etched-glass doors and find yourself in a 15- by 22-foot living room with pale cream walls; a birch, beech, and maple hardwood floor partially covered by a navy blue Chinese rug with border patterns in camel and light blue; and a birch fireplace with a painted pine mantel. There is a hand-creweled wing chair on each side of the fireplace, and facing it, a tuxedo couch picks up the color scheme of the rug.

French doors lead from the living room to the sunken garden-room, which has a brick floor, a 16-foot vaulted ceiling with exposed cedar beams, and an attached screened-in gazebo featuring handmade latticework. The garden room's appointments include a nineteenth-century walnut pump organ, a heavy rattan couch upholstered in navy and white batik, a 12-foot palm tree, and a glass-topped table that's actually a copper tympany drum.

All guest rooms are done in Laura Ashley wallpapers and fabrics and may contain marble-topped writing desks, a hand-crocheted canopy draped over a queen-size cherry four-poster, an empire couch, a chandelier, or a pair of handmade patchwork comforters.

Guests are served a Continental breakfast of fresh-squeezed orange juice, hot rolls, and tea or coffee—at the time they choose. Complimentary hors d'oeuvres, tea or coffee, and setups are offered in the afternoon.

Accommodations: 7 rooms with private bath. *Smoking:* Permitted. *Children:* Not permitted. *Pets:* Not permitted. *Breakfast:* Included. *Driving Instructions:* From Detroit or Kalamazoo, take Route 94 West to Route 196 North, which runs right through Saugatuck. From Grand Rapids, take Route 196 South.

Union City **MICHIGAN**

The Victorian Villa

    601 North Broadway Street, Union City, MI 49094. (517) 741-7383. *Hosts:* Ron and Sue Gibson.

A little older than the six huge sugar maples in front of it, The Victorian Villa is an 1876 structure with Italianate and Tuscan elements and a square, mansard-roofed tower. A porch, its roof supported by double columns ending in carved buttresses, runs across the front of the house. Ron and Sue recently started planting a salad garden and an orchard that features dwarf and semi-dwarf fruit trees including pear, peach, apple, and cherry trees. They also grow blueberries, red raspberries, and yellow raspberries.

    The guest rooms have wide-board pine floors covered here and there with reproduction Turkish and Oriental rugs. Furnishings are all period Victorian pieces—a walnut turtle-top table inlaid with rosewood and topped with marble; two finger-carved walnut side chairs upholstered in a white mohair; and a white marble fireplace to match the one in the parlor-lounge area.

The Rocow bedroom has a bay window with moldings painted downing sand; an 1860 walnut headboard with a triple-arch design and carved flowers; a handmade quilt in browns and blues; a leaded-glass lamp hanging from a bronze chain; a carved-walnut armoire; a three-drawer marble-topped washstand; and a window facing a hundred-year-old-pine tree.

The house features all-walnut woodwork, a three-story winding staircase with walnut banisters and spindles, and double-thickness walnut doors leading into both parlors.

The Continental breakfast includes fresh-fruit compote, applesauce coffee cake, tea or coffee, and fresh muffins.

Accommodations: 4 rooms with shared bath. *Smoking:* Not permitted. *Children:* Permitted. *Pets:* Not permitted. *Breakfast:* Included. *Driving Instructions:* Union City is on Route M-60, 7 miles west of its junction with Route I-69.

"Old Frontenac" (*Bed & Breakfast Upper Midwest*)

Minneapolis Area **MINNESOTA**

Lake Nakomis. This guest house within blocks of Lake Nakomis has a large yard where guests may relax. The area has many parks, as well as several lakes. *Represented by:* The Bed & Breakfast League, Ltd., (202) 232-8718. $20–$28.

Lake of Isles. This guest house has a greenhouse and a gazebo, as well as a convenient location: The Walker Art Center, the Guthrie Theatre, and shopping and restaurants are close by. *Represented by:* The Bed & Breakfast League, Ltd., (202) 232-8718. $30–$38.

Minneapolis (Downtown). Although its exterior has been modernized, this 1880s Victorian remains almost entirely original inside. The downstairs area is marked by oaken woodwork (wainscoting, ball and stick work, and so forth), and the living room has stained-glass windows. Hosted by teachers, the house is furnished with period antiques, and at times is filled with classical music. The dining room has an attached conservatory. The Minneapolis Institute of Art is close by, as is the Dudley Riggs Brave New Workshop. *Represented by:* Bed & Breakfast Upper Midwest, (612) 535-7135. $20.

Minneapolis Area **MINNESOTA**

Old Frontenac. Two blocks from the Mississippi, in a historic neighborhood, this late-nineteenth-century house was built by the Westervilles, one of the founding families of Old Frontenac. It is furnished with a combination of antiques and simple but comfortable pieces. The hosts are artists, and they enjoy referring guests to the studios of other artists in the area. *Represented by:* Bed & Breakfast Upper Midwest, (612) 535-7135. $38–$54.

St. Louis Park. Open to families traveling with children, this guest house features a fireplace and a library stocked with books and games. The hosts make a canoe and a bicycle available to guests, and their home is only a block from the bus. *Represented by:* The Bed & Breakfast League, Ltd., (202) 232-8718. $30–$38.

Winnetonka. Twenty-five minutes from Minneapolis and three minutes from Lake Winnetonka, this guest house consists of two geodesic domes, both solar-active and furnished with modern pieces. The structure is situated on an acre of wooded land, and the host— the artistic director of a theater company—enjoys cooking and serves a full breakfast. *Represented by:* Bed & Breakfast Upper Midwest, (612) 535-7135. $20.

"Winnetonka" (*Bed & Breakfast Upper Midwest*)

Rochester MINNESOTA

Canterbury Inn Bed and Breakfast
  723 Second Street, S.W., Rochester, MN 55901. (507) 289-5553.
Hosts: Mary Martin and Jeffrey Van Sant.

A red 1890s Victorian trimmed in cream and black, Canterbury Inn has a porch on two sides and nine and a half gables. It is on a street currently under consideration as a historic landmark and is five minutes from the Mayo Clinic and IBM's Rochester facility.

  The house, which Mary and Jeffrey restored themselves, has a large turned-oak spindle staircase; stained-glass windows in the living room, parlor, dining room, and on the staircase landing; oaken floors; Oriental rugs; and numerous period and family antiques.

  The central living room has a blue Oriental rug with a pattern in rose, green, and beige; a fireplace; a blue linen sofa; an 1880s oaken platform rocker; a mahogany lawyer's table; a pine Shaker table stained buttermilk; and several heirloom oil paintings. The foyer also has two small Oriental rugs and an 1830s walnut hall tree. The downstairs bath has a large-enough-for-two clawfooted tub.

The guest rooms, each with a private bath with tub, come with an antique walnut or oak dresser. One room has a pineapple four-poster, another has twins made of walnut, and a third has a king-size bed with a pine headboard that used to be a door.

Breakfast, served at guests' convenience, is designed to meet dietary and gastronomic needs and predilections, and ranges from omelets to eggs Benedict to pancakes to waffles. Afternoon tea includes hors d'oeuvres, tea, coffee, and other beverages.

Accommodations: 4 rooms with private bath. *Smoking:* Not permitted in rooms. *Children:* Over 12 permitted. *Pets:* Not permitted. *Breakfast:* Included. *Driving Instructions:* From Minneapolis, take Route 52 south for 85 miles to the exit at Second Street southwest; turn left and proceed to number 723, which is on the left.

Natchez **MISSISSIPPI**

The Burn

712 North Union Street, Natchez, MS 39120. (601) 445-8566.

Hosts: Major Tony and Loveta Byrne.

An 1832 Greek Revival structure with four Doric columns and a paneled doorway surrounded by five glass insets, The Burn is beautifully appointed. One guest room features hand-carved Prudent Mallard furniture, an Aubusson carpet, a chandelier, and an elaborate fireplace with a huge gilt-framed mirror on its mantel. Another guest room has an acanthus carved bed and dressing table, two wing-chairs upholstered in a tufted gray fabric, a fireplace, a circular gilt-framed wide-angle mirror complete with an eagle, and elaborate valenced curtains in the same fabric draped over the four-poster bed.

The music room features laminated and carved Belter furniture (a love seat and several chairs covered in a tufted gold fabric), a crystal chandelier, a large gilt-framed mirror on the fireplace mantel, a large classical painting, and a harp. The entrance hall is furnished with New York Empire pieces, a brass and crystal chandelier, a wide-angle gilt-framed mirror with an eagle perched on top, several Oriental rugs and a large, sinuous spiral staircase with two eighteenth-century Mannerist paintings halfway up it. The Byrnes offer a complimentary breakfast.

Accommodations: 6 rooms with private bath. *Smoking:* Permitted. *Children:* Over 6 permitted. *Pets:* Not permitted. *Breakfast:* Included (dinner on request). *Driving Instructions:* Take Route 61 to Great River Road, and take North Union Street next. The Burn is on North Union between Bee and Oak streets.

Port Gibson **MISSISSIPPI**

Oak Square Country Inn
   1207 Church Street, Port Gibson, MS 39150. (601) 437-4350, -5771, -4239. *Hosts:* Mr. and Mrs. William D. Lum.
In Port Gibson, a history-drenched Southern city that Union General U. S. Grant characterized as "too beautiful to burn," Oak Square is an 1850 Greek Revival structure with six 22-foot fluted Corinthian columns supporting the roof's overhang. Its name derives from the many 100-foot-plus red oaks sprinkled about the grounds, which also feature a courtyard, a gazebo, and a fountain.

   Drawing on a wealth of family antiques, Mr. and Mrs. Lum have furnished their home entirely with period pieces. The double parlor includes: a white marble fireplace with a gold-leaf French mantel mirror above it; a brass and crystal chandelier; elaborately draped windows topped with pressed-brass cornices; a Victorian sofa with matching chairs upholstered in a tufted rose material; and gleaming pine floors. The parlor adjoins the dining room, which also has a brass and crystal chandelier and pine floors. Beneath the chandelier is a mahogany table large enough to seat twelve, and matching mahogany chairs. The library has an 1850 Empire sofa and Chickering piano, a brass gasolier, a Prudent Mallard early-Victorian secretary, and a tufted Victorian lady's chair covered in velvet.

One bedroom features an enormous 1830 mahogany bed with four posts—of at least 8 inches in diameter—holding up a large mahogany top frame. The bed is covered with a hand-crocheted bedspread. The room also has a brass and crystal chandelier and a Victorian parlor set upholstered in rose.

Accommodations: 10 rooms with private bath. *Smoking:* Not permitted. *Children:* Permitted. *Pets:* Not permitted. *Breakfast:* Included. *Driving Instructions:* Port Gibson is on Route 61, halfway between Natchez and Vicksburg, Mississippi.

Kansas City Area **MISSOURI**

Kansas City. Less than 2 miles from the Country Club Plaza, this bed and breakfast was featured in a local 1983 homes tour. The hosts are interested in antiques and are more than willing to direct guests to the best local antique sources. The hosts, one of whom is a gourmet cook and cookbook editor, serve guests a full breakfast. *Represented by:* Kansas City Bed & Breakfast, (913) 268-4214. $38–$40.

Kansas City. Hosted by a Kansas City policeman and an airline professional, this bed and breakfast town house is in a residential area between Kansas City and the airport, and is furnished with many antiques. One host is a gourmet cook who turns out Belgian waffles for guests; the other is an avid fisherperson who can tell interested anglers about the fishing possibilities of Smithville Dam. *Represented by:* Kansas City Bed & Breakfast, (913) 268-4214. $35–$40.

Kansas City. Fifteen minutes from downtown, on a large wooded lot, this bed and breakfast is close to the Kansas City Museum of History and Science. The host's catering business specializes in supplying entertainment to small parties, and the hostess has interests in gardening and interior design. Two guest rooms are on the second floor; the third floor, equipped with sleeping bags, is set up to accommodate children. *Represented by:* Kansas City Bed & Breakfast, (913) 268-4214. $27–$30.

Kansas City. An older home in a residential area just south of Country Club Plaza, this bed and breakfast is hosted by a registered nurse who runs a health clinic and is interested in tennis, bridge, baseball, and classical music. The house has hardwood floors and a fireplace, and its guest bedrooms open onto private porches. *Represented by:* Kansas City Bed & Breakfast, (913) 268-4214. $35.

Kansas City. Hosted by an ex-engineer and long-time resident of the area, this bed and breakfast is a two-story contemporary home slightly north of the Missouri River. The house, furnished with a mixture of contemporary and antique pieces, has a large backyard with numerous mature trees. The hosts offer guests two rooms and serve a full breakfast. *Represented by:* Kansas City Bed & Breakfast, (913) 268-4214. $30–$35.

Liberty. Near William Jewell College, this guest house is a restored antebellum structure. The ground-level guest room has a private bath, and guests can arrange to engage a second room with

Kansas City Area **MISSOURI**

a sofa that opens into a queen-size bed. During the week the host serves a Continental breakfast; on the weekends, a full one. *Represented by:* Kansas City Bed & Breakfast, (913) 268-4214. $32–$37.

Parkville. On 88 acres of Missouri hillside, this bed and breakfast is an earth-integrated structure with an indoor pool and an exercise room. A jogging path winds around the perimeter of the property. A separate entrance leads to the four guest rooms, each with a private bath. The hosts, who welcome children and well-behaved pets, serve a full breakfast, in bed, by the pool, or in the dining room. *Represented by:* Kansas City Bed & Breakfast, (913) 268-4214. $48–$50.

Kirkwood (Bed & Breakfast St. Louis)

St. Louis Area   **MISSOURI**

Restored Historic Home. A *ca.*-1900 renovated Gothic Victorian made of sandstone, this bed and breakfast is convenient to numerous St. Louis attractions—St. Louis University, Washington University Medical School, and the theater, midtown, and downtown districts. One guest room has a queen-size bed and adjacent sun porch/lounge; another has a four-poster bed. There's also a two-room suite with a king-size bed and a private bath. *Represented by:* Bed & Breakfast St. Louis, HO-44, (314) 868-2335. $35–$50.

N.E. Suburb. In a northeast St. Louis suburb, this ranch-style bed and breakfast is in a private, wooded area. The living room has a fireplace and opens onto a screened-in porch overlooking a stand of pines—and, from time to time, a procession of quail. There's a woodburning stove in the family room, and the guest room has a private bath and a cherry bedroom set with a high headboard. *Represented by:* Bed & Breakfast St. Louis, RE-16, (314) 868-2335. $35–$40.

Kirkwood. Surrounded by redbud, flowering bushes, and dogwood, this bed and breakfast is an 1853 historic house furnished primarily with period antiques. There are heirloom quilts in the

Pasedena Hills (Bed & Breakfast St. Louis)

St. Louis Area   MISSOURI

guest room, along with needlepoint accessories and Godey prints. The hostess, who prides herself on her knowledge of the historic aspects of St. Louis, serves guests a full breakfast. *Represented by:* Bed & Breakfast St. Louis, CR-30, (314) 868-2335. $35–$39.

Ladue. On grounds with magnolia trees and featuring a full-size swimming pool, this bed and breakfast is a Tudor-style home. There are a grandfather clock tucked into the curve of the entrance hall's circular stairway, a formal parlor, and a screened-in porch. One guest room has an antique oaken bed; the other has three exposures and a private bath. *Represented by:* Bed & Breakfast St. Louis, RI-39, (314) 868-2335. $35–$45.

Pasedena Hills. A 1940s brick Tudor-style home with enclosed porches on its first and second floors, this bed and breakfast is convenient to the University of Missouri and minutes from the downtown waterfront. Two guest rooms are available, both with country furnishings and leaded stained-glass windows. The arrangement here is most suitable for couples traveling together or families with children. *Represented by:* Bed & Breakfast St. Louis, HA-72, (314) 868-2335. $30–$40.

Omaha Area **NEBRASKA**

Blair. This chalet-style home, 10 miles north of Omaha and 6 miles south of Blair, is on a private lake that has two swimming beaches. Guests are invited to use the hosts' boat and fishing equipment. The hosts—who enjoy hunting, fishing, and gardening—have one guest room, which has a double bed and antique furnishings as well as a private bath. The hosts serve a full breakfast, and have a large redwood deck overlooking their garden and lake. *Represented by:* Bed & Breakfast of Nebraska, #5, (402) 564-7591. $30.

Fort Calhoun. This ninety-two-year-old three-story house is on 9 acres of wooded land 12 miles north of Omaha, not far from the DeSoto Bend wildlife refuge. The larger rooms in the house feature stained-glass windows, sandstone fireplaces, oak parquet floors, and carved woodwork. The hosts serve a full breakfast and invite guests to share their living room. *Represented by:* Bed & Breakfast of Nebraska, #4, (402) 564-7591. $25–$30.

Elkhorn. Ten minutes from the major shopping areas in Omaha and Boys Town, this bed and breakfast is a contemporary ranch-style house on an acre of land. A full-time homemaker, the hostess here makes her own jams and jellies, and confesses to an almost overpowering interest in gardening. The house features a recently redone family room, and the hostess welcomes pets. *Represented by:* Bed & Breakfast of Nebraska, #3, (402) 564-7591. $15–$30.

Omaha. Built in 1894, this chateau-style house was designed by the architect Ives Cobb. Unlike nearly every other building on the block, it survived the Easter Sunday tornado of 1913. Legend has it that during the storm an open decanter of sherry was carried 35 feet from a sideboard in the dining room to the living room—and not a drop was spilled. There is a great deal of carved woodwork: oak in the entry hall, mahogany in the living room, walnut in the dining room. There are fireplaces in the living room, the dining room, and two of the bedrooms. Furnished with antiques, the bedrooms vary—one has a carved wood bed; another has a brass bed and a fireplace; another has a three-quarter bed and a fireplace. The hosts, a fashion illustrator and her musician son, invite guests to use the barroom if they like, and they serve a Continental breakfast in the dining room. *Represented by:* Bed & Breakfast of Nebraska, #1, (402) 564-7591. $36–$55.

Omaha. This bed and breakfast on an acre of looked-after grounds is a contemporary split-level home that's very convenient

Omaha Area **NEBRASKA**

to Route I-80. The guest room features a king-size water bed and a private half-bath. The hosts, who have traveled across the continent staying in bed-and-breakfast places, serve a full breakfast and welcome children and pets. *Represented by:* Bed & Breakfast of Nebraska, #10, (402) 564-7591. $20–$30.

Imlay   **NEVADA**

Old Pioneer Garden

Unionville 79, Imlay, NV 89418. (702) 538-7585. *Hosts:* Mitzi and Lew Jones.

One way to avoid the pressure of keeping up with the Joneses is to live in a ghost town, which is exactly what Mitzi and Lew Jones decided to do. The Old Pioneer Garden is a genuine ghost town, which Mitzi and Lew have been restoring.

The main farmhouse was built in 1861, when mining for silver, gold, antimony, and copper attracted prospectors and businessmen to the area. The old Arizona mine, which virtually made the town of Unionville, is a short walk from the property. The grounds are bound to please nature lovers—there are a trout stream, a pond, and spectacular mountain views. The elevation here is 6,000 feet plus; from the farmhouse porches one can view the fruit trees and animals and the snow-covered mountains in the distance.

The Joneses raise sheep, goats, pigs, chickens, geese, guineas, and ducks. "We raise much of what we eat," says Mitzi. They're more than generous when it comes time to feed the guests. Their rates include a full ranch-style breakfast.

Accommodations: 9 rooms, 5 with private bath. *Smoking:* Tolerated. *Children and Horses:* Permitted. *Pets:* Permitted if well behaved. *Breakfast:* Included. *Driving Instructions:* From Winnemucca take Route I-80 south to Mill City; take Route 400 south for 16 miles, then turn right on the gravel road and go 3 miles.

NEW HAMPSHIRE

Hancock. This 1790 farmhouse in the small village of Hancock has been authentically restored—Indian shutters cover the windows, wide pine-boards, the floors, and original stenciling, the walls. Off the kitchen there's an herb garden that the host harvests to make the jams, jellies, and vinegars she sells at a farm stand in the fall. The barn contains a cider mill, whose output guests get to enjoy. There's a private living room for guests, who are invited to watch the television in the country kitchen. *Represented by:* New Hampshire Bed & Breakfast, #540, (603) 279-8348. $35–$40.

Franklin. This 1830s farmhouse, part of a 200-acre farm, is on the shore of Webster Lake. Its grounds include a private beach, clay tennis courts, and a gazebo. The barn has a pool table, a Ping Pong table and a mirrored dance/exercise area. The house is slightly less than two hours from Boston, and the area offers a host of New Hampshire lakes region attractions. *Represented by:* New Hampshire Bed & Breakfast, #231, (603) 279-8348. $30–$40.

Meredith. Hosted by a retired teacher with a penchant for bridge, this bed and breakfast sits among pines on the shore of Lake Winnipesaukee. The grounds feature a private beach and dock, and the house has a living-room deck overlooking the mountains and the lakes; the living room itself includes a baby grand piano and an organ. *Represented by:* New Hampshire Bed & Breakfast, #215, (603) 279-8348. $35–$50.

Ossipee. This eighteenth-century farmhouse on a 500-acre working farm has five fireplaces, Indian-shuttered windows, floors of wide pine boards, and exposed-beam ceilings. It is furnished with many antiques, and the hosts pride themselves on expertly preparing their organically grown foods. North Conway is a short drive from here, as are numerous dining and antiquing possibilities. *Represented by:* New Hampshire Bed & Breakfast, #201, (603) 279-8348. $35.

Whitefield. Hosted by two teachers, this mid-nineteenth-century restored farmhouse is on the northern slopes of the White Mountains. The house has three fireplaces—one in its large country kitchen and one in each of two living rooms—and mountain views from all eighteen rooms. Furnished with period antiques, the house offers five guest rooms. Both living rooms and the television are there for guests' use, and the hosts offer limited kitchen privileges.

NEW HAMPSHIRE

Represented by: New Hampshire Bed & Breakfast, #101, (603) 279-8348. $30.

Wilton. A quarter of a mile from the highest waterfall in New Hampshire, this bed and breakfast is an 1812 Federal home. Decorated with period antiques, the living room features Moses Eaton stenciling; a den/library has a television set and a fireplace. The equestrian host has two box-stalls available for horses or pets, and two double-bedded guest rooms with private bath for other guests. *Represented by:* New Hampshire Bed & Breakfast, #545, (603) 279-8348. $30–$45.

Ashland   **NEW HAMPSHIRE**

Cheney House Bed and Breakfast

40 Highland Street, Ashland, NH 03217. (603) 968-7968. *Hosts:* Mike and Daryl Mooney.

Situated on 3.5 acres planted with maple, catalpa, spruce, and butternut trees, Cheney House is an 1895 Victorian brick structure, its upper stories painted beige. The entrance foyer, which is rather the centerpiece of the house, has oaken floors and wainscoting, stained-glass windows, and a carved oaken balustrade. Breakfast is served in this foyer and consists of such items as oven pancakes stuffed with poached eggs, bacon, or sausage, or perhaps homemade blueberry pancakes with real maple syrup.

The guest rooms are decorated wtih country furniture. One has an antique handmade quilt covering a queen-size bed, dark brown wall-to-wall carpeting, Currier and ives prints on the walls, and a window overlooking the lawns and garden. All of the guest rooms have views of lawn, flowers, and trees.

Cheney House is within walking distance of a Squam Lake beach and tennis courts.

Accommodations: 3 rooms with shared bath. *Smoking:* Permitted. *Children:* Permitted. *Pets:* Not permitted. *Breakfast:* Included. *Driving Instructions:* From I-93 North exit at Ashland, bear left at Cumberland Farms, and take the first left onto Highland Street.

Hampton Beach   **NEW HAMPSHIRE**

The Grayhurst

11 F Street, Hampton Beach, NH 03842. (603) 926-2584. *Hosts:* Peter and Judy Chaput.

Eighty feet from the ocean, the Grayhurst is an 1890 gambrel-roofed Cape Cod–style structure with porches on the first and second floors and a 40-foot row of flowers in front of it. The front yard and the 3-foot deep flower boxes on the porch are filled with petunias, geraniums, and marigolds. Old-time residents of the area remember one of the house's former residents—an opera singer who on Sunday mornings took up a position on a porch and burst into high-volume song. That porch usually gets a cool breeze.

From May through October Peter and Judy Chaput offer several efficiency apartments that feature private baths, television, and complete cooking facilities, as well as a cottage with 3 rooms and a private porch. The rooms are simply furnished.

One apartment has a nonworking fireplace with a hundred-year-old 3- by 4-foot seascape hanging above it, wall-to-wall carpeting, an antique oaken bureau, antique oaken chairs, and tasseled Colonial curtains.

Peter, who has a master's degree in business, currently teaches business and accounting courses at New Hampshire College.

The Grayhurst is in the center of Hampton Beach, which has

numerous attractions and can be quite noisy and congested during the high season.

Accommodations: 13 rooms with shared bath, 3 apartments, and 1 cottage. *Smoking:* Permitted. *Children:* Permitted. *Pets:* Not permitted. *Driving Instructions:* The Grayhurst is in the center of the beach area.

Jackson **NEW HAMPSHIRE**

Stone Fox Lodge

Tin Mine Road, Box 406, Jackson, NH 01581. (203) 383-6636.

Hosts: Ed and Alice Bannon.

Built around 1880 as a summer home, Stone Fox is a Victorian shingled structure with rock pillars and foundation. Legend has it that a friendly ghost named Murphy inhabits the house, but you're more likely to be awed by the natural beauty of the house's setting than worried by any of its supernatural denizens. The views from the guest rooms and the building's wraparound porch are nothing less than spectacular: One looks across Mount Washington and sees the Presidential Range of the White Mountains.

The living room has a large stone fireplace, antique wooden paneling, and Oriental rugs, both on the floors and displayed on the walls. Off the living room are two dining rooms with pine paneling and fireplaces. There are green plants in these rooms and nearly all the others.

The guest rooms are furnished with a combination of antique and 1930s and 1940s pieces, and on the landing leading to the rooms is a miniature John Thomas grandfather clock. Some of the guest rooms have Oriental rugs, and the halls and the bathrooms contain many green plants.

The lodge has a restaurant that serves meals to the public by reservation only, and Ed and Alice put out tea and cakes for their guests. The restaurant features entrées such as cinnamon duck, Stone Fox steak, veal Bosco, and Chateaubriand for two.

The lodge is closed in April and May and from the end of the fall-foliage season through Christmas.

Accommodations: 5 rooms with shared bath. *Smoking:* Permitted. *Children:* Young ones discouraged. *Pets:* Check in advance. *Breakfast:* Included. *Driving Instructions:* Take Route 16B into Jackson, and turn up Tin Mine Road at the sign for the Tyrol Ski Area and the Stone Fox Lodge.

Littleton **NEW HAMPSHIRE**

1895 House

75 Pleasant Street, Littleton, NH 03561. (603) 444-5200 or (609) 652-8634. *Hostess:* Susanne Watkins.

Built in the year of its name, 1895 House is a white Victorian structure with green shutters and a wraparound porch. The building is situated on half an acre of land, planted with sugar maples and 20-foot lilac bushes. The backyard of 1895 House is contiguous with a park that has a baseball diamond, tennis courts, and, close to the house, a gazebo.

A massive oak door with beveled glass insets opens into a foyer that has an oaken floor and hand-carved woodwork on the walls. The stairway leading upstairs is also made of oak, and its banister posts were carved by hand.

The living room has sliding oaken doors with brass knobs, a Chippendale camelback couch upholstered in silver gray velvet, two Queen Anne chairs, and a tan, beige, and coral Oriental rug. The room has bay windows that overlook the porch and the town of Littleton, and the walls are hung with Oriental prints, such as original Japanese woodcuts, from Susanne's collection. The living room has a stereo, on which Susanne plays classical music. (Beethoven and Bach are two of her favorite composers, and she takes particular delight in the playing of Vladimir Horowitz.)

A pair of sliding oaken doors lead to the dining room, which has a brick fireplace with a carved oaken mantel incorporating a mirror inset and the head of Old Man Winter in bas-relief, an oaken dining table with rope legs, and a set of bay windows that overlook the high lilac bushes.

The guest rooms have oaken floors, oaken armoires and dressers, braided and Oriental rugs, quilts that Susanne made by hand, and Priscilla tieback curtains. The third-floor guest rooms have slanted walls.

Accommodations: 6 rooms, 1 with private bath. *Smoking:* Permitted except in dining area. *Children:* Permitted. *Pets:* Sometimes permitted—check in advance. *Driving Instructions:* From I-91 take Route 302 east into Littleton, then turn left off Main Street onto Pleasant Street.

Conover's Bay Head Inn

646 Main Avenue, Bay Head, NJ 08742. (201) 892-4664. *Hosts:* Carl and Beverly Conover.

Bay Head, situated at the beginning of the inland waterway to Florida, was a resort as far back as the sixteenth-century, when the Leni-Lenape Indians summered here. Conover's Bay Head Inn is a large, shingled 1910 cottage-style structure with several small gables on its roof. The grounds, planted with geraniums and azaleas, contain a picnic area that guests may use.

The living room has a white stone fireplace with an antique walnut clock on its mantel, beige Bargello-pattern carpeting, a walnut couch upholstered in a dark beige fabric and brightened with needlepoint throw pillows, which Beverly made, and a mahogany table. The room is filled with plants.

One guest room has a bed with a lacy canopy and a matching spread, a chandelier with a Tiffany shade in greens and yellows, and a hand-painted night table. The third-floor guest rooms have dormer windows, and two of them have water views. One third-floor room, which has a view of the Bay, has a large Victorian bed and delicate buttercup wallpaper that matches the pillows and the bedspread. Each guest room is color-coordinated, with matching wallpaper, pillows, and spreads. The guest rooms are further enhanced by doilies Beverly crocheted herself. One room reflects Carl's preoccupation with steam engines (he used to own one) and is decorated with all manner of gauges.

Carl and Beverly serve their guests complimentary wine, as well as a Continental breakfast that includes fresh-baked breads, which Beverly varies from day to day. The inn is open from February 15 through December 15.

Accommodations: 12 rooms, 4 with private bath. *Smoking:* Permitted. *Children:* Well-behaved older children permitted. *Pets:* Not permitted. *Breakfast:* Included. *Driving Instructions:* Take the Garden State Parkway to exit 98, pick up Routes 34 and 35 South, and continue to Point Pleasant Beach. Bay Head is the next town.

276

Cape May   **NEW JERSEY**

The Abbey

Columbia Avenue and Gurney Street, Cape May, NJ 08204. (609) 884-4506. *Hosts:* Jay and Marianne Shatz.

The Abbey was built in 1869 by a wealthy coal baron and politician, a man who doubtless cherished spectacular views. The city of Cape May and the Atlantic Ocean seem almost to have been designed for viewing from the Abbey's Tower Room, high in the structure's 60-foot tower.

Stenciled and ruby-glass arched windows, 12-foot mirrors, fireplaces, carved walnut beds, marble-topped dressers—appointments like these are found throughout the Abbey. Jay and Marianne Shatz have assembled a stunning collection of ornate gaslighting fixtures, which run on electricity these days and seem to show up in every room.

The back parlor features a slate fireplace with a huge gilt-framed mirror rising from its mantel, an 1840 Swiss harp made of mahogany and fruitwood, a heavily tufted green velvet parlor set carved out of walnut and inlaid with rosewood and tulip wood, ornate frieze wallpaper bordering the multicolored ceiling molding, and white-curtained bay windows. All of the fourth-floor guest rooms have private baths and small refrigerators. "I couldn't find any Victorian refrigerators," Marianne claims. The other guest rooms share a 15- by 15-foot bathroom with an Oriental rug, a claw-footed tub, a pedestal sink and a brass chandelier. The Abbey is closed from December through March.

Both Jay and Marianne have marketing backgrounds in the chemical industry, and they opened the Abbey in a spirit of elegant revenge—they had both stayed in too many motels.

Accommodations: 7 rooms, 4 with private bath. *Smoking:* Permitted but no cigars. *Children:* Over 12 permitted if well behaved. *Pets:* Not permitted. *Breakfast:* Included. *Driving Instructions:* Take the Garden State Parkway to its end, turn left on Ocean Street, then left again on Columbia Avenue.

Cape May **NEW JERSEY**

Barnard-Good House

238 Perry Street, Cape May, NJ 08204. (609) 884-5381. *Hosts:* Nan and Tom Hawkins.

An 1869 Second Empire structure with a mansard roof, Barnard-Good House was sold at a sheriff's auction for one hundred dollars—the year, 1937. The house has never been structurally altered and retains its original picket fence, wraparound veranda with gingerbread trim, and unusual bone-shaped flower bed.

Provided their legs are strong enough to pump it, guests frequently play the parlor's antique pump organ. The room also has a hand-carved and tiled fireplace that was put in way back when for purely decorative reasons (it doesn't function, never did, but looks rather stunning). Lace curtains, a tasseled valance, and antiques dress up the room. The dining room has an iron, pewter, and brass gasolier; a large table covered with lace; an 1870 sideboard with griffin-shaped solid-brass pulls; an 1868 marble-topped server; a bay window with lace curtains; and a Victorian tufted sofa with matching ladies' and gentlemen's chairs.

Guest rooms feature such appointments as an appliquéd oaken dresser and wardrobe; twin four-posters put together to make a king-size bed; an antique double brass bed; elegant wallpapers; a ceiling fan; and iron and brass beds.

Breakfast here is substantial and completely homemade. Typical menu entries include double cheese puffs filled with ham and Mornay sauce; crepes with apple and sour cream and raisin fillings; chilled blueberry/raspberry soup . . . Get the idea?

Accommodations: 6 rooms, 3 with private bath. *Smoking:* Permitted, but not happy about cigar smokers. *Children:* Not permitted. *Pets:* Not permitted. *Breakfast:* Included. *Driving Instructions:* Follow the Garden State Parkway to the end. Go over the bridge and follow Lafayette Street through two traffic lights; turn right at Collier's liquor store to the next light.

Cape May NEW JERSEY

The Brass Bed Victorian Guest House
   719 Columbia Avenue, Cape May, NJ 08204. (609) 884-8075.
   Hosts: John and Donna Dunwoody.
So named because each guest room has one, The Brass Bed is an 1872 Gothic Revival structure. As John and Donna Dunwoody restored the old house they came across a good deal of dusty furniture that had obviously belonged to the original owner: His name appeared on shipping tags still attached to it.

   The house has a 32-foot porch with white wicker furniture and long-backed rocking chairs fashioned of long-grained pine. The garden's flowers—two groupings of coleus and a mix of geraniums and begonias—complement the colors of the house: gold, sand, and chocolate brown.

   The central parlor—where guests read, talk, or cajole John Dunwoody into playing his rosewood Graphola—has 12-foot French doors; an 1840 drop-leaf oaken desk with a 1900 Corona typewriter perched on it; a spoon-carved Lady Eastlake platform rocker; and an Indian rug with an abstract design in oranges and blues. The hall and dining room have ornate plaster ceiling medallions, and a curved mahogany banister leads up to the second floor. The Congress Hall room features a blue Oriental rug with a floral pattern in golds, creams, and browns, an 1872 poplar armoire, and a late-nineteenth-century mahogany leaf table.

John and Donna serve a complimentary breakfast of fresh fruit, juices, cereal, coffee, and cake.

Accommodations: 8 rooms, 2 with private bath. *Smoking:* Permitted. *Children:* Under 13 not permitted. *Pets:* Not permitted. *Breakfast:* Included. *Driving Instructions:* Take the Garden State Parkway south to its end, turn left on Ocean Street, then left again on Columbia Avenue.

Cape May   **NEW JERSEY**

Captain Mey's Inn

202 Ocean Street, Cape May, NJ 08204. (609) 884-7793. *Hostesses:* Carin Feddermann and Milly Laconfora.

This 1890 Victorian structure, built by a homeopathic physician, is named after Cornelius J. Mey, the founder of the Cape May community. "'Tis better to govern by love and friendship than by force," said he.

Carin and Milly, who do things like commission analyses to determine the original paint color of their house, furnished Captain Mey's Inn with stunning antiques. The parlor has a Gothic bookcase hand-carved out of dark oak; a lighter shade of hand-carved oak encircles the Tiffany stained glass and matching-shell-design tiles incorporated into the vestibule. The living room has a leaded-glass bay window, complete with a window seat, chestnut oak paneling, and a crowned, molded ceiling, as well as a fireplace.

The guest rooms tend to contain marble-topped dressers, 5-foot high and 200-year-old beds (some of oak and some of walnut), lace curtains, handmade quilts and afghans, Oriental carpets, and freshly cut flowers.

As do many people with taste, Carin and Milly play Mozart during breakfast, which they serve, idiosyncratically, by candlelight—in a dining room with a fireplace, or on the front porch.

Accommodations: 10 rooms, 3 with private bath. *Smoking:* Permitted. *Children:* Over 12 permitted. *Pets:* Not permitted. *Breakfast:* Included. *Driving Instructions:* Take the Garden State Parkway to the Cape May exit; cross the bridge to Lafayette Street and go straight to the second red light; make a left onto Ocean Street.

Cape May   **NEW JERSEY**

The Dormer House International

800 Columbia Avenue, Cape May, NJ 08204. (609) 884-7446.

Hosts: Bill and Peg Madden.

An 1895 Colonial Revival structure, the Dormer House was originally the private home of a Philadelphia marble dealer. The house, which the U.S. Navy used as a rehabilitation center between 1918 and 1920, has been a guest house for well over half a century. It was converted into apartments in the early 1970s. The house features a large front porch with a glassed-in area, and period furniture.

All the guest apartments, some of which are available only on a weekly basis, are fully equipped, although Bill and Peg don't supply linens (towels, sheets, pillowcases, and so on), maid service or breakfast.

One apartment, which accommodates six, has a private porch, a kitchen separated from the living room by an island counter with a maple butcher-block top, and a bedroom with two exposures. Some apartments have private entrances; some have rooms with three exposures; one has a fireplace; and another, a marble bathroom.

Bill and Peg supply guests with a tranquil garden, hibachis and charcoal, coin-operated laundry facilities, and beach tags (for a small contribution). No meals are served, but shopping is nearby and each apartment has a kitchen.

Accommodations: 7 apartments with private bath. *Smoking:* Reluctantly permitted. *Children:* Permitted. *Pets:* Dogs permitted if approved in advance. *Driving Instructions:* The Dormer House is in the middle of Cape May, two blocks from the fire station.

Cape May **NEW JERSEY**

The Queen Victoria

102 Ocean Street, Cape May, NJ 08204. (609) 884-8702. *Hosts:* Dane and Joan Wells.

The Wellses recently restored this large 1881 Victorian structure to its original appearance. The Sherwin-Williams Company has pointed to the house as perhaps the best example of color placement in Cape May. Joan used to be the executive director of the Victorian Society in America, and her fascination with Victoriana manifests itself throughout the house.

The bedrooms are furnished with authentic Victorian pieces,

mostly of walnut, wicker, oak, and pine, along with fresh flowers and colorful quilts. The parlor, which features a large fireplace, and the dining room are furnished with the Wellses' personal collection of Mission furniture. William Morris wallpapers, reproduced by hand-printing, cover the walls. The wallpaper in the dining room was designed for Queen Victoria, and Morris incorporated into the design the queen's initials and the imperial crown.

For guests who feel like exploring the town of Cape May or observing the ocean from a moving perspective, bicycles—one of them even built for two—are available. Farm eggs and cream, fresh fruit, homemade breads, and imported coffees and teas constitute the Wellses' complimentary breakfast. The Wellses serve guests tea each afternoon.

Accommodations: 12 rooms, 4 with private bath. *Smoking:* Permitted in parlor only. *Children:* Not permitted. *Pets:* Not permitted. *Breakfast:* Included. *Driving Instructions:* Take the Garden State Parkway to its end; continue straight on Route 109, which becomes Lafayette Street; in town, turn left at the second stoplight, Ocean Street, and proceed three blocks.

Cape May   **NEW JERSEY**

The 7th Sister Guesthouse

10 Jackson Street, Cape May, NJ 08204. (609) 884-2280. *Hosts:* Bob and JoAnne Myers.

Listed in the National Register of Historic Places, The 7th Sister is an 1888 Victorian Renaissance Revival structure with an imposing circular central staircase. The house, scarcely a hundred feet from the ocean, has a living room and several guest rooms that overlook the Atlantic.

The furnishings are 85 percent original, and to the original decor Bob and JoAnne have added a wicker collection of more than fifty pieces, a profusion of plants, and many of JoAnne's paintings. The parlor has its original coal-grate fireplace, and a sun porch faces the ocean. The side yard is taken up by a lawn and flowers.

Whether you're a history buff or love the outdoors, there's plenty to do in Cape May—swimming, sailing, canoeing, tennis, and antiquing are all major pastimes here.

Accommodations: 6 rooms with shared bath. *Smoking:* Permitted. *Children:* Over 7 permitted. *Pets:* Not permitted. *Driving Instructions:* Take the Garden State Parkway to its end; continue on Lafayette Street until it comes to a *T*, then make a left.

(Lower) Delaware River Valley **NEW JERSEY**

Gardenville (Pennsylvania). Previously part of the adjoining Gardenville Farm Dairies, this 1732 Bucks County stone house is on 24 acres of partially wooded meadow. From the grounds you can see the Holsteins grazing on nearby meadows, and you can sometimes hear them mooing in harmony. A retired attorney and an antique dealer are hosts of the house, which is furnished with a mixture of country antiques and contemporary pieces. Three guest rooms are available—two with a shared bath and one with a private bath. During the summer months guests are invited to use the in-ground swimming pool. *Represented by:* Town and Country Bed & Breakfast, (609) 397-8399. $50.

Lambertville. Furnished with antiques, this brick town house is hosted by two area artists whose paintings, mainly landscapes and portraits, hang throughout the home. Guests are offered a two-room suite that has a bedroom with a three-quarter-size antique oak bed, a sitting room, and a private bath. The host serves a Continental breakfast, and the house is in a historic area known for its many fine restaurants. *Represented by:* Town and Country Bed & Breakfast, (609) 397-8399. $50.

Lambertville. One guest room in this restored Italianate-style townhouse features a large mahogany bed, a matching mahogany wardrobe, and a view of York Street Park with its gazebo and cannon. Fluent in German, the host is a local antiques dealer, and the house is furnished entirely with antiques. Both guest rooms share a bath and have working fireplaces. The living-room floor features two marble fireplaces, an eclectic collection of antiques, and a good stereo. The host doesn't serve breakfast, but guests are free to make themselves coffee and tea and to store things in the refrigerator. *Represented by:* Town and Country Bed & Breakfast, (609) 397-8399. $50–$55.

Three Bridges. On 6 acres fronting the Raritan River, this guest house is a *ca.* -1830 restored frame gristmill, which is furnished with a mixture of antiques and contemporary pieces. The host, a consultant who occasionally conducts seminars at the mill, has four rooms available for guests. The guest rooms share a large bath and are on the third floor, which also has a sitting room complete with television and a Betamax. Guests are invited to view whatever movies the host has at the time, and if you check in advance, you might be able to arrange to see one of your favorites. Compleat anglers

Three Bridges (Town & Country Bed & Breakfast

Lambertville (Town & Country Bed & Breakfast)

(Lower) Delaware River Valley NEW JERSEY

should, of course, bring along their fishing poles. *Represented by:* Town and Country Bed & Breakfast, (609) 397-8399. $60.

Washington Crossing. On 8 acres, 2 of them landscaped and 6 wooded, this eighteenth-century stone manor house has been in the same family for eighty years. Also on the property is a restored stone gristmill, now an antique shop. Hosted by a retired schoolteacher and assistant principal, the house is furnished entirely with antiques. Washington Crossing is a picturesque, historic area. The host serves a Continental breakfast. *Represented by:* Town and Country Bed & Breakfast, (609) 397-8399. $60.

Stockton   **NEW JERSEY**

The Woolverton Inn

    Woolverton Road, Stockton, New Jersey. Mailing address: Box 233, R.D. 3, Stockton, NJ 08559. (609) 397-0802. *Hostess:* Deborah Clark.

Situated on 10 acres of grounds that include parts of a sheep pasture and a formal garden, which Whitney North Seymour planted, the Woolverton Inn is a three-story Victorian stone manor house with an Italianate mansard roof. The house was built in 1793 by John Prall, the owner of a local quarry for whom Prallville, which is what Stockton used to be called, was named. There are porches on the first and second floors.

    Deborah Clark, who used to raise Siberian tigers for the Chrysler Marine Corporation, furnished the Woolverton Inn entirely with antiques. The living room has a fireplace with a wooden fanned mantel, an antique baby-grand piano, a 1930s French reproduction Louis XV chair upholstered with needlepoint, an Oriental rug in shades of blue and red, and etchings and drawings on the walls.

    One guest room is a suite with three exposures, a king-size bed, and walls lined with bookcases, which contain some rare books. Each guest room features something different: There are a canopied bed with a matching cover and dust ruffle, a pair of 6-foot-tall fourposters, an Empire rocker, and Oriental rugs.

    Deborah serves a Continental breakfast that includes fresh fruit, juices, and croissants and fancy breads.

    Accommodations: 9 rooms with shared bath. *Smoking:* Permitted. *Children:* Not permitted. *Pets:* Permitted. *Breakfast:* Included. *Driving Instructions:* Take Route 29 north to Stockton, and then Route 533 for ¼ mile; turn left on Woolverton Road.

Silver City   **NEW MEXICO**

Bear Mountain Guest Ranch

P.O. Box 1163, Silver City, NM 88062. (505) 538-2538. *Hostess:* Myra B. McCormick.

Someone characterized Myra McCormick as a woman likely to have flapjacks in one hand and binoculars in the other. She is an active and erudite ornithologist and botanist. Hummingbirds sip nectar at her window feeders, and she has established a national reputation as a Wildplant Seekers Guide.

At an elevation of 6,250 feet, Myra's rambling hacienda features seven guest rooms with private bath; a four-bedroom house; a one-bedroom house; and a cottage. All guest rooms have porches with southern exposures.

Myra serves complimentary breakfast, lunch, and dinner and will prepare sack lunches for anyone who feels like exploring the countryside. Bear Mountain Guest Ranch is close to such natural wonders as hot springs and the Gila National Forest.

Accommodations: 7 rooms with private bath, 3 guest houses. *Smoking:* Permitted. *Children:* Permitted. *Pets:* Dogs on a leash permitted. *Breakfast, lunch, and dinner:* Included. *Driving Instructions:* From Silver City take Route I-80 toward Glenwood; turn right on Alabama Street, then turn left on the dirt road just beyond the cattle guard.

(North Country Bed & Breakfast CI-5)

(North Country Bed & Breakfast PH-14)

The Adirondack Region **NEW YORK**

Lake George. Built in 1906 for one Royal Peabody, this bed and breakfast, a mansion constructed of wood and stone, stands right on the shore of Lake George. Six guest rooms are available; all have private baths with marble tubs and showers. Oriental rugs and velvet settees set the formal tone of the decor here. Four rooms overlooking the lake have private balconies, and the reception room and the main living room have marble fireplaces. Fishing, boating, waterskiing, and swimming are all popular Lake George activities. *Represented by:* North Country Bed & Breakfast, #ADK-4, (518) 523-3739. $65–$75.

Lake Placid. A contemporary Swiss-style chalet built of wood and generous amounts of glass, this home is in a new but heavily wooded area of town. The hosts, fluent in German, Spanish, and French, are active skiers and take an interest in community activities. The house is furnished with modern pieces—Scandinavian furnishings and glass and chrome predominate. A double and a single room are available for guests, as well as a small apartment that has a large private bath and a sitting room with television. The house is close to the Northville-Remsen trail, which winds its way from central New York to the Canadian border. *Represented by:* North Country Bed & Breakfast, (518) 523-3739. $25–$35.

Lake Placid. A 1920s Colonial painted white and trimmed black, this home has a porch running all across the back of the house. Its backyard is wooded with mature Eastern white pines and white birches. One host is director of the Alpine Training Center at Whiteface Mountain, and the other, a legal secretary. Overstuffed country furnishings constitute the decor, and there is a woodstove between the living and dining rooms. Each of the thirteen guest rooms has wood paneling and built-in twin-size bunk beds. Skiers are invited to use the equipment room, which has waxing paraphernalia and other skiing essentials. The hosts serve a full breakfast, and their home is about two blocks from the Olympic Arena. *Represented by:* North Country Bed & Breakfast, #CI-5, (518) 523-3739. $12.

Lake Placid. This bed and breakfast, a mile from the center of town, is called the "Rose Mobile." The hostess is a silk-screener who enjoys bobsledding, and her wooden mobile home with various additions (one contains a sauna), is in a wooded area beside a stream, which a rear deck overlooks. The hostess collects old clothes and

The Adirondack Region **NEW YORK**

hats, some of which are displayed, and her decor is suggested by touches like a white couch, a blue, brown, and rust Oriental rug, and numerous framed photographs of Lake Placid. She serves a Continental breakfast. *Represented by:* North Country Bed & Breakfast, #PH-14, (518) 523-3739. $30.

Lake Placid. Standing directly on the west bank of Lake Placid, this guest house consists of some twenty log cabins, each with an Adirondack stone fireplace. The cabins are furnished with rustic wooden pieces topped with overstuffed pillows. Several cabins have views across Lake Placid and of the mountains in the distance. There are one- and two-bedroom cabins, the latter with small porch/decks. The property includes an eighteen-hole golf course, four tennis courts, a sand beach, and a dock for swimming. Guests are served a full breakfast in the central dining room. *Represented by:* North Country Bed & Breakfast, (518) 523-3739. $45–$85.

Lake Placid. A *ca.* 1895 barn, this guest house has been renovated and, of course, painted red. Although in a residential area half a mile from town, the barn has a large field in front of it, and beyond the field are mountains. The house features gold and rust wall-to-wall carpeting, exposed beams, stucco ceilings, a woodburning stove, and many country antiques, including old farm tools that hang on the walls. Four guest rooms, each with an antique bed, share two baths. The house is very close to all kinds of cross-country skiing opportunities. *Represented by:* North Country Bed & Breakfast, #PH-2, (518) 523-3739. $35.

Albany Area **NEW YORK**

Albany. A short walk from just about anything in the district of the capitol, this guest house is a sixth- and seventh-floor duplex penthouse. The apartment has two exposures: one faces Washington Park and the other faces the capitol. There are a skylit entry hall, oaken floors, a living room with a fireplace, a greenhouse and porch area, and a friendly German shepherd. The host is an independent insurance agent who specialized in annuities and estate planning. The guest room has a king-size bed and a panoramic view of the park, which has tennis courts. *Represented by:* Bed & Breakfast USA, Ltd., (914) 271-6228. $50.

Brunswick (Troy). On 72 acres including a fenced-in play area, an old cemetery and a pond, this bed and breakfast is an 1830 farmhouse with planked floors, beamed ceilings, an enclosed porch, a Franklin stove, air conditioning, television, and stereo. The host, a retired professor, enjoys reading, bird-watching, history, and word games. Guests are invited to ski cross-country on the property, or to take the host's canoe on the pond. *Represented by:* Bed & Breakfast USA, Ltd., (914) 271-6228. $20–$30.

Hoosick Falls—Boyntonville. This is a contemporary, Colonial-style home fifteen minutes from Bennington, Vermont, on 100 acres complete with an in-ground pool and a stream-fed pond that contains bass. The grounds also include a playground set and lots of children's toys; the hosts' daughter, age five, enjoys sharing her room with other little girls. The hosts also have two young boys, eight and ten, as well as a cat, a German shepherd, a canary, and a rabbit. The guest rooms have sofas that open up to king-size beds, and the hosts will consider giving up their deluxe master bedroom if guests are celebrating a special occasion. *Represented by:* Bed & Breakfast USA, Ltd., #34, (914) 271-6228. $30–$50.

Glenmont. Seven minutes from the Albany Symphony and the Capitol Repertory Theater, this guest house is hosted by a public relations senior vice-president and a former interior-design entrepreneur recently returned to school. The house is in a new development that has a pool and tennis courts, which guests are invited to use. The guest suite has a large bedroom, a sitting room with a sofa bed, and a private bath. The suite has television, a radio, and a desk. The hosts—particularly knowledgeable about cultural events, gardening, and travel—usually greet guests with a snack or

Albany Area **NEW YORK**

wine, and they always serve a full breakfast. *Represented by:* Bed & Breakfast USA, Ltd., (914) 271-6228. $30–$40.

Menands. A white split-level contemporary brick house, this bed and breakfast is hosted by a commodities trader, who loves to cook, and the director of volunteer services for the Department of Correction. There's a baby grand piano in the living room and a pool in the backyard, which is overlooked by the private enclosed porch of the guest suite. The suite has a bedroom, a baby's room adjoining, and a private bath. For a small fee, guests are invited to play golf at the host's club. The hosts serve a full breakfast and will pick guests up at the airport or the bus or train station. *Represented by:* Bed & Breakfast USA, Ltd., (914) 271-6228. $30–$50.

Burdett **NEW YORK**

The Red House Country Inn and Store

Picnic Area Road, Burdett, NY 14818. (607) 546-8566. *Hostesses:* Sandra Schmanke and Joan Martin.

Although Sandra and Joan own only seven acres, another 13,000 acres of undeveloped forest surround their 1844 red and white-trimmed farmhouse. It is the only structure in the Hector Land Use Area, which Congress recently declared a national forest and will probably dub "Finger Lakes National Forest." The area, most of it at an elevation of 2,000 feet, has 28 miles of hiking trails and thirty ponds (eight of them stocked), and is thick with black walnut, red and white pine, white weeping birch, oak, hemlock, and cedar.

The house, furnished with a combination of period and reproduction antiques, has sixty-one windows, all of which have views. The main den includes a large open-hearth brick fireplace fitted out with a woodburning stove; maple floors partially covered with a dark ruby carpet; a 4-foot-tall seventeenth-century ceramic vase from China; two easy chairs upholstered in leather; a collection of Flo Blue china on the mantel; and a large collection of pewter.

The 25- by 21-foot Blue Room has an 1855 pencil-post bed fashioned out of cherry and covered with a handmade Amish quilt; wall-to-wall teal blue carpeting; a Federal-style striped wallpaper that picks up the color of the carpet; an antique love seat covered in dusty rose velvet; a deep maroon hand-hooked rug; an antique cherry dresser; six windows; and an alcove with an antique table covered with plants. Another guest room has an open-hearth brick fireplace and a bed and dresser made of oak and inlaid with pewter.

Sandra and Joan raise Samoyeds, and even have a racing sled they might be talked into taking you for a ride on. They also have horses as well as room for those their guests might bring.

The breakfast is a full one—eggs come from nearby farmers, the sausages are homemade, as are the jams, jellies, and granola.

Accommodations: 4 rooms with shared bath (each guest room has a "marine toilet" concealed behind a three-section walnut screen). *Smoking:* Permitted. *Children:* Over 7 permitted. *Pets:* Check in advance. *Breakfast:* Included. *Driving Instructions:* From the intersection of Franklin and Fourth streets in Watkins Glen, take Route 414 for 8.7 miles to Schuyler County Road #2; turn right and proceed for 3.4 miles—the inn is on your right.

Catskills & Hudson River Valley **NEW YORK**

Earlton. This 1830 Colonial home on 20 acres is in the process of being restored. The property includes a small pond, ideal for skating when the weather's cold, at which time, since the hosts raise lambs, guests may also get to see lambs being born. Guest accommodations feature a sitting room with a fireplace, a bedroom with an iron bed, and a private bath with shower. The Catskill Game Farm is 12 miles away, and numerous Catskill resorts are close by. The hosts welcome children, and will baby-sit. *Represented by:* Bed & Breakfast USA, Ltd., #43, (914) 271-6228. $20–$30.

Germantown. Hosted by a history buff who plays bridge, gardens, does needlepoint, and runs her church's thrift shop, this bed and breakfast is a large Victorian home a little way down the road from the home of Frederick Church, the Hudson River School painter. Claremont State Park, which features formal gardens and concerts of medieval music, is close by, as is the Livingston estate. In October there's a German Fest in Germantown. *Represented by:* Bed & Breakfast USA, Ltd., (914) 271-6228. $20–$30.

Highland Falls. Listed on the National Register of Historic Places, this bed and breakfast is a *ca.* -1880 Victorian house on the banks of the Hudson River, overlooking Buttermilk Falls. The host, an engineer who enjoys mountain climbing and running, did a splendid job of restoring the interior of the house himself and is about to start on its exterior. Two double rooms, one of which has a water bed, are available for guests. West Point is within walking distance, and Bear Mountain and the Storm King Arts Center are close by. *Represented by:* Bed & Breakfast USA, Ltd., #9, (914) 271-6228. $20–$40.

Saugerties. A three-story brick Federal-style home filled with antiques, this bed and breakfast is next to an open green affording an unobstructed view of the Catskill Mountains. There's a swimming pool in the backyard. Antique stores line both sides of Main Street in Saugerties, and the host here sells antiques, by appointment only, in one of the downstairs parlors. The house is close to the Catskill Game Farm, Hunter Mountain, Hyde Park, and New Paltz. *Represented by:* Bed & Breakfast USA, Ltd., (914) 271-6228. $20–$30.

Spring Valley. Hosted by a novelist who claims his library of more than three thousand volumes guarantees you'll have something

Catskills & Hudson River Valley **NEW YORK**

to do on a rainy day. This bed and breakfast is a large suburban home on 2 acres. Its grounds include an in-ground swimming pool, a jogging track, and a gazebo. Inside, there's a stone fireplace, an excellent stereo, three television sets and a videotape recorder. The host enjoys reading, music, and gardening, and considers himself an expert bargain-hunter. He can point guests who thrive on thrift to the choicest of markets. *Represented by:* Bed & Breakfast USA, Ltd., (914) 271-6228. $20–$30.

Cold Spring **NEW YORK**

The Antique Mews

73 Main Street, Cold Spring, NY 10516. (914) 265-3727. *Host:* Jack Kelly.

The Antique Mews is a four-story brick Federal structure that has been, over the years, a warehouse, an insurance company's offices, and a girls' finishing school. Today it's a combination antique shop and guest house.

Host Jack Kelly told me there's no knowing what kind of furnishings the front room and living room are likely to have at any given time, because antiques move in and out of his house like chess pieces. During my last visit, the living room contained an 1860s Third Empire gilded alcove bed, an early-American desk, and a Wedgwood music cabinet.

One of the guest rooms is done in Art Deco and features an overstuffed sofa upholstered in a wine-colored velvet, chevron-design fabric curtains, and an armoire and coffee table that Jack designed himself. The other guest room, which has a working fireplace, sports walls covered in a Paisley fabric and is furnished in wicker.

Jack serves his guests a full breakfast, which consists of some sort of hot bread (such as popovers or biscuits), juice, melon, eggs or French toast, and bacon or sausage.

Accommodations: 2 rooms with private bath. *Smoking:* Permitted: *Children:* Permitted. *Pets:* Not permitted. *Breakfast:* Included. *Driving Instructions:* The Antique Mews is in the center of Cold Spring.

Cold Spring **NEW YORK**

One Market Street

1 Market Street, Cold Spring, NY 10516. (914) 265-3912. *Hosts:* Philip and Esther Baumgarten.

Philip and Esther have a *circa*-1830 Federal-style house with a large yard shaded by mature trees. The house is one block from the Hudson River. Guests are welcome all year.

The guest suite has a small sitting room, a convertible couch, air conditioning, and a fully equipped kitchen, which is stocked with coffee and other morning essentials. The bedroom features a bed with a bamboo headboard, an old rocker and an old wicker chair, a 1930s radio that still works, and a grass rug on the floor. The walls are papered in a light and dark beige paper with a jungle-leaf pattern worked into it, and two large windows, with bamboo curtains, overlook a picturesque street. Each morning Philip and Esther bring their guests a newspaper, fresh buns, and fresh orange juice.

Accommodations: 1 suite with private bath. *Smoking:* Permitted. *Children:* Permitted. *Pets:* Not permitted. *Breakfast:* Included. *Driving Instructions:* The house is in the center of Cold Spring.

Corning — **NEW YORK**

Laurel Hill Guest House

2670 Powderhouse Road, Corning, NY 14830. (607) 936-3215.
Hosts: Dick and Marge Woodbury.

In a wooded area, on 2½ acres sprinkled with oaks and hemlocks and pines, Laurel Hill Guest House is a 1968 Cape Cod structure. It features a screened-in porch, filled with and surrounded by greenery, where guests take their breakfast when the weather permits. Weather permitting or not, finches and nuthatches and cardinals also breakfast on the porch, albeit on the other side of the screen. Dick and Marge's bird feeders make quite a hit, even though Marge feeds the birds cracked seeds instead of the Laurel House butter—a mixture of sweet butter, grated orange rinds, powdered sugar, and Cointreau—that she offers to guests.

The house is furnished with a mixture of antique and contemporary pieces. The living room has a parlor organ, a grand piano, a stereo, and an extensive and eclectic record collection (jazz, ragtime, classical, opera). There's a hooked rug on the floor, pine molding near the ceiling, handwoven cushions on the sofa, and a brick fireplace that has a hearth large enough to rest your feet on.

One bedroom has a Victorian walnut table, an antique oaken table with ladder-back chairs; a Salem rocker and a Windsor chair; a contemporary maple bed and dresser; and walls and eaves covered with a subtle floral-print paper. Both guest rooms come with fresh flowers and fruit.

Inspired by staying in many bed-and-breakfast places, Dick and Marge decided to try one of their own after attending two weddings and finding both of their daughters living elsewhere. Whale and his mother, a pair of regulation gray and white cats, are still single and live in the house.

Accommodations: 2 rooms with shared bath. *Smoking:* Permitted. *Children:* Permitted. *Pets:* Permitted if well-behaved. *Breakfast:* Included. *Driving Instructions:* From Route 17, exit at Walnut street in Corning and drive 1.7 miles south on Powderhouse Road.

Corning   **NEW YORK**

Rosewood Inn

134 East First Street, Corning, NY 14830. (607) 962-3253. *Hosts:* Dick and Winnie Peer.

The trees surrounding it date back only to 1880 or so, but the Rosewood Inn itself was built in 1860. Architecturally it is something of a hybrid, with elements of both Victorian and English Tudor design.

The house is a couple of short blocks from Corning's restored Market Street; a quick stroll across Centerway Bridge brings you to the Corning Glass Museum, which isn't made of glass but certainly houses a fascinating collection of it. Outdoor people will marvel at the beauty of New York's Finger Lakes region; indoor people will appreciate the area's many wineries, which feature free tastings and tours.

Winnie and Dick serve a complimentary breakfast, which includes homemade muffins and their special rosewood butter, in their paneled dining room.

Accommodations: 5 rooms, 3 with private bath. *Smoking:* Permitted. *Children:* Permitted. *Pets:* Permitted if well behaved. *Breakfast:* Included. *Driving Instructions:* One block south of Route 17, on East First Street.

Garrison's Landing **NEW YORK**

The Golden Eagle Inn

Garrison's Landing, NY 10524. (914) 424-3067. *Hosts:* George and Stephanie Templeton.

Something of an architectural hybrid, a rectilinear Colonial of sorts with a slight Georgian feeling, the Golden Eagle is an 1848 brick building with eight square columns, four on a floor, supporting a roofed porch and second-floor veranda. The lawn extends from the front porch to the Hudson River, which flows by with a kind of lazy majesty. You can participate in the river's flow by watching it from your room or the veranda; or, if you wish, George and Stephanie will lend you a canoe and instruct you in its use. The inn is closed from January through March.

Parts of the movie *Hello Dolly* were filmed on location at the Golden Eagle, which is decorated with a combination of genuine antiques and period reproductions. George and Stephanie used to be designers, and George's paintings, mostly of yachts, hang in the inn.

"We try to treat each of our guests as a houseguest and not just another body," says George. He and Stephanie especially enjoy sharing cocktails or wine with their guests before dinner. The Templetons serve a full complimentary breakfast, which guests can take in their room or on the veranda. Served with china and silver, it usually consists of freshly ground and brewed coffee, fresh fruit, warm croissants, and a selection of jams.

Accommodations: 6 rooms, 4 with private bath. *Smoking:* Permitted (cigars outdoors only). *Children:* Not permitted. *Pets:* Not permitted. *Breakfast:* Included. *Driving Instructions:* Take Route 403 to Route 12; follow Route 12 to its end and cross a small bridge; turn left and proceed 100 feet.

Geneva **NEW YORK**

The Cobblestones

R.D. 2, Geneva, NY 14456. (315) 789-1896. *Hosts:* Mr. and Mrs. Lawrence Gracey.

Constructed of sandstone cobbles, lake-washed and sorted according to size and color, The Cobblestones is an 1848 Greek Revival building. Four huge columns with Ionic capitols support the overhanging triangular pediment. Two smaller structures attached to the main house on either side also have columns holding up overhanging structures—in both cases, gabled roofs. The grounds comprise an acre of well-trimmed lawns with hedges and bushes.

Guest rooms are furnished primarily with antiques and period reproductions. The upstairs bedrooms still have their original old latches, and Oriental rugs appear all over the house.

Geneva is in one of New York State's lovelier areas, a lake region very active in agriculture. The New York State Agricultural Experiment Station, a branch of Cornell University, is close by, as are the Finger Lakes for fishing, boating, and swimming.

Accommodations: 3 rooms with shared bath. *Smoking:* Permitted. *Children:* Permitted. *Pets:* Permitted if well behaved. *Driving Instructions:* Take the New York State Thruway to exit 42 or exit 44 and continue into Geneva; then take Routes 5, 7, and 20 west for 3.5 miles.

The Hamptons **NEW YORK**

Bellport. A gray turn-of-the-century farmhouse, this bed and breakfast is on a quiet rural lane that somehow manages to be within walking distance of everything. Its two guest rooms are both large—one has a king-size bed; one twin beds. Public tennis courts and a public golf course are close by, as is a ferry (nominal fee) to the beaches. *Represented by:* Hampton Bed & Breakfast, (516) 288-3390, $48–$54.

East Moriches. A teacher is hostess of this ranch-style bed and breakfast, elegantly furnished and appointed. Two guest rooms are available—one with a double bed, one with twin beds. Breakfast, served on the deck when weather permits, includes homemade muffins and breads. *Represented by:* Hampton Bed & Breakfast, (516) 288-3390. $48–$50.

East Moriches. Surrounded by fields, this Cape Cod structure is furnished with contemporary pieces and dressed up with enormous ferns. The guest room has a private bath, air conditioning, and television; the grounds include an all-weather tennis court. *Represented by:* Hampton Bed & Breakfast, (516) 288-3390. $45.

East Moriches. An engineer and a teacher are hosts of this bed and breakfast, a *circa* 1884 Cape Code–style house on the shore of West Cove, which runs into Moriches Bay, and the hosts are willing to give guests sailing lessons. The house is furnished with a mixture of antique and contemporary pieces, and the hosts offer two guest rooms—a double and a single, both with shared bath. *Represented by:* Hampton Bed & Breakfast, (516) 288-3390. $45.

East Quogue. One guest room here is actually a suite with private bath and a small living room with television; the other has twin beds and a private balcony. The house is within walking distance of shops and restaurants, and the grounds feature an in-ground pool that guests are invited to use. *Represented by:* Hampton Bed & Breakfast, (516) 288-3390. $80.

Hampton Bays. Hosted by a retired couple willing to give guests wind-surfing lessons, this ranch-style bed and breakfast has a terrace and is right on the bay. The house is furnished with contemporary pieces and features many Mexican accents, such as wall hangings and tapestries. With sufficient notice the hosts will prepare meals other than breakfast. *Represented by:* Hampton Bed & Breakfast, (516) 288-3390. $48.

The Hamptons **NEW YORK**

Remsenburg. A contemporary Colonial-style structure, this bed and breakfast features central air conditioning, hardwood floors, modern furnishings, and a free-form, in-ground pool surrounded by gardens. Three guest rooms, one with private bath, are available. Remsenburg is a rural village about six minutes from Westhampton Beach. *Represented by:* Hampton Bed & Breakfast, (516) 288-3390. $60.

Sag Harbor. This small yellow Cape Cod structure is a short walk from the village of Sag Harbor and the fishing docks. One of its guest rooms adjoins a sun-deck, and has a private bath, a refrigerator, a hot plate, and television. Sag Harbor has plenty of dining, shopping, and sightseeing opportunities. *Represented by:* Hampton Bed & Breakfast, (516) 288-3390. $54.

Southampton. This white Cape Cod home is two blocks from the village of Southampton, and a mile from the Southampton beaches. The hostess, a part-time nurse, offers guests a large air-conditioned room and invites them to make full use of her patio and garden. The house, furnished with contemporary pieces, is within walking distance of shops and restaurants. *Represented by:* Hampton Bed & Breakfast, (516) 288-3390. $54.

Southampton. A short walk from the bay and six minutes from both village and beach, this bed and breakfast is on a wooded hill in the Shinnecock Hills section of Southampton. A self-contained cottage, separate from the main house, is available for guests. It has a bedroom, a living room with sleeper sofa, pine paneling, a kitchenette, and a fireplace. *Represented by:* Hampton Bed & Breakfast, (516) 288-3390. $90–$120.

Westhampton Beach. This white 1884 Colonial bed and breakfast is furnished primarily with period antiques. The hosts have three double rooms available for guests—one with an antique brass bed covered with a handmade quilt—and serve a Continental breakfast including homemade breads and rolls. The house is within walking distance of the many shops and restaurants in the village of Westhampton Beach, and the beach is less than a mile away. *Represented by:* Hampton Bed & Breakfast, (516) 288-3390. $30–$60.

High Falls   **NEW YORK**

House on the Hill

Box 86, High Falls, NY 12440. (914) 687-9627. *Hosts:* Shelly and Sharon Glassman.

Surrounded by locust, maple, evergreen, ash, and hickory trees, this eyebrowed Colonial structure was built in 1825. In 1856, a hand-forged iron fence appeared along the front lawn's perimeter; sometime after that, a Colonial-style porch was added to the house. The property also contains a two-story wood-pegged barn, a smokehouse constructed of pink bricks, and a two-sided outhouse. The grounds feature thickly wooded areas and a pond.

Of the three suites, one has a private bath, sitting room, and dressing room; the other two share a bath, and each has a sitting room. Every bed in the house is covered with a handmade quilt, and each guest room is furnished in Colonial style and comes with a bowl of fruit and freshly cut flowers.

The House on the Hill is minutes away from Lake Mohonk, New Paltz, Hurley (famous for their many restored stone houses), and historic Kingston, which maintains a symphony orchestra.

Shelly and Sharon serve a full complimentary breakfast. When it's cold out, guests take it in the keeping room, which has the house's original fireplace and irons. Some guests prefer to eat breakfast on the glassed-in porch that faces the pond; others prefer it outdoors under the evergreens.

Accommodations: 3 suites, 1 with private bath. *Smoking:* Permitted in the sitting room. *Children:* Permitted. *Pets:* Sometimes permitted; check first. *Breakfast:* Included. *Driving Instructions:* Take the New York State Thruway to exit 18 (New Paltz); take Route 299 West to the center of town; make a right onto Route 32 North; take Route 213 West into High Falls.

Keene   **NEW YORK**

The Bark Eater

Alstead Mill Road, Keene, NY 12946. (518) 576-2221. *Hosts:* Joe-Pete Wilson and Harley McDevitt.

In the old days the Adirondacks were controlled by the Iroquois and Algonquian tribes who dominated the area's prime hunting grounds. Smaller, less powerful Indian tribes competing for space in these mountains were called "adirondacks," an Indian word that means "bark eater," referring to people whose hunting privileges were such that they could exist only by eating bark.

The Bark Eater, a 150-year-old farmhouse, is on 200 acres of land in the High Peaks region of the Adirondacks. There are five 100-foot sugar maples outside the house, which overlooks mountains 3,600 feet high. The central living room features a fieldstone fireplace, maple floors, country antique furnishings, a piano, Oriental scatter rugs, and plenty of books. The fireplace in the dining room is made of cobblestones, as is its mantel. The dining room also has two large mahogany tables, matching chairs covered with a pale green fabric, Oriental throw rugs, and two breakfronts—one of mahogany, one of oak. Guest rooms are named after animals. "Bear" features maple floors, Oriental rugs, a carved and painted mahogany bed, a mahogany dresser and side table, and a view of hayfields and woods.

Joe-Pete, an Olympic cross-country skier and coauthor of a book about the sport, is on hand to give cross-country skiing instructions and maintains a complete ski shop where one can rent equipment.

At The Bark Eater a complimentary breakfast of hot cereal and homemade granola is always available; Irish soda bread, homemade morning-glory muffins, and eggs with bacon frequently appear. Packed lunches and family-style dinners are available for a slight fee, and if you're into eating bark, there's plenty of that around too.

Accommodations: 12 rooms with private bath. *Smoking:* Permitted. *Children:* Permitted. *Pets:* Permitted. *Breakfast:* Included. *Driving Instructions:* The Bark Eater is 1.5 miles west of Keene on Route 73.

Lake Placid NEW YORK

The Stagecoach Inn

Old Military Road, Lake Placid, NY 12946. (518) 523-9474.
Hosts: Sherry and Pete Moreau.

The Stagecoach Inn was once a tavern where "people held elections, gathered for sport and horse trading, drank hard cider and sometimes liquids of a more stimulating character." The 1830 farmhouse was also once a post office and a sanctuary for one of Brigham Young's fleeing wives. The building was once owned by the man who invented the Dewey Decimal System (Melvil Dewey), and later by a president of Syracuse University.

Today the building is owned by Sherry and Peter Moreau, who have restored it—and have captured something of its more stimulating character. The building is in almost original condition. The Common Room, where guests tend to recount the events of their lives, has two fireplaces, one with a flintlock rifle hanging above it, and a birch log balcony spanning the length of the room. Some guest rooms feature brass beds or fireplaces or furniture original to the house.

Accommodations: 7 rooms, 3 with private bath. *Smoking:* Permitted. *Children:* Permitted. *Pets:* Not permitted. *Breakfast:* Included. *Driving Instructions:* Take Route 86 or Route 73 to Old Military Road.

East 60s. In an East Sixty-second Street building with doorman, this bed and breakfast is hosted by a former opera singer who is fluent in French and Italian as well as English. The apartment's numerous period antiques include an eighteenth-century Italian armoire, a nineteenth-century German dining table, and an assortment of Oriental rugs. There's a grand piano in the living room, and the guest room has a queen-size bed and private bath. *Represented by:* The B & B Group (New Yorkers at Home), #85, (212) 838-7015. $30–$50.

Tudor City. Hosted by a British businessman and his wife who formerly ran a bed and breakfast in England, this Tudor City apartment is a block from the United Nations. Its guest room features a double bed and a private bath; it is convenient to midtown, especially the East Side. *Represented by:* The B & B Group (New Yorkers at Home), #75, (212) 838-7015. $35–$55.

East Twenty-fourth Street. In Waterside Plaza, a large, modern complex of buildings directly on the East River, this bed and breakfast is a complete one-bedroom apartment. The living room overlooks the river, and for a fee the complex offers a health club with a swimming pool. Buses stop right at the complex, and there's a car service in one of the buildings. *Represented by:* The B & B Group (New Yorkers at Home), #113, (212) 838-7015. $65–$75.

West Side. This two-bedroom, two-bath apartment is in Lincoln Towers, on West Sixty-sixth Street. Lincoln Center is a short walk away, and visitors to New York will probably like the myriad shops and restaurants on Columbus Avenue. The host, a literary agent, offers the entire apartment to guests. *Represented by:* The B & B Group (New Yorkers at Home), #69, (212) 838-7015. $100.

Roosevelt Island. A twin-bed room and a double-bed room, both with private bath, are available in this duplex apartment of a clothing-store manager. The apartment is on Roosevelt Island, a small and luxuriously developed island in the East River between the boroughs of Manhattan and Queens. Access to Manhattan, which is approximately 150 yards away, is either by car or (for those who enjoy convenience or a good view) via a monorail tramway that glides over the East River and in ninety seconds or so deposits you at Fifty-ninth Street and Second Avenue—one block from Bloomingdale's. *Represented by:* the B & B Group, (212) 838-7015. $35–$55.

New York City (*Urban Ventures* #109)

New York City (*Urban Ventures* #410)

New York City

The 80s on Lexington. Hosted by a dealer in eclectic antiques who also does some television acting, this guest room with a private bath is in a building a short walk from the Whitney Museum and Gimbels East. *Represented by:* The B & B Group, (212) 838-7015. $40–$55.

Featured in "Redbook." Your hostess, who has a degree in education, arranges the curriculum for a New York City high school, operates a catering service, and conducts cooking classes. Her home, recently featured in *Redbook*, is a two-story brownstone in the West 80s. The house contains such niceties as wainscoting and cherry-wood paneling. Her upstairs living room can be used as a sitting room and bedroom. Share bath. No smoking. *Represented by:* The B & B Group, (212) 838-7015. $35–$55.

Riverside Drive. Filled with antiques, craft pieces, and paintings, this nine-room apartment is hosted by a portrait artist and fashion-handbag designer. Two guest rooms are available, with windows overlooking the Hudson River and Riverside Park. If only one bedroom is being used, the bath is private. *Represented by:* The B & B Group (New Yorkers at Home), #95, (212) 838-7015. $35–$50.

Fifty-seventh and Lexington. A pair of enthusiastic New Yorkers and a shaggy dog are hosts of this bed and breakfast, which offers a king-size bedroom with a private bath. The building has a doorman and is in perhaps the city's prime shopping area: Bloomingdale's is two blocks away, and Burberry's, Bendel's, and Tiffany's are right up Fifty-seventh. *Represented by:* Urban Ventures, #25, (212) 662-1234. $44–$62.

East Fifty-sixth Street. A studio so large it has room for a separate sleeping area that's fitted out with a queen-size *futon,* this bed and breakfast is an entire apartment. Furnished with contemporary pieces, it has a small but full kitchen and a choice East Side location. *Represented by:* Urban Ventures, #21, (212) 662-1234.

West 57th Street. This accommodation features a thirty-story-high panoramic view of New York City. The views are even better from the roof, where there is a health club accessible to guests. *Represented by:* Urban Ventures #306, (212) 662-1234. $44–$52.

The Fort Greene Historic Section. This guest accommodation is in a nineteenth-century brownstone that has leather wall coverings here and there. Your hosts serve a full breakfast, and their guest

Featured in Redbook (*The B & B Group*)

New York City **NEW YORK**

room, furnished with antiques, includes a sitting room. *Represented by:* Urban Ventures #304, (212) 662-1234. $27.

East Sixty-sixth Street. A chic modern apartment featuring architectural built-ins, this bed and breakfast is next door to numerous movie theaters and boutiques. The guest room has a private bath; a sleeping loft makes it suitable for a third person. *Represented by:* Urban Ventures, #206, (212) 662-1234. $56–$75.

34th Street. Close to Macy's, Orbach's and Altman's, this bed and breakfast is an entire apartment on West Thirty-fourth Street. Simply but comfortably furnished, it has two beds, a kitchen, and as convenient a location as any serious shopper could ask for. *Represented by:* Urban Ventures, #36, (212) 662-1234. $65.

The West 90s. You can sun yourself on the balcony of this nineteenth-floor apartment if you like; but even if you came to New York for something other than the sun, this accommodation has a beautiful view of New York and Central Park. The guest room, a double, has a canopy bed. "Of course use the kitchen." *Represented by:* Urban Ventures #16, (212) 662-1234. $40–$52.

East Seventy-eighth Street. This accommodation, which has a bathroom and a kitchen behind a hardly noticeable partition, has a working fireplace. The beds here are *futons*—a kind of Japanese sleeping quilt with which many are replacing their current mattresses. Near Central Park. *Represented by:* Urban Ventures, Apt. #20, (212) 662-1234. $65.

East Seventy-second Street. The designer host of this strikingly decorated four-room apartment uses it as a pied-à-terre or makes it available to guests. The apartment features a full bedroom, living, dining room, and kitchen. East Seventy-second Street is as fashionable as it is convenient. *Represented by:* Urban Ventures, Apt. #2, (212) 662-1234. $90.

Fifty-fifth off Fifth. A guest house that's convenient if you like to shop, or eat well, or visit the Museum of Modern Art and other Fifth Avenue attractions. Your hostess has decorated her home with the many handicrafts she brought from her native Hungary. *Represented by:* Urban Ventures #31, (212) 662-1234. $38.

East Eighty-fourth. This one-bedroom apartment, half a block from the Central Park Reservoir, is in an 1892 mansion convenient to the Metropolitan Museum of Art, the Madison Avenue boutiques,

New York City (*Urban Ventures* #304)

New York City **NEW YORK**

and the Guggenheim Museum. *Represented by:* Urban Ventures Apt. #24, (212) 662-1234. $90–$115.

Near Lincoln Center. "The highlight [of my trip] was the owner, who offered me a soft drink when I arrived—and was very friendly. On both mornings she brought coffee and toast to my room and even remembered I like to drink lots of ice water."—*The Travelbug.* This accommodation on the nineteenth floor of a high-rise is ten minutes from Lincoln Center. *Represented by:* Urban Ventures #105, (212) 662-1234. $40–$52.

East Sixty-fifth. Your host, who has traveled the world taking photographs for *National Geographic,* offers guests a large bedroom with two exposures. This accommodation requires that you walk up five flights of steps; but the stairs, if it's any relief, are beautifully polished. *Represented by:* Urban Ventures #27, (212) 662-1234. $34–$45.

View of Park. This guest room has a commanding view of a church spire, Central Park, and myriad New York City skyscrapers. Your host, an artist, responded: "Use the kitchen? Of course. Front room too—I'm so rarely home." *Represented by:* Urban Ventures #117, (212) 662-1234. $50.

Next to the Dakota. On West Seventy-Third Street, this accommodation, whose hosts are both in the theater, features a superb collection of Eastern and Western decorative art pieces. Walk to Lincoln Center or Central Park. *Represented by:* Urban Ventures #115, (212) 662-1234. $50.

Near Lincoln Center. This accommodation is in an elegant, television-monitored building. All guests are announced. Your host is an advertising executive. *Represented by:* Urban Ventures #109, (212) 662-1234. $50–$56.

Rensselaer   **NEW YORK**

The Tibbitts House

    100 Columbia Turnpike, Rensselaer, NY 12144. (518) 472-1348.
    Hosts: Herb and Claire Rufleth.

This converted farmhouse dating from the 1850s, constructed of massive timbers fastened with square nails, is on the old Knox Trail (now Routes 9 and 20). The trail made it possible for General Knox and his troops, with a little help from a team of oxen, to drag a huge cannon, which the British would have preferred they had left at home, from Fort Ticonderoga to Boston.

The house is surrounded by trees, flower boxes with lilies and petunias, and manicured beds of iris and violets. Family owned and operated for the past fifty-five years, The Tibbitts House now features an 84-foot porch where Herb and Claire serve breakfast during the warmer months. The lounge, a converted keeping room, has exposed tree-trunk beams in the ceiling, a 12-foot oak and walnut church pew, a raised-hearth fireplace in the corner, and numerous hand-hooked scatter rugs.

Accommodations: 5 rooms with shared bath. *Smoking:* Permitted. *Children:* Not permitted. *Pets:* Not permitted. *Breakfast:* Not included. *Driving Instructions:* On Routes 9 and 20 in Clinton Heights.

Rochester Area **NEW YORK**

Fairport. Furnished with a mixture of period and reproduction antiques, this bed and breakfast is a *ca.*-1834 Colonial painted medium green. Its grounds have an old barn, tall shade trees, and the fruits of the host's hobby—gardening. Antique shops, restaurants, and the Old Barge Canal, which is still in use, are a short walk from here; downtown Rochester is a fifteen-minute drive away. *Represented by:* Bed & Breakfast Rochester, (716) 223-4733. $30–$38.

Fairport. On 7 acres of rolling hills, this 1825 farmhouse is furnished entirely with antiques. The property contains several large barns that are also filled with antiques—the hostess is an antique dealer. The host is the owner of several MGs. This farmhouse, totally restored and painted gold, was one of the original homes in the area. *Represented by:* Bed & Breakfast Rochester, (716) 223-4733. $22–$30.

Fairport. Constructed in 1975 and furnished with American country pieces of pine, this bed and breakfast is on 5 acres and surrounded on all sides by undeveloped land. One of the house's two fireplaces is in the hostess's studio, where she makes stone mosaics. Accommodations here include a little cottage, completely self-contained and set in a clearing in the woods. It has a cathedral-ceilinged living room and such amenities as a full kitchen and a washer/dryer. *Represented by:* Bed & Breakfast Rochester, (716) 223-4733. $24–$50.

Penfield. Twenty-five minutes from downtown Rochester, this contemporary ranch-style home is hosted by a vegetarian who loves gardening. It is surrounded by rolling countryside and has a living room that features a fireplace and a baby grand piano. Furnishings consist of comfortable contemporary pieces, and the specialty of the hostess is home-baked apple muffins. *Represented by:* Bed & Breakfast Rochester, (716) 223-4733. $20–$30.

Shelter Island **NEW YORK**

The Bowditch House

166 North Ferry Road, Shelter Island, NY 11965. (516) 749-0075 or (516) 887-1898. *Hosts:* Jim and Nora Furey.

Originally part of a farm, the Bowditch House was built in 1854 and added to over the years. It currently has eighteen rooms. The house was built by Nathaniel Bowditch, who wrote *The American Practical Navigator,* and to be sure, Shelter Island is a place for practical navigators: A ten-minute ferry ride brings you to the island, which is just about traffic-free and has 57 miles of waterfront. Many guests leave their cars at home and use bicycles when they're on the island.

The guest rooms have fabric-covered walls and wide-board pine floors and are decorated individually with many antiques. One guest room has a carved oaken bed and dresser, a marble-topped night table, and an oaken reclining rocker. Another has a hand-painted bedroom set.

The living room, where Nora serves wine and tidbits in the afternoon, has a Victorian carved mahogany couch, maple floors, floor-to-ceiling windows that retain their original blown glass, and a child's desk and chair over in the corner. The room also has a nonworking fireplace and always has fresh flowers in it—as does every room in the house.

The Bowditch House is open weekends only from Memorial Day till Mid-June. From then on, it is open every day through Labor Day.

Accommodations: 9 rooms sharing 3 baths. *Smoking:* Permitted. *Children:* Under five not permitted. *Pets:* Not permitted. *Breakfast:* Included. *Driving Instructions:* The Shelter Island Ferry lets you off on North Ferry Road near the Bowditch House.

Stone Ridge   **NEW YORK**

Baker's Bed and Breakfast

R.D. 2, Box 80, Stone Ridge, NY 12484. (914) 687-9795. *Hosts:* Fran Sutherland Baker and Doug Baker.

A 1780s stone farmhouse, Baker's Bed and Breakfast is on 16 acres of fields and woods. The property has a pond large enough for a hockey game and is wooded mostly with maples, cedars, and hemlocks. In the latter, "On Lincoln's Birthday," claims Fran, the resident owls lay their eggs. Orioles flit about here too, and the environs are patrolled by domestic geese and ducks.

The central living room has wide-board pine floors with scattered Oriental rugs; a down-filled Chippendale sofa upholstered in needlepoint; two antique oaken wing chairs with leather seats; a Franklin stove; and a southeast exposure facing fields, woods, and the Shawangunk Mountains. Another fine mountain view is available to those who choose to stand up in the in-ground hot tub and—their collarbones hot, their chins dry—gaze through a pane of greenhouse glass framing Mohonk Mountain and the famous Mohonk Mountain House. The greenhouse, 19 feet long, is furnished with wicker chairs and settee, sheepskin rugs, pillows positioned against the wall, and a great deal of light.

The guest rooms have wide-board pine floors covered with more Oriental scatter rugs, antique four-poster beds with down comforters and antique spreads, lamps fashioned from antique jugs, white linen curtains, and beautiful views. The house also has a solarium that features Fran's paintings, landscapes she classifies as mildly abstract-expressionistic.

Accommodations: 5 rooms with shared bath. *Smoking:* Not permitted. *Children:* Permitted during the week. *Pets:* Not permitted. *Breakfast:* Included. *Driving Instructions:* Take the New York State Thruway north to exit 18, turn left on Route 299 West, then turn right on Route 32 North; proceed to Route 213 West, turn left and go 3 miles to Route 209; drive for a mile, then make a left on Old King's Highway—Baker's Bed and Breakfast is the first house on your right.

Westchester County **NEW YORK**

Crestwood. A block from the Crestwood railroad station (Grand Central Station is 25 minutes away), this two-story brick home is hosted by a retired businessman who is now a master beekeeper. Breakfast always includes honey. The hostess paints, and various of her works hang throughout the house. Five bedrooms are available for guests—four with shared bath and one with private bath. *Represented by:* Bed & Breakfast USA, Ltd., (914) 271-6228. $32–$44.

Croton-on-Hudson. Hosted by a psychologist and the head of a computer consulting firm, this bed and breakfast is a six-bedroom Victorian. The house features a 35-foot sun-room with 60 feet of windowed walls overlooking an apple orchard and the Hudson River. The grounds include a swimming pool, and the house comes with two fireplaces, cable television, a baby grand piano, and two French bulldogs who probably have some English. The hosts' four-year-old daughter enjoys showing her toys and swing set to playmates. The hostess grows raspberries in her garden and serves them in pancake form. *Represented by:* Bed & Breakfast USA, Ltd., (914) 271-6228. $30–$50.

Croton-on-Hudson. A ca.-1880 farmhouse on 8 acres, this bed and breakfast is adjacent to a 300-acre nature preserve with 12 miles of hiking trails. For those who prefer swimming, the property includes a heated pool. Furnished with many antiques, the house boasts numerous stained-glass windows, one of them made by one of the hosts, a stained-glass artist. Two rooms are available for guests—a double with private bath and a single with a shared bath. The double room has a picture window overlooking the woods. The hosts serve a full breakfast. *Represented by:* Bed & Breakfast USA, Ltd., (914) 271-6228. $30–$50.

Eastchester. Guests arriving here find brie, crackers, a full ice bucket, and little bottles of mixers waiting in their rooms. In the morning the hosts leave a thermos of coffee before the guest bedroom door, for those who enjoy having a cup of coffee in bed. This Victorian home is thirty minutes from New York City and convenient to Sarah Lawrence, Iona, and New Rochelle colleges. The furnishings, including gilded headboards, have been in the family for generations. Breakfast is served either before the fireplace in the kitchen or on the screened-in porch. *Represented by:* Bed & Breakfast USA, Ltd., (914) 271-6228. $30–$40.

Westchester County **NEW YORK**

New Rochelle. Fifteen minutes from the corporate section of White Plains, this Tudor-style structure is in the Wykagyl section of New Rochelle, which is close to numerous golf courses, hiking trails, and the Long Island Sound. The hostess, an avid bridge player, raises prize-winning Shih Tzus, three of whom are in residence. The house has a screened-in porch, and the grounds include a shaded patio. *Represented by:* Bed & Breakfast USA, Ltd., (914) 271-6228. $30–$40.

Ossining. Constructed in 1787 and added to during the 1920s, this rounded-front brick Georgian is hosted by a professor of English literature and furnished primarily with antiques. The house is in a historic area near the Sleepy Hollow Restorations (remember Ichabod Crane?), and the host is president of the local historical society. You can walk here from the Judson line of Metro North (New York City is forty-five minutes away), and, weather permitting, eat your full breakfast under a brick-archway on a patio that overlooks a terraced garden. *Represented by:* Bed & Breakfast USA, Ltd., (914) 271-6228. $30–$40.

Tarrytown. Close to Marymount College and convenient to White Plains, this brick Georgian home is hosted by a woman who writes a daily column for a major Westchester newspaper. The guest room has a private bath, and the grounds feature a dog run, which your pet might well appreciate. The hostess is interested in gardening, art, music, and tennis. *Represented by:* Bed & Breakfast USA, Ltd., (914) 271-6228. $30–$40.

Kill Devil Hill NORTH CAROLINA

Ye Olde Cherokee Inn
 P.O. Box 315, Kill Devil Hill, NC 27948. (919) 441-6127. *Hosts:* Phyllis and Bob Combs.

Painted pink and trimmed white, Ye Olde Cherokee Inn was originally built as a hunting and fishing lodge. The house, which features a wraparound porch, is a hundred yards from the ocean, which several of the guest rooms overlook.

Six guest rooms are totally paneled, ceilings as well as walls, in wideboard cypress. The seventh guest room, though not entirely paneled in cypress, has cypress wainscoting and a large exposed beam in the ceiling. Guest rooms, which are spotlessly clean, feature private baths, wall-to-wall carpeting, color cable television, and simple but tasteful country furnishings. The beds are covered with print bedspreads, and curtains soften the light that pours into the rooms.

Ye Olde Cherokee Inn is surrounded by natural and historical attractions—you can see the Wright Brothers Memorial from the house, and Roanoke, the site of the famous Lost Colony, is a ten-minute drive away. The Cape Hatteras National Seashore, where one can sight a peregrine falcon and thousands of ducks and geese, is also ten minutes away.

Bob describes Phyllis and himself as "a couple of Yankees who couldn't take the cold anymore." They could also be described as two of the warmest people you could meet.

Accommodations: 7 rooms with private bath. *Smoking:* Permitted. *Children:* Permitted but not encouraged. *Pets:* Not permitted. *Breakfast:* Included. *Driving Instructions:* Take Route 158 into Kill Devil Hill; if proceeding from the north, take a left onto the road opposite the one leading to the Wright Brothers Memorial; if coming from the south, make a right. Proceed to the beach road and turn right. Go about a block and look for the pink house.

Ocracoke **NORTH CAROLINA**

The Beach House

P.O. Box 443, Ocracoke, NC 27960. (919) 928-6471. *Hosts:* Tom and Carole Beach.

Something of an architectural hybrid, The Beach House is a New England-style cottage with slight suggestions of Victorian and Georgian design. Painted gray and trimmed white, it sits on 1¼ acres bordering directly on Silver Lake. The lake is filled, especially in autumn, with all manner of waterfowl: egrets and herons, ducks and geese. Live oaks and cedars sprinkle the grounds.

One guest room's pine floor is partially covered by two small area rugs (one braided, one wool), a pine bed, an antique pine table stained dark mahogany, and a view of Silver Lake and the Ocracoke Lighthouse. Another bedroom has an iron bed painted black, a handmade brown-on-white floral-design quilt, pine floors, a gold sofa bed that picks up the colors of a braided rug, a coffee table made of antique wood salvaged from an old barn, and a view of the Ocracoke Coast Guard Station. On the wall is a sketch of the view from this room, left by a guest who stayed in it.

During the summer months Tom and Carol serve a full country breakfast in their dining room, which is furnished with many antiques as well as a collection of blue Copenhagen plates and a collection of Ward Brothers hand-carved decoys.

Accommodations: 3 rooms with shared bath. *Smoking:* Permitted. *Children:* Permitted. *Pets:* Not permitted. *Breakfast:* Included. *Driving Instructions:* The Beach House is on Route 12 at Silver Lake.

Tryon   **NORTH CAROLINA**

Mill Farm Inn

P.O. Box 1251, Tryon, NC 28782. (704) 859-6992 or 859-6242. *Hosts:* Chip and Penny Kessler.

A 1939 stone structure, Mill Farm Inn is on 3 ½ wooded acres. The property, wooded primarily with ash, birch, and enormous white pines, has as its rear boundary the Pacolet River. There are a couple of stone benches down by the river and in the yard.

The inn's central living room features a stone fireplace, sand-plaster walls, exposed chestnut beams on the ceiling, gold shag wall-to-wall carpeting, and a casement window overlooking the lawn. The room is furnished with new, traditional-style pieces: a couch upholstered in yelow and gold print on a black background; a pair of wing-back chairs covered in a fabric of yellow and green; and a 25-inch color television with a videotape recorder hooked up to it (guests are invited to use the video file).

Guest rooms are also carpeted wall-to-wall and furnished with new, traditional-style pieces, such as high-poster beds and porcelain lamps. The rooms are decorated with prints, and each has a rocking chair.

At an oaken table, which seats twelve, guests partake of a buffet breakfast that includes dry cereal, preserves, and pumpkin or banana bread, as well as coffee or tea.

Accommodations: 8 rooms with private bath. *Smoking:* Reluctantly permitted. *Children:* Permitted. *Pets:* Not permitted. *Breakfast:* Included. *Driving Instructions:* Tryon is 2.5 miles off Route 126 right at the North Carolina–South Carolina state line.

Waynesville **NORTH CAROLINA**

The Swag

Route 276, Box 280-A, Waynesville, NC 28786. (704) 926-0430 or 926-9978. *Hosts:* Dan and Deener Matthews. Closed from November through late May.

The Matthewses saw the land on a topographic map and acquired it; then they built a 2.5-mile road so they could get to it. They took apart six antique structures (including an old log and stone church), and from four states flatbed trucks carried construction materials to the building site, 250 acres separated from Great Smoky Mountains National Park by a split-rail fence. The views from here are spectacular—you can see Mounts Mitchell and Pisgah, and the Blue Ridge Parkway. The grounds offer a racketball court, a trout pond, a small dock and a boat, a treehouse, and easy access to the national park.

The house was built about 1970 of heavy two-hundred-year-old hand-hewn logs (poplar, ash, and chestnut). Guests are accommodated in two structures, The Swag and the Chestnut Lodge. The latter features wormy chestnut paneling and a living room 20 feet high. Furnishings in both structures include many antiques—the beams in the cathedral-ceilinged Swag living room, the handmade patchwork quilts, the cherry and walnut cannonball beds, the player piano. There are handmade rockers, sofas, and country wing chairs, real pewter plates, handwoven mats, linen napkins. Even the bath mats are handwoven. Each room is stocked with fresh flowers and a fruit basket.

Currently the rector of Saint Luke's Episcopal Church in Atlanta, Dan used to be the pastor of an Episcopal church in Knoxville. It was during his tenure there that he and Deener built The Swag. They used it originally as a second home as well as a place for retreats, and opened it to the public in 1982.

Accommodations: 12 rooms, 6 with private bath. *Smoking:* Permitted. *Children:* Permitted. *Pets:* Not permitted. *Breakfast:* Included, as well as dinner. *Driving Instructions:* From Asheville, take Route I-40 West to exit 20 (Route 276 South); go 2.8 miles and look for the Swag sign.

Wilmington **NORTH CAROLINA**

Anderson Guest House

520 Orange Street, Wilmington, NC 28401. (919) 343-8128. *Host:* Connie Anderson.

Some people in this world are blessed with wonderful Rabelaisian, infectious laughter. Connie is one, and perhaps by way of making sure you join in, she serves you the cocktail of your choice the afternoon you arrive. She also gives guests a tour of her house, an 1853 stuccoed-brick Italianate structure that has the original, functioning gas-electric chandeliers and sconces; parquet floors; a recessed tile fireplace with a cherry mantel and a mirrored top; a bay window with cherry window seats and stained glass in the top panes; a seventy-five-year-old Oriental rug woven in blues and whites and golds; a modern Italian table made of mahogany and surrounded by mahogany Chippendale chairs; a dining room ceiling that's 14 feet high and vaulted, large amounts of cherry woodwork, and . . .

There's a hundred-year-old magnolia in front of the main house, which isn't where the guest rooms are located. They are both in a house that's at the same time old and new—new on the outside, old within—and have private entrances as well as working fireplaces.

One guest room has pine floors and a wide-board-pine ceiling painted avocado green; an 1860 brass and iron canopy bed; a white ceiling fan; a white wicker chair upholstered in a pink, blue, and green floral pattern against a white background; mint green walls; a hand-carved Indian table painted white; and a Pakistani Bokhara rug woven primarily in yellows and pinks. Both bathrooms have footed tubs with showers added, and private entrances.

Breakfast—served on the piazza or in the gaslit dining room, depending on weather—might consist of fruit crepes in cream sauce, eggs Mornay, or . . . well, leave it to Connie.

Accommodations: 2 rooms with private bath. *Smoking:* Permitted. *Children:* Permitted. *Pets:* Not permitted. *Breakfast:* Included. *Driving Instructions:* Anderson Guest House is in downtown Wilmington, at the corner of Sixth and Orange streets.

Akron **OHIO**

Portage House

601 Copley Road, Akron, OH 44320. (216) 535-9236. *Hosts:* Harry and Jeanne Pinnick.

A large 1917 Tudor structure, the Portage House is on an acre that used to be part of the Perkins farm. The Perkinses were the founding family of Akron, and their original house as well as the stone wall surrounding it still stand. A plaque on the stone wall notes that this piece of land was, in 1785, the western boundary of the United States. The Summit County Historical Society maintains the Perkins mansion, as well as the John Brown House, and conducts daily tours.

Harry and Jeanne Pinnick offer guests a variety of accommodations, including a kitchenette apartment with a private bath and a large bedroom with a fireplace and a private bath. Harry and Jeanne serve a complimentary Continental breakfast; for the truly hungry they will cook a full morning meal for a slight charge.

The Portage House is next door to museums and near the Blossom Music Center (the summer home of the Cleveland Orchestra) and the Football Hall of Fame.

Accommodations: 5 rooms with private bath. *Smoking:* Permitted. *Children:* Permitted. *Pets:* Permitted. *Breakfast:* Included. *Driving Instructions:* Take Route I-77 to Route 162 (Copley Road), and proceed 2 miles east on Copley Road.

Bellville **OHIO**

The Frederick Fitting House

72 Fitting Avenue, Bellville, OH 44813. (419) 886-4283. *Hosts:* Rick and Jo Sowash.

This 1863 Victorian structure, with elaborate filigree and arched shutters on every window, was built by Frederick Fitting, a prominent Bellville citizen. Another prominent citizen, Johnny Appleseed, left his mark in the nearby forests.

Rick is the executive director of Mansfield's historic Renaissance Theatre, a published novelist, and an award-winning classical composer. Jo has degrees in English and registered nursing.

The living room is warmed by a large fireplace and has a library containing more than three thousand volumes. The house features 11-foot ceilings; a free-standing staircase of walnut, butternut, and oak; an elaborately hand-stenciled dining room; and a bathroom with Victorian fixtures—claw-foot tub, a pedestal sink, and an Italian tile floor with matching wallpaper. The Sowashes serve a complimentary breakfast. As Rick puts it, "Our home is our hobby,"

Accommodations: 3 rooms with shared bath. *Smoking:* Not permitted. *Children:* Permitted. *Pets:* Permitted but not in the house (there is a large fenced-in yard). *Breakfast:* Included. *Driving Instructions:* Midway between Cleveland and Columbus, Bellville is 3 miles east of Route I-71 on Route 97. Enter the village on Route 97 and turn left at Fitting Avenue.

Cleveland Area **OHIO**

(East). Twenty minutes from downtown and the East Side's cultural attractions, this large 1913 house is hosted by a couple who speak seven languages between them. A household of many tongues, this bed and breakfast has in permanent residence a Great Dane, who has a little English. The hosts offer two guest rooms, both with private bath. *Represented by:* Private Lodgings, Inc., (216) 321-3213. $25–$65.

(East). On a large, country-like wooded lot, this bed and breakfast is convenient to shopping, restaurants, and Cleveland's major traffic arteries. The hostess, a pianist with a great interest in the performing arts, frequently shows her guests around town. Two guest rooms are available, one with a shared bath and one with a private bath; and there's a living room where everyone tends to congregate. The hostess is willing to accept children over ten and pets if she's notified in advance. She serves a full breakfast on weekends, a Continental one during the week. *Represented by:* Private Lodgings, Inc., (216) 321-3213. $25–$65.

(East). This Tudor-style home in a residential neighborhood offers a two-room suite that used to be the servants' quarters. Decorated in Early American style, the suite was obviously designed for privacy and comes with a private bath and a private entrance. The house is convenient to Cleveland's business district as well as its major cultural and recreational attractions. *Represented by:* Private Lodgings, Inc., (216) 321-3213. $25–$65.

(East). A 1920s Tudor-style home listed in the National Register of Historic Places, this bed and breakfast is surrounded by a large landscaped lot. A professional couple, the hosts have spent the better part of their leisure traveling. They offer guests bedrooms as well as suites; most rooms have private baths. A full breakfast is served. *Represented by:* Private Lodgings, Inc., (216) 321-3213. $25–$65.

(West). Furnished with many antiques, including the guest room's doll collection, this bed and breakfast apartment is hosted by a woman interested in interior decorating. Guests staying here are invited to use the facilities including indoor and outdoor pools, a game room, an exercise room, a whirlpool, a sauna, tennis courts, a running track, and the lake. Depending on the inclinations of her guests, the hostess serves either a Continental or a full breakfast. *Represented by:* Private Lodgings, Inc., (216) 321-3213. $25–$65.

Cleveland Area **OHIO**

(West). Convenient to both the airport and public transportation, this red-brick Tudor stands right on the Lake Erie shore. The house has a fireplace, as well as a large backyard/patio area. The hostess, who cooks "the natural way," will prepare breakfast and, with notice, other meals for guests. The one guest room has a private bath. *Represented by:* Private Lodgings, Inc., (216) 321-3213. $25–$65.

(West). Furnished with many period antiques, this bed and breakfast is a large, bright condominium not far from the airport and downtown Cleveland. The guest room has a double brass bed and a private bath. The host, a self-employed professional, doesn't serve breakfast but puts out all the ingredients for one. *Represented by:* Private Lodgings, Inc., (216) 321-3213. $25–$65.

(East). Oaken floors, dark birch trim, simple white walls, and lots of green plants characterize this bed and breakfast, hosted by a busy career woman. One guest room, furnished with Early American pieces and sharing a bath, is available for guests. The hostess serves a Continental breakfast. *Represented by:* Private Lodgings, Inc., (216) 321-3213. $25–$65.

(West). This three-story home in a rural suburban area is hosted by a couple who got a taste of bed and breakfasting in England, Germany, and California and decided to try it out under their own roof. They will arrange transportation to and from the airport and serve a full breakfast (guests can arrange for other meals by advance notice). *Represented by:* Private Lodgings, Inc., (216) 321-3213. $25–$65.

Spring Valley **OHIO**

3 Bs Bed and Breakfast

103 Race Street, Spring Valley, OH 45370. (513) 862-4241. *Hosts:* Patricia and Herbert Boettcher.

Surrounded by flower beds filled with petunias and marigolds, and mature maples and pines, 3Bs Bed and Breakfast is a late-nineteenth-century two-story farmhouse painted entirely white. The barn in the backyard is entirely red. Spring Valley is a village of 450 people, and the house is on a half acre that separates it from its neighbors.

The family room has wall-to-wall carpeting; a brick fireplace with a hearth large enough to sit on; a deacon's bench; an easy chair upholstered in a blue fabric; an antique mahogany rocker; and a bobsled. The bobsled, which the Boettchers acquired while living in Germany, is fitted with cushions and serves now as a bench that faces the fireplace. The walls in this room are decorated with etchings of German scenes, an heirloom photograph of Canada's Banff National Park, and several shelves full of knickknacks—mugs from Germany, delicate plates from France, and so on. The guest parlor has three overstuffed easy chairs, an overstuffed sofa, an overhead fan, television, an antique rocker, and a painting of the red barn.

One guest room has a bird's-eye maple bedroom set that includes a bed with tall head- and footboards, a matching dresser with a mirror, and a straight-backed chair. This room has a red carpet, white walls with blue trim, and views of cornfields and farmland.

Breakfast includes homemade muffins and breads, juice, coffee or tea, and omelets with bacon or sausage.

Accommodations: 3 rooms with shared bath. *Smoking:* Permitted. *Children:* Permitted. *Pets:* Not permitted. *Breakfast:* Included. *Driving Instructions:* From I-70 West, exit at Route 68 South to Xenia; turn right at the courthouse onto Route 42 South and proceed 5 miles.

Zoar OHIO

The Cider Mill

Second Street, P.O. Box 441, Zoar, OH 44697. (216) 874-3133.

Hosts: Ralph and Judy Kraus.

The entire village of Zoar is listed in the National Register of Historic Places. The Cider Mill, a banked barn whose first and second floors both have a ground-floor entrance, was built in 1863. The first floor houses an antique and gift shop; the second floor is a Victorian living room; and the guest rooms and owners' quarters are on the third floor. Guests travel from one floor to the other by way of a spiral staircase.

All of the building's original beams have been exposed, as have the sandstone wall in the antique shop and the brick wall in the living room. The two guest rooms share a bath.

Ralph and Judy serve a full complimentary breakfast, permit children, and even arrange for baby-sitters. They permit pets, too, providing the visiting animals are compatible with the resident three dogs and a cat. Many attractions are nearby, including eight old buildings maintained by the Ohio Historical Society that are open to the public from April through October.

Accommodations: 2 rooms with shared bath. *Smoking:* Permitted. *Children:* Permitted. *Pets:* Permitted if compatible with resident animals. *Breakfast:* Included (gourmet meals provided at an additional charge). *Driving Instructions:* Located 3 miles east of Route I-77 and 15 miles south of Canton.

OREGON

Arch Cape. Less than a block from the ocean and with an unobstructed view of it, this contemporary house is 6 miles from Cannon Beach, an artists' colony with many shops and a summer theater. You can see the ocean while breakfasting. *Represented by:* Northwest Bed & Breakfast, #302, (503) 246-8366 or 246-2383. $25–$30.

Bandon. You can see whales, sea lions, and fabulous sunsets from the large deck that wraps around the ocean side of this house, which is perched on a bluff about 40 feet above the ocean, to which you can easily walk. The hosts, whose hobbies include wine-making and rock-polishing, welcome contract-bridge players. *Represented by:* Northwest Bed & Breakfast, #310, (503) 246-8366 or 246-2383. $25–$36.

Bend. Seven miles east of Bend, this bed and breakfast is a 40-acre working cattle ranch hosted by educators interested in backpacking, cross-country skiing, fly fising, bird-watching, sailing, and river-running. Breakfast consists of fresh eggs and homemade breads, and is served in a dining room with a view of the Cascade Mountains. *Represented by:* Northwest Bed & Breakfast, #456, (503) 246-8366. $18–$28.

Depoe Bay. Depoe Bay and the Pacific come into panoramic perspective when viewed from this home on a hillside. The hosts welcome women, couples, and families. *Represented by:* Northwest Bed & Breakfast, #305, (503) 246-8366 or 246-2383. $25–$30.

Dexter. A farm homestead 14 miles south of Eugene, this accommodation features a hot tub, which is on a deck that overlooks a meadow. The house has a pool table, which guests are invited to use. A professional couple, the hosts enjoy organizing activities. *Represented by:* Northwest Bed & Breakfast, #432, (503) 246-8366 or 246-2383. $18–$40.

Eugene. A replica of an original homestead, this two-story ranch on an 80-acre working farm was designed by the architect owner and his wife. Cattle, lambs, poultry, and cutting horses roam the land, and the grounds include a small pond (with a rowboat) populated by frogs and ducks. The house has hand-hewn timbers and high ceilings (including a copper one in the entranceway). The host, a licensed hunting and fishing guide, can organize float trips on the McKenzie River and other such outings. The hosts will pick up guests at the Eugene depots. *Represented by:* Northwest Bed & Breakfast, #434, (503) 246-8366. $25–$38.

Gleneden Beach. An ideal location from which to watch whales, this home is on the oceanfront, near a beach, and you needn't go far for golf or indoor tennis. Guests are invited to use the whirlpool tub. *Represented by:* Northwest Bed & Breakfast, #304, (503) 246-8366 or 246-2383. $25–$30.

Newport. A retired professor and his wife welcome guests to their antique-furnished home, which overlooks the ocean and Yaquina Head. The house, near a golf course, features a fireplace. The hosts' hobbies are working in stained glass and baking. *Represented by:* Northwest Bed & Breakfast, #307, (503) 246-8366 or 246-2383. $18–$30.

Redmond. This house, built and designed by the owner, features a deck that faces nearby mountains, offering spectacular views of Black Butte and the Cascades. *Represented by:* Northwest Bed & Breakfast, #453, (503) 246-8366 or 246-2383. $20–$30.

Ashland **OREGON**

Ashland's Main Street Inn

    142 North Main Street, Ashland, OR 97520. (503) 488-0969.

    Hostesses: Roanne Lyall and Dorothy Walker.

Shaded by three tall maples, Ashland's Main Street Inn is an 1883 Victorian painted beige and trimmed in brown. Roanne and Dorothy planted flowers along the walkways, and pots of flowers dress up the house's three porches.

The central living room has flooring fashioned of several woods but mostly fir and pine, a reproduction Victorian sofa made of mahogany and upholstered in satin brocade, a piano, an antique china closet, two deep green rugs, Oriental prints, a framed tapestry, a curved staircase with carved posts against a far wall, and an antique bric-a-brac case.

Each guest room has a predominating color scheme. The Blue Room has blue carpeting and drapes, a bay window, an oaken table and two oaken chairs, an oaken armoire, and a balcony. Another balcony is off the Gold Room, which overlooks the mountains. The Red Room has a bay window, red wall-to-wall carpeting, red drapes, a red bedspread, and a rounded dresser.

Roanne and Dorothy serve sherry in the afternoons and will bring a Continental breakfast to the guest rooms.

Ashland's big attraction is the Shakespearean Festival that runs from spring through fall. The festival usually includes eight or nine full-length dramas, which range from Shakespeare to O'Neill to the work of contemporary playwrights. At one point the town has three theaters operating simultaneously.

Accommodations: 3 rooms with private bath. *Smoking:* Permitted. *Children:* Check in advance. *Pets:* Permitted. *Breakfast:* Included. *Driving Instructions:* When Route 99 enters Ashland, it becomes Main Street.

Eugene/Leaburg **OREGON**

Marjon

44975 Leaburg Dam Road, Leaburg, OR 97489. (503) 896-3145.
Hostess: Margie Haas.

Margie Haas's real name is Countess Margaret Olga Von Retzlaff Hass, but her house seems much more the work of a Japanese empress than a German countess. A chalet-style structure built entirely of cedar, Marjon is on two acres bordered by the McKenzie River. A small creek runs through property, rife with flowers, including seven varieties of violets, and wooded with 200-foot Douglas firs. A small footbridge spans the creek, and Margie has a dock that floats lazily on the McKenzie.

Margie's living room, a 60- by 60-foot X-shaped room, has 21-foot ceilings; a fireplace constructed of 16 tons of hearthstone; a watermelon-colored curved sofa that seats twenty; a 30-foot wall of glass; teak furniture from Japan; and a black lacquer chest inlaid with soapstone figurines whose faces are carved from ivory.

The smaller of Margie's guest rooms measures 15 by 18 feet and has a robin's-egg-blue, turquoise, and avocado-green carpet matching the colors of the McKenzie River; a teak, hand-carved Chinese table; an 8-foot-tall weeping fig tree; a queen-size bed with a hand-crocheted spread; a Sojii screen made of rice paper with flowers and leaves hand-pressed into it; and a large window overlooking a hundred-year-old apple tree. The apple was grafted long ago, and by now one half of it blooms, then, just when the petals are falling, the other half blooms. The bath in this room—done in whites and butter yellows with silver fixtures—has what Margie calls a "fishbowl shower": it's completely enclosed in glass, and when you're taking a shower you can look out through one of its sides at the river.

The larger guest room is 24 feet square (its bath is 10 by 18 feet), and has a 6- by 9-foot window overlooking the river. The window has a hand-carved fretwork screen in front, and the room is done in bone-white French Provincial reproduction pieces. The room has a chair and a love seat upholstered in white fur, and a 7- by 12-foot bed covered with a custom-made quilt (large pink and red roses and tiny violets on a white background) that picks up the colors in Margie's formal Japanese garden. The bath in this room has etched gold-leaf fixtures and a sunken tub.

The Countess offers a full breakfast and excellent conversation.

Accommodations: 2 rooms with private bath. *Smoking:* Permitted. *Children:* Not permitted. *Pets:* Not permitted. *Breakfast:* Included. *Driving Instructions:* From Eugene, take Route 126 East for 24 miles; then turn right onto Leaburg Dam Road, which ends, after a mile, at Marjon.

Jacksonville **OREGON**

Judge Touvelle House

435 North Oregon, Jacksonville, OR 97530. (503) 899-8223.

Hosts: Verne and Tom Beebe.

Painted white and trimmed forest green, Judge Touvelle house is an 1856 farmhouse. Converted in 1916 into a craftsman-style structure, the building features a wraparound porch furnished with antique white wicker pieces. The house sits on a rise on 4 acres of land sprinkled with fir, redwood, and oak trees, in among which are a swimming pool and a hot tub.

The central living room has 15-foot ceilings with exposed ash beams, an antique brass and frosted glass chandelier, and a fireplace of "Jacksonville" stone. The room has 10-foot ash wainscoting, a cherry Victorian rocker upholstered in navy blue velvet, a nineteenth-century Oriental screen, off-white wall-to-wall carpeting partially covered by an Oriental rug in reds and blues and beiges, a tuxedo couch upholstered with a tiny floral print on powder-blue fabric, and walnut chests and tables topped with marble.

One guest room features a 12-foot walnut bed inlaid with burl, a tiny white floral print on navy blue Laura Ashley wallpaper, a beige, blue, and pink Oriental rug, a pair of Victorian host and hostess chairs and a matching sofa covered in white satin, and needlepoint pillows, as well as a private terrace.

Breakfast, served on antique china with silver utensils, features Verne's jams and homemade croissants as well as fresh fruit in season. Verne likes to serve fresh raspberries and wild blackberries in cream or in half a canteloupe.

Accommodations: 4 rooms, 1 with private bath. *Smoking:* Permitted but not encouraged. *Children:* Not permitted. *Pets:* Not permitted. *Breakfast:* Included. *Driving Instructions:* From Medford take Route 23, which becomes California Street in Jacksonville. Proceed on California Street to Oregon and turn right, then go 1 block.

Jacksonville **OREGON**

Livingston Mansion Inn

4132 Livingston Road, Box 1476, Jacksonville, OR 97530. (503) 899-7107. *Hosts:* Wally and Sherry Lossing.

A 5,000-square-foot English-style mansion dating from 1915, Livingston Mansion Inn is on 4 acres of land overlooking Roque Valley. Its grounds feature a swimming pool.

One guest room has a fireplace, a private entrance, and French doors leading to a screened-in porch. Another room, done in shades of burgundy and rose and furnished with white wicker, has an unobstructed view of the valley as well as of the swimming pool. A third guest room, done in blues, has French doors opening into a bath that retains all its original fixtures, including the original oaken stool.

European period antiques—from Belgium, Norway, Sweden, and England—appear throughout the house, as do fresh flowers, down comforters, and elegant wallpapers.

Breakfast consists of Sherry's special blend of coffee, breakfast cookies crammed with raisins, granola, and nuts, and fresh crepes. Wally travels a great deal; after staying in a great many bed-and-breakfast places, he suggested to Sherry that they open one themselves—which Sherry had sort of been thinking of doing anyway.

Accommodations: 3 rooms with private bath. *Smoking:* Not permitted in bedrooms. *Children:* Permitted. *Pets:* Not permitted. *Breakfast:* Included. *Driving Instructions:* Livingston Mansion Inn is 5 miles west of Medford on Route I-5. Call or write for specific instructions.

Portland Area **OREGON**

Terrace and Antiques. Built in 1910, this traditional house is on a tree-lined street in a quiet residential neighborhood. The house, furnished with many antiques, has a fireplace and a terrace where, weather permitting, breakfast is served. The guest rooms are on the upper level and have private baths. The host, who sings in a choir, is interested in music, art, photography, and—being a descendant of early Oregon settlers—local history. *Represented by:* Northwest Bed & Breakfast, #352, (503) 246-8366. $20–$25.

Quilts and Jellies. The north, south, and west exposures of this bed and breakfast overlook the Pacific Ocean, which is a few hundred feet away. The host is a retired executive who currently designs quilts and makes jams and jellies. One guest room, with a private bath, is available for guests. *Represented by:* Northwest Bed & Breakfast, #331, (503) 246-8366. $20–$25.

Deck and View. Guests in this traditional home tend either to sit on the deck and take in the view of the 200-acre Hoyt Arboretum and downtown Portland, or, especially the children, to play Ping Pong or video games. The house is a mile from Washington Park Zoo, the Forestry Center, and the Oregon Museum of Science and Industry. The hosts speak a little Russian. *Represented by:* Northwest Bed & Breakfast, #364, (503) 246-8366. $20–$30.

Pool and Garden. When the weather's good, the hosts serve breakfast by their pool, which is surrounded by a garden. Literature and art—as well as swimming, of course—appeal to the hosts, a business-and-professional couple. *Represented by:* Northwest Bed & Breakfast, #362, (503) 246-8366 or 246-2383. $18–$34.

Airville PENNSYLVANIA

Spring House
 Muddy Creek Forks, Airville, PA 17302. (717) 927-6906. *Hostess:* Ray Constance Hearne.

Ray Hearne prefers the aesthetic to the practical, which explains (at least partially) why she undertook to restore singlehandedly a 1798 stone house that one realtor called a "stone ruin," why she does all her cooking on and heats her house exclusively with wood stoves, why she commissioned an artist to do stencil work on her walls, and why she lives in a town whose population is 17.

All of the guest-room beds are covered with handmade quilts and coverlets. One room has a spool model bed and a wood stove. For those allergic to electric blankets, Ray offers a solution to cold sheets—she warms them with heated soapstones, which she leaves, safely wrapped, at the foot of your bed.

The house features floors of oak or pine, numerous Oriental rugs, some preserved 1840s stencil work, many original paintings, and whitewashed walls. Ray's complimentary breakfast is full—sausage, eggs, fruit, homemade muffins, coffee, and juice. Spring House is closed for a month each winter.

Accommodation: 3 rooms with shared baths. *Smoking:* Not permitted. *Children:* Permitted. *Pets:* Occasionally permitted. *Breakfast:* Included. *Driving Instructions:* Take Route 74 south to the village of Brogue, turn right at the post office, and go 5 miles to Muddy Creek Forks.

Reminder: Rates and credit-card information are listed in the index.

Gettysburg **PENNSYLVANIA**

The Homestead
    785 Baltimore Street, Gettysburg, PA 17325. (717) 334-2037.
    Hostess: Ruth S. Wisler.

Located at the edge of Gettysburg Battlefield, the Homestead was built in 1869 as the annex to an orphanage. The story has it that after the Battle of Gettysburg someone found in the hand of a dead soldier a daguerreotype of that soldier's three children. This prompted the citizens of Gettysburg to build an orphanage, and when three years later the increasing numbers of orphans required another building to house them, the citizens erected the Homestead. The third floors of both buildings served as dormitories, the original building (a museum now) housed the dining room and kitchen, and the school was in the annex. The Homestead has on display reproductions of early photographs of the orphanage and its occupants. Shortly after its last director was dismissed for mistreating the children (there's a dungeon in the cellar where the children were punished) the orphanage closed and the buildings became private dwellings.

    Today The Homestead is furnished with heirloom antiques, some dating from as far back as the early nineteenth century. Much of the furniture was brought here from Germany by hostess Ruth Wisler's grandparents. The living room has an antique drop-leaf table, an old Boston rocker, a set of Ruth's grandmother's ladder-back chairs, several electrified kerosine lamps (including two revitalized nickel Rayo lamps), a corner cupboard, an organ, and an antique dry sink. The guest rooms are simply but comfortably furnished.

    Accommodations: 2 rooms with shared bath. *Smoking:* Permitted. *Children:* Permitted. *Pets:* Not permitted. *Breakfast:* Not included. *Driving Instructions:* The Homestead is on Route 97, near the National Cemetery.

New Hope **PENNSYLVANIA**

Wedgwood Inn

111 West Bridge Street, New Hope, PA 18938. (215) 862-2570.
Hosts: Nadine Silnutzer and Carl Glassman.

Situated on an acre of landscaped property—with five sugar maples in the front yard and a black walnut, a black elm, a hemlock, and a blue spruce out back—the Wedgwood Inn is an 1870 Victorian structure with a wraparound veranda featuring scrolled-wood brackets and turned posts. The building also has a porte cochere and a gazebo.

The inn's central living room contains a 9-by-12 Oriental rug woven in shades of maroon and blue; oaken flooring; a cherry desk with two glass-enclosed bookcases attached to it; an antique light oaken table surrounded by eight ladder-back chairs; a rattan couch and two matching chairs upholstered in a Wedgwood-blue country fabric; a marble lamp with a linen shade; a red burl slab table; an oak and wrought-iron umbrella stand; bay windows; a picture rail encircling the entire room; wood trim painted Wedgwood blue; and a small collection of Wedgwood pieces.

One bedroom has a walnut four-poster covered with a delicate lace canopy; two walnut side tables; a 9-by-12 blue wool rug; a blue and rose hand-embroidered bedspread; and three 7-foot-tall windows—two facing north, one, east. Another bedroom features an antique brass bed with a curved footboard; an antique white bedspread; a Pennsylvania Dutch quilt in greens and yellows; a chestnut bureau with curved drawers; an 1862 Victorian lady's folding chair upholstered in a maroon and gold needlepoint.

The Wedgwood Inn features a great deal of original art, most of it the work of Nadine's great-aunt Sara Winston, a painter whose abstracts have been exhibited extensively— at the Smithsonian, the National Academy, and so on. There is also a collection of antique gum-ball machines (the gum balls themselves are more modern), fresh flowers and a carafe of Amaretto in every room, mints waiting on the pillows of turned-down beds, and a complimentary Continental breakfast.

Accommodations: 8 rooms, 6 with shared bath. *Smoking:* Permitted in the parlor if no one is inconvenienced. *Children:* Permitted. *Pets:* Selectively permitted—call to inquire. *Breakfast:* Included. *Driving Instructions:* In New Hope, take Main Street to Bridge Street, then turn west.

Paradise **PENNSYLVANIA**

Maple Lane Guest House

505 Paradise Lane, Paradise, PA 17562. (717) 687-7479. *Hosts:* Edwin and Marion Rohrer.

In the heart of Pennsylvania Dutch country, the Maple Lane Guest House is part of a 250-acre working farm that has 180 head of cattle, a hundred or so of them milk cows. The farmland here consists of rolling valley meadows (you can see for 40 miles from above one of them) with patches of wooded areas. A stream winds through the property, and 2 acres of lawn and a few mature maple trees surround the main farmhouse, a modern Colonial-style home painted green and beige.

The living room has white walls trimmed in Williamsburg blue, a curved walnut Victorian sofa upholstered in a rose- and shell-colored tapestry fabric, an antique cherry smokestand end table, off-white carpeting, and an electric organ. Like the living room, the guest rooms are furnished primarily with antiques, and every bed in the house is covered with a handmade quilt. Marion, like many of her Amish neighbors, makes quilts by hand and does needlepoint.

Across from the new farmhouse is the old farmhouse, where Marion and Edwin's son now lives—an 1875 fieldstone structure built by a German immigrant.

The Maple Lane Guest House is close to any number of Pennsylvania Dutch-country attractions: A wax museum, the Pennsylvania Farm Museum, and the Robert Fulton House are all nearby. The farm itself is an attraction, especially around milking time, and guests are welcome to watch the doing of farm chores.

Accommodations: 4 rooms, 2 with private bath. *Smoking:* Not permitted. *Children:* Permitted. *Pets:* Not permitted. *Driving Instructions:* From Strasburg, turn south on Route 896 and proceed for 1.5 miles. Look for the sign of the Timberline Lodge, which is on Paradise Lane.

Philadelphia Area **PENNSYLVANIA**

Society Hill Town House. This three-story town house, on a quiet street in the middle of Philadelphia's Historic District, offers two guest rooms, both with air conditioning and television and sharing a bath. Decorated in Colonial style, the living room has sliding glass doors that overlook the patio. Your hostess, a businesswoman, knows the city and its surrounding areas well. Full complimentary breakfast. *Represented by:* Bed & Breakfast of Philadelphia, (215) 884-1084. $30–$35.

Lansdowne International. A mile and a half from the city line, thirty-five minutes by bus to the center of town, this accommodation is in a large house that contains a stone fireplace as wide as the room it's in. There's a grand piano in the living room (your hosts love classical music), and an eighteenth-century canopied bed in the guest room. For a mileage fee, your host, a member of the Scottish Historical Society, chauffeurs/guides international visitors. He welcomes cats and dogs, speaks German, and serves a full breakfast. *Represented by:* Bed & Breakfast of Philadelphia, (215) 884-1084. $18–$25.

Radnor Charm. Twenty-five minutes by train from central Philadelphia, this 107-year-old house offers two guest rooms, both with a television set and a private bath, as well as tile-faced fireplaces and large low-sill windows facing high tree-branches. Your hosts serve a full breakfast, either in their Colonial breakfast room or on their screened-in porch. *Represented by:* Bed & Breakfast of Philadelphia, (215) 884-1084. $25–$30.

Jarreton Farmhouse. This 150-year-old farmhouse, thirty-five minutes by train from the center of town, offers up to four guest rooms (sometimes the children visit). Wood stoves heat the sitting room, the family room, and one bedroom. The water is solar-heated. Excepting the three midweek days she works, your hostess serves a full breakfast—the rest of the time do-it-yourself ingredients are available. *Represented by:* Bed & Breakfast of Philadelphia, (215) 884-1084. $20–$28.

Strafford Village. A public relations/advertising manager and business/craftswoman are your hosts in this Colonial home seven minutes from Valley Forge National Historic Park. During the summers they serve breakfast in their lush garden, under a yellow umbrella. *Represented by:* Bed & Breakfast of Philadelphia, (215) 884-1084. $25–$33.

Philadelphia Area **PENNSYLVANIA**

Valley Forge Apartment. Forty-five minutes from the center of Philadelphia, this apartment offers a balcony and an indoor/outdoor swimming pool. Your hostess teaches at a technical school and has a collection of San Blas Indian *molas* in her living room. *Represented by:* Bed & Breakfast of Philadelphia, (215) 884-1084. $18–$25.

Pineapple Hill—New Hope. The dining room here has a fireplace and 18-inch-thick walls. Guests are invited to use the pool, which is in the ruins of a stone barn. The guest rooms, most with sloping walls, have brass or spool beds and simple country furnishings. *Represented by:* Bed & Breakfast of Philadelphia, (215) 884-1084. $40.

West Chester circa 1840. Forty-five minutes by bus from town, surrounded by old trees, this accommodation is in a "summer home" that sits on a curved knoll. There are high ceilings, tall windows, and a fireplace in the den. With a large corporation until recently, your host knows the area well, especially activities at the University of Pennsylvania. *Represented by:* Bed & Breakfast of Philadelphia, (215) 884-1084. $25–$35.

Philadelphia PENNSYLVANIA

Society Hill Hotel

Third and Chestnut streets, Philadelphia, PA 19106. (215) 925-1394. *Hosts:* David DeGraff and Judith Baird Campbell.

The Society Hill Hotel is an 1832 red-brick building across the street from the Federal Visitor's Center and Independence Historic National Park. The building is trimmed in Williamsburg red, except those parts of it that are made of marble, such as the front steps.

The guest rooms have pale gray walls and charcoal gray wall-to-wall carpeting, burgundy hand stenciling and crown moldings, and brass double beds. Historical prints and lithographs appear in all the rooms, which are furnished with a combination of antique and traditional furnishings. All of the guest rooms have private baths, some of which retain their antique brass fixtures, and each bath comes complete with a hair dryer and Euro-bath soap. There are fresh flowers in every room.

Breakfast is served on a wicker tray decorated with fresh flowers and brought to your room at the time you request. The Society Hill Hotel has a bar-restaurant characterized by light woods, stained glass, and plenty of plants.

Accommodations: 12 rooms with private bath. *Smoking:* Permitted. *Children:* Permitted. *Pets:* Not permitted. *Breakfast:* Included. *Driving Instructions:* The hotel is in the heart of Philadelphia's Old City and Society Hill, directly across the street from the Federal Visitor's Center.

The Poconos **PENNSYLVANIA**

Joe Jefferson Cottage. Joe Jefferson, the famous nineteenth-century American actor, wrote his popular dramatic adaptation of Washington Irving's *Rip Van Winkle* while staying in this 1850 Pennsylvania farmhouse. The hosts here enjoy bird-watching and hiking, and frequently take guests on tours of the mountains. The Camelback ski area is less than a half hour from here. The hosts welcome children and don't mind supervising them for limited stretches. *Represented by:* Bed & Breakfast Pocono Northeast, Inc., (717) 472-3145. $20–$27.

June's Place. In 1756 the hostess's great-great-great-grandfather tried to settle here, on the bank of Brodheads Creek, but was evicted in advance by a tribe of local Indians. In 1764 he returned and had the distinction of being the first settler of this community. The hostess is interested in antiques, crafts, and travel, and her eclectic collection of objects and curios is almost a travelogue. Camelback ski area is 14 miles from here; Tanglewood, 12. The hostess will supervise children during the dinner hour. *Represented by:* Bed & Breakfast Pocono Northeast, Inc., (717) 472-3145, $22–$35.

Weekend Getaway Suite. The second-story deck of this bed and breakfast has a 35-mile view of the Poconos. It offers guests a suite with a private entrance, a deck, a living room with a sofa and television, two bedrooms, and a private bath. The house has a recreation room with a pool table, a bar, a dartboard, and other diversions. Skiing and golfing are twenty minutes away. *Represented by:* Bed & Breakfast Pocono Northeast, Inc., (717) 472-3145. $25–$90.

Powder Mill Farms. This bed and breakfast is on 42 acres adjoining state game lands. Right outside the 1826 lodge are large maples and stone walls. The property also contains a pond and a stream that runs through the ruins of a Civil War gunpowder mill, among which trout tend to congregate. The lodge is 3 miles from Elk Mountain ski area, and guests are invited to cross-country ski or ice skate right on the property. The hosts provide a refrigerator for guests and invite them to barbeque on a screened-in deck. *Represented by:* Bed & Breakfast Pocono Northeast, Inc., (717) 472-3145. $20–$27.

Southeastern Region **PENNSYLVANIA**

Barto. An 1830 brick house on a 23-acre working farm, this bed and breakfast is hosted by a semiretired couple involved in a mail-order business. The hostess restores old quilts and makes new quilts to order, and both hosts are antique-buffs who invite their guests to join them on antique outings. Guests may also fish in the property's pond, or, if properly licensed, try their luck at Tulpehoken Creek, which is a hundred yards away and stocked by the state. Hawk Mountain is 15 miles away. *Represented by:* Bed & Breakfast of Southeast Pennsylvania, (215) 845-3526. $27–$40.

East Greenville. A large Cape Cod house surrounded by woods, this bed and breakfast is on 45 acres, 20 of which have walking trails. One of the guest rooms is a private suite on the second floor, immediately across the hall from the family television room, which guests are invited to use. The host is a chemist, and the hostess an expert with yeast (makes her own sweet rolls), and fluent in German. The hosts welcome children and will even permit a small dog or cat. *Represented by:* Bed & Breakfast of Southeast Pennsylvania, (215) 845-3526. $30–$40.

Quakertown Area. Hosted by a sales representative for Bethlehem Steel and a social worker, this bed and breakfast is a stone farmhouse with an 1850 guest wing. The two-story wing has a private entrance, a sitting area with a queen-size sofa bed, and a bath downstairs. Up a winding staircase is a bedroom with twin beds. There is an in-ground swimming pool that guests are invited to use. *Represented by:* Bed & Breakfast of Southeast Pennsylvania, (215) 845-3526. $27–$40.

Reading. In the historic district of downtown Reading, this bed and breakfast, hosted by a woman who manages an art gallery, consists of two apartments. One has a bedroom with a queen-size bed, a kitchen/dining area, and a living room, with television, that opens onto a backyard with a patio and a picnic table. The hostess stocks the apartments with breakfast supplies, and guests are welcome to shop and prepare their other meals in the apartments. *Represented by:* Bed & Breakfast of Southeast Pennsylvania, (215) 845-3526. $25–$40.

State College Area **PENNSYLVANIA**

Centre Hall. Thirteen miles from Penn State, this *ca.* -1860 structure has been entirely restored by the hosts, a second-grade teacher and a personnel director. Every room in the house has antique furnishings, and the grounds include a built-in swimming pool that guests are invited to use. Breakfast includes fresh baked muffins, and each evening at nine the hosts set out sweets and sherry for their guests. *Represented by:* Rest & Repast, #4, (814) 355-4910. $25–$40.

Pine Grove Mills. A 1950s contemporary-style structure on an acre of wooded land, this bed and breakfast is hosted by a Penn State professor of forestry, and a secretary for the State College area school district. The grounds feature a nature walk, complete with labeled trees, that the professor designed. Three guest rooms are available, two with shared bath and one with private bath. The breakfast here is a full one, served, weather permitting, on an enclosed deck off the kitchen. *Represented by:* Rest & Repast, #1, (814) 355-4910. $45.

Potters Mills. Ten miles east of Penn State, this 1824 structure is in the National Register of Historic Places. The house is furnished primarily with period antiques, and all but two rooms have been completely restored. The hosts, a teacher and the president of an instrumentation firm, raise cows, chickens, pigs, horses, and other farm animals. The guest rooms are furnished with antiques, and the house features a study with a bay window that overlooks the Alleghenies. *Represented by:* Rest & Repast, #2, (814) 355-4910. $25–$40.

Spruce Creek. This *ca.* -1820 farmhouse about halfway between Altoona and State College has five working fireplaces, deep windowsills, a curving staircase in the main hall, wide-board pine floors, and elaborate woodwork. It is on a 100-acre farm, and one of the hosts, who has a master's degree in animal science, raises Angus cattle. The guest rooms, which share a bath with the hosts, are furnished with late-nineteenth-century antiques and have working fireplaces. *Represented by:* Rest & Repast, #3, (814) 355-4910. $25–$40.

Newport **RHODE ISLAND**

Sunnyside Manor. Hosted by an attorney and his wife, this guest house is on a quiet, tree-lined street. In back of the house is a large garden surrounded by woods. Each room is furnished differently, according to a theme. The "Turkish Room" features a large canopy bed and various accessories, such as the large hookah pipe on the wall, that suggest the Middle East. *Represented by:* Newport Travel Service, (401) 846-1615. $40–$95.

Ellery Park. Mike and Margo, who work for *Cruising World* magazine, have a Colonial-style home in downtown Newport. Furnishings are a combination of antique and contemporary Colonial pieces, and there are such niceties as hooked rugs scattered on hardwood floors and a fireplace in the central living room. *Represented by:* Newport Travel Service, (401) 846-1615. $40–$55.

Fitch House. Near Ocean Drive, on landscaped grounds with flowering fruit trees and gardens, Fitch House is a white Cape Cod structure with four rooms for guests. Betsy has furnished her home with comfortable contemporary pieces, and she prepares guests for the day by serving a full breakfast. *Represented by:* Newport Travel Service, (401) 846-1615. $40.

The Writers' House. Surrounded by trees at the end of a long driveway, this 1844 Gothic Revival structure is hosted by a couple who have written books on the country inns of Great Britain and Ireland. There are antiques in every room, and the grounds feature a swimming pool that guests are invited to use. *Represented by:* Newport Travel Service, (401) 846-1615. $35–$55.

Newport **RHODE ISLAND**

The Brinley

23 Brinley Street, Newport, RI 02840. (401) 849-7645. *Hostesses:* Amy Weintraub and Edwina Sehest.

The Brinley is an 1871 Victorian home that was originally built by one Joseph Tews, a man who seems to have eluded history, albeit there's a nearby street named after him.

The guest rooms, which come with fresh flowers and turned-down beds with mints on their pillows, are furnished with a combination of contemporary pieces and Victorian antiques. Three of these rooms have nonworking fireplaces; some feature 9-foot-wide bay windows; all have matching bedspreads and curtains. The parlor has a Victorian curved, claw-footed couch covered in mauve fabric, side tables covered with lace, a floral Sarouk rug, and an elaborately carved Victorian rocker.

An executive producer for NBC and a doctor of psychology with a practice, Amy and Edwina decided to chuck their careers and open an inn. So they came to Newport and took over the Brinley. They distributed their collection of antique miniature kerosine lamps throughout the bedrooms. They also have a number of antique miniature candlesticks. The parlor features a collection of books on art, architecture, antiques, and photography.

Accommodations: 17 rooms, 5 with private bath. *Smoking:* Permitted. *Children:* Under 10 not permitted. *Pets:* Not permitted. *Breakfast:* Included. *Driving Instructions:* The Brinley is near the center of Newport.

Dennis Guest House

59 Washington Street, Newport, RI 02840. (401) 846-1324. *Host:* The Reverend Henry G. Turnbull.

Dennis House is a 1740 Colonial structure, with an elaborate pineapple-front doorway and a widow's walk (the only flat one in Newport). The house is also the rectory of Saint John's Episcopal Church.

Father Turnbull, who has been rector of Saint John's for more than twenty years, decided to turn the rectory into a guest house because the costs of maintaining the building were getting out of hand. "Now," Father Turnbull proudly says, "the rectory supports itself so well I've removed it from the parish budget."

Father Turnbull told me that his guest house is not religiously oriented. "It's nice to have a little break from solely religious matters," he said, "and meeting with as many people as I have has been an absolutely ecumenical experience."

In addition to being a rector, Father Turnbull is also something of an antique collector. The guest rooms feature such items as Victorian-reproduction stripe and print wallpapers, country antiques, kilimlike Yugoslavian rugs, and in one room, a 9- by 12-foot blue-and-gray Oriental rug. Two of the guest rooms have working fireplaces.

The parlor, which Father Turnbull calls the hospitality center, features electrified wrought-iron wall sconces, a wall of exposed brick, built-in bookcases, and a view of Narragansett Bay and the Newport Bay Bridge.

Accommodations: 3 rooms and 1 suite, all with private bath. *Smoking:* Permitted. *Children:* Permitted. *Pets:* Permitted. *Breakfast:* Included. *Driving Instructions:* Dennis House is in the center of Newport, next to Saint John's Episcopal Church.

Newport **RHODE ISLAND**

The Walsh's

300 Gibbs Avenue, Newport, RI. (401) 842-4441. *Hosts:* Mary and Alex Walsh.

This twenty-two-room 1882 house was built by Arthur B. Emmons, a coal baron from Boston who obviously had a weakness for large houses and elaborate woodwork. Mary and Alex bought the home twenty-six years ago, when it was auctioned by the Bank of New York because Mrs. Emmons, who lived to be six months short of a hundred, had no heirs.

Mrs. Emmons was a horticulturist, and the 4 ½ acres of grounds show it—there are red cedars, a copper beech, flowering crab apples, rare Japanese spruces, and other exotic trees, all over a hundred years old.

Mary and Alex wound up buying the furnishings as well, except for Mrs. Emmon's art collection, which she had left to a New York museum, providing they wanted it. When a curator came and saw, among other pieces, Renoir's *Bay of Naples,* he said they wanted it. The house is full of antiques, many of them restored, along with lots of polished woodwork. The dining room and living room have 6-foot-high wainscotting and built-in shelving and cabinetry. The living room has an elaborate oak-paneled ceiling.

Two guest rooms have fireplaces, one has a private porch, and all have antique furnishings. The music room includes a baby grand piano, a fireplace, and formal upholstered antique couches. Without its extension the oaken table in the dining room seats twenty.

This may all sound very formal, but the atmosphere is casual and relaxed—coffee in the kitchen, and so forth.

Accommodations: 4 rooms, 3 with private bath. *Smoking:* Permitted. *Children:* Permitted. *Pets:* Ask in advance. *Breakfast:* Included. *Driving Instructions:* Take Avenue of the Americas south to Memorial-Boulevard (the post office is at this corner), turn left and proceed to Gibbs Avenue, which is at the top of the hill; turn left on Gibbs and go two blocks—the house is on the northeast corner of Gibbs and Catherine.

Newport **RHODE ISLAND**

"Wayside"

Bellevue Avenue, Newport, RI 03840. (401) 847-0302. *Hosts:* Al and Dorothy Post.

When the tall ships were scheduled to appear in Newport back in 1976, the mayor asked the citizens to open their doors to visitors. So Al and Dorothy Post—restaurateurs and in the hospitality business anyway—said, "Why not?" Their doors are still open, and there's a mansion behind them—an 1876 beige-brick Georgian trimmed with white stone, on an acre and a half of land. The shutters are black, and there's a veranda on one side of the building, a porch in back, and a tall copper beech in front. There's a pool outside, and a pool table within.

The front hall, paneled in oak, has a winding staircase. The entrance adjoins the central living room, which features a large granite fireplace that Dorothy has filled with plants—she's lined the hearth with mirrors that reflect the plants. The living room is also paneled oak and features a 15-foot ceiling; a love seat covered in a beige and brown floral print that picks up the tones of the oak; marble-topped side tables; a hutch; and windows that look out on the beech tree. In a lounge area, guests often shoot pool or watch color television.

One guest room has a queen-size bed made of cherry and covered with a canopy and a dust cover, both of them yellow. The yellow is picked up by the cushions on the wicker couch and chair set in the sitting area. The room has a marble fireplace and oaken floors (all the floors here are of oak). Each guest room has a sitting area. There's also a simply but comfortably furnished two-bedroom apartment available.

Accommodations: 7 rooms with private bath, 2 rooms with shared bath and sitting room. *Smoking:* Permitted. *Children:* Permitted. *Pets:* Not permitted. *Breakfast:* Included. *Driving Instructions:* "Wayside" is on Bellevue Avenue, between Parker Dickson and Arragansett.

Newport **RHODE ISLAND**

The Yankee Peddler Inn

113 Touro Street, Newport, RI 02840. (401) 846-1323. *Hostess:* Ellen Retler.

Painted beige and trimmed in white, the Yankee Peddler Inn is a mansard-roofed 1830s Greek Revival structure. The house is on the same block as the Newport Historical Society and the Touro Synagogue, the oldest in the country.

The parlor, which at one time was the basement, has foot-thick walls, a fireplace, pine floors covered here and there with Oriental throw rugs, and, right at the flower level, windows trimmed with fieldstone. The room, furnished with a mixture of antiques and contemporary pieces, is simple but comfortable.

One guest room features a fireplace, a queen-size bed covered with a quilt that matches the curtains, wall-to-wall carpeting, an antique rocking chair, a collection of photographic portraits hanging on the wall, and a couple of Scandinavian dressers. Hostess Ellen Retler also has a suite for guests. The living-room area features a fireplace, a navy blue sleeper sofa, a pair of antique straight-backed chairs, a round table covered with beige linen, and a mahogany coffee table with a marble inset.

Ellen, who used to own a restaurant, serves a complimentary breakfast that usually includes bagels, English muffins, an assortment of jellies, cream cheese, and coffee. For tea drinkers she offers a choice of tea leaves, which she told me, she never reads.

Accommodations: 20 rooms, 18 with private bath. *Smoking:* Permitted. *Children:* Permitted. *Pets:* Not permitted. *Breakfast:* Included. *Driving Instructions:* From the Newport Bridge, take the Scenic Newport exit, turn right off the ramp, and proceed past three traffic lights, then turn left.

Beaufort SOUTH CAROLINA

Bay Street Inn

601 Bay Street, Beaufort, SC 29902. (803) 524-7720. *Hosts:* David and Terry Murray.

Listed in the National Register of Historic Places, the Bay Street Inn is an 1852 mansion with six Ionic-over-Doric columns supporting two verandas. During the Civil War the house functioned as a Union officers' club and, when things got worse, as a hospital.

Each guest room is furnished with antiques, which range from period French pieces to a grand old Carolina rice bed, and each has a fireplace and a sitting area. The public rooms feature fine plaster- and woodwork, high ceilings, and two fireplaces with black marble mantels.

The Murrays include in their rates a great many complimentary extras—breakfast, the morning paper, a fruit basket, a decanter of sherry, evening chocolates, and bicycles. David and Terry serve breakfast on china, with crystal and sterling.

The house, whose grounds contain azalea, dogwood, and crepe myrtle, overlooks South Carolina's intercoastal waterway.

Accommodations: 5 rooms with private bath. *Smoking:* Permitted. *Children:* School-age children permitted. *Pets:* Not permitted. *Breakfast:* Included. *Driving Instructions:* From Savannah, take Route 17-A north; then take Route 120 into Beauport.

Barrett House (*Historic Charleston Bed & Breakfast*)

Charleston **SOUTH CAROLINA**

Jeffords House. An 1843 Greek Revival structure, Jeffords House features a wrought-iron gate that leads to a private patio. The patio, in turn, leads to a garden next to an old carriage house that now serves as the guest quarters. Both houses are furnished with a blend of antique and modern pieces. *Represented by:* Historic Charleston Bed & Breakfast, (803) 722-6606. $75–$120.

Barrett House. Built in 1875, Barrett House has a porch and a veranda that overlook its private garden, to which each of the

Watkins–Thomas House (Historic Charleston Bed & Breakfast)

Jeffords House (Historic Charleston Bed & Breakfast)

Charleston **SOUTH CAROLINA**

three guest rooms has access. The house's original oven and kitchen fireplace are still there, as are the wide-board wooden floors. Each guest accommodation (all of them restored) has its own living room. *Represented by:* Historic Charleston Bed & Breakfast, (803) 722-6606. $75.

Watkins-Thomas House. A *circa*-1720 structure, Watkins-Thomas House has a carriage house available for guests. This carriage house is listed in the National Register of Historic Places and features exposed-beam ceilings and a clay-tile roof. The grounds include a formal garden. *Represented by:* Historic Charleston Bed & Breakfast, (803) 722-6606. $100–$150.

Chapman House. Chapman House, built in 1795, has two rooms for guests. A sunny third-floor garret room contains antique French twin beds, and a second-floor room has an antique four-poster. Breakfast is served on silver trays. *Represented by:* Historic Charleston Bed & Breakfast, (803) 722-6606. $45–$50.

Leopard's House. Furnished with a combination of antiques from Leopard's Shop and period reproductions, this 1890s structure is in the heart of Charleston's antique district. The guest quarters feature a private piazza where guests may take their breakfast. *Represented by:* Historic Charleston Bed & Breakfast, (803) 722-6606. $65.

Charleston   **SOUTH CAROLINA**

Two Meeting Street Inn

    2 Meeting Street at the Battery, Charleston, SC 29401. (803) 723-7322. *Hostess:* Marceline Murphy.

To prevent plaster from falling onto the food during earthquakes (the Charleston quake of 1886 having leveled the building previously occupying the same site), its builders specified that the dining room and foyer of this 1892 Queen Anne Victorian mansion have ceilings made of oak. Worried though they might have been about falling plaster, they didn't worry at all about breaking glass: The dining room has a 6-foot sunburst stained-glass window above a built-in china cabinet; and the living room, dining room, foyer, and staircase landing all have Tiffany stained-glass windows.

    The building is surrounded on two sides by arched piazzas that face the Battery Park across the street. The columned bandstand in the park was presented to the city of Charleston by this inn's original owners, a family enamored of listening to concerts while sipping mint juleps on their piazza.

    Five of the guest rooms have private baths, as well as seventeenth-century Dutch-tiled fireplaces. The furnishings throughout the house include such goodies as Persian and other Oriental rugs, old blue-and-white Canton china, brass chandeliers, carved oaken paneling, and easy chairs covered with needlepoint. The entire building is centrally air-conditioned and heated.

    Accommodations: 7 rooms, 5 with private bath. *Smoking:* Permitted. *Children:* Under 6 not permitted. *Pets:* Not permitted. *Breakfast:* Included. *Driving Instructions:* Take Route I-95 to Route I-26 East, and exit at its terminus onto Meeting Street.

Memphis Area **TENNESSEE**

Downtown. A large open apartment in a recently renovated and architecturally distinctive warehouse, this bed and breakfast is on the bank of the Mississippi River. The host, president of a management consulting firm, travels often, and the entire apartment is frequently available for guests. Furnished with contemporary pieces, it features a large open kitchen with a work/eating area; throughout the apartment are Oriental carpets and lots of plants. *Represented by:* Bed & Breakfast in Memphis, MM-0403, (901) 726-5920. $34–$40.

Central Gardens. Hosted by a marketing executive with a major bank, this bed and breakfast is an older home in midtown Memphis. Its guest area has twin beds, a private bath, a small stove, and a refrigerator; guests are invited to use the sitting area downstairs. The house is convenient to the Memphis Medical Center, Southwestern University, and many dining and shopping possibilities. *Represented by:* Bed & Breakfast in Memphis, MM-0403, (901) 726-5920. $34–$40.

East. Surrounded by mature trees, this white frame house with its porch complete with a porch swing, is in a quiet residential neighborhood in Memphis's Walnut Grove/Goodlett area. The hostess, a vitamin distributor and portrait painter, offers two guest rooms. These, and their baths, are furnished with period Victorian pieces, and the layout is particularly suited to couples traveling together. Dixon Galleries and Gardens is close to here, as are many restaurants and a public golf course. *Represented by:* Bed & Breakfast in Memphis, ME-1701, (901) 726-5920. $26–$32.

Cordova. Authentic even to its furnishings, this bed and breakfast is a log cabin twenty minutes from midtown Memphis. Weather permitting, guests are invited to fish, hike, swim, or cook out on the patio. The house features a river-rock fireplace, a double featherbed for guests, and a fully stocked kitchen. It is close to Germantown, which has plenty of shops and restaurants, and the hosts are commercial and residential interior designers. *Represented by:* Bed & Breakfast in Memphis, MC-1801, (901) 726-5920. $80–$120.

Millington. This bed and breakfast in northwest Memphis is a 47-acre farm. Guests who bring their own gear are invited to fish on the property, and horses are available at a nearby public stable. The hostess enjoys writing country-music lyrics, farming, and cook-

Memphis Area **TENNESSEE**

ing. She serves breakfast in a screened-in plant/sitting room that overlooks a stand of mature trees. Numerous dogs romp about the property, and one is in residence in the house. The guest room has a canopied bed and a private bath. *Represented by:* Bed & Breakfast in Memphis, MN-5301, (901) 726-5920. $34–$40.

Nashville **TENNESSEE**

Near Centennial Park. Fifteen minutes from the airport and three minutes from "Music Row," this apartment couldn't be closer to Nashville's famous night spots. Centennial Park and Vanderbilt University are also close by. The hostess—who welcomes women, couples, or families with a small child—enjoys accompanying her guests on weekend tours around town. *Represented by:* Nashville Bed & Breakfast, A-0301, (615) 298-5674. $21–$35.

Near "Music Row." Hosted by a young professional couple, this house is in a complex with a swimming pool. Two free tennis courts are just down the street. Between them, the hosts speak French, German, and Spanish, as well as English. "Music Row" and downtown Nashville are near. *Represented by:* Nashville Bed & Breakfast, A-0503, (615) 298-5674. $26–$35.

Former Church. This building used to be a church, and what used to be a choir loft is now a guest room with a Jacuzzi. The Tennessee Historical Commission cited this home as a creative example of adaptive restoration. The hosts speak French and Spanish, as well as English, and their home is fifteen minutes from downtown Nashville. *Represented by:* Nashville Bed & Breakfast, A-2101, (615) 298-5674. $34–$40.

Twenty Minutes from Opryland. This guest house features an accommodation with its own living room, bedroom, kitchen, and private entrance. Children are welcome. *Represented by:* Nashville Bed & Breakfast, C-7502, (615) 298-5674. $28–$34.

Mini-Farm. A mini-farm with horses, this home has guest quarters that are detached from the main house. The guest quarters have a bedroom, a small refrigerator, and a private bath. When they're home, the hosts allow guests to ride their horses. Opryland is only twenty minutes away. *Represented by:* Nashville Bed & Breakfast, D-2703, (615) 298-5674. $26–$32.

Renovated Barn with Tree House. Twenty minutes from Opryland and situated on 8 acres, this guest house is a renovated barn. The ground floor has a living room and a kitchen, and what used to be the hayloft is now a bedroom with a bath. The grounds feature a tree house that overlooks a creek, and the hostess doesn't charge for extra guests who bring their own bedding. *Represented by:* Nashville Bed & Breakfast, D-2704, (615) 298-5674. $44–$56.

Land, Lots of Land. Each of the guest rooms here opens onto

Nashville **TENNESSEE**

a deck that overlooks a trout stream and the woods surrounding it. Both retired navy people, the hosts raise Tennessee walking horses, and if you know how to ride, there are 100 acres of land to do it on. *Represented by:* Nashville Bed & Breakfast, E-3701, (615) 298-5674. $34–$40.

Leawood—The Williams

Shiloh **TENNESSEE**

"Leawood"—The Williams Estate

P.O. Box 24, Shiloh, TN 38376. (901) 689-5106. *Hosts:* Jay, Felix, and Margaret Williams.

Situated in a grove of white pines and surrounded by 80 acres of forested land with a profusion of live and white oaks, The Williams Estate is an imposing Tudoresque building in the style of those found on English country estates. The grounds are covered with nature trails and feature a 4-acre stocked and spring-fed lake with a 20-by-50 swimming pool right next to it.

Built in the 1930s, the house is constructed of brown river rock and logs, which compose the second floor. The place was built by gangsters, who used it as a hideout. We should all have such a place to hide out.

The great hall is 70 feet long and has a 35-foot vaulted, exposed-oak-beam ceiling surrounded by a second-floor hanging balcony. The room features a 12-by-40 Oriental rug woven primarily in golds, a stone fireplace that goes all the way to the ceiling, hardwood flooring, marble-topped coffee and end tables, one 12-by-15 and two 8-by-10 Oriental rugs in golds and reds, a couch and some wing chairs, and a good stereo.

There's also an 80-foot screened-in veranda with a "bring your own bottle" bar.

The guest rooms are carpeted wall to wall and, like the rest of the house, furnished with a mixture of antique and contemporary pieces. Every room has a view. Nine of the thirteen rooms are suites with a bedroom, a sitting room, and a bath.

For breakfast there are eggs with bacon or sausage, hot biscuits covered with flour gravy, Danish pastries, preserves, and coffee or tea.

Accommodations: 13 rooms, 4 with shared bath. *Smoking:* Permitted. *Children:* Permitted. *Pets:* Not permitted. *Breakfast:* Included. *Driving Instructions:* Shiloh is 15 miles north of Corinth, Mississippi, on Route 22, or 12 miles south of Savannah, Tennessee, on Route 142. Call or write for specific directions to "Leawood."

"Driftwood" (Sand Dollar Hospitality)

Corpus Christi Area **TEXAS**

"The Driftwood." A spacious two-story contemporary with four bedrooms for guests, this bed and breakfast faces the fairway of a private golf course. The guest bedrooms share a lounge area with television, a game table, and a refrigerator, which guests are invited to use. The hosts, interested in square dancing and entertaining, welcome children over twelve and extend limited kitchen and laundry privileges to guests. The house, not far from Corpus Christi Bay, is ten minutes from Padre Island National Seashore. *Represented by:* Sand Dollar Hospitality, Bed and Breakfast, (512) 853-1222. $40–$50.

"Las Palmas." Hosted by a geologist and a tennis coach, this bed and breakfast is in the process of being renovated inside and out by a Floridian specialist in Art Deco restoration. The house is half a block from Ocean Drive, a scenic route that runs along the bay, and fifteen minutes from Padre Island National Seashore. The hosts speak English, French, and Spanish, welcome children and pets, and have two guest rooms available—one with private bath and one with shared bath. *Represented by:* Sand Dollar Hospitality, Bed and Breakfast, (512) 853-1222. $30–$35.

"Las Palmas" (Sand Dollar Hospitality)

Corpus Christi Area **TEXAS**

"The Islander." A half hour from downtown and minutes from Corpus Christi's best beaches, this bed and breakfast is on a waterfront lot on a tropical Padre Island canal. The guest room has a queen-size water bed, a private bath, and a private entrance. The hosts' interests are fishing, boating, hunting, and water-skiing (a boat dock adjoins the property). They serve a Continental breakfast and extend television and laundry privileges to guests. *Represented by:* Sand Dollar Hospitality, Bed and Breakfast, (512) 853-1222. $40–$50.

"Ebbtide." This bed and breakfast is on Corpus Christi's southside, fifteen minutes from Padre Island National Seashore. The hosts, a dentist and his wife, have three rooms for guests. One has twin beds and an adjoining bath, as well as a private entrance leading out to the pool and patio. The other two rooms share a bath and have furnishings imported from Spain. The hosts, who welcome children and pets, have three dogs. They extend limited kitchen and laundry privileges to guests. *Represented by:* Sand Dollar Hospitality, Bed and Breakfast, (512) 853-1222. $30–$35.

Dallas/Fort Worth Area **TEXAS**

Dallas— "Iris." A large brick structure (complete with historical marker) not far from downtown, this guest house has two rooms available. One comes with a king-size bed, the other, with a double. Both beds have canopies, which might prove useful in the morning—the host prepares breakfast downstairs but serves it in the guest rooms. Grounds around the house include a swimming pool that guests are invited to use. A cat patrols both outside and inside the house. *Represented by:* Bed & Breakfast Texas Style, (214) 298-5433 or 298-8586. $40–$45.

Dallas— "The Rose." The guest room here is furnished completely with antiques—an armoire, a dresser, a luggage rack, and an antique telephone that actually works. The antique bed is covered with a rose quilt the host's mother made. The room has a private bath and a private entrance, which is off a circular porte cochere. The house has a historical marker; its host, whose hobby is quilting, prepares a Continental breakfast for guests. *Represented by:* Bed & Breakfast Texas Style, (214) 298-5433 or 298-8586. $40–$45.

Dallas— "Highlands." Close to Southern Methodist University, Northport Mall, and the Greenville Avenue nightspots, this bed and breakfast is hosted by a school librarian who backpacks, sails, and plays bridge. The guest room, a double, has a private bath. During the school year the hostess prepares a Continental breakfast for guests. *Represented by:* Bed & Breakfast Texas Style, (214) 298-5433 or 298-8586. $30–$35.

Dallas— "Texas Queen." On the shore of Lake Ray Hubbard,

Dallas/Fort Worth Area **TEXAS**

this guest house is thirty-five minutes from downtown Dallas. One guest room has a king-size bed covered with a handmade quilt, and a private bath. Chandler's Landing, where one can catch the paddleboat steamer, is close by. Monarch butterflies—who migrate each spring and fall from northern Canada to southern Mexico—stop by for a few weeks to rest here. The hosts serve a breakfast that includes homemade muffins. *Represented by:* Bed & Breakfast Texas Style, (214) 298-5433 or 298-8586. $32–$38.

Dallas— "Tranquility." Not far from Southfork Ranch of *Dallas* fame, this bed and breakfast is hosted by a musician who often performs on one of his instruments for guests, at their request. The guest room has a queen-size brass bed, Impressionist art on the walls, many books for insomniacs, and a private bath. The host serves a Continental breakfast in the Atrium Room. *Represented by:* Bed & Breakfast Texas Style, (214) 298-5433 or 298-8586. $35–$40.

Dallas— "Fan Room." They call it the "Fan Room" because the focal point of this twin-bedded guest room with private bath is a black antique fan. The hosts, a church secretary and an entrepreneur who works out of the house, traveled in England and Scotland, where they developed a taste for bed and breakfasts. Their breakfast, a full one, includes a jalapeño muffin (make sure there's a glass of water around before eating a jalapeño anything). *Represented by:* Bed & Breakfast Texas Style, (214) 298-5433 or 298-8586. $35–$40.

Fort Worth— "Eclectic." Named after its combination of modern, Louis XIV, Oriental, and rattan furnishings, this bed and breakfast in southwest Forth Worth is ten minutes from downtown. Its guest room has a double bed, a sitting room, and a roll top desk. The hosts, who have traveled extensively and lived overseas, prepare a full breakfast including homemade breads and jellies. For a slight fee they will take guests on a tour to Billy Bob's and the Botanical Gardens. *Represented by:* Bed & Breakfast Texas Style, (214) 298-5433 or 298-8586, $30–$34.

Forth Worth— "Yellow Rose." Fifteen minutes from downtown and thirty minutes from historic Granbury, this bed and breakfast is hosted by a couple who lived in Germany for six years, and the home is full of German artifacts. Two guest rooms are available, as well as a very full breakfast—cinnamon apple muffins, baked eggs, fruit, and coffee or tea. *Represented by:* Bed & Breakfast Texas Style, (214) 298-5433 or 298-8586. $30–$35.

Houston Area **TEXAS**

Bacliff. Close to Galveston and Texas City, this guest house is a couple of yards from a bay where guests can go fishing, swimming, or boating. Guests are invited to use the hosts' pool and patio. The host, in the catering business, prepares a full breakfast for guests. *Represented by:* Bed & Breakfast Society of Houston, B9, (713) 666-6372. $40–$50.

Baytown/Tri-Cities Beach. A contemporary plantation-style house furnished primarily with antiques, this bed and breakfast is bordered on two sides by San Jacinto Bay. The grounds feature a couple of barns, a 70-foot pier, a windmill, and a greenhouse; the home itself has porches on all four sides. Each of the five guest rooms has a private bath and air conditioning. *Represented by:* Bed & Breakfast Society of Houston, BC2, (713) 666-6372. $40–$50.

Bellaire. This Bellaire bungalow is convenient to downtown Houston, the Texas Medical Center, the Galleria area, and the Astrodome. The host, who has traveled widely, stocks the refrigerator with fresh fruit, juice, eggs, and other breakfast ingredients, which guests are invited to prepare as they will, and when. *Represented by:* Bed & Breakfast Society of Houston, BC1, (713) 666-6372. $25–$35.

Braeswood. A brick house with a landscaped backyard that features a hot tub, this bed and breakfast is near Loop 610, which makes it very convenient to Astroworld and the Astrodome. The two guest rooms share a television/sitting room. One host has a model-train collection, which interested guests can easily entice him to demonstrate. The other host, whose business is real estate, is always willing to provide any special assistance her guests might require. *Represented by:* Bed & Breakfast Society of Houston, B10, (713) 666-6372. $25–$35.

Champions. Hosted by an engineer and a schoolteacher, this bed and breakfast is in Houston's FM 1960 area, a suburban section close to shopping malls and a large commercial district. Guests are invited to use the small swimming pool in the backyard and are given a choice of two rooms—one has a double and the other matching twin beds. *Represented by:* Bed and Breakfast Society of Houston, C8, (713) 666-6372. $25–$35.

Houston Suburb. Close to a freeway that runs directly into downtown Houston, this bed and breakfast is a suburban town house in a complex with a swimming pool that guests are invited to use.

(Bed & Breakfast Society of Houston M14)

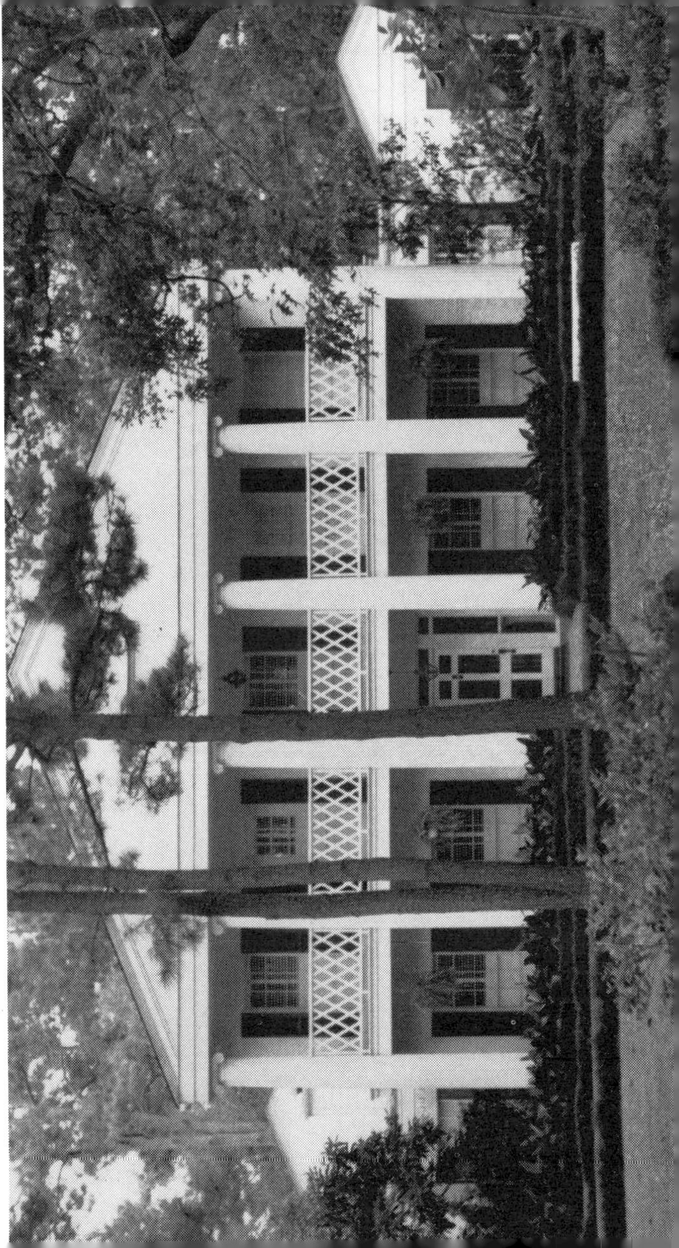

Houston Area **TEXAS**

Two rooms are available for guests, one of which has cable television, a sitting area, a coffee maker, and a private bath. The host serves a full country breakfast and bakes fresh bread daily. *Represented by:* Bed and Breakfast Society of Houston, TC5, (713) 666-6372. $25–$35.

Memorial. This scaled-down replica of an 1840 Louisiana plantation home (the hosts named it Madewood II) is smack in the heart of Houston, minutes away from Memorial Park and the Galleria. Its grounds have a swimming pool and a small games court. The hostess, who frequently uses the house for wedding receptions and parties, always leaves at least two guest rooms available, both with private entrances and use of the second-floor balconies. *Represented by:* Bed & Breakfast Society of Houston, I14, (713) 666-6372. $50–$85.

Memorial. Hosted by a career counselor, this bed-and-breakfast home is built on a square design around a landscaped atrium. In the greenhouse off one side of the living room, the hostess grows many species of bromeliads. The decor here is primarily American Indian. Two guest rooms, which share an adjoining bath, are available. *Represented by:* Bed & Breakfast Society of Houston, M30, (713) 666-6372. $25–$35.

Montrose. Hosted by a social worker and furnished with many family antiques, this bed and breakfast is convenient to much of Houston—the theater district, museums, the medical complex, numerous city parks, and finer restaurants. The guest room here has twin beds and an adjoining bath. Mauve rugs and burgundy accents suggest the decor. *Represented by:* Bed & Breakfast Society of Houston, M2, (713) 666-6372. $25–$35.

Spring Branch. Owned by an antiques dealer and her husband, this bed and breakfast is a simple brick house that is full of antiques. The two guest rooms are furnished with period American antiques, and guests are invited to peruse the hosts' various collections as well as their extensive library. The house also has an old player piano and a hot tub/spa in the backyard. The hosts serve a full breakfast, greet their guests with a welcoming drink, and place a basket of fruit in each guest room. *Represented by:* Bed & Breakfast Society of Houston SB22, (713) 666-6372. $25–$35.

Jefferson **TEXAS**

Pride House

    409 Broadway, Jefferson, TX 75657. (214) 665-2675. *Hostess:* Ruthmary Jordan.

Pride House is a Victorian building with stained-glass windows in every room. A certain Mr. Brown built the house for his daughter in 1888, and he used a great deal of hardwood in its construction. The trim, the cabinetry, the wainscoting, and the moldings are all testimony to Mr. Brown's love of wood (not to mention the fact that he owned a sawmill).

In addition to the rooms in the main house, guest accommodations are available in a small saltbox building that used to be a kitchen house. That house features a queen-size rope bed, the kitchen's original drainboard and flour bin, and an attic room with an antique desk, an Oriental rug, and walls hung with primitive watercolors.

Ruthmary's breakfast varies, sometimes including exotic melons, baked apples, or stuffed pears, and always including juices, homemade breads, jams, and coffee. Ruthmary, who used to run a restaurant, told me that her change of business was quite easy to make, adding, "I'm not professional at anything. I just do things 'cause I like 'em." Ruthmary likes running a bed-and-breakfast place.

Accommodations: 6 rooms with private bath. *Smoking:* Permitted. *Children:* Permitted in cottage only. *Pets:* Permitted in cottage only. *Breakfast:* Included. *Driving Instructions:* From Route 59 take Route 49 (Broadway) east for five blocks.

San Antonio. Hosted by a legal secretary, this bed and breakfast is twenty minutes from downtown San Antonio. The house and its decor have a decidedly Spanish influence, although one of the three guest rooms has a Governor Winthrop desk. Another has a queen-size bed and a private entrance (the bath is also private if the other guest rooms are not being used). *Represented by:* Bed & Breakfast Texas Style, (214) 298-5433 or 298-8586. $32–$38.

San Antonio. A simple brick house with a landscaped yard bordered by shrubs and flowers, this bed and breakfast is twenty minutes from the Alamo. The guest room here is decorated with a yellow-daisy theme picked up by the wallpaper, the drapes, and the spread on the king-size bed. The house is convenient to Lackland and Kelly Air Force bases. *Represented by:* Bed & Breakfast Texas Style, (214) 298-5433 or 298-8586. $38.

New Braunfels. Hosted by a couple who will advise on how to canoe or tube your way down the Guadalupe River, this bed and breakfast reflects another of the hosts' interests—restoring antique furniture. There are many antiques in the house, and the guest room has a brass bed. The hostess specializes in ethnic food, with a repertoire that includes German wurst and Mexican *taquitos. Represented by:* Bed & Breakfast Texas Style, (214) 298-5433 or 298-8586. $42–$48.

New Braunfels. Convenient to tennis and golf, this bed and breakfast is in the hot-air-balloon capital of Texas and five minutes from Southfork Ranch. The guest room has antique cherry furniture, lots of green plants, and a private bath. The hosts serve a full breakfast. *Represented by:* Bed & Breakfast Texas Style, (214) 298-5433 or 298-8586. $35–$42.

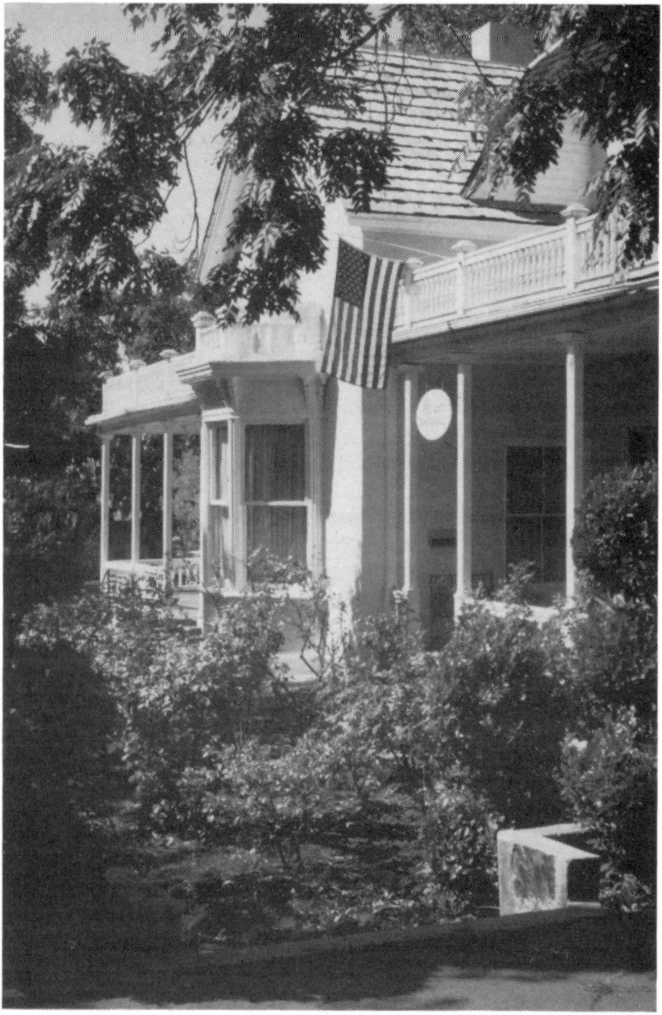

St. George **UTAH**

Seven Wives Inn

217 N 100 W, St. George, Utah, 84770. (801) 628-3737. *Hosts:* Donna and Jay Curtis.

When Donna and Jay were renovating the Seven Wives Inn, they discovered in a closet a secret passageway to the attic. Rumor has it that the original builder of their house, an 1873 Colonial, incorporated into the structure an escape route for polygamists, whom federal agents pursued with vigor in those days.

All seven bedrooms were named after the wives of Donna's polygamous great-grandfather—a closet case, perhaps, but not in any ordinary sense. One bedroom has 12-foot ceilings; a fireplace with a pine mantel painted to look like marble; a queen-sized bed with an oaken headboard 8 feet high; a 10-foot oaken armoire; and a tin tub trimmed in oak. Another bedroom features an oval-mirrored oaken dresser, two overstuffed Victorian chairs, and two beds—a queen-size one made of brass, and another fashioned of white iron trimmed with brass. Other bedrooms include such items as handmade quilts, antique pine or mahogany beds, a wood-burning stove, a fireplace, or a Franklin stove. All guest rooms come with bowls of fresh fruit and vases of roses grown in the garden.

The 20-by-30 central parlor has an oaken parquet floor; a medallioned ceiling with a brass chandelier; elaborate pine woodwork surrounding windows cut into 18-inch-thick walls; a love seat with carved lion's-head arms and red velvet upholstery; a fireplace with a painted pine mantel and a gold-framed antique mirror suspended above it; and a view of the Brigham Young home.

Donna and Jay serve a full breakfast of fresh orange juice, German apple pancakes, scrambled eggs with bacon and ham, and tea or coffee.

Accommodations: 7 rooms, 6 with private bath. *Smoking:* Not permitted. *Children:* Permitted if well behaved. *Pets:* Permitted if well behaved. *Breakfast:* Included. *Driving Instructions:* From Salt Lake City or Las Vegas, take Route I-15 to the St. George exit. Follow the signs to the Brigham Young home—Seven Wives Inn is catty corner from it.

Salt Lake City **UTAH**

Brigham Street Inn

1135 East South Temple, Salt Lake City, UT 84102. (801) 364-4461. *Hosts:* John and Nancy Pace.

An 1896 Victorian structure with Queen Anne and Classical Revival elements, Brigham Street Inn won awards from The American Institute of Architects, the Utah Heritage Foundation, and the Utah Historical Society. The building was the site of Salt Lake City's first "Designers Showcase," in which every room was put together by an interior designer. In other words, Brigham Street Inn is a showcase—an elegant juxtaposition of old and new.

The parlor has a bird's-eye-maple fireplace with a built-in mirror and acanthus-leaf carving, beige and maroon Dutch tiles, and a cast-iron cover. The fireplace is flanked by an Areca palm and a Ficus exotica; in front of it is a custom-made bird's-eye-maple coffee table with a glass top, surrounded by sleek modern furniture upholstered in beige. There's a brass vase on either side of the mantel, a brass pharmacy lamp, deep maroon vases and matching lamps, a beige carpet bordered in burgundy, and other visual treats.

The living room features a Steinway grand piano, glossy black walls highlighted by artwork and bordered by an oaken picture molding and rising to a cream-on-white ceiling. The room is indirectly lit by four cordera lamps and has a Dutch-tile fireplace with a red oak mantel, oaken floors partially covered by a cream area rug, and a hooded porter's chair upholstered in black horsehair.

The dining room features a bay window with red oak woodwork; a two-hundred-year-old tapestry woven by Tibetan nuns; a Chapman brass chandelier hanging over a large oaken dining table; a navy blue rug bordered in white; navy blue lacquered chairs upholstered in a jute herringbone; and red oak wainscoting.

The guest rooms are as beautifully appointed as the common rooms. In a word, the place is lovely.

Accommodations: 9 rooms with private bath. *Smoking:* Permitted. *Children:* Over 12 permitted. *Pets:* Not permitted. *Breakfast:* Included. *Driving Instructions:* From the east, take Route I-80 and exit on Seventh Street East, then go north to South Temple Street.

VERMONT

East Burke. A yellow contemporary ranch-style house with white trim, this guest house is on 3 secluded acres. Furnished with a combination of antique and contemporary pieces, the house has views of Burke Mountain and is 4 miles from the ski area there. *Represented by:* American Bed & Breakfast, #21, (802) 524-4731. $18–$35.

Enosburg Falls. On 600 acres of rolling hills in northern Vermont, this meticulously remodeled farmhouse is close to the Stowe, Smugglers Notch, and Jay Peak ski areas. There's also a nearby golf course and swimming hole. The hosts' children enjoy taking guests on hikes. The house is furnished with a mixture of antique and contemporary pieces. *Represented by:* American Bed & Breakfast, #2, (802) 524-4731. $18–$35.

Killington. This ski-lodge structure sits on 2 wooded acres at the base of Killington Mountain. In addition to the trees, its grounds are sprinkled with chickens, ducks, donkeys, and horses, and guests can arrange to be taken on a horse-drawn buggy ride. The Killington gondola, minutes away, operates all year—the panorama includes the Green, White, and Adirondack Mountains. *Represented by:* American Bed & Breakfast, #29, (802) 524-4731. $18–$35.

Barnet **VERMONT**

Old Homestead Inn

P.O. Box 35, Barnet, VT 05821. (802) 633-4100. *Hosts:* Robert and Mary Gordon.

Built around 1880, Old Homestead Inn is a large Colonial structure painted white with black shutters. A postman and a housekeeper, Robert and Mary Gordon dreamed of opening an inn; so they moved here from Long Island and did just that. Their house is situated on 22 acres thick with pine trees, and their property includes several streams and a waterfall.

The lounge and dining area have dark pine floors and reproduction Colonial furnishings. Mary's paintings, landscapes and seascapes influenced by Van Gogh and Gauguin, hang in the lounge area. Off the dining area there's a sun parlor with wooden walls, floors, and ceiling and with windows that overlook the mountains. The lounge area also has a bar, and Robert and Mary are happy to provide their guests with setups.

Two large guest rooms overlook the Connecticut River and the White Mountains and are furnished for the most part in oak. One room has an iron bed, a big old oblong antique mirror, and an oaken night table. Both rooms have wide-paneled maple floors, white quilts, and white ruffled curtains. They share a bath that has a pedestal sink and all of its old fixtures still intact.

Mary's breakfast includes juice, English muffins and freshly baked doughnuts, and coffee. For those with appetites still unsatisfied, Mary is willing "to make 'em something."

Accommodations: 5 rooms, 2 with private bath. *Smoking:* Permitted. *Children:* Pemitted. *Pets:* Not permitted. *Breakfast:* Included. *Member:* American Bed and Breakfast Program. *Driving Instructions:* Old Homestead Inn is 10 miles south of St. Johnsbury on Route 5.

Woodruff House

13 East Street, Barre, VT 05641. (802) 476-7745. *Hosts:* Robert R. and Terry L. Somaini.

Woodruff House is an 1883 Queen Anne structure that was remodeled years later by a wealthy granite manufacturer. Across the street from a park, it is surrounded by a well-trimmed lawn with beds of flowers and numerous trees.

Bob and Terry Somaini filled their home with an eclectic combination of furniture, which ranges from the comfortable to the formal. They have three living rooms, one of which is 18 by 24 feet, with a white-painted Georgian fireplace in one wall and built-in bookcases taking up another. The room has some pieces dating back to the late eighteenth century. There are a pair of Louis XVI chairs upholstered in striped tapestry, a couple of wing chairs, and two Oriental rugs. Another living room has key-design mahogany parquet floors, an antique piano, a couple of carved walnut panels, and a walnut Eastlake sofa covered with a navy blue pin-dot velvet.

One guest room is furnished entirely with Empire pieces, including a mahogany armoire, a mahogany sleigh bed, and a chair upholstered in tapestry. The room has a mahogany-and-oak parquet floor.

Woodruff House is close to the state capitol, the Kent Museum, and the world's largest granite quarries. Downhill skiing, cross-country skiing, and other sports are all nearby.

Accommodations: 2 rooms with shared bath. *Smoking:* Not permitted. *Children:* Permitted. *Pets:* Not permitted. *Breakfast:* Included. *Member:* American Bed and Breakfast Program. *Driving Instructions:* Woodruff House is near the center of Barre, adjacent to the park.

Brandon **VERMONT**

Stone Mill Farm
P.O. Box 203, Brandon, VT 05733. (802) 247-6137. *Hosts:* Eileen and Charles Roeder.

Federal in design, Stone Mill Farm's main farmhouse was built in 1773 by Salmon Farr, who added a guest ell in 1786. The 10-acre grounds feature a swimming pool and a logging trail, which runs through cedars and ends at the third tee of the Neshoe Golf Course.

The Roeders raise pigs, chickens, ducks, and geese, who stroll or flap around the property. They also raise berries and make maple syrup.

The house is furnished with English and American antiques, a collection the Roeders assembled during Charles's previous career as an antiques dealer and auctioneer. One guest room, furnished in antiques and wicker, has double glass doors leading onto a balcony that overlooks the pool and the neighboring dairy farm. The Roeders serve a complimentary breakfast on their porch.

Accommodations: 3 rooms, 1 with private bath. *Smoking:* Permitted. *Children:* Permitted. *Pets:* Not permitted. *Breakfast:* Included. *Member:* American Bed and Breakfast Program. *Driving Instructions:* Take Route 7 North; turn right on Route 73 East, then turn left on Dirt Lane; cross the bridge and bear right.

Craftsbury **VERMONT**

Gary-Meadows Farm

R.R. 1, Craftsbury, VT 05826. (802) 586-2536. *Hostess:* Nicki Houston.

On 700 acres of land, Gary-Meadows Farm, a computerized dairy farm with 650 registered holstein cows, includes a rambling 1884 Cape Cod-style farmhouse with a Vermont-style sun parlor. Behind the house there's a still-water pond (fed entirely by rain) where guests may go fishing and boating.

The guest room, which is available from May through October, has wide-panel pine floors, light blue walls decorated with watercolors done by a friend of the Houstons', a large wooden bed covered by a brown, blue, and beige sunburst quilt, a drop-leaf maple table, two ladder-back chairs, a maple bureau and nighttable, and two large windows with twelve panes of glass each. The living room features a walnut Empire hutch and a bureau, a walnut spool cabinet, and a series of braided rugs.

Nicki is an ex-teacher now in the process of raising three children, but she manages to find time to involve herself in the publicity activities of the Vermont Country Players, a local drama group, and to show people around her and her husband's farm.

On pressed-paint dishes, a breakfast large enough for anybody appears each morning: Juice, homemade coffee cake or muffins, three kinds of cereal, homemade jams and jellies, and coffee are part of the fare.

Accommodations: 1 room with shared bath. *Smoking:* Permitted. *Children:* Permitted. *Pets:* Not permitted. *Breakfast:* Included. *Member:* American Bed and Breakfast Program. *Driving Instructions:* Gary-Meadows Farm is 1 mile from Craftsbury Village, 500 feet off Route 14 North.

East Burke **VERMONT**

House in the Wood

R.F.D. Kirby Road, East Burke, VT 05832. (802) 626-9243.

Hosts: Jerry and Elaine Derry.

Built of four by fours, House in the Wood is a 1976 wooden-frame house. The entire structure has wooden walls and floors. Three rooms are done in butternut, one in white ash, one in brown ash, one in cherry, and the two bathrooms are done in oak. Where did all this wood come from? Host Jerry Derry, who designed the house, manages a sawmill.

The house has a 30- by 16-foot living room with seven windows that face Burke Mountain, which is a 3-minute drive from the house. The living room, carpeted wall to wall, is furnished with contemporary pieces and a few antiques such as an oaken secretary with a glass inset. There is also a large recreation room with a stone fireplace, a shuffleboard set, wall-to-wall carpeting, television, and plenty of books. Three of the guest rooms have views of Burke Mountain. Guests are invited to use any part of the house they choose, including the kitchen.

Jerry and Elaine moved into their house four years ago and realized that the two of them didn't need so much room. Renting the three bedrooms worked out so well that they transformed their attached garage into another two guest rooms.

Accommodations: 5 rooms, 2 with private bath. *Smoking:* Permitted. *Children:* Permitted. *Pets:* Not permitted. *Member:* American Bed and Breakfast Program. *Driving Instructions:* House in the Wood is on Kirby Road ¾ mile north of East Burke Village.

Essex Junction **VERMONT**

Varnum's

143 Weed Road, Essex Junction, VT 05452. (802) 899-4577.

Hosts: Todd and Sheila Varnum.

Todd and Sheila Varnum have a large 1792 cedar shake farmhouse on more than 10 acres of land. One of the oldest buildings in the area, the Varnums' place, local legend has it, used to be a tavern that catered to the passengers of one of Vermont's stagecoach lines. The property is surrounded by mountains and affords a splendid view of Mount Mansfield.

One enters Varnums' through a large country kitchen, which has a wood-burning stove and an inexhaustible supply of hot chocolate. From there one passes through a dining room and a study to enter an 18- by 33-foot living room, which has traditional furniture, ruffled curtains, and a piano.

The guest rooms are off the upstairs hallway, which has a floor of 18-inch-wide pine boards (hidden beneath plywood until recently). One guest room, done in reds, features a reproduction antique pine bed covered with a handmade quilt; and the other room, done in yellows, has an antique brass-and-iron bed.

Also off the upstairs hallway is the Varnums' spa room, which has a passive solar shower and a hot tub that seats six. This room has lots of plants and an entire wall of windows looking out on trees and mountains.

Accommodations: 2 rooms with shared bath. *Smoking:* Not permitted. *Children:* Not permitted. *Pets:* Not permitted. *Breakfast:* Included. *Member:* American Bed and Breakfast Program. *Driving Instructions:* From Essex Junction, take Route 15 east 5.7 miles, and turn left on the dirt road. Varnum's is the first house on the left. The name is on the mailbox.

Fairfax **VERMONT**

Foggy Hollow Farm

Route 104, Fairfax, VT 05454. (802) 849-6385. *Hosts:* Mr. and Mrs. Jean-Paul Bouthillette.

A working dairy farm with some seventy-five cows, Foggy Hollow Farm consists of 400 acres of land. The farmhouse was constructed sometime around 1857 and later had the distinction of being the first home in the area to be wired for electricity.

The entire farmhouse is furnished in antiques, and the ambience is substantially enhanced by the many craft pieces Mrs. Bouthillette made. Her repertoire of skills includes sewing, embroidery, millinery, patchwork, and macramé. The house is filled with plants suspended in macramé hangers.

One guest room has an antique iron bed, an oaken night table and an oaken dresser, and a brown, peach, and beige carpet. The other contains an old maple bed, a sprinkling of antique furnishings, and a navy blue and white carpet. The walls are covered with a delicate brown-on-beige calico print wallpaper. The beds are covered wtih ruffled spreads.

Mrs. Bouthillette told me that in addition to her other skills, she is also a hair stylist, although I never found out whether or not she practices that skill on guests. "I do a little bit of everything," said she.

Accommodations: 1 room with shared bath. *Smoking:* Not permitted. *Children:* Permitted. *Pets:* Not permitted. *Breakfast:* Included. *Member:* American Bed and Breakfast Program. *Driving Instructions:* Take I-89 to the St. Albans exit, then pick up Route 104 East; proceed for 8 miles—it's the white house with black shutters.

Franklin

Fair Meadows Farm Bed and Breakfast

Route 235, Franklin, VT 05457. (802) 285-2132. *Hosts:* Phil and Terry Pierce.

Fair Meadows Farm has been in Phil Pierce's family since 1853. A fire some years after that destroyed the farmhouse, but the family rebuilt it in 1896. Phil and Terry still have the only piece of furniture that survived the blaze—a parlor chair with a wicker seat.

Fair Meadows is a 480-acre working dairy farm, so don't be surprised if you run into a cow while you're taking a stroll around the property. The Pierces' land has two ponds, but the animals have them pretty well tied up, which is to say that the ponds are more for seeing than for swimming.

The guest rooms are furnished with a mixture of heirloom antiques and contemporary pieces, and each room has at least two windows, which overlook the Green Mountains, the farm's rolling hills, and the plethora of big old maple trees that surround the house and the dairy barn. The guest-room floors are particularly interesting: Phil and Terry arranged carpet remnants into what you might call mosaics. The guest rooms are filled with green plants, of which the house contains more than a hundred.

The living room, carpeted in shades of green, is comfortably furnished and contains a television set guests are invited to watch. (The Pierces will lend a portable set to guests who crave late-night movies.)

Breakfast is a treat: You can choose from bacon and eggs, blueberry muffins, pancakes, and french toast, the last two served with real maple syrup.

Accommodations: 3 rooms with shared bath; 1 with half bath. *Smoking:* Permitted. *Children:* Permitted. *Pets:* Permitted if well behaved. *Breakfast:* Included. *Member:* American Bed and Breakfast Program. *Driving Instructions:* Take I-89 north to the Swanton exit, turn right, proceed 4 miles, turn left after Nadeau's Grocery, and go 8.1 more miles.

Grafton **VERMONT**

The Hayes House

Grafton, VT 05146. (802) 843-2461. *Hostess:* Margery Hayes Heindel.

In addition to running a guest house and raising Chesapeake Bay retrievers, Margery is currently serving her fifth term as chairman of Grafton's Board of Selectmen, a local elected body with the powers of a mayor. Her house is an 1803 shingled clapboard farmhouse on land that used to contain two sawmills, both constructed about 1793. The house has two porches.

Margery's living room overlooks a field, a garden, and a covered bridge that spans the Saxtons River. The focal point of the room is a brick fireplace with a fieldstone hearth. Other features are a three-legged coffee table whose top is a 4-inch-thick slab of teak, a Second Empire-period couch with carved swan heads and velvet upholstery, a brass coffee table from India, and a maroon Oriental rug with a floral design in various shades of blue. The room's ambience reflects Margery's having lived for several years in the Orient; and the stone rubbings she made while in Thailand, which hang in this room and others, suggest her eclectic—Oriental and traditional—taste in decor.

One guest room has a corner fireplace with a fieldstone hearth, an antique rope bed with a matching chest of drawers, wide-board pine floors, and a countercross-stitch floral bouquet on the wall.

Margery's breakfasts include homemade muffins, bread, and jellies, and she keeps a pot of soup on her stove in winter.

Accommodations: 4 rooms, 1 with private bath. *Smoking:* Permitted except in bedrooms. *Children:* Permitted. *Pets:* Dogs permitted. *Breakfast:* Included. *Driving Instructions:* The house is in the town of Grafton, near the covered bridge.

Randolph **VERMONT**

Windover House

R.F.D. 2, Randolph, VT 05060. (802) 728-3802. *Hosts:* George and Shirley Carlisle.

Windover House used to be called the Mid-State Villa, after geologists had ascertained that this 1800 New England farmhouse stood on the exact geographic center of Vermont and a statewide contest had been held to find a name for it. Curiously enough, this house feels like the very center of Vermont when you're relaxing on its terrace and contemplating the 5 wooded acres that surround it. The Carlisles have some of the oldest trees in Vermont on their property. The lounge, which looks onto the terrace, has cherry paneling, a fireplace, and a color television set, and there is an enclosed porch with a fireplace and an outer terrace. Each light and airy guest room has a fine view.

Although the Carlisles don't serve complimentary meals, they offer a sort of cafeteria to guests, who can make themselves coffee or tea whenever they like.

Accommodations: 8 rooms with shared baths. *Smoking:* Permitted. *Children:* Permitted. *Pets:* Not permitted. *Driving Instructions:* Take Route I-89 to exit 4. Turn left, and go 1 ¼ miles to Randolph Drive. Turn right at the Windover House sign, and continue to the corner.

Stowe **VERMONT**

Guest House Christel Horman

Mountain Road, Stowe, Vermont. *Mailing Address:* R.R. 1, Box 1635, Stowe, VT 05672. (802) 253-4846. *Hosts:* Christel and Jim Horman.

Built in 1980, Christel and Jim's house looks like a large Swiss chalet. A balcony encircles the entire house, situated among pine trees in the beautiful Green Mountains. The grounds contain an outdoor swimming pool, lawn games, and a trout stream. When it's cold, you can begin cross-country skiing from the Hormans' front door; or you can drive 10 minutes to Stowe, one of the Northeast's best downhill-skiing areas.

All guest rooms have private baths, two double beds, wall-to-wall carpeting, and individually controlled thermostats. The parlor—where guests congregate for coffee or hot apple cider and exchange stories of frozen slopes or fish that got away—has a fireplace, wall-to-wall carpeting, contemporary early American furniture, and plenty of books and magazines. The Hormans offer a full complimentary country breakfast.

Accommodations: 8 rooms with private bath. *Smoking:* Tolerated. *Children:* Permitted. *Pets:* Not permitted. *Breakfast:* Included. *Driving Instructions:* Take Route I-89 to Waterbury; take exit 10 toward Stowe; turn left at the traffic light onto Mountain Road (Route 108) and proceed 6 miles.

Waitsfield **VERMONT**

Lareau Farm Country Inn

Route 100, P.O. Box 563, Waitsfield, VT 05673. (802) 496-4949.

Hostess: Annie Salvant.

In a meadow and with an unobstructed view of the Green Mountains, Lareau Farm Country Inn is a *circa*-1830 farmhouse, painted gray and trimmed in green and white. The grounds comprise some 45 acres bordering Camel's Hump State Forest and the Mad River ski area, which is perhaps 100 feet from the house. The major activity around here is skiing (Sugarbush is five minutes away), but if you're not inclined to slide down the side of a mountain, you might be able to talk Annie into taking you for a ride in her sled, which is propelled by two horses. The only other animal on the place is Pig, a tricolored cat with a weakness for mice.

The house is heated entirely by wood, and Annie cooks on a woodstove in the kitchen. She makes, as she shamelessly describes them, "the best pancakes in the world . . . light as air." She whips the egg whites, then douses the pancakes with real maple syrup.

All the guest rooms have antique beds—some brass, some wood, some hand-painted—and the entire house has wide-board pine flooring. One guest room is done in beiges and browns, with an antique oaken rocker, a bed and dresser made of ash, an oaken table, a brown and green Oriental throw rug, and two windows, one of which overlooks a knoll and the river.

Accommodations: 6 rooms with shared bath. *Smoking:* Permitted, but not in bedrooms. *Children:* Permitted. *Pets:* Check in advance. *Breakfast:* Included. *Driving Instructions:* Lareau Farm Country Inn is on Route 100, ¼ mile south of its junction with Route 17.

Waterbury **VERMONT**

Schneider Haus

Route 100, Box 283A, Waterbury, VT 05676. (802) 244-7726.
Hosts: George and Irene Ballschneider.

Well back from the highway and surrounded by forested mountains, Schneider Haus is a Tyrolean-style chalet that George and Irene Ballschneider built by themselves. They picked out and carried home each stone in their fireplace; they dragged lumber to the building site with a snowmobile. It took them two and a half years to build their chalet, with money they received from the sale of their New York City delicatessen. "I wanted a house like one of those hideaways you find in the Austrian Mountains," says Irene.

Each guest room, furnished with early American antiques and period reproductions, has a door leading to the balcony that wraps around the entire house. In addition to its large stone fireplace, the lounge has 21 feet of windows overlooking brilliant foliage or knee-deep snow or summer forests you can't see for the trees. George and Irene also offer tennis courts, a color television set, a sauna, a hot-tub, and a game room for the children.

Accommodations: 10 rooms, 2 with private bath. *Smoking:* Permitted. *Children:* Over 4 permitted. *Pets:* Not permitted. *Breakfast:* Included. *Member:* American Bed and Breakfast Program. *Driving Instructions:* Proceeding southward from Waterbury on Route I-89, take exit 10, 5 miles south of Waterbury.

Blue Ridge Area **VIRGINA**

Berryville. A contemporary reproduction of a Williamsburg Colonial, this bed and breakfast is on the bank of the Shenandoah River, right at the base of the Blue Ridge Mountains. The house is furnished with period antiques, and the hosts offer two guest rooms, both with king-size beds. In addition to enjoying the scenery, guests can fish or hunt if they like. *Represented by:* Blue Ridge Bed & Breakfast, (703) 955-3955. $30–$40.

Bluemont. Owned way-back-when by a Lady Paradise, this bed and breakfast is a late-eighteenth-century cabin on 35 acres next to the Appalachian Trail. The hosts, a State Department official and a computer specialist, serve a full breakfast when they're in attendance and will also prepare dinner on request. When they're elsewhere, they will rent the entire cabin, which is large enough for a family of six. *Represented by:* Blue Ridge Bed & Breakfast, (703) 955-3955. $35–$45; $300 per week for entire cabin.

Boyce. The hosts here, retired special-education professionals, like to take their guests' children on horse-and-buggy rides. They offer guests two rooms that share a bath, an arrangement suitable for a family of four or two couples traveling together. The grounds are rural and offer an unobstructed view of the Blue Ridge Mountains. *Represented by:* Blue Ridge Bed & Breakfast, (703) 955-3955. $30–$40.

Purcellville. Hosted by an electronics-industry marketing representative with a weakness for horses, this bed and breakfast, a hundred-year-old Victorian, is decorated entirely with period antiques. The three guest rooms all have rope beds. Purcellville is a small country town just east of the Blue Ridge Mountains and a little more than an hour east of Washington, D.C. *Represented by:* Blue Ridge Bed & Breakfast, (703) 955-3955. $40–$50.

Warrenton. Guest accommodations here consist of a private suite with its own entrance and porch. The house is in the foothills of the Blue Ridge Mountains, a short drive from the Skyline Drive. The hosts, previously with the Ford Foundation and the United Nations, serve a full breakfast and will prepare other meals on request. *Represented by:* Blue Ridge Bed & Breakfast, (703) 955-3955. $25–$45.

Charlottesville Area **VIRGINIA**

Chaumine. On top of a mountain 9 miles west of Charlottesville, Chaumine is a contemporary wood, stone, and glass cottage. The living room/dining room, bath, and kitchen are around a massive stone fireplace. From a deck you can see woods. Two bedrooms, a double and a king-size, are available. *Represented by:* Guesthouses Bed & Breakfast, (804) 979-8327 or 979-7264. $80–$148.

Windhaven Farm. Overlooking the Blue Ridge Mountains, Windhaven Farm offers accommodation in a private wing of a recently constructed Georgian-style home. The guest wing has a country kitchen with a wood stove, two bedrooms, a bath, and a deck. There are stables for those who bring horses, and guests can arrange to use a hot tub for a small fee. *Represented by:* Guesthouses Bed & Breakfast, (804) 979-8327 or 979-7264. $100.

Coleman Cottage. Coleman Cottage is a redecorated servants' house on Seven Oaks Farm, an antebellum estate 15 miles west of Charlottesville. At the base of Afton Mountain (the junction of the Skyline Drive and the Blue Ridge Parkway), the cottage features three bedrooms, living and dining rooms, a kitchen, a bath, and two porches with views of the spacious grounds and the surrounding mountains. *Represented by:* Guesthouses Bed & Breakfast, (804) 979-8327 or 979-7264. $155–$210.

Bavarian-style House. This split-level Bavarian-style house is 16 miles west of Charlottesville, in the Blue Ridge foothills. Each of its two guest rooms opens onto a back patio. The house is furnished mainly with antiques. *Represented by:* Guesthouses Bed & Breakfast, (804) 979-8327 or 979-7264. $40–$44.

Melrose. Halfway between Charlottesville and the Skyline Drive, this home is a composite of two eighteenth-century structures, *circa* 1738 and 1797, that were dismantled, moved, and reassembled. The guest suite has a private entrance and hallway, a fireplace, eighteenth-century paneling, kitchen privileges, and the use of a balcony overlooking the grounds, which were on the 1979 Virginia Garden Tour. *Represented by:* Guesthouses Bed & Breakfast, (804) 979-8327 or 979-7264. $56–$72.

Georgian. This large Georgian home was built in the early 1900s for the first president of the University of Virginia. A physician and his wife, your hosts, have daily help and make sure that Southern hospitality lives on. *Represented by:* Guesthouses Bed & Breakfast, (804) 979-8327 or 979-7264. $52–$56.

Charlottesville Area **VIRGINIA**

Slave Quarters Suite. The guest suite, upstairs in the former slave quarters, consists of a sitting room and two bedrooms. Your hosts, an antique dealer and his wife, have furnished their home with a combination of antiques and contemporary pieces and maintain a bonzai garden. Private entrance. *Represented by:* Guesthouses Bed & Breakfast, (804) 979-8327 or 979-7264. $52–$56.

Ednam. Conveniently as well as scenically located, this brick split-level home overlooks the Boar's Head Inn. Guest quarters have doors leading onto a patio with a private entrance. Each guest room has a private bath and shares a recreation room that has a fireplace. *Represented by:* Guesthouses Bed & Breakfast, (804) 979-8327 or 979-7264. $52–$56.

Bellair. This French country home 2 miles west of the University of Virginia has a garden, a heated pool, and two guest rooms, one with a private entrance. *Represented by:* Guesthouses Bed & Breakfast, (804) 979-8327 or 979-7264. $52–$56.

Farmington Area. This single-story Williamsburg brick structure is adjacent to the prestigious Farmington Country Club golf

Coleman Cottage (*Guesthouses Bed & Breakfast*)

"Georgian" (*Guesthouses Bed & Breakfast*)

"Georgian" (*Guesthouses Bed & Breakfast*)

Charlottesville Area **VIRGINIA**

course. Guests here occupy a private wing with a studio living room, a bedroom with twin beds, a kitchenette, and a private entrance. The rooms are furnished with American and English antiques and a collection of artifacts the hosts gathered on their extensive travels. Guests can arrange to use a pool in summer. *Represented by:* Guesthouses Bed & Breakfast, (804) 979-8327 or 979-7264. $52–$64.

Ingwood. Situated on 6 wooded acres near the sixteenth tee of the Farmington Country Club golf course, this is a lower-level apartment in a villa. The apartment features a private drive and a private entrance, a fireplace, a built-in bar in the living room, balloon curtains, and mirrored doors in the bedroom. Both the bedroom and the living room have glass-paneled sliding doors that open onto a secluded outdoor sitting area. *Represented by:* Guesthouses Bed & Breakfast, (804) 979-8327 or 979-7264. $52–$64.

Whippoorwill Farm. This early-nineteenth-century frame structure, to which a large drawing room was added in 1962, is on a horse farm in the foothills of the Blue Ridge Mountains. Guests are invited to use the private tennis court and can fish, canoe, or swim in Moorman's River, which adjoins the property. The house, which has three guest rooms, is furnished with antiques. *Represented by:* Guesthouses Bed & Breakfast, (804) 979-8327 or 979-7264. $56–$64.

Old Ordinary. The oldest section of this early-eighteenth-century frame structure is a log cabin. The guest room, which has a private entrance and a private bath, contains primitive American accessories and a walnut double bed with an early-American quilt hanging on the wall behind it. For a small fee, guests can arrange to play tennis or swim at a nearby private club. The home has been featured in the Virginia Garden Tour. *Represented by:* Guesthouses Bed & Breakfast, (804) 979-8327 or 979-7264. $48–$52.

Laurel Ridge. This 1830s log cabin is on the saddle of the West Branch of Piney Mountain, at the edge of woods. The view from here is panoramic, and guests like to breakfast on the large deck that sweeps across the west side of the cabin. The first floor has a large studio living-and-dining room with a queen-sized convertible sofa and a wood stove. Upstairs is a loft, with a double and a single bed, that overlooks the living room. *Represented by:* Guesthouses Bed & Breakfast, (804) 979-8327 or 979-7264. $80.

Downing's Cottage. Reproduced from a design by A. J. Downing, a renowned early-nineteenth-century architect, this is a picturesque country cottage. Furnished with country antiques, it offers a complete kitchen, a full bath with a shower, and a sitting area with a sofa bed. Guests are invited to use the pool—provided they don't mind sharing it with Annie, a Labrador retriever. *Represented by:* Guesthouses Bed & Breakfast, (804) 979-8327 or 979-7264. $80.

Chincoteague Island **VIRGINIA**

Year of the Horse Inn

600 South Main Street, Chincoteague Island, VA 23336. (804) 336-3221. *Hosts:* Jean and Carlton Bond.

A rambling Colonial-style structure probably built in the 1940s and added to since, painted white and trimmed black, the Year of the Horse Inn is a little less than 20 feet from Chincoteague Sound. Three of the guest rooms, all with private entrances onto the balcony, overlook the water. During breakfast on the balcony one might see a couple of hundred brants, a few industrious oyster catchers, a gaggle of snow geese, and a few cormorants. During wine at dusk, a great blue heron was seen landing on a nearby pylon.

Jean told me she thinks of her decor as having a sense of humor. Observing a life-size decoy of a whistling swan, a claw-footed mahogany fainting couch, and a flocati and ceramic rocking camel capable of supporting a 180-pound person—one must agree. But she also decorates with a certain elegance: the central parlor has a walnut Victorian washstand inlaid with burl and topped with marble, a nickel-plated hatstand complete with gargoyles, a Pakistani rug, a tuxedo couch upholstered in brown velvet, a cane couch from the 1930s upholstered in a purple fabric with a blue and white floral design and covered with a hand-crocheted bedspread, and an old lithograph of a lion.

The spotless guest rooms are simple but comfortably furnished, with wall-to-wall carpeting, light and colorful fabrics, some antiques, and private baths. One room has a full kitchenette, and a two-bedroom apartment is available.

The Year of the Horse Inn is five minutes from Chincoteague National Wildlife Refuge, which has 16 miles of undeveloped beach, large pure stands of loblolly pine, all manner of waterfowl, and Assateague's famous herd of wild ponies.

Accommodations: 3 rooms with private bath, 1 two-bedroom apartment with private bath. *Smoking:* Permitted. *Children:* Permitted. *Pets:* Not permitted. *Breakfast:* Included. *Driving Instructions:* Take Route 175 onto Chincoteague and turn right on Main Street; The Year of the Horse Inn is about ¼ mile down the road on the right.

North Gardens **VIRGINIA**

Crossroads Inn

P.O. Box 36, North Gardens, VA 22959. (804) 293-6382. *Hosts:* Stephen and Shirley Ramsey (Kirsten Wilson, manager).

A typical old brick tavern, the Crossroads Inn was built in 1818, when this area, at an elevation of 2,800 feet, was something of a trade route. After the James River Canal was destroyed in the Civil War, the flow of trade through here stopped, and the once-important thoroughfare where the Crossroads stands turned into a quiet country road. But the flow of guests continues.

Surrounded by 150-feet-tall red oaks, the Crossroads Inn is at the edge of rolling pastures sprinkled with Black Angus cows. What used to be its keeping room is now the living room, which features exposed hand-hewn pine beams on the ceiling, a checkerboard painted floor, and a brick fireplace with a pine mantel. An 1850 country sofa upholstered in a blue-and-white striped fabric, a pair of wing chairs covered in a red and blue print, a pine sugar chest, and other country antiques are evidence of Stephen's antique business.

With the exception of the bathrooms, fitted with assiduously concealed plumbing pipes and electrical wiring, the inn is completely authentic. Many of the walls feature wide-board pine paneling, the floors are their original pine, and the doors and mantels retain their original paint decoration.

Four of the guest rooms have working fireplaces, as does the cottage, a two-story accommodation that features brick floors, a brick cooking fireplace, an exposed-beam ceiling, Laura Ashley curtains, an upstairs bedroom with exposed-beam ceiling, and a deck overlooking the pastures and the grazing cattle.

The inn serves a full country breakfast.

Accommodations: 4 rooms, 2 with private bath. *Smoking:* Permitted, but not wholeheartedly. *Children:* Permitted. *Pets:* Permitted with prior approval and arrangements. *Breakfast:* Included. *Driving Instructions:* From Charlottesville, take Route 29 south for 10 miles, turn right on Route 692, and proceed about 200 yards.

"Historic Church Hill" *(Bensonhouse of Richmond)*

Richmond Area   VIRGINIA

Historic Church Hill. This 1870s Victorian structure features four working fireplaces, exposed wood and brick walls, and several skylights. Filled with plants, the house contains baskets and other craft pieces from all over the world, especially from Brazil, a past home of the owner. Your hostess, a snorkler and shell collector, draws finely detailed studies of pine cones, shells, and other natural phenomena. This home has been featured on the Church Hill Tour. *Represented by:* Bensonhouse of Richmond, (804) 648-7560 or 321-6277. $32–$40.

University of Richmond Area. Adjacent to the James River Golf

Richmond Area **VIRGINIA**

Course of the Country Club of Virginia (the brick porch in front faces the ninth green), this guest house is a two-story, brick Georgian minutes away from the University of Richmond. The house has a formal living room, a formal dining room, and a paneled study. Three guest rooms are available, all with private baths and one with a fireplace. *Represented by:* Bensonhouse of Richmond, (804) 648-7560 or 321-6277. $60–$72.

Ginter Park. Not quite as tall as the stately old magnolia that dominates its front yard, this 1920s two-story white frame house has a slate roof, an arched fireplace in the living room, double crown moldings in the living and dining rooms, and brass fixtures almost

"Hanover County" *(Bensonhouse of Richmond)*

Richmond Area **VIRGINIA**

everywhere. Your hostess, a woman whose interests include duplicate bridge and canoeing, serves homemade bread with her complimentary breakfast. *Represented by:* Bensonhouse of Richmond, (804) 648-7560 or 321-6277. $28–$36.

Hanover County. A 1790 clapboard cottage, not far from the main house on a 200-acre estate, this accommodation consists of three rooms on three levels, each with a fireplace. Furnished with antiques, the cottage has a kitchen area with exposed brick walls, an 1800 yellow-pine painted bed, thick monogrammed towels, and maid service on weekdays. Your hosts, competitive snow-skiers with careers in real estate and insurance, invite guests to use the estate's swimming pool. *Represented by:* Bensonhouse of Richmond, (804) 648-7560 or 321-6277. $80–$100.

Historic Fan District. This 1914 red-brick structure was designed by Duncan Lee, a turn-of-the-century Richmond architect. The garden room has a marble floor, and furnishings throughout are a blend of genuine antiques and period reproductions. To complement the traditional furnishings, your host has used unusual window treatments that create an open and airy effect, and has added to the decor colorful works of contemporary art. Currently in real estate, he has lived in France, Newfoundland, and New York. A skier and traveler, he has been involved in a number of Fan District renovations. *Represented by:* Bensonhouse of Richmond, (804) 648-7560 or 321-6277. $40–$48.

Fan District. The hosts totally renovated this 1910 row house, removing walls to open up the space, exposing brick, and refinishing the original pine floors and custom-milled French doors. Oriental rugs appear among a mixture of antique and contemporary pieces. The house's 13-by-29-foot kitchen was featured in the September 1982 issue of *Better Homes and Gardens. Represented by:* Bensonhouse of Richmond, (804) 648-7560 or 321-6277. $40–$48.

Clark Row. In 1900, Maben Clark, an early-twentieth-century photographer, built four connecting houses known now as The Clark Row. This home is one of these and features stained glass and old chandeliers, hollyberry-red walls in the living rooms, and fine woodwork throughout. Your hosts, university professors, are urban archaeologists who have gathered a collection of aged wood—weathered gable peaks, porch posts, fretwork—that they have incorporated into their home's decor. They have also gathered a col-

Richmond Area **VIRGINIA**

lection of cats. *Represented by:* Bensonhouse of Richmond, (804) 648-7560 or 321-6277. $32–$40.

Monument Avenue. With an attorney and a designer of custom banners as hosts, this house was designed in 1915 by Duncan Lee and served for more than thirty years as a nursing home. The hosts incorporated artifacts from demolished buildings into their renovation design. Owned at one time by a wealthy tobacconist, the house

Fan District (*Bensonhouse of Richmond*)

Richmond Area **VIRGINIA**

has entertained such guests as Charles Lindbergh, Lady Astor, and Simon Guggenheim and contains a sun-room where the decision to repeal prohibition in Virginia was reached. *Represented by:* Bensonhouse of Richmond, (804) 648-7560 or 321-6277. $52–$66.

Monument Avenue. Some of the furnishings in this 1924, cottage-style house were acquired at the 1922 Davanzanti Palace sale in Florence, Italy. Among the heirlooms here are genuine Renaissance pieces including tapestries and rugs. The main rooms have Art Deco cornices with a running design of vines or flowers, and each opens through French doors onto the marble-paved loggia (now enclosed) or the garden. *Represented by:* Bensonhouse of Richmond, (804) 648-7560 or 321-6277. $40–$48.

NOTE: For a fee, Bensonhouse of Richmond can arrange for their guests to have a luxurious breakfast in bed—bamboo trays, linen napkins, a complimentary bottle of champagne, smoked salmon, quiche lorraine, chocolates for the ladies and cigars for the gentlemen—all this delivered to the Bensonhouse accommodation you stay in by a man in a tuxedo and a woman in a French maid's outfit.

Tidewater Area **VIRGINIA**

Eastern Shore. A contemporary reproduction of a two-story Colonial Virginia home, this bed and breakfast is 4 miles from the entrance to the Chesapeake Bay Bridge–Tunnel. The house has an unobstructed view of the bay, and a private beach reserved for family, guests, and, unavoidably, such shore birds as gulls and sandpipers. The house, with wide-board pine floors, is furnished with traditional pieces as well as many antiques. The guest rooms have pines right outside their windows and share a private entrance. *Represented by:* Bed & Breakfast of Tidewater Virginia, (804) 627-1983 or 627-9409. $35–$40.

Chesapeake. This bed and breakfast is directly on a river, 20 minutes from downtown Norfolk and Portsmouth. Two guest rooms are available, each with a private bath. The hosts not only allow but urge their guests to use their all-weather tennis court. *Represented by:* Bed & Breakfast of Tidewater Virginia, (804) 627-1983 or 627-9409. $40–$45.

Norfolk. An 1893 town house opened to the public during Garden Week in Virginia, this bed and breakfast is right in the middle of Norfolk's Ghent section. The guest room has twin beds, sunlight during the day, and a fire at night (there are seven fireplaces in the house). *Represented by:* Bed & Breakfast of Tidewater Virginia, (804) 627-1983 or 627-9409. $30–$40.

Virginia Beach. On 5 acres of well-tended grass, this brick ranch-style structure is 12 miles from the ocean. The hosts, a practicing veterinarian and a retired nurse, are interested in golf and sailing. Virginia Beach affords myriad activities along its splendid beach, as well as many dining and shopping possibilities. *Represented by:* Bed & Breakfast of Tidewater Virginia, (804) 627-1983 or 627-9409. $30–$35.

Williamsburg Area **VIRGINIA**

Two Miles from Historic Area. On a large wooded lot, this two-story brick Colonial guest house has grounds with a sculptured English garden featuring meticulously trimmed hedges and many varieties of flowers. The hosts, a retired physician and his wife, have interests in architecture, archeology, history, and gardening. They also have a boat, which they keep on the lake adjacent to their backyard. The house is furnished entirely with period antiques; each guest room has a canopy bed. Guests are invited to use the library with its good stereo, television, and many books. *Represented by:* The Travel Tree, #171, (804) 229-4037 or 565-2236 evenings and weekends. $50–$60.

Four Miles from Busch Gardens. In a heavily wooded residential area, this one-and-a-half story brick Colonial features a porch and a large backyard and garden. The house is near the Colonial Parkway that connects Jamestown and Yorktown (Williamsburg, 2 miles away, is between the two towns). Furnishings combine contemporary Colonial and traditional pieces, and a collection of antique artifacts is displayed in the living room. The guest rooms on the second floor have dormer windows, small table and chair sets, and throw rugs partially covering hardwood floors. One has a four poster. *Represented by:* The Travel Tree, #113, (804) 229-4037 or 565-2236 evenings and weekends. $35.

Brick Rambler. On landscaped grounds in a wooded area, this guest house is a rambling, contemporary brick structure. There's a small lake half a block away. The hosts, seasoned travelers, have decorated their home with furnishings and accessories from all over the world. The upstairs guest room has a king-size bed, a private bath, and a private entrance; the downstairs room features twin beds and a private bath. There are nice views from just about everywhere in the house. *Represented by:* The Travel Tree, #133, (804) 229-4037 or 565-2236 evenings and weekends. $50.

WASHINGTON

Burien. Surrounded by gardens and lawns, this New England-style structure has a living room with a cathedral-style ceiling, a balcony, and an antique pump organ. The hosts, professional people, are involved in church activities and enjoy gardening and playing pool. *Represented by:* Northwest Bed & Breakfast, #152, (503) 246-8366 or 246-2383. $20–$30.

Olympia. This large 56-year-old house on 2.5 wooded acres adjacent to Puget Sound features easy access to a beach and a view of Mount Rainier. Public-health professionals, the hosts are enamored of classical music, cooking, and wines. *Represented by:* Northwest Bed & Breakfast, #106, (503) 246-8366 or 246-2383. $18–$34.

Deer Harbor **WASHINGTON**

Palmer's Chart House

P.O. Box 51, Orcas Island, Deer Harbor, WA 98243. (206) 376-4231. *Hosts:* Majean and Donald Palmer.

Seasoned, compulsive travelers with backgrounds in dance and education, Majean and Donald have a contemporary cedar bungalow with two decks overlooking Deer Harbor, a quiet, yacht-filled waterway bordered by fir-lined rock bluffs. Majean and Donald offer guests the view of the house from the water by taking them, when the skipper is available, for rides on their Rhodes-design, 33-foot Pearson sloop.

Furnished with contemporary pieces, the guest rooms feature refrigerators, wall-to-wall carpeting, thick comforters and designer sheets, private baths, and entrances onto a sun deck overlooking the water.

Rates here include dinner as well as breakfast, and before and after these meals guests may congregate in the Palmer's living room, which contains artifacts from all over the world: woodcarvings from places like Tahiti, Bali, and Haiti; a hand-carved Oriental chest made of teak; an Oriental hand-carved rosewood lamp; a leather Chesterfield couch and a matching wing chair; a pair of Italian easy chairs upholstered in oyster-colored velvet; a brick fireplace; and a collection of paintings of the Northwest.

The meals here, served family style, are substantial. Dinner is likely to consist of fresh seafood casseroles with plenty of local shrimp and crab, fresh salmon when they're running, Indonesian chicken, or some other specialty of the cook's choice.

Accommodations: 2 rooms with private bath. *Smoking:* Permitted. *Children:* Not permitted. *Pets:* Not permitted. *Breakfast:* Included along with dinner. *Driving Instructions:* From Route I-5 take Route 20 to Anacortes; then board the ferry to Orcas. Call for more specific instructions.

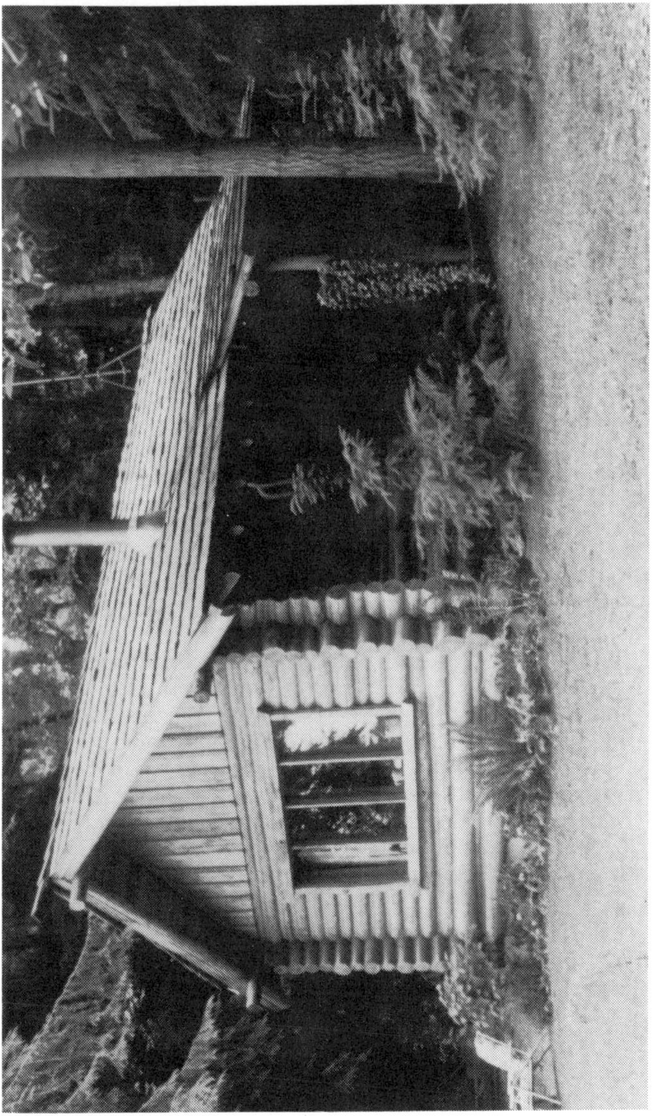

Greenbank **WASHINGTON**

Guest Houses Bed and Breakfast

835 East Christenson Road, Greenbank, WA 98253. (206) 678-3115. *Hosts:* Donald and Mary Jane Creger.

Situated on 15 heavily wooded acres complete with a private pond and a variety of firs and cedars, Guest Houses Bed and Breakfast has three private cottages including a log cabin and a carriage house. All have fireplaces, full kitchens and baths, skylights, stained glass, and antique furnishings.

The Carriage House features a stained-glass arched entry door, two skylights, a full picture window that looks out at a thickly wooded hillside; knotty-pine decor with Early American furnishings and antiques, wall-to-wall carpeting, color television, and an ornate antique double brass bed.

Hansel and Gretel, the log cabin, has stained-glass windows, a skylight, a sleeping loft bordered with log rails, Early American and oaken furnishings, wall-to-wall carpeting, trees all around, and a pond in front.

The cottages contain pull-out beds, which makes them quite suitable for four people.

The cottages can be rented with or without breakfast, which is delivered to your door the night before—cold or hot instant cereal, cream, fruit juice, an egg in an eggcup, coffee, croissants or home-baked breakfast rolls, cheeses, butter and jam, and fresh fruit in season. On Sundays, a gourmet breakfast is available.

Greenbank is on ruggedly beautiful Whidbey Island, which contains the nation's first historical reserve, 17,400 acres of it.

Accommodations: 3 cottages with private bath and 2 rooms with shared bath. *Smoking:* Permitted outside only. *Children:* Under 15 not permitted. *Pets:* Not permitted. *Breakfast:* Not included but optional. *Driving Instructions:* From Mukilteo, take the ferry to Whidbey Island and follow Route 525 for 16 miles; watch for the Twin View Realty sign on the left—Christenson Road is the next road. Make a left there and enter the first loggated driveway on your right.

Langley **WASHINGTON**

The Saratoga Inn

4850 South Coles Road, Langley, WA 98260. (206) 221-7526.

Hosts: Debbie and Ted Jones.

On 25 acres of woods and meadows crisscrossed by paths, The Saratoga Inn is a 1982 two-story shingled structure, with sunbursts on its gables, beveled glass around its entrance, a front porch complete with an old church pew, and a side deck that overlooks the garden. The house itself overlooks the Saratoga Passage, a strait that separates Whidbey Island and the Washington mainland.

The central living room features a brick fireplace, oaken floors partially covered by a navy blue and white striped carpet, a walnut dining table surrounded by Chippendale chairs, 10-foot-high ceilings, and French doors that lead onto the deck, which overlooks Saratoga Passage.

One guest room has a Franklin stove on a brick hearth, a blue ceiling and blue windows, a mahogany Chippendale chair upholstered in needlepoint, a bent-willow bed complete with down pillows, and a view of Saratoga Passage. Most rooms here have views, whether of the water, the Cascade Mountains, or the meadows surrounding the house. One has a fireplace.

For the arboreally inclined, Debbie and Ted have a treehouse large enough for four and all but invisible when the trees have their leaves.

The hosts serve a Continental breakfast including homemade muffins and homemade jams and jellies. They also have bicycles that guests are invited to use.

Accommodations: 5 rooms with private bath. *Smoking:* Not permitted. *Children:* Not permitted. *Pets:* Not permitted. *Breakfast:* Included. *Driving Instructions:* From Seattle, take Route I-5 north to the Whidbey Island–Mukilteo Ferry exit (189); continue on to Mukilteo and catch a ferry to Whidbey Island. Follow the signs to Langley. From the north, cross the Deception Pass Bridge on Route 20 and take Route 525 south to Langley.

Leavenworth **WASHINGTON**

Brown's Farm

11150 Highway 209, Leavenworth, WA 98826. (509) 548-7863. *Hosts:* Steve and Wendi Brown.

Steve and Wendi, with a little help from their children, built this cedar and log structure themselves. They cut and peeled the logs (primarily Douglas fir and lodgepole pine) and hauled the granite for the fireplace all the way from Icicle River valley. Steve figures he and Wendi saved the Forest Service a small fortune by removing the granite, which falls off the cliffs and sometimes blocks the roads.

The fireplace takes up half a wall of the Brown's living room, which is furnished with country antiques and such family heirlooms as a hand-carved covered wagon that Steve's father made for his mother (who was born in a covered wagon). The room has exposed logs on the ceiling, wall-to-wall carpeting, old Charles Russell prints, two Early American-style couches, an oaken rocker, an antique piano, and a hand-braided rug in front of the hearth.

The guest rooms are also furnished with country antiques and heirlooms. One room has an antique pine chest with a rooster carved into it, an Oriental rug, a rocker, a down comforter, and a quilt Steve's great-grandmother made hanging on the wall. The room overlooks the yard, where the Browns' horses often play, and in the distance you can see the Wenatchee National Forest, which adjoins the Brown's property.

The Browns have twenty chickens that supply fresh eggs for breakfast, a pony, a horse, six rabbits, some dogs, cats, and a rooster that holds forth briefly at 5:30 A.M.

Accommodations: 2 rooms with shared bath. *Smoking:* Permitted, but not in guest rooms. *Children:* Permitted. *Pets:* Not permitted. *Breakfast:* Included. *Driving Instructions:* Brown's Farm is off Route 2, a mile and a half from Leavenworth—call for specific instructions.

Leavenworth **WASHINGTON**

Edel Haus Bed and Breakfast

320 Ninth Street, Leavenworth, WA 98826. (509) 548-4412. *Hosts:* Mark and Betsy Montgomery.

A white stucco, two-story Bavarian-style structure built in the 1930s, Edel Haus originally served as a boardinghouse for doctors working at a nearby hospital. The grounds are sprinkled with forty-year-old trees—juniper, maple, blue spruce, a ponderosa pine with a very crooked neck, a flowering crab apple—and hundreds of tulips, as well as roses, daffodils, petunias, and peonies.

The central living room has its original light green wool carpeting; a fireplace with a pine mantel and a hearth of porcelain tiles in varying shades of red; an old globe that opens into a bar; two Early American couches (one upholstered in orange corduroy, the other in a striped cotton); and a huge bay window overlooking the Wenatchee River. Another window affords a view of the Enchantment Peaks, part of the Cascade Mountains. Indirect track-lighting over the fireplace illuminates a 3-foot-high Bavarian cuckoo clock made from five different kinds of wood.

Two of the guest rooms have wrought-iron balconies, one of which overlooks the riverfront park. The other balcony, opened onto by French doors, looks out at the Cascades. Furnished with many antiques, the rooms are light, airy, and comfortable.

Mark and Betsy also have a secluded patio with stunning views and a hot tub. Mark gives instruction in cross-country skiing and has equipment that guests can rent.

Breakfast includes fresh fruit, homemade sweet breads, French toast with cinnamon butter, and blackberry pancakes with sour cream and honey.

Accommodations: 4 rooms, 1 with private bath. *Smoking:* Not permitted in the bedrooms, but there's a smoking area for guests. *Children:* Permitted in the room with private bath. *Pets:* Not permitted. *Breakfast:* Included. *Driving Instructions:* Leavenworth is due east from Seattle on Route 2.

Leavenworth **WASHINGTON**

Haus Rohrbach Pension

12882 Ranger Road, Leavenworth, WA 98826. (509) 548-7024.

Hosts: Bob and Kathryn Harild; Greg and Sharon Lunz.

Inspired by stays in European pensions, William Rohrbach built this Bavarian-style chalet in 1975. The house, on 15 acres at the base of Tumwater Mountain, has three levels of balconies that overlook farmlands and the town of Leavenworth, an elaborate reconstruction of a Bavarian village.

Many of the guest rooms have doors that open onto a balcony. The rooms themselves are spare and simple, with brown wall-to-wall carpeting and platform beds with firm foam mattresses. The rooms feature a great deal of woodwork, which Mr. Rohrbach and his sons apparently labored at—the platform beds, some of which sport down comforters, were made by hand, and of fir.

The central living room is 36 by 24 feet and has dark-stained pine wainscoting, an exposed-beam ceiling of fir, two davenports, and a wood stove sometimes used as a fireplace. Haus Rohrbach also features an outdoor heated pool and a Jacuzzi-style hot tub large enough for eight. Cross-country skiers, who can rent equipment and get lessons here, use the hot tub even in winter. You can also use the pool in the winter, if you can deal with the air temperature when you finish swimming.

The breakfast is a full one: homemade cinnamon rolls, eggs with ham or sausage, sourdough pancakes, coffee or tea.

Accommodations: 13 rooms, 2 with private bath, and a private chalet that sleeps six. *Smoking:* Permitted in the common room only. *Children:* Permitted. *Pets:* Not permitted. *Driving Instructions:* Leavenworth is due east from Seattle on Route 2; slightly west of town, look for an Arco station and take Ski Hill Drive 1 mile north; then turn left on Ranger Road.

Port Townsend **WASHINGTON**

The James House

1238 Washington Street, Port Townsend, WA 98368. (206) 385-1238. *Hosts:* Rod and Deb La Montagne.

An 1889 Victorian structure, the James House was built by Francis Wilcox James, a wealthy English capitalist who had careers as a customs inspector, an Indian agent, and an assistant lighthouse keeper. Mr. James built the house to retire in, but his wife died just seven weeks after the two of them moved in. Not a man enamored of spending time alone, Mr. James, shortly after his loss, married his housekeeper, a 24-year-old woman 53 years his junior. The marriage later ended in divorce.

The house that Mr. James built has sweeping views of Port Townsend, Mount Rainier, Quimpec Sound, and the Cascades. It contains such stuff as ornately carved fireplaces in both the parlor and the library, parquet floors fashioned of oak, walnut, and cherry, and carved brass door hinges.

What used to be the master bedroom is now the bridal suite: a pair of rooms with parquet floors, a fireplace, a small private balcony, and a view of Puget Sound. The guest rooms, most of which have water or mountain views or both, are decorated with antiques and plants. Among the accommodations to choose from are two garden suites, one with a wood-burning stove, each of which has two rooms and views of the water.

Accommodations: 12 rooms, 4 with private bath. *Smoking:* Permitted. *Children:* Under 12 not permitted. *Pets:* Not permitted. *Breakfast:* Included. *Driving Instructions:* The James House is on the bluffs in Port Townsend.

Port Townsend **WASHINGTON**

Lizzie's

731 Pierce Street, Port Townsend, WA 98368. (206) 385-4168 or (206) 385-9826. *Hostsess:* Thelma Scudi.

Lizzie's is an 1887 Italianate mansion secluded by hedges and shaded by mature plantings such as a pear tree and a plum tree that are as old as the house. Lizzie's is owned and operated by Thelma Scudi, whose careers have included running a construction company, working in the aerospace industry, and designing kitchens.

Thelma once owned an antique business, which perhaps explains how she managed to acquire some of her furnishings. The parlor has a Chinese red wall-to-wall carpet, a hand-painted metal fireplace with a navy blue leather Chesterfield couch facing it, a red leather

Chippendale wing chair, and a Queen Anne wing chair and ottoman upholstered in a navy and cream blazed chintz. The room has its original wall and ceiling papers, a Knabe rosewood grand piano, and on either side of the fireplace a tapestry that came from the original production of *Flower Drum Song*. A life-size statue of a Chinese temple guard watches over all of this, and so does Thelma, whose conversation I recommend.

The rooms, most of them with water views, are furnished with antiques, and Thelma has a local chemist make glycerine soaps and apricot lotions and bubble baths for her guests.

Breakfast here is served at the whim of the cook; seconds are encouraged.

Accommodations: 7 rooms, 2 with private bath. *Smoking:* Permitted. *Children:* Permitted "if they can function graciously in an adult environment." *Pets:* Not permitted. *Breakfast:* Included. *Driving Instructions:* Lizzie's is one block from Puget Sound and six blocks from the edge of the Port Townsend bluffs.

Seattle Area **WASHINGTON**

Private Beach. Surrounded by a landscaped garden, this contemporary home has views of Puget Sound and the Olympic Mountains. A trail leads from the house to a private beach where the hosts and their guests often go for walks at low tide. The hosts, who have interests in gardening, tennis, and hiking, invite guests to use their canoe and rowboat as well as their library. *Represented by:* Northwest Bed & Breakfast, #180A, (503) 246-8366. $24–$28.

Near the University. This bed and breakfast in a quiet residential neighborhood is a *ca.* 1920 house with a large yard and a deck. It is a mile from the University of Washington and the Medical School, where the host, a research biologist, teaches. The Seattle Yacht Club, the University Arboretum, and the Japanese Gardens are all close by. The host is interested in social and peace issues, and in music, theater, and art. He has a dog who usually hangs around in the house, and two cats who live primarily outdoors. *Represented by:* Northwest Bed & Breakfast, #178, (503) 246-8366. $20–$28.

Condominium. Six minutes from downtown Seattle, this large condominium has views of the mountains, a lake, and the city. Guests are invited to use the pool and sauna at the condominium complex. The hosts, fluent in Norwegian, will pick up guests in Seattle. *Represented by:* Northwest Bed & Breakfast, #174, (503) 246-8366. $25–$35.

View. Your hosts—conversant in French and fond of opera, sports, and travel—have a contemporary home that affords spectacular views of Lake Washington. The bedroom has a television set, and the hosts are willing to pick guests up at the airport. *Represented by:* Northwest Bed & Breakfast, #150, (503) 246-8366 or 246-2383. $22–$30.

Vashon **WASHINGTON**

The Swan Inn

Route 5, Box 454, Vashon, WA 98070. (206) 463-3388. *Hosts:* Dick and Jeri Bain.

Built in the mid-1970s, The Swan Inn is a beautiful reconstruction of a fourteenth-century Tudor inn—the Crown Inn of Surrey, England, as a matter of fact. Although the house is new, it was constructed in large part from antique materials salvaged from older structures. Most of the windows, for example, are of either stained or leaded glass (every bedroom in the place has a stained-glass window, as does the living room) that was brought here from England.

The house sits on 10 acres of land sprinkled with Douglas firs, birches, and maples; and the Bains raise cows, chickens, and ponies.

The living room features an exposed-beam (some salvaged antiques, some new) Douglas fir ceiling; a brick Rumford fireplace; a large Persian Heriz rug woven primarily in blues, browns, and ivories; a Pakistani Bokhara rug; wide-board pine floors stained dark walnut; a 1775 oak and mahogany grandfather clock with a brass dial; two English Windsor chairs flanking a small oaken table; a contemporary overstuffed couch that picks up the colors of the Heriz; and artwork including antique brass rubbings, Hogarth prints, and a large oil painting of the Crown Inn. On the way to the bedrooms, on the stairway landing, is another grandfather clock, this one made in 1790.

One bedroom has a New York State four-poster bed made of mahogany and covered with a white-on-white bedspread and an afghan; stained- and leaded-glass windows; an oaken Georgian-style tilt-top table; a large mahogany English dresser; a Queen Anne side table; an Austrian shaving stand; and a solid fir door.

Accommodations: 3 rooms, 1 with private bath. *Smoking:* Permitted. *Children:* Over 10 permitted. *Pets:* Not permitted. *Breakfast:* Included. *Driving Instructions:* The Swan Inn is on Route 5, 2½ miles west of Vashon, on an island in Puget Sound.

Reminder: Rates and credit-card information are listed in the index.

Milwaukee **WISCONSIN**

Tudor Style—Private Entrance. A contemporary Tudor-style home in Milwaukee's northeast lakeshore area, this bed and breakfast is a block from the University of Wisconsin at Milwaukee, about fifteen minutes by bus from downtown. A former New Yorker, the hostess is a social work director at a Milwaukee Hospital and offers guests a third-floor bedroom with a private entrance and bath. The room, done in warm reds and white, has a slanted ceiling, lace doilies here and there, and lots of hanging flowering plants. *Represented by:* Bed & Breakfast of Milwaukee, (414) 342-5030. $40–$45.

Antiques. Furnished with mid-eighteenth-century antiques, the guest room here features a small rose-patterned wallpaper and a private bath, and overlooks a garden. The house, a traditional Milwaukee bungalow with a large front porch and a sloping roof, is about three quarters of a mile from the lake. The hostess, a lawyer who works in the health field, is assisted in most matters by her eight-year-old son. A short walk will get you to the University of Wisconsin at Milwaukee, and a bus that runs directly into downtown stops a block away. *Represented by:* Bed & Breakfast of Milwaukee, (414) 342-5030. $35–$40.

Cedarburg. Furnished with early American antiques, this bed and breakfast is an 1860s structure built of cream city brick, a local material. Twenty minutes from downtown Milwaukee, Cedarburg is an historic town that features a converted mill that now houses craft shops boutiques as well as a former brewery currently full of artists' galleries. This house is right off Main Street and features a fireplace in the living room and a woodburning stove in the kitchen. Ideal for a family or two couples traveling together, the accommodations include two bedrooms with a shared sitting room. *Represented by:* Bed & Breakfast of Milwaukee, (414) 342-5030. $30–$50.

Sturgeon Bay **WISCONSIN**

White Lace Inn

16 North Fifth Avenue, Sturgeon Bay, WI 54235. (414) 743-1105.

Hosts: Bonnie and Dennis Statz.

So named for its profusion of white lace curtains, White Lace Inn is a 1903 Eastlake Victorian painted white and trimmed in green. The house has a hexagonal tower and a wraparound, column-supported porch, which is furnished with white wicker pieces and dressed up with hanging flower baskets. The house is in a residential area, on slightly less than an acre—in front of it there's a lawn and two clumps of white birches. The grounds also contain an 1883 Victorian, which Bonnie and Dennis had moved here—they're currently restoring the house, each of whose rooms has a fireplace.

The central living room has a hardwood maple floor, oaken woodwork, a bay window covered with white lace curtains, a brass fireplace, and many antiques. A carved-oak archway leads from the living room to the parlor, which has a floral-print Oriental rug in shades of burgundy and plum. One guest room has a brass bed with a hand-crocheted canopy, a green rug partially covering its maple floor, floral-print wallpaper, and access to the tower room, which has a desk and a few chairs. All the guest rooms contain some antiques and have private baths and, of course, white lace curtains.

Sturgeon Bay and its environs, Door County, are on a peninsula that juts into Lake Michigan, forming 250 miles of shoreline.

Accommodations: 5 rooms with private bath. *Smoking:* Permitted. *Children:* Ask in advance. *Pets:* Not permitted. *Breakfast:* Included. *Driving Instructions:* From Green Bay, take Business Route 42–57 North into Sturgeon Bay; cross the bridge into downtown, at which point you'll be on Michigan; proceed along Michigan to Fifth Avenue and turn left—White Lace Inn is on your right.

CANADA

40 Acres of Parkland (*Alberta Bed and Breakfast*)

Country Living (*Alberta Bed & Breakfast*)

ALBERTA

40 Acres of Parkland. Twenty minutes from downtown Edmonton, this contemporary home has a backyard that's contiguous with 40 acres of parkland. The park has a man-made lake stocked each year with trout, which are yours to take and eat if you can catch them. In winter, guests can ski cross-country or skate on the lake. The hosts enjoy taking guests on tours and will arrange for a baby-sitter or baby-sit themselves. *Represented by:* Alberta Bed & Breakfast, (403) 462-8885. $20–$35.

Two-Bedroom Suite. This contemporary home is in a quiet residential neighborhood, 20 minutes by public transportation from downtown Edmonton. The house has a large garden and a patio, both of which guests are invited to use, and the guest suite has two bedrooms, a rumpus room with a Hide-a-Bed, a private bath, and a private entrance. *Represented by:* Alberta Bed & Breakfast, (403) 462-8885. $20–$35.

Country Living. Situated in the wide-open spaces, this contemporary home has a small greenhouse beside it and numerous bird feeders, which are easily seen through the house's many large windows. The guest room, done in yellows and golds, has a private bath. There's plenty of room on the property for guests to bring along a trailer or a boat. *Represented by:* Alberta Bed & Breakfast, (403) 462-8885. $20–$35.

Airport Pickup. The host, the director of the local Senior Citizen Day Centre, is willing to pick guests up at the airport and also to conduct tours and arrange for baby-sitting or do it himself. Three guest rooms available, one with a private bath. Public transportation stops at the front door. *Represented by:* Alberta Bed & Breakfast, (403) 462-8885. $20–$35.

Vancouver Area **BRITISH COLUMBIA**

Third Avenue near Alma. Mrs. Darragh offers guests a large bedroom that opens onto a rear garden. This accommodation, one block from a bus stop, is convenient to beaches, the University of British Columbia, and the planetarium. Mrs. Darragh offers a Continental breakfast and, if you check with her in advance, may well let you bring your pet. Call Mrs. Darragh, (604) 224-3854. Member of Town & Country Bed & Breakfast in B.C. $20–$35.

Twenty-seventh Avenue near McKenzie. Mrs. Smith, a Scotswoman, has a 1945 West Coast-style house surrounded by evergreens, birches, poplars, and a garden. There is a large patio on the grounds, and the house has a spacious deck that overlooks the city. From elsewhere in the house there are views of the mountains and the ocean. The guest quarters consist of a bedroom with a private bath and a private entrance, and guests may use the recreation room, with its fireplace, books, games, small pool table, and television. Call Mrs. Smith, (604) 738-9160. Member of Town & Country Bed & Breakfast in B.C. $25–$40.

Ladner. Featured in a promotional film about bed-and-breakfast places, this guest house recently received a Heritage Restoration Award. Host Joan Hoar has a Victorian farmhouse, as well as a barn, situated on 200 acres. One guest room has a view of fields; and the other, a view of the mountains. The house, simply but comfortably furnished, is 5 minutes from the Victoria Ferry to Vancouver Island. Call Joan Hoar, (604) 946-7886. Member of Town & Country Bed & Breakfast in B.C. $30.

Mountroyal and Skyline. Perched at the 900-foot level of Grouse Mountain, this guest house features a great deal of glass and a wraparound balcony and garden patio that overlook Vancouver and the harbor from the north. The house, which has something of an Oriental feeling about it, was designed by one of the hosts, an engineer. The living room has 12-foot ceilings, and the entrance hall has cathedral ceilings. You can walk to the Grouse Mountain Skyride from here, and the Baden Powell Trail is a mile away. Call Mrs. Copes, (604) 987-8988. Member of Town & Country Bed & Breakfast in B.C. $20–$30.

Cliffridge and Clements. Twenty minutes north of downtown Vancouver and 5 minutes from the ocean, this contemporary house offers guests a combined bedroom and sitting area with a brick fireplace that has a slate hearth. The walls are wood-paneled, the

Vancouver Area **BRITISH COLUMBIA**

floor is covered with a red shag carpet, and the room overlooks the garden, which has rhododendrons, an azalea bush, and large hedges. The house is in a scenic area near a salmon hatchery. Call Mrs. Hansen, (604) 988-5307. Member of Town & Country Bed & Breakfast in B.C. $20–$30.

St. James and Mahon. Architecturally something of a Colonial structure, this guest house has three rooms for guests. Decorated primarily in yellows, two of the rooms have views of the garden (planted with roses, rhododendrons, begonias, and geraniums), and the other room, which has a fireplace, faces the mountains. There's public recreation two blocks from the house—a pool, a sauna, tennis courts, and other recreational facilities are available to guests. Call Mr. or Mrs. Poole, (604) 987-4594. Member of Town & Country Bed & Breakfast in B.C. $35.

ONTARIO

Caledon. Situated on 3 acres near Caledon, Lothlorien is a restored Victorian farmhouse. A spiral staircase leads to the guest rooms. Hosts Gord and Joan are interested in cooking and their two Irish setters, among other things. Their house is close to cross-country and downhill skiing facilities, and the Bruce Trail is nearby. *Represented by:* Country Host, (519) 941-7633. $28-$35.

Hockley Valley. Paul and Ingrid have a bungalow on 2 acres of grounds not far from scenic Hockley Valley, which is popular among bird-watchers and photographers. First-rate trout fishing is less than a mile away, and golf is also close by. Paul and Ingrid offer guests two double rooms. *Represented by:* Country Host, (519) 941-7633. $28-$35.

Orangeville. The garden of this split-level home opens onto the Minora Conservation area, an all-season recreation area with both a beach and cross-country ski trails. Nearby Orangeville Raceway will appeal to racing fans, as well as anyone who enjoys a first-rate buffet. *Represented by:* Country Host, (519) 941-7633. $28-$35.

Shelburne. This restored 1907 house is on a 116-acre farm that has both donkeys and ponies. Fond of children, hosts Hilda and Cecil frequently take them for donkey, pony, or hay rides. The area offers excellent fishing and hiking, and Wasaga Beach, on Georgian Bay, is only 20 miles distant. *Represented by:* Country Host, (519) 941-7633. $28-$35.

Ottawa Area **ONTARIO**

Downtown. This turn-of-the-century Victorian-style house is conveniently located in downtown Ottawa. Constructed of brick and trimmed in beige, the house has a gabled roof, as well as gable-roofed porches on the second floor. The guest room has twin beds and a private bath, and on the second floor is a private sitting room for guests. *Represented by:* Ottawa Area Bed & Breakfast, #B-13, (613) 563-0161. $25–$30.

Ashton. A few miles outside the village of Ashton in rural eastern Ontario and 30 miles from downtown Ottawa, this guest house is a meticulously restored 1851 stone structure on 75 acres of cedar bushes, maples, and farmland. It is furnished with Colonial pieces, such as cannonball beds, many of them antiques. Surrounded by small historic villages, the property offers miles of walking trails. The hosts are fluent in both English and Dutch. The guest rooms have private sitting rooms and baths. *Represented by:* Ottawa Area Bed & Breakfast, #B-107, (613) 563-0161. $25–$30.

North Gower. On a hillside and surrounded by maples, this guest house is a modern, white brick structure with black shutters and a redwood deck. It sits on 25 acres of land, which is used, primarily, to keep horses and make maple syrup. Hosted by two retired farmers and their sister, the house is twenty minutes from downtown Ottawa. *Represented by:* Ottawa Area Bed & Breakfast, #B-103, (613) 563-0161. $25–$30.

Nepean and Ottawa. This stone-and-stucco bungalow is 15 minutes from the Parliament Buildings and the Arts Centre. The front yard contains three large spruce trees and a mature beech, and the backyard and patio are totally enclosed by a 10-foot-high cedar hedge. Inside there's wall-to-wall carpeting, teak furniture, and a recreation room. *Represented by:* Ottawa Area Bed & Breakfast, #B-28, (613) 563-0161. $25–$30.

Linhenlea. This 1927 two-story red brick structure is hosted by a National Museums of Canada strategic planner and a marketing administrator. It is within walking distance of Government House and the prime minister's residence. One can also walk to the National Arts Gallery from here. Furnished with a combination of antique and traditional pieces, the home features hardwood floors covered here and there with area rugs. *Represented by:* Ottawa Area Bed & Breakfast, #B-30, (613) 563-0161. $25–$30.

Eglinton and Kipling. This accommodation, located at the highest point in Toronto, commands a unique view of the city. It is in a condominium apartment with a carpeted terrace, air conditioning, a heated pool, a sauna, a gym room, laundry facilities, and security parking—all for the use of the guests. Call Marguerite Beaven, (416) 248-5722. Member of Toronto Bed & Breakfast, (416) 233-3887 (evenings and weekends only). $30–$45.

Dupont and Spadina. This late-nineteenth-century antique-filled house has four guest rooms, one of them with a queen-size brass bed. Near Taylor Park and Toronto's Greek section, this guest house is 20 minutes from downtown. Call Ms. Fox, (416) 690-5549. Member of Toronto Bed & Breakfast, (416) 233-3887 (evenings and weekends only). $45.

Bathurst and College. In the Kensington area, which is convenient to all of downtown Toronto's attractions, this accommodation consists of three rooms available to guests. One—a large master bedroom with air conditioning and television—has a balcony overlooking the street. Guests are invited to use the backyard's table and barbecue. English, Ukrainian, Polish, and German are spoken. "Come sample our blueberry muffins." Call Dan Martyniuk, (416) 364-7726. Member of Toronto Bed & Breakfast, (416) 233-3887 (evenings and weekends only). $25–$35.

Don Mills and Shepard. Your hosts invite guests to sun in their garden, watch television in their family room, and join them for a cup of tea each evening. These accommodations, twenty minutes from downtown, consist of two rooms for guests. English, French, and Spanish are spoken. Call Ruth or Gerald Maher, (416) 494-5433. Member of Toronto Bed & Breakfast, (416) 233-3887 (evenings and weekends only). $25–$38.

Montreal Area **QUEBEC**

Eight-Room Duplex. This accommodation—either of two rooms in an eight-room lower duplex—comes complete with eggs Benedict for breakfast. Your hosts, a recently retired couple fluent in English and French, make silver jewelry as a hobby. Convenient to public transportation. *Represented by:* Montreal Bed and Breakfast, #4, (514) 735-7493 or 738-3859. $28–$40.

Fireplace. This accommodation offers one single and one twin-bedded room for guests. The living room, accented with oak, has a fireplace. In the northeastern section of Notre Dame de Grace, this six-room semidetached home is two minutes from a subway direct to downtown Montreal. *Represented by:* Montreal Bed and Breakfast, #1, (514) 735-7493 or 738-3859. $25–$40.

La Cité Complex. A short walk from McGill University and just about all downtown Montreal attractions, this bed and breakfast is a twenty-ninth-floor apartment. When atmospheric conditions are right, you'll literally be sleeping in the clouds here, and when it's clear, you'll have a panoramic view of Montreal and the mountains. Health club facilities are available to guests. *Represented by:* Montreal Bed & Breakfast, (514) 735-7493 or 738-3859. $30–$40.

The Boulevard. On the border of Upper Westmount, this Victorian town house is more than a century old and has three fireplaces, a spectacular stairway, an interior of brick and natural wood, a plethora of paintings and antiques, and views of the city. There's a large veranda off the kitchen, and there are extensive grounds in back. The hosts are both attorneys, and they enjoy making arrangements to serve their guests dinner. *Represented by:* Montreal Bed and Breakfast, #9, (514) 735-7493 or 738-3859. $30–$50.

Off Sherbrooke Street. Two minutes from the Vendome Métro station, this seven-room lower duplex features a living-room fireplace and some unusual antique dining-room furniture. The hostess, who is in charge of a television network's library, is interested in art, literature, politics, tennis, and squash. *Represented by:* Montreal Bed and Breakfast, #2, (514) 735-7493 or 738-3859. $28–$40.

Upper Westmount. A family of five and a dog who enjoys company are hosts of this bed and breakfast, a three-story, eleven-room house. The grounds feature a patio, and the hosts offer guests a large family room with two double beds and a private bath. *Represented by:* Montreal Bed & Breakfast, (514) 735-7493 or 738-3859. $50.

Montreal Area **QUEBEC**

Girouard Park. Hosted by an energetic couple in their seventies, this three-story cottage faces Girouard Park. Maria swims regularly and gardens (guests are invited to enjoy the garden behind the house), and her husband is an avid reader. One guest room has a private sun porch, and the house contains a well-stocked library. Between them, the hosts speak eight languages. *Represented by:* Montreal Bed and Breakfast, #3, (514) 735-7493 or 738-3859. $28-$40.

Mount Royal Park. This 1920s stone mansion is at the edge of Montreal's impressive Mount Royal Park. The house has views of the St. Lawrence River and of downtown Montreal, which is a fifteen-minute walk from here. There are jogging and hiking trails just outside the back door. Both guest rooms have private baths and cable television. *Represented by:* Montreal Bed and Breakfast, #6, (514) 735-7493 or 738-3859. $35-$50.

Outremont. This ten-room cottage in the old and elegant section of Outremont has been in the same family for seventy-five years. It is near several of Montreal's prettier parks and the chic Lourier Avenue. Two guest rooms have double beds, and one has twins. There is excellent transportation to downtown. *Represented by:* Montreal Bed and Breakfast, #5, (514) 735-7493 or 738-3859. $25-$35.

Beaconsfield. Overlooking Lake St. Louis, this nine-room cottage has three rooms available to guests—two singles and a twin. The location, twenty minutes by car from downtown, is in the West Island community of Beaconsfield. The household includes two cats and a dog. *Represented by:* Montreal Bed and Breakfast, (514) 735-7493 or 738-3859. $25-$40.

Quebec City Area **QUEBEC**

Ste-Foy. On a hill overlooking the Saint Lawrence River and surrounded by mature maples and flower gardens, this guest house is a French-Canadian two-story structure, painted white and trimmed in gray. It is furnished entirely with antiques, most of them family heirlooms. All the rooms have maple floors partially covered with area rugs, including a pink-and-blue Persian in the living room. The living room features a fireplace, and the guest room, painted pale green, contains antique French provincial furniture. Thérèse, the Hostess, owns and operates the Gîte Québec bed-and-breakfast agency. *Represented by:* Gîte Québec, (418) 651-1860. $30–$50.

Charlesbourg. This gray stone house built in the late 1950s is a replica of a late-nineteenth-century French-Canadian design. Situated on grounds sprinkled with birches and maples, it offers a view of Quebec City, which is 8 miles away. Furnished with a mixture of modern and antique pieces, it has hardwood floors, a stone fireplace in the living room, and many paintings. *Represented by:* Gîte Québec, (418) 651-1860. $30–$50.

Sillery. This guest house with a swimming pool on its grounds is a squarish, modern brick structure. The guest suite has a bedroom and a living-room sitting area. There's a brick fireplace in the living room, and the hosts—a pharmacist and his wife—have planted a profusion of flowers on their grounds. *Represented by:* Gîte Québec, (418) 651-1860. $40–$50.

Old Quebec Bridge. Near the Old Quebec Bridge, this guest house is a 10-year-old traditional-style structure made of stone and wood. Painted white and trimmed in green, it features an outdoor brick fireplace, a large guest room with a private bath, and a mixture of antique and modern furnishings. The hostess, an artist who studied in France, currently works at home in her pottery studio. Many works of art contribute to the house's decor. *Represented by:* Gîte Québec, (418) 651-1860. $40–$50.

INDEX

WITH RATES AND CREDIT CARD INFORMATION

INDEX
WITH RATES AND CREDIT-CARD INFORMATION

These rates reflect the cost per day of a single and a double room; if one rate is given, it represents the cost of double-occupancy accommodations. The rates are subject to change, and some vary according to season.

Credit-card abbreviations:
AE: American Express
D: Diners Club
MC: MasterCard
V: Visa
NCC: No credit cards accepted

Abbey, 277; $50-$75; MC,V
Amherst House, 223; $30-$55; NCC
Anderson Guest House, 329; $55; NCC
Ann Marie's Lodgin' and Gallery, 38; $60; NCC
Antique Mews, 300; $65-$75; MC,V
Asheton House, 238; $30-$60; NCC
Ashland's Main Street Inn, 338; $40-$52; NCC
Asphodel Village, 182; $55-$75; MC,V
Bailey House, 139; $45-$75; AE
Baker's Bed and Breakfast, 321; $58; NCC
Baker's Manor Guest House, 123; $17-$19; NCC
Bark Eater, 309; $21-$30; NCC
Barnard-Good House, 278; $50-$70; NCC
Bay Street Inn, 365; $48-$65; MC,V
Bayberry, 86; $45-$85; AE,MC,V
Beach House, 326; $32-$35; NCC
Bear Mountain Guest Ranch, 291; $38.40-$57.55; NCC
Beazley House, 55; $60-$95; MC,V
Bed and Breakfast Inn, 80; $53-$163; NCC
Bed and Breakfast on Our Farm, 181; $18-$30; NCC
Benjamin Choate House, 237; $35-$55; NCC
Bergman's, 23; $45; NCC
Blackthorne Inn, 36; $40-$80; MC,V
Blue Quail Inn, 87; $36-$75; MC,V
Blue Sky Inn, 120; $38-$48; NCC
Bock's Bed and Breakfast, 81; $28-$38; NCC
Bowditch House, 320; $45-$60; NCC
Bradley House, 103; $40-$60; NCC
Brannon-Bunker Inn, 193; $35-$50; MC,V
Brass Bed Victorian Guest House, 279; $35-$60; NCC
Breezemere Farm, 198; $39-$42; MC,V
Briar Rose Bed and Breakfast, 119; $49-$65; AE,MC,V
Brigham Street Inn, 388; $60-$125; AE,MC,V
Brinley, 359; $30-$75; NCC
Britt House, 74; $65-$95; MC,V
Brown's Farm, 425; $40-$45; NCC
Brunton House, 2; $19-$24; NCC
Bud and Dot Shackelford, 26; $35-$60 daily, $140-$315 weekly

Burgundy House Country Inn, 111; $35-$159; AE,MC,V
Burn, 258; $65-$75; MC,V
Camel Lot, 169; $40-$60; NCC
Camellia Inn, 35; $40-$70; MC,V
Canterbury Inn Bed and Breakfast, 256; $50-$60; AE,MC,V
Captain Mey's Inn, 281; $45-$70; MC,V
Carlisle House, 227; $30-$75; NCC
Carriage House, 42; $60-$80; NCC
Carter House Inn, 27; $55-$75; AE,MC,V
Casa Arguello, 82; $30-$70; NCC
Casa Larronde, 48; $58-$65; NCC
Casita Blanca, 83; $60; NCC
Cheney House Bed and Breakfast, 270; $24-$40; NCC
Chestnut House, 228; $45-$80; MC,V
Chetwynd House, 194; $42-$65; NCC
Cider Mill, 335; $35-$40; MC,V
Cliff Crest, 89; $45-$85; AE,MC,V
Cobblestones, 305; rates on request; NCC
Colonial Hotel, 167; $30-$32; NCC
Conover's Bay Head Inn, 275; $42-$80; MC,V
Cornstalk Fence Guest House, 185; $60-$80; AE,MC,V
Cottage, 76; $40-$50; MC,V
Country House Inn, 101; $45-$55; NCC
Country Inn, 31; $45-$55; AE,MC,V
Court Street Inn, 40; $45-$95; NCC
Crossroads Inn, 412; $45-$65; NCC

Dairy Hollow House, 10; $39-$59; AE,MC,V
De Loffre House, 149; $45-$58; AE,MC,V
Dennis Guest House, 360; $50-$75; NCC
Dormer House International, 283; $25-$53 daily, $155-$440 weekly; MC,V
Dunbar House, 53; $40-$55; NCC
Edel Haus Bed and Breakfast, 426; $30.50-$50; MC,V
Eden Pines Inn, 239; $45-$60; NCC
1802 House, 195; $45-$60; MC,V
1833 House, 129; $22-$52; NCC
1895 House, 274; $15-$60; AE,MC,V
Eliza Thompson House, 150; $68-$88; AE,MC,V
Ellings' Guest House, 220; $38-$45; NCC
Fair Meadows Farm Bed and Breakfast, 399; $20-$26; NCC
Fleming Jones Homestead, 66; $45-$64; NCC
Foggy Hollow Farm, 398; $18-$25; NCC
Foxes in Sutter Creek, 95; $60-$70; AE,MC,V
Frederick Fitting House, 331; $28-$38; NCC
Gallery Osgood, 57; $65; MC,V
Gary-Meadows Farm, 394; $24-$28; NCC
Glendeven, 43; $55-$75; NCC
Golden Eagle Inn, 304; $50-$75; AE,MC,V
Goldminer Hotel, 122; $19-$30; NCC
Goodspeed's Guest House, 192; $35-$45; NCC
Gosby House Inn, 63; $50-$75; NCC
Gramma's Bed and Breakfast

453

Inn, 20; $58-$85; AE,MC,V
Grayhurst, 271; $26-$36 daily, $300-$400 weekly; AE
Green Gables Inn, 65; $70-$105; NCC
Grieder Guest House, 230; $50; NCC
Guest House Christel Horman, 402; $25-$32; MC,V
Guest Houses Bed and Breakfast, 423; $30-$85; MC,V
Gustavus Inn, 5; $70; NCC
Halsam-Fort House, 152; $60-$125; NCC
Hanford House, 97; $45-$100; MC,V
Haus Rohrbach Pension, 427; $28-$48; MC,V
Haven Guest House, 224; $30-$80; AE,MC,V
Hawthorne Inn, 217; $60-$80; NCC
Hayes House, 400; $20-$40; NCC
Headlands Inn, 49; $59-$75; NCC
Heirloom, 37; $40-$60; NCC
Hendrick Inn, 109; $20-$35; NCC
High Tor, 197; $55-$75; NCC
Hobson's Bluffdale, 166; $35 daily, $225 weekly; NCC
Holiday House, 21; $50-$60; NCC
Homestead, 347; $10-$18; NCC
Hope-Merrill House, 33; $50-$60; MC,V
Hotel Brooklyn, 175; $15-$37; NCC
Hotel St. Helena, 70; $50-$95; MC,V
House in the Wood, 396; $12-$26; NCC
House of the Seven Gables, Inc., 231; $55-$90; MC,V
House on the Hill, 308; $45-$65; NCC

Inn on Castro, 84; $60-$75; AE,MC,V
Isis Oasis Lodge and Cultural Center, 34; $35-$50; MC,V
Ivanhoe Country House, 245; $30-$60; NCC
Jabberwock, 51; $70-$105; NCC
Jackson Court City Share, 85; $75-$125; AE,MC,V
James House, 428; $38-$80; MC,V
Judge Touvelle House, 342; $45-$55; NCC
Kalorama Guest House, 132; $30-$50; AE,MC,V
Kimble Cliff, 180; $30; NCC
Lafitte Guest House, 186; $58-$95; AE,MC,V
Lantana House, 242; $32-$47; NCC
Lareau Farm Country Inn, 403; $22-$64; MC,V
Laurel Hill Guest House, 30?; $28-$33; NCC
Leawood—the Williams Estate, 375; $30-$40; MC,V
Liberty Inn, 154; $70-$120; AE,MC,V
Livery Stable, 146; $18-$25; NCC
Livingston Mansion Inn, 343; $65-$75; MC,V
Lizzie's, 430; $46-$79; MC,V
Maple Lane Guest House, 350; $18-$24; NCC
Marjon, 340; $60-$80; NCC
Martin's Guest House, 232; $55-$85; NCC
Mary Lee Guest Accommodations, 156; $50; NCC
Mason House Inn, 173; $40-$75; NCC
Mayfield House, 99; $50-$70; MC,V
Mill Farm Inn, 327; $40-$60; NCC

454

Morey House, 68; $45-$70; NCC
Nantucket Landfall, 233; $30-$40; NCC
Oak Hill Ranch, 105; $45-$65; NCC
Oak House, 225; $45-$65; MC,V
Oak Square Country Inn, 259; $50-$65; MC,V
Old Homestead Inn, 391; $20-$35; NCC
Old Pioneer Garden, 267; $25; NCC
Old Town Bed and Breakfast, 30; $35-$55; MC,V
Olde Rowley Inn, 196; $36; MC,V
Oleander House, 113; rates on request; MC,V
One Centre Street Inn, 247; $35-$45; NCC
One Market Street, 301; $40-$55; MC,V
Outlook Lodge, 121; $25-$35; MC,V
Palmer's Chart House, 421; $30-$60; NCC
Park View Guest House, 187; $30-$55; AE,MC,V
Parsonage, 88; $55-$100; MC,V
Portage House, 330; $18-$24; NCC
Pride House, 383; $37-$60; MC,V
Queen Victoria, 284; $50-$90; AE,MC,V
Red House Country Inn and Store, 297; $32-$47; MC,V
Remshart-Brooks House, 157; $50; MC,V
Rose Victorian Inn, 17; $60-$80; NCC
Rosewood Inn, 303; $30-$40; NCC
Royal Manor Guest House, 234; $25-$50; NCC

San Antonio House, 22; $65-$95; NCC
Saratoga Inn, 424; $55-$75; NCC
Schneider Haus, 404; $14-$23; AE,MC,V
Schofield's Guest House, 219; $36; NCC
Sea Gull Lodge, 218; $15-$18; AE,MC,V
Seacrest Manor, 241; $44-$66; NCC
Seafarer Guest House, 243; $38-$54; NCC
Seven Wives Inn, 387; $20-$50; D, MC, V
1735 House, 133; $45-$80; AE,MC,V
7th Sister Guest House, 286; $38-$48; NCC
Shore Inne, 128; $32-$45; MC,V
623 Ursulines, 188; $45-$55; NCC
Skagway Inn, 6; $35-$45; MC,V
Society Hill Hotel, 353; $60-$90; AE,MC,V
Spring House, 345; $42-$50; NCC
Stagecoach Inn, 310; $25-$35; NCC
Stone Fox Lodge, 273; $42; MC,V
Stone Mill Farm, 393; $30; NCC
Strawberry Inn, 201; $45-60; NCC
Sunnyside, an Urban Inn, 94; $35; NCC
Swag, 328; $80-$98; MC,V
Swan Inn, 434; $40-$55; MC,V
Thistle Dew Inn, 91; $35-$95; MC,V
3 Bs Bed and Breakfast, 334; $20-$25; NCC
Tibbitts House, 318; $18-$25; NCC
Two Meeting Street Inn, 370;

$50-$85; NCC
Union Hotel, 18; $60-$105; AE,D,MC,V
Valley View Citrus Ranch, 61; $35; NCC
Varnum's, 397; $30-$35; NCC
Venice Beach House, 107; $50-$125; AE,MC,V
Victorian, 226; $65-$125; AE,MC,V
Victorian Farmhouse, 45; $60; NCC
Victorian Villa, 252; $40-$65; MC,V
Vintage Towers, 24; $35-$65; MC,V
Walshes', 361; $35-$50; NCC
"Wayside," 362; $55-$65; NCC
Wedgwood Inn, 348; $35-$60; NCC
Wellman General Store Guest Apartment, 248; $35-$100; NCC
White Lace Inn, 438; $48-$65; MC, V
Wickwood, 250; $65-$90; AE,MC,V
Wildwood Inn, 246; $25-$45; MC,V
Williams House Bed and Breakfast, 11; $35-$65; NCC
Willow Springs Country Inn, 93; $30-$58; NCC
Windover House, 401; $25-$30; NCC
Woodruff House, 392; $22-$30; NCC
Woolverton Inn, 290; $45-$65; AE
Yankee Peddler Inn, 363; $35-$95; AE,MC,V
Ye Olde Cherokee Inn, 325; $25-$65; AE,MC,V
Year of the Horse Inn, 411; $27-$55; MC,V
Yesterhouse Inn, 60; $55-$90; V

THE COMPLEAT TRAVELER'S READER REPORT

To: *The Compleat Traveler*
c/o Burt Franklin & Co., Inc.
235 East 44th Street
New York, New York 10017 U.S.A.

Dear Compleat Traveler:

I have used your *Bed & Breakfast: Great American Guest House Book*. I would like to offer the following ☐ new recommendation, ☐ comment, ☐ suggestion, ☐ criticism, ☐ or complaint about:

Name of Guest House/Bed & Breakfast:

_____

Referral service used: _____

Address: _____

_____

Comments:

Date of my visit: _____ Length of stay: _____

From (name): _____

Address: _____

_____ Telephone: _____

THE COMPLEAT TRAVELER'S READER REPORT

To: *The Compleat Traveler*
    c/o Burt Franklin & Co., Inc.
    235 East 44th Street
    New York, New York 10017 U.S.A.

Dear Compleat Traveler:

I have used your *Bed & Breakfast: Great American Guest House Book*. I would like to offer the following ☐ new recommendation, ☐ comment, ☐ suggestion, ☐ criticism, ☐ or complaint about:

Name of Guest House/Bed & Breakfast:

_____

Referral service used: _____

Address: _____

_____

Comments:

Date of my visit: _____ Length of stay: _____

From (name): _____

Address: _____

_____ Telephone: _____